Albert the Great

Center of Tommaso da Modena's *Albertus Magnus* (1352) in the Chapter Room of S. Niccolo at Treviso, Italy.

ALBERT THE GREAT

Commemorative Essays

Edited and with an Introduction by
Francis J. Kovach
and
Robert W. Shahan

University of Oklahoma Press : Norman

By Francis J. Kovach

Die Aesthetik des Thomas von Aquin: eine genetische und systematische Analyse (Berlin, 1961)
Philosophy of Beauty (Norman, 1974)
Bonaventure and Aquinas: Enduring Philosophers (coeditor; Norman, 1976)
Albert the Great: Commemorative Essays (coeditor; Norman, 1980)

By Robert W. Shahan

Bonaventure and Aquinas: Enduring Philosophers (coeditor; Norman, 1976)
David Hume: Many-sided Genius (coeditor; Norman, 1976)
American Philosophy: From Edwards to Quine (coeditor; Norman, 1977)
Spinoza: New Perspectives (coeditor; Norman, 1978)
Essays on the Philosophy of W. V. Quine (coeditor; Norman, 1979)
Albert the Great: Commemorative Essays (coeditor; Norman, 1980)

Library of Congress Cataloging in Publication Data

Main entry under title:

Albert the Great.
   Includes bibliographical references and index.
   1. Albertus Magnus, Saint, Bp. of Ratisbon, 1193?–1280—Addresses, essays, lectures.
I. Kovach, Francis Joseph.   II. Shahan, Robert W., 1935–
B765.A44A64   189′.4   79-6713

This publication has been supported in part by a grant from the Oklahoma University Associates Fund.

Contents

v

Introduction

In 1974 the world commemorated the seven hundredth anniversary of the death of two of the four most outstanding high-scholastic philosopher-theologians—those of Saint Thomas Aquinas and Saint Bonaventure. Six years later another septemcentennial anniversary has arrived, that of the death of Saint Albert the Great.

Of these three most distinguished thirteenth-century schoolmen Saint Thomas has deservedly received the greatest attention from philosophers, theologians, and historians, whereas Saint Albert has been relatively neglected for various reasons. Thus the seven hundredth anniversary of Albert's death offers an opportunity to make up in part for the relative neglect Albert has suffered both doctrinally and historically and to endeavor to reveal aspects of his rich thought that deserve attention even seven centuries after his death.

I

The relative neglect of Albert is ironic indeed, since his works can be characterized as highly impressive, if not overwhelming, in certain respects. That this characterization befits the *length* of the life of Saint Albert can be seen from two historical facts. One is that, whether Albert was born (at Lauingen in Swabia, a little town between Ulm and Regensburg)[1] as early as 1193 (one extreme view on his birth date,

---

[1] That is why Albert sometimes signed his name Albertus de Lauingen. On the other hand, since both Lauingen and Swabia were German-speaking territories, he also used the names Albertus de Alemania and Albertus Teutonicus. The latter name can be found, e.g., on a document of the University of Paris, 1248, and on another in Toulouse, 1258 (see Martin Grabmann, "Der Einfluss Alberts des Grossen auf das mittelalterliche Geistesleben," *Zeitschrift für katholische Theologie* 52 [Innsbruck: F. Rauch, 128] pp. 157–59). On the other hand, Girardus de Fracheto, Albert's contemporary *confrère*, refers to him as *Teutonicus* in his *Vitae fratrum ordinis praedicatorum* of 1260 (see Hieronymus Wilms, *Albert der Grosse* [Mün-

advocated by, e.g., Emil Michael and Hieronymus Wilms) or as late as 1207 (the other extreme view on this question, held by, e.g., J. A. Endres and P. Mandonnet),[2] his life span far surpasses those of the other three high-scholastic giants. Duns Scotus, chronologically the last of the four giants, was born only fifteen years before the death of Albert; yet he outlived Albert by no more than twenty-eight years. Thomas Aquinas was born two or three decades after Albert; yet Albert outlived Thomas by more than six years (Thomas died on March 7, 1274, and Albert on November 15, 1280). Finally, although Bonaventure (who was four years older than Thomas and died four months after him) was himself between fourteen and twenty-eight years younger than Albert, he preceded him in death by more than six years (July 15, 1274).

The other historical fact is that the years of Albert's life witnessed the large majority of events constituting the history of philosophy from the abrupt end of the golden period of Arabic and Jewish philosophy in the twelfth century to the beginning of the disintegration of high-scholastic philosophy at the end of the thirteenth century.[3] For instance, Albert was born no more than nine years after but possibly as much as five years before the death of Averroes (1198); no more than three years after but possibly eleven years before the death of Moses Maimonides; and no more than five years after but possibly as much as nine years before the death of one of the main figures of twelfth-century scholasticism, who preceded Albert in being called *doctor universalis*—Alan of Lille (1202).

At the other end of his life span, Albert died no more than eighteen years before the death of Peter John Olivi, who seems to have introduced the first traces of agnosticism into scholasticism, and only a little

chen: J. Kosel & F. Pustet, 1931], English tr. by A. English and P. Hereford [London: Burnsdates & Washbourne, 1933], p. xix).

[2] For a brief but excellent summary of the views on the actual birth date of Albert see J. A. Weisheipl, "Albertus Magnus and the Oxford Platonists," *Proceedings of the American Catholic Philosophical Association* 32 (1958), p. 124, n. 1.

[3] On the life of Albert my main sources were Wilms, *op. cit.* and Dorothy Wyckoff, "Life of Albert," in her *Albertus Magnus' Book of Minerals* (Oxford: Clarendon Press, 1967), pp. xiii–xxvi. I also consulted F. J. Catania, "Albert the Great," in *The Encyclopedia of Philosophy*, ed. E. Edwards (New York: Macmillan and the Free Press, 1967), 1:64–66; Grabmann, *art. cit.*; Weisheipl, *art. cit.*; and, for additional historical data, among others, F. Ueberweg and B. Geyer, *Geschichte der Philosophie*, (Berlin: E. S. Mittler & Sohn 1928), vol. 2; E. Gilson, *History of Christian Philosophy in the Middle Ages* (New York: Random House, 1955); and F. Copleston, *A History of Philosphy*, (Westminster, Md.: Newman Press, 1950), vols. 2–3.

over two decades before Duns Scotus completed his *Opus Oxoniense*—which contained the seeds of a certain skeptic tendency leading in the first few decades of the fourteenth century, through Durandus and Aureolus, to the well-known nominalism of William of Ockham and to the full-blown skepticism of some logicians and metaphysicians within the Ockhamist movement (Richard Billingham, Robert Holkot, John of Mirecourt, Nicholas of Autrecourt, et al.).

Correspondingly, as the years of Albert's childhood, adulthood, and old age passed, the great majority of the events in the history of high scholasticism took place. For instance, when the *Metaphysica vetus*, the earliest Latin translation of Aristotle's principal work, was completed, and the Provincial Council of Paris forbade the teaching of Aristotle's *Physics* and condemned Amalric of Bene and David of Dinant (later targets of both Albert's and Thomas's severe criticism), Albert was at least three and at most seventeen years of age (1210). Moreover, when Roger Bacon was born (1212), Albert was at least five if not as much as nineteen years old. Also, in 1215, when William of Moerbeke, the great translator into Latin of Aristotle and other great Greek authors, was born; when Alexander of Hales's commentary on the *Sentences* was approved by the Lateran Council; and when Robert de Courcon, the papal delegate, chartered the University of Paris; Albert was between eight and twenty-two years old. Furthermore, when Honorus III by a papal bill confirmed the Order of Preachers (Dominicans) in 1216, Albert was at least nine and possibly as old as twenty-three. In the year 1217, when the Dominican school for advanced studies—the school where Albert himself was to study decades later—was established in Paris, Albert was at least ten and, at most, twenty-four. And in 1221, the year that witnessed the birth of Saint Bonaventure; the appointment of Robert Grosseteste, the highly influential scientist-thinker as chancellor of Oxford University; the death of the founder of the Order of Preachers; and the Dominicans' settling down in Oxford and Cologne, Albert was no more than fourteen or as much as twenty-eight.

On the other hand, in the year 1222, in which the earliest known events occurred in Albert's life, viz., his witnessing some destructive earthquakes in Lombardy and his becoming acquainted with the Dominicans (the order both he and Aquinas were to join eventually), Padua received a university at which Albert later studied philosophy. Also, following the Dominicans, the Franciscans settled down in Oxford in 1224—probably one year after Albert entered the Dominican Order. Jordan of Saxony formally admitted Albert to the Dominican Order and sent him for his novitiate to Cologne (where Albert spent a good portion of his life)[4] in the same year (1229) in which the Dominicans received their first chair of theology at the University of Paris; and William of Auvergne, the first outstanding Franciscan theologian-philosopher, was working on his *De anima*.

It was during Albert's first tenure at Cologne that Philip the Chancellor, the first schoolman to discuss the transcendental properties of being, wrote his *Summa de bono* (ca. 1230); William of Auvergne finished his important *De universo creaturarum*; Gregory IX appointed a commission of theologians to correct Aristotle's prohibited works; the Franciscans obtained their first chair of theology at the University of Paris; and Alexander began teaching there as the first holder of that chair (1231). Around the time that Hildesheim and, subsequently, Freiburg im Breisgau opened Dominican schools (ca. 1234-35)—schools where Albert taught as *lector* after his Cologne tenure—Raymond Lull, one of the most intriguing figures of the century, and Siger of Brabant were born, ca. 1232-35 and 1235, respectively). In 1238, Albert probably attended the Chapter General at Bologna, at which he came close to being elected master general of the order. In the same year Conrad von Hochstein was elected archbishop of Cologne—the prelate whose long-standing feud with the citizens of Cologne was eventually arbitrated by Albert.

Turning to the next decade of Albert's life, one finds that it was probably in 1240, the year of the birth of the Franciscan Matthew of Aquasparta and of Bonaventure's entrance into the Franciscan Order, that Albert visited Saxonia and, according to his own report, saw a great comet there. Two or three years later he was sent by his religious superiors to Paris to study theology at the Dominican School of Advanced Studies (1242-43)—possibly one year before Bonaventure began studying in Paris under Alexander of Hales. The year 1245 was an important turning point in Albert's life: he became master in theology under Gueric of Saint-Quentin, the first German Dominican to achieve this distinction. Immediately afterward he began teaching theology as full professor at the University of Paris. In the same year both Alexander of Hales and John of La Rochelle (Alexander's disciple) died in Paris; Bonaventure continued his studies under Eudes Rigaud and William of Melitva; and Thomas Aquinas began his three-year study in Paris under Albert. In 1247, the second year of Albert's tenure at Paris

[4] For the importance Cologne played in Albert's life see Grabmann, *art. cit.* pp. 157-59. This importance explains the name Albertus Colonienses—the name at least three thirteenth-century authors used in reference to Saint Albert: Siger of Brabant in his *Impossibilia*; Robert Grosseteste (?) in *Summa philosophiae* (for the two see Grabmann, *art. cit.* p. 152, nn. 2, and 1); and Dante, *Paradiso*, X, 98.

as master of theology, Giles of Rome, the great independent schoolman of the century, was born. The next year, 1248, when Bonaventure began lecturing as bachelor of Scripture, the General Chapter of the Dominicans, meeting in Paris, decided to establish a *studium generale* in each of the four Dominian provinces and appointed Albert regent of studies at the school for the Teutonia province in Cologne. Thus in the same year Albert went back to Cologne, ending his professorship in Paris; Thomas Aquinas followed him to that city to continue his own studies under Albert; Bonaventure became biblical bachelor; and Peter John Olivi, the talented but often misinterpreted and tragic Franciscan, was born. It was during Albert's second tenure in Cologne that William of Auvergne, the great Franciscan master, died (1249); Roger Bacon entered the Franciscan Order; and Bonaventure commenced his lectures on the *Sentences* of Peter Lombard (1250).

In 1252, still during his second tenure in Cologne, Albert drew up a judgment on the feud between Archbishop Conrad von Hochstein and the citizens of Cologne. In that year Thomas Aquinas finished his studies under Albert and, probably upon his master's recommendation, was sent back to Paris to begin his lectures as biblical bachelor. In 1253, the following year, while Albert was still teaching at Cologne's *studium generale*, Bonaventure began teaching as regent master in theology at the University of Paris. Robert Grosseteste, the first advocate of an empirical approach to philosphy in the thirteenth century, died the same year. One year later, 1254, Albert was elected prior provincial of the Teutonia province, which then included today's Germany, Austria, Switzerland, Alsace, Lorraine, Luxembourg, Belgium, Holland, and even parts of Poland, Lithuania, and Latvia. The same year Aquinas started his lectures on Peter Lombard's *Sentences*. In his new capacity as prior provincial, Albert began visiting a number of Dominican monasteries in the Teutonia province in 1255—the same year in which Alexander urged Albert to forward missionary work in Prussia and Lavonia; William of St. Amour, a secular professor at the University of Paris, published his *De periculis novissimorum temporum*, thus causing a long-lasting strife between the religious and the secular professors of the university; Thomas composed his *De principiis naturae*; and for the first time all the known works of Aristotle were officially lectured on at the University of Paris. A year later, in 1256, Albert returned from his visitations to Cologne, attended the General Chapter in Paris to discuss the attack of William of St. Amour on the mendicant orders, and then, on the invitation of Alexander IV, departed for Anagni, to testify against William and certain Paris professors before the Commission of Cardinals in the papal curia; he also found time to compose his polemic work directed against Averroes (*De unitate intellectus contra Averroes*). In the same year Thomas completed his great commentary of the *Sentences* and composed his short but profound metaphysical work *De ente et essentia*; Bonaventure wrote his *Breviloquium*; and both Thomas and Bonaventure were appointed to chairs of theology in the University of Paris.

In 1257, after an extensive two-year tour of visitation to many German cities, including such faraway places as Lübeck and (possibly) Riga, Albert lectured, conducted a public disputation, and did research in the papal court (which in the meantime had moved from Anagni to Viterbo). In that year Roger Bacon incurred the suspicions of his religious superiors for certain doctrines and ceased lecturing at Oxford, and Bonaventure resigned his chair at Paris, because he was named minister general of the Franciscan Order. Having been relieved of the office of prior provincial and having assumed the duties of regent of studies in 1258, Albert helped settle a trade dispute between Cologne and Utrecht in 1259 and in the same year attended the General Chapter at Valenciennes, serving on the same committee as Aquinas and discussing the curriculum of the Dominican schools. Meanwhile, Bonaventure composed his *Itinerarium*, and Thomas left Paris for Italy to teach theology at the *studium curiae* attached to the papal court. In 1260, having been appointed bishop by Alexander IV and consecrated as such, Albert entered Regensburg (Ratisbon), and became involved in administrative work in that city. That is also the year in which Meister Eckhart, the most outstanding representative of neo-Platonist mysticism in the fourteenth century, was born and Giles of Rome became the first doctor of the *studium generale* of the Augustinians in Paris.

In the first year of the next decade of his life Albert met Thomas Aquinas and William of Moerbeke in the court of newly elected Pope Urban IV at Viterbo (1261). Thomas was lecturing there, William was working on his translations, and Albert was occupied with writing. In 1263, Urban IV renewed the 1210 prohibition of Aristotle at Paris and, having confirmed Albert's successor as bishop of Regensburg, appointed Albert preacher of the Crusade. Thus Albert began his two-year-long tour of preaching in today's Germany, Holland, and Bohemia, visiting Cologne, among other cities, several times. Toward the end of 1264, after the tour was over, having ended with the death of Urban IV, Albert began an approximately three-year stay with the Würzburg Dominicans, among whom was his own brother, Henry. In the same year Thomas finished his *Summa contra Gentiles*. Three years later, in 1267, Albert traveled from Würzburg to various German cities

(Aachen, Cologne, Strasbourg, etc.)—one year after Clement IV, the new pope, is said to have received the *Opus Maius* from Roger Bacon. In 1268, the year Bonaventure wrote his *De septem donis Spiritus Sancti*, Clement IV ordered Albert to leave for Mecklenburg to settle a dispute over some property involving the Knights of Saint John. This was the journey during which Albert was first allowed to use a vehicle. In the same year, on account of troubles with the Averroists (led by Siger of Brabant), Thomas Aquinas was sent back from Viterbo to Paris as a scholarly troubleshooter; William of Moerbeke stayed at Viterbo and finished his translation of Proclus's *Elements of Theology*. During the first two years of Thomas's second tenure at the University of Paris (1269–71), Albert resided mainly in Strasbourg, where his disciple Ulrich Engelbert (better known as Ulrich of Strasbourg) was acting as lector. However, toward the end of 1272, the year Giles of Rome wrote his *Errores Philosophorum*, Albert returned to Cologne to negotiate a political settlement between Archbishop Engelberg and the citizens—possibly in the same month in which Etienne Tempier, bishop of Paris, condemned thirteen theses of Siger of Brabant.

Albert spent the last decade of his life mainly in Cologne. He was still active—the main fruit of those years being his principal theological work, the *Summa Theologiae*. During Albert's third year in Cologne (1272) several significant events occurred. While Albert sealed still another agreement in Cologne, Robert Kilwardby was elected archbishop of Canterbury, the Faculty of Art in the University of Paris issued a warning to Siger of Brabant, and Thomas was sent back from Paris to Italy—this time to erect a Dominican *studium generale* in Naples. In the subsequent year, 1273, a politically important meeting was held in Cologne; Albert, together with John of Vercelli, the master general of the order, and Ulrich Engelbert, met Rudolph of Hapsburg.

In the meantime Bonaventure was appointed cardinal, and completed his *Collationes in Hexaemeron*, while, in Naples, Thomas wrote two additional Aristotle commentaries (on *De caelo* and on *De generatione et corruptione*) and composed the last *quaestio* of his theological *summa* (*quaestio* XC of *Pars Tertia*). Summoned by Gregory X, Thomas left Naples to attend the Council of Lyon, but he died on his way in Fossanuova (between Naples and Rome) on March 7, 1274. Albert learned this sad news while he himself was traveling to Lyon, where he arrived late for the opening of the council. According to a late account he spoke to the council in June, only thirty-nine days before the death of Bonaventure (July 15, 1274), who was also attending the council. That is also the year during which the Franciscan William of La Mare, the author of the first *Correctorium* of Thomistic doctrines, became master of theology in Paris. One year later, in 1275, Albert was again on a journey around Germany and acted also as arbitrator in Cologne, while Peter of Auvergne, an Aristotelian Thomist opposed by Henry of Ghent, became rector of the University of Paris. The next year, in 1276, following the deaths of three popes (Gregory X, Innocent V, and Adrian V) and the election of John XXI, Albert was in Antwerp attending the Provincial Chapter, at which he met his great disciple Ulrich of Strasbourg for the last time, for Ulrich died on March 7, 1277 (the same day of the year on which Thomas Aquinas had died two years before). The year 1277 is rich in historical events relevant to the history of philosophy in general and Albert's life in particular. It was probably early in 1277 that Albert journeyed to Paris to defend his most famous disciple, Thomas Aquinas, against certain theological charges raised against him by overzealous Augustinian Franciscans. Nevertheless, on the very day of the third anniversary of the death of Saint Thomas (who was indirectly affected by this act), Bishop Tempier issued his famous but hasty condemnation of 219 theses attributed to Siger of Brabant— a disciplinary measure endorsed eleven days later by the English Dominican Robert Kilwardby, archbishop of Canterbury. This condemnation caused Siger of Brabant to leave France for Italy with Boethius of Sweden (Boethius de Dacia). Also in 1277 Peter of Spain (John XXI) wrote his famous *Summula locicales*.

Within the last two years of Albert's life the Augustinian Giles of Rome composed his important polemic work *De gradibus formarum*, rejecting the plurality of forms held by John Peckham; and the Dominican Giles of Lessines (who studied under Albert) wrote his reply to Robert Kilwardby concerning the unicity of form (1278). Early next year, in January, 1279, Albert made his will, describing himself in it as *sanus et incolumen*; he then continued to function on various ecclesiastic occasions. In the same year the Franciscan Matthew of Aquasparta (b. *ca.* 1240) succeeded John Peckham as master in theology at the papal court; the Franciscan Walter of Bruges, author of an important *Quaestiones disputatae*, became bishop of Poitiers; the Dominican Robert Kilwardby died; and Jerome of Ascoli, who condemned Roger Bacon for certain doctrines, completed his tenure as minister general of the Franciscans.

Albert died on November 15, 1280, about three months after the death of Nicholas II, in the year in which Duns Scotus took the habit of the Friars Minor; Raymond Lull, the author of the famous *Ars combinatoria* and the influential *doctor illuminatus*, had his first stay as a missionary in Africa; and, probably, John Quidorf (John of Paris) answered William of la Mare's *Correctorium* in defense of Thomas.

Albert's death occurred two years before the Franciscan Bartholomew succeeded Matthew of Aquasparta as master in theology at Bologna and three years before Peter John Olivi was compelled to retract twenty-two of his doctrines (1283); four years before Siger of Brabant died, and the Franciscan Richard of Mediavilla became master in theolgy at Paris (1284); five years before Giles of Rome and Godfrey of Fontaine became masters in theology at the same university (1285); eight years before Matthew of Aquasparta was named cardinal (1288); twelve years before the death of the Franciscan John Peckham, a bitter opponent of Saint Thomas (1292); and about thirteen years before the death of Henry of Ghent and Roger Bacon, the only contemporary who matched Albert as a scientist (1293).

II

That all the events listed above—that is, the great majority of the highlights of the thirteenth-century scholasticism—took place during the life of a single philosopher, Albert, is in itself impressive.

Admittedly, a number of the works included in the thirty-eight quarto volumes of the August Borgnet edition of Albert's *Opera Omnia* (Paris: L. Vivès, 1890–99) are known to have been written by schoolmen other than Albert (the best known of these works being the *Compendium theologiae veritatis,* by Hugh Ripelin of Strasbourg, one of Albert's first disciples) and Albert's authorship of still other texts included in this edition is doubtful. On the other hand, a number of exegetical, mathematical, astronomical, and rhetorical works by Albert have not yet been found. At any rate, according to the *conspectus* of the critical Cologne edition, presently there are no fewer than sixty-nine extant authentic writings by Albert, not counting his sermons and letters. In fact, the total of his writings is actually seventy, if the *Summa de creaturis* is counted as two separate works, the *De quatuor coaevis* and the *De homine.*

These extant writings cover four generic areas of knowledge: logic, philosophy, theology, and natural science (in the broad sense that includes cosmological and psychological works as well as scientific works in the modern sense). Of these four genera of knowledge, philosophy is exclusively treated in the smallest number of works (eight, five of which are metaphysical and three ethical), followed by the works in logic (nine) and the scientific writings (twenty-two), while theology is the generic topic of no fewer than thirty texts (thirteen of which are exegetical and seventeen sytematic-theological). One must bear in mind, however, that some of the seventeen works on systematic theology contain an enormous amount of philosophical material and that philosophical views are expressed in virtually all the twenty-two scientific works.

Six of the nine logical works deal with and bear the titles of the parts of Aristotle's *Organon*, while the subject of one work is Porphyry's five universals. Among the eight philosophical works the *Metaphysica*, the *Ethica*, the *De causis*, and the polemical *De unitate intellectus* stand out doctrinally.

The twenty-two works on natural science were written according to an elaborate Aristotelian master plan specified by Albert himself in an early part of his *Physics*. There he listed nineteen planned works, all except five of which bear Aristotelian titles. Thus of the twenty-two extant scientific works only six are on topics not treated by Aristotle, while two others, dealing with animals, partly reflect Aristotle's works on animals, and one, the *Mineralia*, treats of a topic Albert believed that Aristotle discussed in a separate work. Philosophically four of the scientific works seem to excel in importance (*Physica, De Caelo et mundo, De generatione et corruptione,* and *De Anima*), while scientifically (to use the term in the modern sense) at least four others appear to stand out (*Meteora, Mineralia, De animalibus* and *Quaestiones super "De animalibus"*).

Finally, among the thirty theological works at least six systematic works are philosophically of great importance: *Summa de creaturis, De natura boni, Super IV Sententiarum, De bono, In Dionysii de divinis nominibus* and *Summa theologiae*.

III

The commemorative essays presented in this collection deal with logical, philosophical, and scientific doctrines of Albert and also consider him historically in terms of both his debts to his predecessors and his influence upon subsequent scholastic thought. Only the theology is left unconsidered.

All of this is done in nine studies. The first considers Albert's theory of universals. The next two contributions deal with two physical theories (time and soul), treated exclusively at what Albert called (with Aristotle) the physical level. Two essays have metaphysical topics, viz., *esse* and God, considered solely at the metaphysical level. The subsequent pair of essays treat of the two topics, the nature of individuum and action at a distance, at both the physical and the metaphysical levels. The last two essays discuss Albert's position on Avicebron's hylomorphism and Albert's influence on Galileo.

The logical paper is Ralph McInerny's "Albert on Universals." The two physical essays are John M. Quinn's "The Concept of Time in Albert the Great" and Ingrid Craemer-Ruegenberg's "The Priority of Soul as a Form and Its Proximity to the First Mover: Some Aspects of Albert's Psychology in the First Two Books of His Commentary on Aristotle's *De Anima*."

The two metaphysical essays are Leo Sweeney's "The Meaning of *Esse* in Albert the Great's Texts on Creation in *Summa de Creaturis* and *Scripta Super Sententias*" and Francis J. Catania's " 'Knowable' and 'Namable' in Albert the Great's *Commentary on the Divine Names*."

The two physico-metaphysical studies are Léonard Ducharme's "The Individual Human Being in Saint Albert's Earlier Writings" and Francis J. Kovach's "The Enduring Question of Action at a Distance in Saint Albert the Great."

Finally, the two historical papers are James A. Weisheipl's "Albertus Magnus and Universal Hylomorphism: Avicebron: A Note on Thirteenth-Century Augustinianism" and William A. Wallace's "Galileo's Citations of Albert the Great." The third part of Francis Kovach's paper is also historical, dealing with the sources and the influence of Albert's theory of action at a distance.

The divisions and sequence of the papers making up this septem-centennial commemorative volume are analogous to the theoretical part of the authentic *corpus Aristotelicum* from the *Categories* to the *Metaphysics*, the first five works being on logic in general, followed by works on physics and, crowning all these writings, a work on metaphysics.

All nine of the essays, whether critical or analytic or both in character, have been motivated by one common desire—to commemorate on the seven hundredth anniversary of Albert's death one of the few persons in history who excelled in philosophy and theology as well as in natural science.

IV

In paying homage to Albert, the authors of the nine essays presented here continue the expressions of admiration and respect that began while he was still alive. The oldest chronicle using the name Albertus Magnus is probably the *Annales Basileenses* of the year 1277.[5] Other chronicles written between the thirteenth and the fifteenth centuries and referring to Saint Albert as *magnus* in some respect include the

---

[5] *In Monumenta Germaniae Historica*, XVII; *Scriptores*, ed. G. H. Pertz (Hannoverae: A. Hahnianus, 1861), p. 202, 10–11.

Alsatian *Annales* (thirteenth century), calling him *magnus praedictor;* the *Annales Halesbrunnenses majores* and the *Flores temporum* of an anonymous Franciscan, both calling him *magnus philosophus;* and the official register of the Dominican Province of Teutonia, which refers to him as *philosophorum maximus.*[6]

Other historical works refer to Saint Albert as Albertus Magnus without any qualification. The earliest known such work is Johann von Victring's *Liber certarum historiarum* (1343), followed by, e.g., the *Annales Wernheri aliorumqûe Tegernseenses* (partly of the thirteenth, and partly of the fifteenth centuries), under the entry for the year 1260, and Luis de Valladolid's *Vita.*[7]

The first theologian-philosopher to call Albert a "great philosopher" (*philosophus magnus*) was probably Raymond Martin;[8] the oldest known philosophical works using the name Albertus Magnus are a Latin Aristotle codex of the first half of the fourteenth century and a theological textbook (*Quaestiones super libros Sententiarum*) of the second half of the same century.[9] Moreover, the humanist John Pico della Mirandola used three laudatory adjectives in characterizing Albert: *priscum, amplum, grande.*[10]

V

Variant forms of praise—those using neither *magnus* nor *maximus*—are equally prevalent, beginning perhaps with the historian Girardus de Fracheto, who, in his *Vitae Fratrum Ordinis Praedicatorum* of 1260, called Albert "a man of extraordinary reputation and great sanctity."[11] In the following year, 1261, Thomas de Chantimpre spoke of Albert "the Celebrated."[12] Another early historian, Heinrich von Herford, remarked that Albert was "honored and venerated by all . . . ," being

[6] See Grabmann, *art. cit.* pp. 164 nn. 1, 4, 5, 6.

[7] For the first two sources see Grabmann, *art. cit.* p. 164; for the third, Wilms, *op. cit.* p. xx.

[8] Raymondi Martini, O.P., *Pugio Fidei adversus Mauros et Judaeos* (1278), III, dist. 2 cap. 2, cum observationibus J. de Voisin (Lipsiae: F. Lanckisus, typis viduae J. Wittigav, 1687), p. 555.

[9] Grabmann, *art. cit.* pp. 164–65.

[10] Johannes Picus de Mirandola, *Apologia XIII Quaestionum,* in *Opera Collecta* (Venetiis, 1496). See M. Grabmann, "Drei ungedruckte Teile der *Summa de creaturis Alberts des Grossen,*" *Quellen und Forschungen zur Geschichte des Dominikanerordens in Deutschland,* XIII) (Leipzig: Otto Harraschowitz, 1919), p. 1.

[11] Wilms, *op. cit.* p. xix.

[12] Thomas Cantipratensis, *Bonum Universale de apibus,* quoted by Wilms, *op. cit.* p. xix.

"the most brilliant sun among all philosophers in all of Christendom."[13] The Swabian Dominican Ludwig Hohentwang of Elchingen praised Albert as "Swabia's unique decor "(*sueviae decus unicum*); the Bavarian Johann Turmair (called Aventinus) considered Albert "the most learned German" (*der gelertiste Teutsche*), and Petrus Marsilius joined in these praises by extolling Saint Thomas Aquinas as the greatest scholar of the Dominican Order next to *frater Albertus philosophus*.[14]

The statements of two additional thirteenth-century thinkers deserve special mention here for various reasons. One of these thinkers is, ironically, Roger Bacon—probably the most bitter and unfair critic of Albert the philosopher. Bacon informed us in his *Opus tertium* that, while he was still alive, Albert was being used and quoted as an authority (*auctoritas*) side by side with Aristotle, Avicenna, and Averroes—a recognition no other philosopher received in the thirteenth century.[15]

The other philosopher at hand is Ulrich Engelberg of Strasbourg, Albert's most loyal disciple. The words of praise he bestowed upon his beloved master best sum up the admiration and respect the *doctor universalis* received from his contemporaries as well as from later schoolmen, and are still valid to some extent after seven centuries:

A man in every science so divine that he could appropriately be called the wonder and miracle of our time.[16]

Norman, Oklahoma
November 15, 1979

[13] "Ab omnibus regularius et secularibus, senioribus, iunioribus, minoribus et maioribus honorabatus et venerabatur"; "philosophorum omnium totius Christianitatis sol preclarissimus." Henricus de Hervordia, *Liber de rebus memorabilioribus sive Chronicon*, Potthast ed. (Göttingen, 1859), pp. 201, 196. See Grabmann, "Der Einfluss Alberts . . .," p. 158, 165 n. 2.

[14] Grabmann, "Der Einfluss Alberts . . .," pp. 163 nn. 3, 4; 165 n. 3.

[15] "Nam sicut Aristoteles, Avicenna, et Averroes allegantur in scholis, sic et ipse [*sc.* Albertus]: et adhuc vivit, et habuit in vita sua auctoritatem, quod nunquam homo habuit in doctrina." Roger Bacon, *Opus tertium*, c. 9, ad obi. 5; ed. J. S. Brewer (London: Longman, Green, et al., 1859), p. 3a. Cf. *ibid.* p. 31. For probably the strangest mixture of high praise and devastating criticism in philosophical literature, see Roger Bacon's remarks on Albert in *Opus minus*, tertium peccatum, ed. cit. pp. 327–28.

[16] "Aliter autem ab omnibus praemissi sentit doctor meus dominus Albertus, episcopus quondam Ratisponensis, vir in omni scientia adeo divinus ut nostri temporis stupor et miraculum congrue vocari possit." Ulricus Engelbertus, *Summa de bono*, IV, tr. 3 c. 9 (Cod. Vat. Lat. 1811 fol 120v and Paris, Bibliothèque Nationale lat. 15900, 336v). See Grabmann, "Der Einfluss . . .," p. 165 n. 1; and Francis J. Lescoe, *God as First Principle in Ulrich of Strasbourg* (New York: Alba House, 1979), pp. 6; 12 n. 48; 41; 48 n. 58.

Part I

Logic

Albert on Universals

RALPH McINERNY
University of Notre Dame

> Hoc enim per rationes logicas ad
> plenum sciri non poterit, sed
> metaphysico determinanda relinquuntur.[1]

To ask after Albert the Great's teaching on the problem of universals, seemingly a pedestrian question, leads one swiftly into a bewildering thicket, but one in which to thrash about is both historically interesting and philosophically worthwhile. Of course we want to know how Albert handled the three Porphyrian questions which constitute the traditional problem of universals, and we expect that his treatment of them will profit from his unparalleled knowledge of the Aristotelian corpus as well as of the Arabs. We are also provided with materials that must influence our judgment of the Platonism of Albert. At the same time, his conception of what logic is and of how it differs from other disciplines is everywhere at work in the passages that must be considered. Once we know Albert's views on the status of the concerns of the logician and the fact that he considers the discussion of universals to be the first task of the logician, we are likely to think that his resolution of the problem of universals is fated and predictable. As we shall see, this is far from being unequivocally or unambiguously so. On this matter, Albert is profound, prolix and unfailingly surprising.

My procedure in this paper is quite straightforward. I shall first set forth Albert's discussion of why universals must interest the logician, in the course of which his view on the nature of logic and the status of its concerns will be sketched. With this in hand, I shall turn to three places in his writings where Albert considers the problem of universals, taking the texts in descending order of importance. The passages in question are (1) the Second Tractate of the work Albert devoted to the *Isagoge*

---

[1] *Liber De Praedicabilibus,* Tractatus 2, cap. 2, p. 20a. I cite this work from the Borgnet edition of the *Opera Omnia,* vol. 1 (Paris, 1890).

of Porphyry, the *Liber de Praedicabilibus*, (2) the Second Tractate of the *De Intellectu et Intelligibili*, and (3) an important passage from Albert's paraphrase of the *Metaphysics*. Although there is intrinsic evidence that Albert wrote the Porphyrean paraphrase after he wrote on the *Physics*,[2] I will not be concerned with questions of chronology, nor, given the constraints of space, will anything be said of the more and less immediate historical sources of Albert's views. All in all, what I have to say will be of a preliminary and largely expository nature, but, given the relative ignorance of Albert's thought, this is as it should be.

I. *The Logic of Universals*

After dutifully repeating Porphyry's demur about discussing in an introductory work the questions that make up the problem of universals, Albert, like so many others before him, launches with gusto into a prolonged discussion of them. Porphyry thought these questions too difficult; Albert, as the motto of this paper indicates, felt that the problem of universals raises questions that are best left to the metaphysician. Nonetheless, he argues that the logician must study universals. Indeed, they are his chronologically first concern. This follows from the nature and scope of logic.

Logic has for its subject argument: "Logicae subjectum est argumentatio."[3] Argumentation involves a plurality of propositions and thus the analysis and understanding of the proposition is a logical task presupposed by the study of argumentation as such. But, if the proposition is an element of argument, the proposition itself can be broken into terms, and thus the logic of the definition of terms comes before the logic of propositions. To cast this point in the framework of the works of the Organon, we see that such books as the *Topics* and *Analytics* presuppose *On Interpretation*, which in turn presupposes the *Categories*.[4] Since Porphyry's little work is an introduction to the *Categories*, Albert, in discussing the five predicables, takes himself to be on the very threshold of logic.

Logic is also—and most frequently—described by Albert as the science or art of coming to knowledge of the unknown through what is already known.[5] It is the mode of all knowledge and/or science[6] and

---

[2] See ibid., cap. 4, p. 28b.

[3] Ibid., Tractatus 1, cap. 4, p. 7b.

[4] See Albert's discussion in the first chapter of the first tractate of his exposition of *On Interpretation: Perihermenias*, Liber 1, ed. cit., pp. 373–76.

[5] See, for example, *De Praedicamentis*, Tractatus 2, cap. 1, p. 149.

[6] *De Praedicabilibus*, p. 2a.

4

concerns itself, not with things, but rather with the way in which things are ordered as we know them.[7] Since our knowledge is expressed in language, the logician must be concerned with language though it does not constitute his essential object.[8] In short, Albert denies that logic is a *scientia sermocinalis*. The logician is essentially concerned with things insofar as they are in the mind of one seeking to come to knowledge of what he does not know through knowledge already had. One can say, accordingly, that logic is not a *scientia sermocinalis* but rather is concerned with second intentions; that is, it bears not on language as such but on the ordering of known things in the mind of a human knower.[9]

Tractatus II of the *De Praedicabilibus* begins by asking why universals, of which the five predicables (genus, species, difference, property, and accident) are instances, should be considered by the logician. The answer derives from the nature of predicability. Only that can be truly and properly predicated of another which is in that of which it is predicated. Now, nothing is in itself, either as the essence or accident of itself, and from this it follows that nothing can be truly or properly predicated of itself. From the fact that what is truly and properly predicated is in another, it necessarily follows that it is communicable to all those things it is signified as being in. To be communicable is to have an aptitude to be in and of many. Whatever is thus in another is for that very reason predicable. The nature itself (*ratio et causa*) of the predicable is that it is universal. Whatever is predicable, in the sense of predicable meant here, is universal. If the first act of one seeking to discover the unknown from the known involves the ordering of the predicables, clearly this presupposes that one knows why the predicable is predicable. Since something is predicable because it is universal, logic begins with the study of universals.

[7] Ibid., p. 9.

[8] "Propter quod logicus et ad se et ad alterum utitur sermone per accidens, et non per se: quia sine sermone designativo procedere non potest ad notitiam ejus quod ignotum est." P. 7a.

[9] "Quia autem logica omnia considerat prout sunt in anima sive in intellectu ejus, qui quaerit per notum sibi venire in notitiam ignoti." Ibid., p. 9a. Richard F. Washell, in "Logic, Language and Albert the Great," *Journal of the History of Ideas* 34 (no. 3): 445-50, criticizes Norman Kretzmann for saying that Albert both challenged the claim that logic is a *scientia sermocinalis* and maintained that it is a science of mental entities (*intentiones*). Kretzmann is undoubtedly on firm ground here. I shall argue later that, however infrequently Albert uses (the phrase) *secundae intentiones*, that phrase best captures his conception of logic. Washell's article as well as his Ph.D. dissertation on Albert's logic (Toronto, 1969) are eminently worth reading, but, in the case of the article, he does not need the bum rap against Kretzmann to make the points he wishes to make.

The universal is that which, though it is in one, is capable of being in many: "Universale autem est, quod cum sit in uno, aptum natum est esse in pluribus."[10] Thus it pertains to the logician to study the universal insofar as it is the basis of predicability. The study of what is universal, insofar as it is a certain nature, a kind of being, falls to the metaphysician.[11] To predicate or to be predicated derives from the mental activity of one ordering and combining predicables according to the proper notion of predicables.

How precisely are we to understand this division of labor between the logician and metaphysician? The logician considers the universal as such, as universal, that is, as predicable, as likely to be in and of many. The metaphysician, on the other hand, considers the universal insofar as it is a certain nature or type of being. Now clearly the nature meant cannot be the nature of the universal properly speaking, since this involves predicability and that is the concern of the logician. It must therefore be the nature known to which predicability attaches, not as such, but *per accidens*: insofar as it is known. The logician considers the nature, not as such, in its ontological constituents, so to say, but just insofar as it is predicable. Speaking of the five predicables, Albert writes, "Per hoc enim accidentia diversum modum accipiunt praedicandi in quid vel in quale."[12] Predicability, universality, is not a constituent of the natures studied by the metaphysician; it is not a feature of real natures as they exist independently of our knowing and talking about them. The logician is thus concerned with the way in which we order and arrange things as we know them in our quest of the unknown through what we already know, an order and arrangement distinct from the order among existent things, the real order. This is Albert's abiding conception of the nature of logical entities, and doubtless that is what Kretzmann had in mind in making the remark to which Washell seems to take exception.

Logic may not be as such a *scientia sermocinalis*, but its concerns cannot be understood apart from language, inner or outer.[13] Albert distinguishes logic's dependence on or concern with language from that of grammar, poetry, and rhetoric. Logic's involvement with language is

10 *De Praedicabilibus*, Tractatus 2, p. 17b.

11 "Et hoc modo prout ratio est praedicabilitatis, ad logicum pertinet de universali tractare, quamvis secundum quod est natura quadam et differentia entis, tractare de ipso pertineat ad metaphysicum. Praedicare enim et praedicari rationis est ordinantis et componentis praedicabilia secundum praedicabilium propriam rationem." Ibid.

12 Ibid., p. 18a.

13 Ibid., p. 7a.

one with its being the mode of moving from the known to the unknown. Then comes this precision:

> The proof of this is that the known (through which knowledge of the unknown is gained) can be considered in two ways, namely as a thing outside the mind of the knower and as a certain notion in the mind of the knower. It is not causative of knowledge of the unknown insofar as it exists outside the mind of the knower, but rather insofar as it is a notion of the thing existing in the knower's mind, for in the latter sense it is significant and grounds for inference, by a perfect comprehension of which the intellect in some way perceives the unknown. It is in this way that the logician considers words significant of things and not otherwise.[14]

The logician is concerned with argumentative or syllogistic discourse and with whatever linguistic constituents of such discourse there may be. That is, he is concerned with simple as well as complex discourse, but with the former as it is presupposed by the latter.[15]

Just as the thing known may be a real thing but the fact that it is known by me (or anyone) is not a constitutive property of it, so for things to be talked about in simple or complex discourse is not a constitutive feature of things:

> Complexity and incomplexity do not belong (*accidunt*) to a thing insofar as it is a thing, nor even to the vocal sound insofar as it is a vocal sound, but they belong to the vocal sound insofar as it is referred to simple or composed understanding.[16]

The basis of this remark is the definition of the *vox significativa* found

[14] "Hujus autem probatio est, quod notum (per quod ignoti scientia accipitur) dupliciter consideratur, scilicet prout est res extra animam noscentis accepta, et prout est notio quaedam in anima noscentis. Non autem facit notitiam ignoti prout est res extra animam noscentis accepta, sed potius prout est notio rei in anima noscentis existens: sic enim significativa est et illativa ejus quod ignotum est: quod ignotum ipsi aliquo modo percipit intellectus perfecta comprehensione. Hoc ergo modo voces significativas rerum considerat logicus et non aliter." Ibid., p. 8a.

[15] In the *De Praedicabilibus*, Albert says that there are two parts of logic based on the division of simple and complex linguistic expressions. "Istae ergo sunt duae partes logicae. Una quidem ut doceantur principia per quae sciatur diffinitio rei et quidditas: ita quod per principia illa doceatur quae sit vera diffinitio, et quae non, et quae videatur esse et non sit. Alia vero ut doceantur principia qualiter per argumentationem probetur enuntiationis veritas vel falsitas." P. 8b.

[16] "Complexio autem et incomplexio non accidunt rei secundum quod res est, nec etiam voci secundum quod vox: sed accidunt voci secundum quod refertur ad intellectum simplicem vel compositum." Ibid., p. 9b.

in *On Interpretation,* and it enables Albert to distinguish the common or universal from the proper name:

> Further the vocal sound insofar as it is referred to the understanding of one seeking to discover the unknown through the known is such that it is divided into the common or universal and the proper or singular, neither of which belong (*accidit*) to it insofar as it is referred to the designated thing. All the things that are sensed and insofar as they are constituted by nature are singular: the note of the common that they take on derives from mind.[17]

Any term that is imposed from a form communicable to many, whether substantial or accidental, whether or not actually shared, is a common or universal term. Singular terms, whether proper names or definite descriptions, signify what can only belong to one.[18]

Given the definition of the universal as that which is predicated of many things, in which it is either substantially or accidentally, Albert provides the following scheme of the five predicables discussed in Porphyry's *Isagoge*:

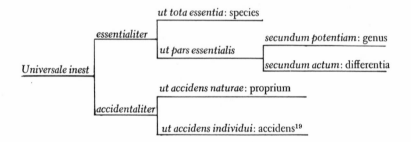

He adds the by now familiar point that he is not here concerned with the things themselves (*res ipsas*) which take on this ordering according to predicability. For things to be genera or species and the like is an accident and not a constituent of them.[20] He seems to contrast the

17 "Adhuc autem vox secundum quod refertur ad intellectum ejus qui quaerit invenire ignotum per notum, habet quod dividitur in commune, seu universale: et proprium, sive singulare: talium enim nihil accidit ei secundum quod ad rem designatum refertur. Res enim omnes sunt singulares quae cadunt sub sensu et secundum quod constituuntur a natura: et commune quod est in eis accipitur ab intellectu." Ibid., p. 10a.

18 Ibid., p. 10b.

19 Ibid., p. 17b–18a.

20 "Sed accidens ipsis rebus, quo eorum primum praedicabilium *generis* habet

predicables with the categories or predicaments, however, as if the former were a concern with the accidents that things take on as known and named by us and the latter a concern with the things themselves. But, if logic is concerned with things as they are known and the *Categories* is concerned with the things themselves, it should follow that the *Categories* is not a logical work. Either that or logic has been badly defined. Albert's thoughts on the matter are easily discovered:

> Because the predicables must be considered insofar as they are signified by vocal sounds, Boethius says that this science, namely that contained in the *Categories*, deals with the ten first words signifying the first genera of things, for this order is not in the things themselves, but it is necessary that reason impose the order, just as it makes composite collections.[21]

Albert seems to go out of his way to stress the point, summarizing the task before him thus: "Cum ergo tam utile sit hoc negotium istarum rerum *prout universalia quaedam sunt,* istarum quinque rerum *prout in ratione sunt,* speculatione sive consideratione tentabo traditionem compendiosam faciens doctrinam monstrare."[22]

Albert's view on the status of the entities with which the logician is concerned seems clear enough. The logician is concerned with that ordering of things known that the mind introduces into its own activity as it moves from the known to the unknown. But, if it is concerned with mental entities, logic is equally and perforce concerned with the linguistic expression of them. And that is Washell's point against Kretzmann. The logician cannot ignore language. To say that the logician "is concerned with discourse only incidentally, if at all" may be taken to set logic off from such *scientiae sermocinales* as grammar, poetry, and rhetoric. Nonetheless, the order among the predicables, for example, "cannot be determined unless the predicable is taken as designated by some vocal sound."[23] "From all this, it is plain what the subject of this book is: it is that which can be ordered according to the notion of the predicable or its subject insofar as this order is signified by

nomen et rationem . . . . Per hoc enim accidentia diversum modum accipiunt praedicandi . . . ." Ibid., p. 18a.

21 "Propter quod praedicabilia oportet considerare secundum quod vocibus significantur: propter quod dicit Boetius quod haec scientia, scilicet liber Praedicamentorum, est de decem primis vocibus prima genera rerum significantibus: ordo enim non est in rebus ipsis, sed oportet quod ratio ponat ordinem, sicut et facit complexionem et collectionem compositorum." *De Praedicamentis,* p. 150a.

22 Ibid., p. 19a.

23 ". . . ordo praedicabilium non potest determinari, nisi secundum quod sub voce habet praedicabile designari." P. 150a.

some vocal sound."[24] In denying that logic is *sermocinalis*, Albert appeals to Avicenna, and, not insignificantly, he points out that, insofar as language is the concern of the logician, namely as *significativus concepti*, it is something a man may engage in with himself as well as with others. That is, as John Damascene suggests, there is an inner as well as an outer language.[25]

It is true that the phrase "second intention" does not often occur in Albert; indeed, so far as I know, it never occurs in the logical writings. But surely the doctrine is there. Universality, predicability of many, is an accident of the nature as abstracted by mind.[26] If the intellectual grasp of a thing by way of abstraction is called an *intentio*, as it is,[27] and if we also find talk of the *intentio generis* and *intentio speciei*, as we do,[28] and if universality attaches to, is accidental to, intentions in the first sense,[29] we have a warrant for calling the universal and its types, genus, species, etc., second intentions. But surely what is important is whether or not Albert holds what is meant by "second intention" and not whether he uses this terminology profusely or at all. Thomas Aquinas is not prodigal with the terminology himself.

By way of summary, we can say that, for Albert, the universal is a concern of the logician because the logician is concerned with argumentation in all its amplitude. This concern embraces all the constituents and presuppositions of argument, propositions, their terms, and the ordering of terms according to predicability and subjectability. A very first concern of the logician, by way of preparation for undertaking the inquiry into the categories, is universality. Universality, predicability of many, is something that attaches to a nature as abstracted by our mind from the individuating and particularizing conditions due to matter. As known, the nature is something one related to the many in

[24] "Et ex his planum est quid sit hujus libri subjectum: est enim subjectum ordinabile in ratione praedicabilis et subjicibilis, secundum quod stat sub voce talem ordinem signante." Ibid. See as well pp. 377b–378a and p. 459: ". . . cum omnis et tota logica sit scientia disserendi . . . ." See too p. 5a and pp. 5b–6a.

[25] "Propter quod dicit Damascenus, quod in duo dividitur, scilicet in encordialem, hoc est, sermonem interius in mente dispositum, et in eum cum ex signis, qui angelus intelligendo est sui cordis nuntius, quia conceptus nuntiat ad alterum. Propter quod logicus et ad se et ad alterum utitur sermone per accidens, et non per se: quia sine sermone designativo procedere non potest ad notitiam ejus quod ignotum est. Ratiocinatione autem utitur per se . . . ." P. 7a–b.

[26] ". . . natura corporis, cui per aptitudinem dicendi de multis accidit universale esse . . .," p. 29a; "Est iterum universale secundum esse naturae simplicis, cui accidit universale esse secundum suam communicabilitatem. . . ." P. 34a.

[27] E.g., p. 10a and p. 22b.

[28] See p. 18b.

[29] See p. 24b.

which it can be found. Just as "to be known by men" is not a constitutive feature of natural things, so "to be talked of by men" is not a constitutive feature of natural things. The relations, properties, and accidents that things take on as known by men are the concern of the logician. Thus logical entities are mental, mind-dependent, and do not enjoy extra-mental existence.

If all this is roughly true, it will seem that Albert is unlikely to have any problem with the ontological status of universals and that he will make short shrift of the three questions of Porphyry that make up the problem of universals. That this is far from being the case, we shall now see.

II. *The Problem of Universals*

Of the three discussions of universals mentioned earlier, that found in Albert's discussion of Porphyry's *Isagoge*, his *Liber De Praedicabilibus*, is by far the most extensive. It is also the most surprising. The whole second tractate of this work deals with the three Porphyrean questions that constitute the problem of universals. In the Borgnet edition, the discussion covers twenty-four pages and comprises nine chapters. The first chapter argues that the logician must handle the question of universals, establishes the number of the predicables as five, and points out the usefulness of the discussion for logic. The second chapter sets forth the three Porphyrean questions and gives several preliminary interpretations of the first question, but not of the second and third. Albert then devotes separate chapters to the discussion of the three questions and adds four more chapters dealing with allied matters. The treatment is anything but perfunctory, therefore, and the reader rightly expects an illuminating and nuanced handling of the issues.

Now it is well known that Porphyry's questions are set forth in such a way that the second presupposes that a certain answer has been given to the first and the third presupposes that the second has been answered in a particular way. That is, the first question asks if genera and species subsist in reality or exist only in concepts, and the second question, presupposing that we have answered the first by saying that genera and species subsist, asks whether they are corporeal or incorporeal. The third question, on the assumption that they are incorporeal, asks if genera and species are found in sensible particulars or exist separately from them. Given Albert's views on the status of logical entities and given that genera and species are logical entities, we might expect that he would handle the first question with a distinction or two and wrap up the whole problem of universals rapidly. *Au contraire.*

Albert devotes a great deal of space to the first question. First, he sets forth seven of the strongest arguments on behalf of the view that genera and species pertain to the conceptual order and are not subsistent entities, arguments that can be roughly characterized as Aristotelian. He follows these with seven arguments on behalf of the view that universals are subsistent entities, and these arguments can be characterized as Platonic. Then, having given his own view, he states that the seven Platonic arguments are valid and necessary and proceeds to refute one by one the seven Aristotelian arguments.

What I propose to do is this: First, I shall set forth Albert's own solution; second, the solution in the *De Praedicabilibus* will be compared with that in *De Intellectu et Intelligibili* and in the paraphrase of the *Metaphysics*; third, I shall comment on Albert's refutation of the seven arguments that deny genera and species subsist; finally, I shall ask how coherent Albert's several treatments of universals are.

1. *Albert's Solution in* De Praedicabilibus

Albert begins by distinguishing three ways in which the universal can be considered, "namely, in itself as a simple invariable nature; as referred to understanding; and as it is in this thing or that."[30] Taken in the first way, it is the simple nature that gives being and definition and a name; it is among the things that are most truly a being, having no alien nature mixed with it, nor is it subject to variation by some other nature. Insofar as it is in this thing or that, many things pertain to it, the first of which is that the nature is particularized and individuated, the second that it is multiplied, and the third that it is incorporated and thereby subject to an infinity of diverse characteristics, since an infinity of things can inhere in matter. Considered in the second way, that is, as in the intellect, one must further distinguish between its reference to the First Intelligence knowing and causing it and its reference to the intellect knowing it by way of abstraction. The First Intelligence causes it to be a ray and light (*radium et lumen*) of itself, to be simple, pure, immobile, incorporeal, both perfectible and moving with regard to the possible intellect. The intellect that does not cause the nature but knows it abstractly confers universality on it by separating it from matter and individuating notes. At this point Albert invokes the Aristotelian dictum: "universale est dum intelligitur, particulare

---

[30] "Nos autem quantum sufficit praesenti intentioni ista solventes, dicimus quod universale triplicem habet considerationem, scilicet secundum quod in seipso est natura simplex et invariabilis: et secundum quod refertur ad intelligentiam: et secundum quod est in isto vel in illo." P. 24a.

vero dum sentitur."[31] Having said that universality pertains to a nature insofar as it is known by such an abstractive intellect as ours, Albert enigmatically adds, "quam de natura sua ante habuit" (which of its own nature it had before).[32] Obviously, universality cannot be both what the nature has of itself and what is conferred on it when it is known by an abstractive intellect. Albert seems to be suggesting that the human intellect, by abstracting the nature from individuating notes, restores it, as it were, to its condition prior to being received in matter.

This interpretation is bolstered by the next distinction Albert draws,[33] that among forms *ante rem*, that is, taken in themselves as being the principles of things, *in re*, that is, taken with the thing in which form exists as individuated and particularized, and *post rem*, as abstracted and separated from individuating conditions and having universality conferred upon them by the mind. The first are the substantial principles of things, the second the substances of things, the third accidents and qualities which are called the notes of things received in the soul.

With these distinctions in hand, Albert can say that

universals, that is, the natures which are called universals, taken in themselves, most truly are and are ingenerable, incorruptible and invariable. They are outside, beyond, bare and pure concepts, as the second group of arguments incontrovertably show; in some sense, however, they are in things and individuated. . . . Furthermore, they enjoy existence in the mind and this in a twofold way, namely, in the intellect which causes and effects them, and in the intellect knowing them by way of abstraction and effecting and educing them through universality.[34]

What then is Albert's answer to the first Porphyrian question? Genera and species, universals, may be considered in three ways and will be said to exist differently according to these different considerations. If we consider the natures or forms that are dubbed universals,

31 P. 24b.
32 Ibid.
33 Ibid.
34 ". . . universalia, hoc est, naturae quae universalia vocantur, secundum se accepta, sunt et verissime sunt ingenerabilia et incorruptibilia et invariabilia. Sunt etiam extra, vel praeter intellectum solum, nudum, et purum, sicut incontradicibiliter probant secundae inductae rationes; secundum autem quoddam esse, in rebus sunt, scilicet secundum esse individuatum . . . . Ad huc autem secundum quoddam esse sunt in intellectu: et hoc dupliciter, scilicet in intellectu per cognitionem causante et agente, et in intellectu cognoscente per abstractionem ea per universalitatem agente et educente." Pp. 24b–25a.

they are, in themselves, changeless, neither coming to be nor passing away. Moreover, they are not mere concepts. This is decisively settled, according to Albert, by the second set of seven arguments. The natures or forms which are called universals are not mere features or creatures of our mind. These forms or natures can be considered as they exist in matter, and there they are particularised and individuated. Thus, insofar as they exist in particulars, natures are particular and not universal. Finally, natures can be considered with reference to intellect, and it is with respect to a mind knowing them in an abstract way, as something one over and above the many particulars, that universality is effected. The short answer would thus seem to be that to be a universal, to be a genus or species, happens to natures as they are abstractly known by such a mind as ours. But Albert exhibits singular reluctance to state and settle for this short answer. And, to the reader's vast surprise, he embraces without question seven Platonizing arguments and undertakes to refute Aristotelian arguments.

2. Other Albertine Solutions

When we turn to the second tractate of Albert's *De Intellectu et Intelligibili*,[35] we seem to be moving in a somewhat different ambience. The opening chapter asks whether only the universal is the object of understanding and Albert provides two sets of arguments, but this time he prefers the set that is compatible with Peripatetic philosophy. The second chapter poses, in effect, the first Porphyrian question. Albert sets down four arguments on behalf of the view that the universal exists in the soul and only three on behalf of the view that universals must enjoy an extra-mental existence. This time Albert does not choose sides, but characterizes his own view as midway between those represented by the two sets of arguments: ". . . we say that the essence of anything can be considered to exist in two ways."[36] In the first way, the nature is taken to be different from matter or any subject in which it is found; in the second way, it is considered as in matter, as individuated. Each of these ways is further subdivided:

> And the first way can be further subdivided into two. First, insofar as it is a certain essence absolute in itself, and thus it is called *essence*, and it is one something existing in itself, nor does it have any other being than that of essence, and thus it is one alone. Second, as com-

[35] The text is found in Borgnet, vol. 9, pp. 477–502, with the second tractate on pp. 490–97.
[36] "Nos autem in ista difficultate mediam viam ambulantes, dicimus essentiam uniuscujusque rei dupliciter esse considerandum." P. 493a.

14

municability according to aptitude belongs to it: and this pertains (*accidit*) to it from the fact that it is an essence apt to give being to many, even if it never does so, and thus it is properly called a *universal*.[37]

The particularized nature may be said to have the aptitude of being in many, but only in the mind is the reference to many actuated: "That is why the Peripatetics say that the universal is only in the mind, meaning by universal that which is in and of many actually and not merely by way of aptitude."[38]

There is certainly a family resemblance between this treatment and that in *De Praedicabilibus*, but the differences are remarkable. One is struck by the phrase *essentia quaedam absoluta in seipsa*, a harbinger of Aquinas's *natura absolute considerata*. Furthermore, the distinction given above seems to avoid the ambiguity between the nature dubbed a universal because of what happens to it as known by us and the nature spoken of with respect to its intrinsic constituents. Just as a physical object can be referred to by way of an accidental property, e.g., "the red one," or substantively, e.g., "the checker," so a nature can be referred to as a universal or as a kind of being, e.g., human. It is one thing to ask whether the nature which takes on, when known, the property of universality can exist outside the mind and quite another to ask whether the nature considered as having the property of universality can exist outside the mind. In this second text, Albert observes this distinction far more faithfully than he does in the *De Praedicabilibus*.

In his presentation of the seventh book of the *Metaphysics*, Albert provides a crisp account.[39] Identifying the substance of man as that which is expressed in the definition, he notes that this substance can be considered in two ways, in itself and with respect to the accidents it takes on. In the second sense, one is concerned with the existence the substance takes on by comparison with something other than itself. Thus to consider the nature or substance as it exists in the mind or as

---

[37] "Et primo quidem modo adhue dupliciter consideratur. Uno quidem modo prout est essentia quaedam absoluta in seipsa, et sic vocatur *essentia*, et est unum quid in se existens, nec habet esse nisi talis essentiae, et sic est una sola. Alio modo ut ei convenit communicabilitas secundum aptitudinem: et hoc accidit ei ex hoc quod est essentia apta dare multis esse, etiamsi numquam det illud, et sic propie vocatur universale." P. 493a.

[38] ". . . et ideo dixerunt Perpitatetici quod universale non est nisi in intellectu, referentes hoc ad universale quod est in multis et de multis secundum actum existendi, et non secundum aptitudinem solam." P. 493b.

[39] *In 7 Metaphysicorum* (ed. B. Geyer; Cologne, 1960), Tractatus V, cap. 1.

it exists in matter is to see it taking on properties or accidents which are not essential constituents of it. To speak of the universal as being in one way or the other is not to assert that it is something *per se existens*. Of course, these remarks in the *Metaphysics* cannot be disengaged from the problematic of that work, but it could be argued that they state a clearer position than that found in the *De Praedicabilibus*.

3. *Albert's Refutations*

When we look at Albert's refutation of the seven arguments he had set down on behalf of the claim that universals do not enjoy separate existence, outside the mind, we find him not at his best. The first argument had maintained that whatever exists is numerically one thing. In reply, Albert says that universals do not exist as do the products of natural processes. Furthermore, he suggests that the nature is itself one, even numerically one.[40] Of course, humanity is one nature and equinity is another, but it seems odd to equate this with numerical unity, particularly when the claim is supported by saying that many men are one in nature. Surely they are numerically many and specifically one.

A similar oddity is found in his refutation of the second argument. That argument had held that whatever exists separately must be a subsistent thing (*hoc aliquid*) whereas the nature is a kind (*quale quid*). Albert suggests that we distinguish two senses of "having separate existence." If it means undivided in itself and divided from all others, the objection holds, but if it means having independent existence, the objection fails, "because the universal, separate in this way, enjoys existence in reality although it is not a subsistent thing."[41] This could mean something as tame as: the nature which takes on universality as known enjoys existence in particular things. Nothing in the first set of seven arguments suggests that so tame an interpretation is being contested and one wonders what Albert means to say.

In refuting both the fifth and sixth arguments, Albert seems guilty of the fallacy of the *per accidens*. The sixth argument had likened the universal to the form in the mind of the artisan which relates to many exemplars, but as exemplified it is always singular and particular. In refuting this, Albert makes the point that what is true of the nature as it exists in individuals is only *per accidens* true of the nature, that is, is not true of it as such. He then goes on to say that to be universal and common belongs to the nature as such (*secundum se*). To this it must

[40] *De Praedicabilibus*, p. 25a.
[41] Ibid.: ". . . quia universale sic separatum, habet esse in natura, et tamen non est hoc aliquid."

be said that to be universal is equally accidental to the nature as such, something Albert himself elsewhere insists on. The same fallacy of the *per accidens* is committed in Albert's refutation of the seventh argument where he asserts that to be common belongs to the nature *secundum se*.[42]

It is difficult to avoid the thought that, in writing the *De Praedicabilibus*, Albert was insufficiently in command of the necessary clarity to deal effectively with the Porphyrean questions. The whole drift of his presentation of the nature of logic and of the status of the concerns of the logician suggests a quite different treatment of the problem of universals from what we in fact find. That drift suggests that Albert should have embraced the first set of seven arguments, those we have characterized as roughly Aristotelian. One can only wonder how he would have gone about showing that the second or Platonic set incontrovertibly establishes the separate existence of universals. In seeking to refute the first set, Albert seems to argue against the grain of his own views and is led into patently fallacious reasoning. We learn from Albert the necessity of distinguishing between what belongs to the nature as such and what happens to it as it is known by an abstractive intellect like ours. And then we see him smudging this distinction and attributing to the nature as such what is only true of it as known abstractly. Later, in the *De Intellectu et Intelligibili*, he proceeds with sureness and clarity and explicitly rejects the Platonic position.

III. *Conclusion*

It is unavoidable to conclude that Albert only gradually won through to a clear position on the problem of universals. In the *De Praedicabilibus* we find a complicated and often incoherent outlook that is notably different from that of the *De Intellectu et Intelligibili*. It is noteworthy that, in the former work, the threefold distinction of forms as *ante rem*, *in re*, and *post rem* is presented by Albert in his own name whereas in the latter he identifies it as a Platonic distinction and is critical of it.[43] One finds adumbrations of the far clearer outlook of Aquinas in reading Albert—we have mentioned the seeming harbinger of the Thomistic *natura absolute considerata*[44]—but any comparison of the two giants of the thirteenth century leads inexorably to the conclusion that Albert, great though he undeniably was, is a precursor of his famous disciple.

[42] Ibid., p. 26a.
[43] Chap. 5, p. 496.
[44] See M.-D. Roland Gosselin, *Le 'De Ente et Essentia' de S. Thomas d'Aquin* (Paris, J. Vrin, 1948), pp. 24–29.

Doubtless he is someone without whom Thomas would have been far less than he was, and it would be churlish not to grant him the admiration he richly deserves. But, as this brief glance at his treatments of the problem of universals suggests, there is a groping, prolix, and unsure aspect of Albert's thought that cannot be denied.

Part II

Physics

The Concept of Time in Albert the Great

JOHN M. QUINN, O.S.A.
Villanova University

The wide range of Albert's knowledge of natural phenomena was surely one of the reasons some medievals dubbed him *stupor mundi,* a wonder of the world, an individual of boundless energy with an astonishingly prehensile mind ever bent on running down clues concerning how things go whether in the domain of animals, birds, flowers, or minerals. But Albert was no mere drudging collector of bags of facts after the fictitious model of Francis Bacon. Matching his prodigious powers of assimilation was a sharpness not to be appeased till it fastened on general and specialized whys of natural events (and too their metaphysical and theological ramifications)—a rigorous pursuit quite influential in enabling Latin Aristotelianism to turn a corner in the thirteenth century. Though the fruits of his feel for fact are at work in the background, Albert's analytical shrewdness accounts for the greater part of the finesse he brings to an original, generally deft handling of natural time, a question as substantially knotty and vexing to medievals as it is to our contemporaries. Indeed the principal issues canvassed in the Albertine theory of time are not matters insulated within the lexicon of the high Middle Ages. Their pondering and adjudication can be livingly brought to bear on the meaning of time for contemporary philosophy of nature. As is well known, Newtonian absolute time is no longer regarded as tenable, for it makes time over into a quasi-mathematical coordinate. Neither quantum theory nor relativity theory, each a great revolutionary turn in twentieth-century physics, provides groundwork for an adequate natural-philosophical picture of time. Quantum theory does not lend extrinsic or conjectural countenance to any particular philosophical view of time.[1] In the bed of relativity theory has grown a variety of philosophical proposals, one invoking its

[1] E. J. Zimmerman, "Time and Quantum Theory," especially pp. 492–99, in J. T. Fraser, ed., *The Voices of Time* (New York: Braziller, 1966).

authority for the claim that time is spatialized and another, its contrary, proving in its light that space is dynamized.[2] Special relativity theory itself has recently come under fire, for its two postulates seem flawed by a massive contradiction—within the same frame of reference clock A may be read as faster and slower than clock B.[3] Even apart from possible inherent defects, relativity theory is strictly not an analysis of time but a specialized theory concerning its measurement. In walking step by step with Albert in his inquiry, we are then not only helping recover some of his physical riches but also regaining one elucidation of the Aristotelian conception that remains a stimulating live option for understanding physical time today.

Our perusal mainly follows the systematic treatment in the commentary on the latter part of Book IV of the *Physics*. After engaging in dialectical preliminaries, we shall look at the definition of time, the meaning of the now, properties of and beings in time, the relation of time to the soul, the ubiquity and oneness of time, and, as a final expository item, a metaphysical addendum concerning eternity. A last section examines difficulties that seem to beset Albertine time.[4]

[2] Olivier Costa De Beauregard, "Time in Relativity Theory: Arguments for a Philosophy of Being," pp. 417–33, and Milic Capek, "Time in Relativity Theory: Argument for a Philosophy of Becoming," pp. 434–54, both in ibid.

[3] Herbert Dingle, "Time in Relativity Theory: Measurement or Coordinate?" pp. 455–72, in ibid. Dingle refines and expands his attack in *Science at the Crossroads* (London: Martin, Brian, and O'Keeffe, 1972), including a searching criticism of the aphysical character of Minkowski's now popularized mathematical invention named space-time. Drawing on, among others, earlier papers by Dingle, L. Essen's *The Special Theory of Relativity: A Critical Analysis* (Oxford: Clarendon Press, 1971) argues that the special theory still lacks experimental confirmation and is seriously blemished by an irresolvable clock or twin paradox, which Einstein's equivocations and later illogicalities by way of apologia only made graver.

[4] Albert's commentary, *Physica* (composed 1245–48), is in vol. 3 of his *Opera omnia* edited by Auguste Borgnet (Paris: Vivès, 1890–99). (We are following the formulation of titles and the dating suggested by James A. Weisheipl, O.P., in "Albert the Great, St.," *New Catholic Encyclopedia*, vol. 1, pp. 257–58.) Unless otherwise indicated, references to his other writings come from this edition; "otherwise" denotes citations of three works from the Cologne edition (1951–). Unlike that of Averroes, Saint Thomas, and Giles of Rome, Albert's exposition, as *Phys.*, I, tr. 1, c. 1, pp. 1b–2a avows, is not a line-by-line commentary on the text (this is true also of his treatises on other parts of the Aristotelian corpus). It seems misguided to claim, as some do, that his version is neither commentary nor paraphrase but a wholly original work. Quasi-commentary seems more just since its ideas are so geared to the Stagirite's order and doctrine that secondary additions to and subtractions from the text are plainly discernible.

Elsewhere in his physical reflections, Albert remarks (*Phys.*, IV, tr. 3, c. 6. p. 318b), he ordinarily takes his cue from Latin thinkers but here he finds the in-

Dialectic of Time

Since unhistorical clichés die hard, it may still come as a surprise to some that members of the Aristotelian school were not, no more than was their mentor, blindly dogmatic and rigidly deductivistic. Every problem is first dealt with problematically, and it is part of the business of dialectic (the branch of the *Organon* that demonstrates ways of grappling with what escapes demonstration) to dialogue with previous thinkers, to explore disputatively questions already mooted about what is under investigation.[5] Here, in short, dialectic formulates the problematic of time. Since it concerns only introductory matters whose solution calls for only common arguments, its inferences, however compelling their guise, remain extrinsic to the proper determination of

sights of the Arabs sure (c. 7, p. 320b echoes this: "and we follow the Arabs *per omnia*, in every solution, as we have said above"). As Augustin Mansion notes in "Les temps chez les péripatéticiens médiévaux, *Revue néo-scolastique de Philosophie*, 36 (1934); 288 and 296–97 (Mansion restricts consideration of the dependence of Albert and Thomas on Averroes to the single problem of temporal unicity), for the bulk of his exposition Albert relies heavily on Averroes. In favor of a time qualifying the primary motion and against the psychologizing of time Albert lists the support of six "men distinguished in philosophy": Avicenna, Alexander, Themistius, Averroes, Theophrastus, and Porphyry (c. 4, p. 313b). Mansion (p. 289) breaks down this apparently ill-assorted line-up of Arabian and Greek antecedents into three subclasses: Avicenna, a primary source; Averroes, who acquaints Albert with the opinions of Alexander of Aphrodisias and Themistius; Theophrastus's and Porphyry's notions, Mansion surmises, may have been channeled through Alfarabi, cited many times in the interpretation of the *Physics*. If, on Mansion's word, we count Averroes's influence pervasive, we may generally confine ourselves to putting our finger here and there on evidences of Avicennian derivation. Albert's already achieved formidable authority might well function as an *a priori* premise for inferring that his thinking on time left a lasting impress on the next generation. According to Mansion (p. 299), Aquinas's handling of unicity leans on Albert's distinction between time as intrinsic number of the first motion and extrinsic number of all other motions. A nuanced tracing of what Albert bequeathed to Thomas, however, lies outside our present scope. It does not seem irrelevant to mention also that Albert's discussion exerted a strong impact on Giles of Rome. A two-installment essay by this writer, "The Concept of Times in Giles of Rome," published in *Augustiniana*, 28–29, fasc. 3–4, 1978 and fasc. 1–2, 1979, touches, on the side, on some of Giles's legacy from Averroes (frequently cited) and Aquinas (never cited). Giles's debt to Albert, it now appears, is more than skimpy—a connection best reserved for scrutiny in another place.

[5] *Topica* (dated 1248–64), vol. 2, I, c. 1 (*Proemium*), pp. 233–34. As *docens* or doctrinal, dialectic is a science that lays down exact modes of arguing with probability, but as *utens*, as actually employed, it always falls short of analytical certitude (p. 235). See also *Metaphysica* (produced 1261–66), ed. Bernhard Geyer (Münster Westfalen: Aschendorff, 1960), t. 16 (pt. 1), III, tr. 3, c. 6, p. 145a–b; IV, tr. 1, c. 7, p. 170b.

time.[6] After dialectically disposing of false approaches, we are still faced with the task of satisfactorily dissecting time.

Dialectic propounds questions and then tentatively counters their doubts and fuzziness concerning the reality of time and the now, the nature of time, and the independence of time from the soul.

1. Though time, along with motion, seems sensorily observable, critical reflection casts suspicion on its existence and that of the now, its acknowledged central factor. Or granted that it somehow exists, so opaque does its configuration appear that time is put down as an I-know-not-what.[7]

Expectation that a divisible like time contains parts apparently goes unfulfilled. No one of the familiar triad, past, future, and present, can assert legitimate title to actual physical existence. The past has ceased to exist, the future is yet to be, and the present as indivisible is not a part of time (in spite of the currency of certain mathematical-philosophical curiosities in our day, no divisible can be composed of indivisibles). Nor can we equate the now with a *pars non aliquota* (two is such with respect to seven) because, while not multipliable by an integer to obtain a certain number, such a part does compose a whole with another part.[8]

In addition, difficulties crowd in when we try to classify the now as permanent or successive. Pluralized nows cannot simultaneously co-exist; otherwise they would not be many, and time would be frozen into one static segment. A succession of nows also labors under inconveniences. A segment of time that is part of a greater segment is always included in the larger part (as an hour in a day), but one now containing several nows is unthinkable, for one indivisible manifestly cannot contain another indivisible. Nor can we conceive of a new now following upon the corruption of its predecessor. A now can be corrupted neither in itself nor in another now. Not in itself: clearly a thing cannot both exist in something and be corrupted in it. Not in an ensuing now: this would have to follow, either immediately or not immediately, the first now. No now can immediately follow another now; a span always intervenes, for no indivisible, lacking continuity, can be right next to or continuous with a preceding indivisible. The supposed corruption cannot occur in a now not following immediately because the line in between the first and the second now (wherein it is assumed to corrupt) contains an infinite number of nows, in which the first or past now

6 *Phys.*, IV, tr. 3, c. 1, p. 305a–b.

7 Ibid., p. 305b

8 Ibid., p. 306a.

24

will perdure and with which it will therefore be simultaneous; and obviously no now can be really identified with its successors. Besides, the merger of past, present, and future nows effectively does away with any succession of nows.[9] Recourse to a now everlastingly the same, on the other hand, looks no more promising. For one thing, a finite continuum has to have more than one terminus; we cannot regard time as divisible without regarding it as bounded by two terminals. Again, a totally unpluralized now so blends before and after that what happened a thousand years ago would be eventuating today.[10]

2. Three opinions on the nature of time receive quick review and rejection. According to the first, time is the movement of the first sphere. But while part of time is time, part of a circular motion is not equivalent to the whole of a circular motion. Too, on this reckoning, if there were several heavens, there would be several times. It is unjust to read into Aristotle the incongruity that if there were two first mobiles there would be two times. The thrust of his criticism is contextual: coexistence of several times is one paradoxical spinoff from hypothesizing several mobiles within the setting of this false definition. Indeed, once we posit several times, we posit, in effect, an infinite number of times. Yet, Albert cautiously avers, we may venture a simultaneity of two times if we ground this in the common now of one or other time.[11]

The second hypothesis, which identifies time with the primary sphere, is coarsely fallacious. In concluding that time is the same as the sphere (because the sphere is that in which all things are and time is that in which all things are), it is guilty of the crude logical mistake of using two affirmatives in the second figure. Too, the middle term is equivocal, for "that in which all things are" refers to place as regards the sphere

[9] Ibid., pp. 306a–307b.

[10] Ibid., p. 307a–b.

[11] Ibid., pp. 307b–308b. Albert ascribes this view to Plato very probably in dependence on Averroes; see *Aristotelis de Physico Auditu libri octo cum Averrois Cordubensis Commentariis* (Venice, 1562–74; Minerva reprint, Frankfurt, West Germany, 1962), IV, com. 92, fol. 176D. According to W. D. Ross, ed., *Aristotle's Physics* (Oxford: Clarendon Press, 1936), p. 596, Plato advocates this definition in the *Timaeus*, 39c5–d2. It is from Avicenna's *Sufficientia* (Venice, 1508; Minerva reprint, 1962), II, c. 10, fol. 33C, that Albert borrows the inconsequence of an infinite number of times. In *Summa theologiae* (written sometime after 1270), vol. 31, pt. I, tr. 5, q. 23, membrum 3, a. 2, obj. 2 in contrarium, pp. 188b–189a, Albert clarifies the thrust of Avicenna's reasoning. Two times would be simultaneous in the same time, i.e., a third time; but three times can be simultaneous only within a fourth time, and so on ad infinitum. A plurality of nonsimultaneous times issues in the same absurdity, for nonsimultaneous times are relatable only in terms of an intermediate time, the number of which multiplies indefinitely.

and to number as regards time. Again, it illicitly assumes that all things are in the sphere and in time.[12]

The opinion that time is motion or change has the most surface probability and widest acceptance. But change lies in what is changed or moved; whereas time is present in all temporals. Moreover, fast and slow are said of motion but time remains uniform, neither fast nor slow. These are attributes of motion measured by time, but time itself is clearly not measured by time.[13]

3. Detouring from his broad gloss on the text, Albert briefly mulls over an allied dialectical concern, the contention that time has no real existence outside the soul. Refusal to identify time with the primary sphere or motion, some hold, implies only the denial of the physical existence of time, leaving the way open to its solely psychic existence. In marking the before and after points of a moving thing and in distinguishing these from the route between them, the soul confers existence upon time. From this standpoint, as Avicenna notes, time is nothing but a cluster of moments, a serial order hanging on the decision of the designater of the moments.[14]

(i) The prior and posterior supposedly numbered in time are correlated by intentional activity. Prior and posterior are taken together as terminals of time only because the soul preserves the prior, now past, to join it to the posterior point yet to be.

(ii) Number is the outcome of two causal factors, numerable matter (prior and posterior) and a soul that numbers: the number that is time is actualized by the soul.

(iii) As Aristotle states, we perceive time only by perceiving motion in the soul—the dependence of time on the soul is plain.

(iv) If time were subjectified in the motion of the heaven, all its parts would be moved together. The consequent being clearly false, a time without actual simultaneity of prior and posterior has to exist in the soul.

(v) According to Galen, if time were in the motion of the heaven, individuals living underground would be deprived of a sense of time—an implication contrary to experience.

[12] Ibid., p. 308b. The first and third items in Albert's rebuttal are taken from Avicenna (*Sufficientia*, II, c. 10, fol. 33H), while the charge of equivocation is gleaned from Averroes, *In phys.*, IV, com. 94, fol. 1761.

[13] Ibid., pp. 308b–309a. At this point, Albert remarks, he glides over, because not germane, the differences setting motion apart from *mutatio* or substantial change (generation and corruption), six reasons for which differences he spells out in ibid., V. tr. 1, c. 3, pp. 360a–362b.

[14] Ibid., 309b–310a. Avicenna, *Sufficientia*, II, c. 10, 33A and 33D.

26

(vi) Saint Augustine defines time as a distension of the soul because past, present, and future show no durational foothold in nature.

(vii) In arguing for a time potentially in motion but actually in the soul, Averroes appears to recommend a strictly psychic time. Several thinkers have mounted a flanking attack on a sheerly nonphysical time.[15]

(i) If absence of the prior and posterior were sufficient to psychologize an entity, motion also would have to be disallowed residence outside the soul. To put it positively, if motion is sensorily observable *in rerum natura*, time also enjoys physical existence.

(ii) It seems to court absurdity to situate time, a continuous quantity, solely in a simple entity like the soul that is devoid of quantity.

(iii) Time as a property of the soul would be unable to share in the properties of continuous and discrete quantity—which prima facie strikes one as awry.

(iv) If the parts of motion that time numbers are in the soul, the soul itself would undergo local motion.

(v) Wholly psychologized time narrows the scope of time-related motion, whereas time subjectively measures the primary motion and applicatively measures all other motions. But these counter-forays are suasive rather than coercive. Once we determine the nature of time and the now, we will be equipped to probatively bulwark the claim of an extra-psychic time.[16]

Definition of Time

Just as it is dialectically clear that time is not the same as motion, so it is sensorily evident that where there is no motion there is no time.

[15] Ibid., pp. 310a–311a. Argument (v) summarizes two distinct subarguments reported by Averroes, who credits Plato with the objection concerning the unawareness of physical time in those living underground (Averroes, *In phys.*, IV, com. 98, fol. 178H) and attributes to Galen the view that we know time only through certain movements of the psyche (ibid., 179E). Averroes's resolution of the question of time's relation to the soul is offered in ibid., com. 131, fol. 202C–H, to which Albert devotes attention in c. 16, p. 339b (see n. 48 below and related matter in our text). A work perhaps slightly earlier than the *Physica*, *De quatuor coaequaevis* (dated 1245–50), vol. 34, tr. 2, q. 5, a. 1, obj. 5 (first set), pp. 365b–366b, quoting key passages from the eleventh book of Augustine's *Confessiones* specifiable in the contemporary edition of M. Skutella (Paris: Desclée De Brouwer, 1962) as parts of 15.20, 20.26, 26.33, and 28.37, tends to injudiciously equate Augustine's delicately wrought position with that turning time into a collection of moments, cited by Avicenna (see n. 14 above).

[16] Ibid., p.311a–b. "Avicenna and several other philosophers" (these latter left unnamed), Albert says, pose these five objections against an exclusively psychic time, but it is not easy to dig them out of the *Sufficientia*.

Should no change occur or should we be unaware that change is occurring, no time seems to occur. Change in our psychological state signalizes a passage of time. A psychologistic approach to the tie-in between awareness of change and the reality of time that relegates time to the mental mode is powerless to explain the overwhelming conviction that we perceive time as a feature of nature. An alternative course seems preferable; as we are interiorly changed, we perceive motion and so perceive the occurrence of time.[17] To couch it negatively, when deep slumber or engrossment in pleasure blots out awareness of change, we detect no passage of time. Legendary heroes who slept through several years without perceiving that time was passing fused the now at the start of dormition with that at the moment of awaking.[18] Occasionally when the mind stays fixed in one and the same indivisible experience, no time seems to flow. Feasting on their Beloved alone, saintly individuals in transport lose all sense of time as their soaring spirits are intoxicated with interior joys that inhibit perception of change.[19] Only speciously can the coperception of time and motion be built into a brief for a soul-produced time. Dephysicalized time carries with it an inconceivable simultaneous existence and nonexistence of time (inasmuch as various souls do and do not attend to it) and the proliferation of times unto infinity.[20]

Hence time is not locked within the soul but properly modifies the movement of the primary mobile, which causes and is therefore graspable in all other motions as a cause operative in its effects.[21] In laying

[17] Ibid., c. 4, p. 312a–b. Following Averroes (*In phys.* IV, com. 98, fol. 179E–F), Albert lists a second faulty proposal, that exterior motion elicits a change in the soul, which he discards because it does not involve direct perception of time.

[18] Ibid., 312b. Ross, *Aristotle's Physics*, p. 597, retails some of the conflicting stories woven about these fabulous sleepers. Albert's biochemical explication of the sluggishness inducing sleep (pp. 312b–313a)—a combination of unreleased internal vapors and a constriction of the pores—obviously would not pass muster today. However, the fact that he does hypothesize a natural scientific analysis of deep slumber appears noteworthy.

[19] Ibid., p. 313a. A kindred experience of loss of time awareness happens "aliquibus hominibus divinis" (*Sufficientia*, II, c. 10, fol. 33F), an expression duplicated in Albert's "homines divini." A severely limited but genuine participation in eternity, he adds, is the reason why godly men are emancipated from awareness of flux and time. *Phys.*, IV, tr. 4, c. 2, p. 348a and c. 3, p. 349a.

[20] Ibid., p. 313a–b.

[21] Ibid., p. 313b. Here Albert calls upon the six worthies spoken of previously (n. 4) to attest to the situation of time in the primary motion. *Sufficientia*, II, c. 13, fol. 36E mentions this, which Averroes enlarges on in *In phys.*, IV, com. 98, fol. 179F. Themistius recognizes the principal temporal residence in *Paraphrasis in Physica*, trans. Hermalaus Barbarus (Venice, 1499), IV, fol. 53a. The Latin version

hold of any motion whatsoever (whether or not we explicitly advert to a causal nexus), we effectively apprehend the first motion. The presence of the first motion, through its causal impress, in every other motion nullifies Galen's objection that lifelong under-the-earth dwellers would be robbed of all sense of time, for subterranean denizens would be regularly cognizant of the primary motion in its effects. Plainly then time is not motion nor simply motion in the soul. Evidently also, time is not knowable, because not really possible, without motion. Even when sitting motionless in the dark, cloistered from all impinging sensory influences, we apprehend time in the apprehension of movements in imagination or intellect. Conversely, every awareness of time tells of the presence of motion.[22]

The primary motion already mentioned as (and later to be proved to be) the primary seat of time traverses a continuous magnitude. Too, motion itself is continuous because it occurs according to change of position—it is a sort of flowing where. The continuity of local motion derives from that of magnitude, and, in turn, the continuity seen in alteration or growth reflects that of local motion. Motion is then observably per se quantified, but motion according to its formal intelligibility does not possess continuity derived from space, else all motion would be nothing but local motion. In any case, the continuity of local motion sprouts from a double root, one proximate, the other primary; the proximate is the unbroken transit of the mobile being according to place, and the primary is continuous space itself. Moreover, as motion draws its continuity from magnitude, so time owes its continuity to motion. Prior and posterior parts are marked off as a particular segment of space by two boundary points apiece that number magnitude. This induction lays the first foundation of the definition of time: space is continuous and denumerable. Moreover, motion exhibits prior and posterior parts available, like their spatial counterparts, for numeration, each part being similarly bounded by two indivisibles called moments. This yields the second fundament: prior and posterior parts bounded by moments number motion. However, motion delimited by the prior and posterior is not synonymous with motion as such; essential

here is a rather free rendering of the Greek available in *Themistii in Physica Paraphrasis*, p. 342, ll. 1–5 (pagination according to the L. Spengel edition, 1866) in *Commentaria in Aristotelem Graeca*, ed. Heinrich Schenkl (Berlin: George Reimer, 1890), 1:163. I have not been able to locate this view in Theophrastus. Alexander's physical glosses seem no longer directly available (Ross, *op. cit.*, p. 103), and all of Porphyry's Aristotelian works save the *Isagoge* and a commentary on the *Categories* have apparently perished.
22 Ibid., p. 314a.

hospitality to such discrete quantities would awkwardly land motion in the category of quantity.[23]

A further, final step achieves an assured concept. As we discriminate the parts of space and motion by terminal points, so we experience time by numbering it at boundary points named nows. As with the spatial boundaries, the four terminals reduce to two. We become aware of time once the soul says the nows are two; knowledge of two nows delimiting a motion continuum is knowledge of time. When, however, we do cognize not two nows but one alone, as if stationary, we are bereft of a sense of time. It is when the now divides into prior and posterior that we remark the lapse of time. This brings us to an adequate definition: "Time is the number taken from the prior and posterior existing in motion." Number, the genus or formal feature, bespeaks number inhering in motion. "Taken from the prior and posterior existing in motion" denotes the units grouped to constitute the number of motion.[24] The rendering of Themistius, according to whom time numbers the prior and posterior of time (whereas the prior and posterior are counted with reference to motion), makes the definition circular: the

[23] Ibid., pp. 314b–315b. In ibid., VI, tr. 1, cc. 1–2, pp. 405–11, Albert shows that spatial continuity, of which motion and time partake, is not composed of indivisibles. Ibid., V, tr. 2, c. 3, pp. 381–83, takes a look at other modes of continuity, such as corporal continuity (in mixed bodies) and colligative continuity (in flesh, veins, and nerves). Ibid., III, tr. 1, cc. 4–5, pp. 190–94, expounds and proves the definition of motion.

[24] Ibid., pp. 315b–316a. On Albert's reckoning, we attain the two nows not directly but stepwise. At first we grasp the time-line roughly as follows:

(nows one and two bound the prior segment, and nows three and four the posterior segment). A second insight reduces the nows from four to two

(we really know time when the first of the prior nows and the second of the posterior nows [assigned the number four in the time line above] delimit the one line). The original four nows correspond to the two prior and two posterior points of space and the two prior and two posterior moments of the motion continuum (p. 315a–b).

According to *De quatuor coaequaevis*, tr. 2, q. 5, a. 2, p. 369b–370a, the time of the theologians, which is the measure of any motion whatsoever, corporeal or spiritual (the latter is a discontinuous series of nows), differs from that of the philosophers, which is continuous.

30

prior and posterior of time are defined in virtue of time, and time itself is defined through the prior and posterior of time.[25]

That time determines the more and less in motion confirms its specific role as number of motion. But in what sense is time number? Real number is distinguished into the material and formal, material referring to things actually or potentially number and formal to that by which we number—number in the usual sense. Time as number occupies a region in between these two kinds of number. Unlike two or three, it is not absolute number but numbered number, and in this respect it is an existential quantity, a being of nature, not classifiable as number except in a relative manner. But insofar as it is applied to motion as a form to matter, time is also formal or numbering number. Its status as numbered number, however, is accidental to time taken strictly, for as the construction of the definition revealed, time is substantially, i.e., essentially, number. The markings on a wooden ell (roughly a medieval equivalent of a meter stick), e.g., indicate that it is quantified, yet the fact that it is something measured is incidental to its work as a measuring device. It is essentially a measuring rod, designed to tell the quantity of natural objects. So with time: considered as numbered number, it is a measured ingredient of nature; considered essentially, taken as numbering number, it functions as the measure of all motion.[26] Another example corroborates time's numerical character. Two motions, one faster than the other in coming to term, may nevertheless be deemed equal in regard to a certain quantity; i.e., each has the power to pass from potency to act. Since we cannot ascribe this quantity to other motions (these are

[25] Ibid., p. 316a–b. Avicenna vaguely identifies the vicious-circle interpreter as "one of the disciples"; *Sufficientia* II, c. 11, fol. 34D. Making no mention of Themistius, Averroes adopts Alexander's caution that the prior and posterior numbered exist in motion. After conceding Galen's contention that the prior and posterior in the definition belong to time, Themistius in *Paraphrasis in Physica*, IV, fol. 50a disclaims the implication that the concession is circular by arguing that the prior and posterior nows simultaneously number diverse motions in Athens, Corinth, and elsewhere. For the original see p. 321, l. 16 to p. 322, l. 15 in the Schenkl edition (cited in p. 21 above), p. 149. However, as *De quatuor coaequaevis*, tr. 2, q. 5, a. 2, ad 8, p. 372a evidences, an earlier Albert, not altogether unsympathetic to Themistius, proposes two senses in which the prior and posterior can be parts of time without risk of vicious circularity.

[26] Ibid., c. 6, pp. 316b–317b. In *De quatuor coaequaevis*, tr. 2, q. 5, a. 3, ad 2, p. 374 substance, we are told, conveys the import of both essence ("quod quid erat esse") and that which the thing is ("id quod est res"). For Albert, following Averroes (*In phys.* IV, com. 101, 181E), number is the substance, i.e., the essential factor, in the definition. It is both material and formal number; material (or numbered) because it is physical, not mathematical; formal (or numbering) because "it is applied to motion as form to matter" (p. 317a). See also *De quatuor coaequaevis*, tr. 2, q. 5, a. 2, ad 1, ad 2, ad 3 and ad 4, pp. 370b–371b.

unequal), to space (unequally traversed), or to mobiles (unequal mobiles can move equally), the equal quantity in all motions has to be time, which is equally present because it numbers motion.[27]

A word should be said to balance the discrete and continuous aspects of time. As already remarked, not motion as such (else motion would be subsumed under quantity) but local motion is continuous. While motion as such is incidentally continuous, time is per se continuous, for prior and posterior are not actually separated in its flow. Yet because it numbers the continuum, it is discrete. Thus time is formally discrete and materially (but truly) continuous. Since time is formally number, it is disclosed more through the discrete than through the continuous. Absolutely, time numbers "the parts of the continuum of an undivided exit," i.e., in terms of an undivided unit. Relatively, time numbers the parts of the continuum seen as dividedly emergent, i.e., seen as parts proceeding one after another to make a line.[28]

The foregoing analysis enables us to disentangle perplexities that dialectically worried us, according to which time does not exist because time cannot be made up of a departed past, partless present, and a not-yet-existent future, or, from another angle, cannot be composed of in-divisible nows. A key distinction topples these barriers: nature is the habitat of successive beings as well as permanent beings. Time patterned after something permanent becomes a hopeless riddle, but if considered, as it is, successive, the enigmas beclouding its existence evaporate. Like motion, time is an admixture of potency and act, which, as its course unfolds, is always varied. From the vantage point of permanent being, the parts of time lack physical existence, but rendered continuous through an ever-present indivisible unit, the parts of the time continuum do enjoy existence. Indeed the polemic against the physical reality of time proves too much; were it sound, it would wipe out the physical character of motion, which is of course an incontestable deliverance of the senses. Undoubtedly, moreover, the now is not a part of time, but as its underlying nucleus it ultimately grounds temporal ubiquity. Yet *secundum esse*, existentially, i.e., in its fluency that makes time, the now is invariably varied. These few exiguous-seeming reflec-

[27] Ibid., pp. 317b–318a.
[28] Ibid., p. 318a–b (also, *De quatuor coaequaevis* tr. 2, q. 5, a. 5, sol. and ad q. 1 and ad q. 2, pp. 377b–378a). Ibid., III, tr. 1, c. 2, pp. 180b–181a proves that motion cannot be categorized as quantity but is analogously said of its species in diverse predicaments. Albert recognizes his indebtedness to Avicenna for the reversal of roles of motion and time with respect to continuity. Although deriving its continuity from motion, time is primarily and per se continuous; motion is only secondarily and relatively continuous insofar as it is numbered by time: *Sufficientia* II, c. 11, 34E and 34F.

tions become luminous when meditated in the light of the nature of the now, a topic to which we now turn.[29]

Meaning of the Now

The nettlesome problem whose solution we just outlined serves as a point of departure: is the now one and the same, or is it pluralized? The answer lies in a fresh probing of motion, the substratum of time. Just as motion can be judged continuous or numbered, so a mobile thing can be inspected from a twofold perspective. Under its proper form a thing moved remains subjectively the same throughout and therefore is numbered by this changeless unity. Under the form of motion, i.e., as the producer of motion, a mobile being occupies successive positions, so that its path is numbered by the plurality of the prior and posterior. Coriscus at home, albeit the same person, differs locally from Coriscus in the forum. Formally taken, the subjective unity of the mobile is the now of time, and, formally taken, its diversification into prior and posterior is the number that is time. Consequently, the now that makes time is related to time as the mobile that produces motion is related to motion. By its very passage the mobile divides prior and posterior parts of motion; analogously, the now, its quantifying adjective, demarcates the parts of time as past and future.[30]

If next we momentarily acquiesce in the impossible assumption that geometrical imagination records mathematical fact, if we suppose that the line generated by a moving point is really impermanent, part successively ceding place to part, then the now would be totally similar to a point. Like a point imagined to be moving, the actually traveling now, remaining substantially the same throughout, causes time, the prior and posterior parts, and the intermediary section they delimit. While the now cannot be a part of time, the time line could not be apart from the now. Thus an additional proportional relationship catches the eye: as time is the number of motion, so the now is the unity of the mobile. The key to penetrating the now, the subjectively one continuator and cause of time, is the mobile. As permanent, the mobile is more knowable than motion both in itself and in regard to our mode of knowing; and motion is, in turn, more known than time. The mobile, we saw, engenders motion by coursing from prior to posterior place, and the number resulting from these parts is time. The flowing quantitative

29 Ibid., c. 7, pp. 318b–319a.

30 Ibid., pp. 319b–320a. According to ibid., c. 12, pp. 332b–333a, the now in common speech ordinarily refers to a slice of time adjacent to the present. See also *De quatuor coaequaevis*, tr. 2, q. 5, a. 3, pp. 373b–374a.

33

duplicate of the mobile's subjectivity is the now. Within the framework of time the now is identified with the mobile; it is the temporalized oneness of the mobile. Subjectively invariant because the primary mobile brooks no alteration or corruption, the one now is *secundum esse*, existentially, pluralized insofar as it touches diverse junctures, prior and posterior, in the stream of time. The duality of the now, its subjective oneness and existential plurality that image the substantial unchangingness and localized change in the mobile, dissipates paradoxes concerning the now, ruminated during the dialectical introductory, that branch off from a spotty portrayal of time.[31]

The now also measures time for the simple reason that it causes the measure of motion that is time. As the temporalized quantitative modification of mobile being, the now divides motion into the before and after and thereby becomes the measure of time itself. Its pluralization that makes the time line makes the very measure that is time: as the principle and cause making temporal measurement a reality, the now is deservedly called the measure of the measure that is time.[32] Withal, though it measures time and numbers the mobile, the now is more one than many. Like the substance that is mobile being, the now is primarily a one and indivisible subject. A rolling stone, because material, is divisible, but in its very substantiality it is formally one and indivisible; so, correspondingly, is the now in its nature or innermost character. In strolling from the theater to the forum, Coriscus of course changes (which change the Sophists misconstrue as substantial), and did he not move locally, it would be senseless to assert that he becomes other. But more basically, if he were not subjectively one, he would be unable to become aspectually different. So, again, with the now: it is its oneness that is actualized into plurality. Motion, we remarked, becomes known to us through the mobile that is being moved. Similarly, inasmuch as the now in its oneness undergoes pluralization, we note the prior and posterior segments of the time line. The now is more known than time because it perdures unchanged through the succession of before and after. Just as number springs from the one, so the variegated positions of the now spring from the subjective oneness of the now. Considered under the form of number, considered as actually number,

[31] Ibid., p. 320a–b. According to *De quatuor coaequaevis*, tr. 2, q. 5, a. 3, ad. 2, p. 374, substance may mean either essence or subject (see n. 26 above). Obviously the now is not the essence of time. Rather, it is the substance of time in the sense that it is the subject of time analogous to the mobile that is the subject of motion: ". . . the unity of the mobile borne through the whole of a motion is the substance of the now itself, which by its flow causes time flowing from prior to posterior . . . ." (p. 320a).

[32] Ibid., p. 320b.

the now is unceasingly other. But it is at bottom substantially one now. Knowing motion through the mobile and time through motion, we know the successive numbered continuum that is time through what is more known, the permanent, subjectively indivisible unity that is the now. We have already resolved the incompatibilities apparently stemming from the oneness and pluralization of the now. Here, it may be mentioned also, our analysis settles the subproblem concerning the corruptibility of the now. The now is corruptible neither in itself nor in another. It suffers corruption only relatively, in the sense that it has to forsake a prior position by the very fact that it reaches a posterior position.[33]

The analogical affinity of the now to time and the mobile opens the door to its explicit definition, a meaning that helps us describe its dissimilarity from as well as its similarity to a point. Their natures inextricably intertwined, time and the now are defined in a partially isomorphic way. Time is the number of motion and, correspondingly, the now is the number of the mobile.[34] But the analogical symmetry must be somewhat qualified, for the now numbers mobile being in this precise respect: it is the unity of the number of the mobile. As touched on several lines back, the now, moreover, resembles a point. The geometrical indivisible continues and divides the parts of a line by terminating one segment and principling its closest neighbor. Likewise, the now, in behaving as the common term of past and future, makes time continuous and, in demarcating time into past and future, divides time. But the similarity breaks down from the angle of the now in motion. A point can be taken twice over, regarded once as term of a prior part, then as principle of a posterior part. Were a point not a motionless indivisible, it could not be doubly aspectual; a successive anterior part not longer existing cannot have a term, and a posterior part not yet existing cannot have a starting point. To press the now-to-point analogy too far converts the flowing now into a static point and congeals time into a wholly spatialized line. Since the now begetting time is always diverse, it requires more than one now—in truth, four nows, two sets of two boundary points—to properly discriminate past from future.[35]

33 Ibid., pp. 320b–321b and c. 1, p. 307a. De quatuor coaequaevis, tr. 2, q. 5, a. 3, ad q. 2, p. 375a.

34 Ibid., p. 322a.

35 Ibid., pp. 322a–323a. Recourse to four rather than two nows to fix past and future squares with the use of four indivisibles to mark off prior and posterior parts in space, motion, and time: ibid., pp. 315a–316a; see nn. 23–24 above. De quatuor coaequaevis, tr. 2, q. 4, a. 3, ad 1, p. 374a–b also develops the case against a now taken twice over, an argument stemming from Sufficientia, II, c. 12, fol. 35M.

Its punctual character underlies another reason why the now is strictly not a part of time. Like a point, the now is a nonpartitive divisor. *Qua* subjectively one, the now also terminates a particular segment of time, for a term properly belongs to what it terminates. But it is responsible for a task far larger than that of mere term. As the number of mobile being, it causes the very number that is time. Like the number ten, which, after being applied to horses, remains predicable of any ordered aggregate, the now as number embraces all numerables falling under it. This broader temporal ambit of the now is rooted in its subjectivity. The one now making the number that is time indirectly witnesses to the universal and formal character of number whereby it is temporally significant beyond the termination of any particular segment of time. As number, time itself is also endowed with this wide range of applicability. Beyond doubt it is a continuum, yet as materially continuous and formally discrete, it may be more accurately named continuous number.[36]

Though essentially and existentially interdependent, time and the now part company as regards the subordination of the continuous to the discrete. As number, time, we showed, is formally discrete; as imbedded in motion, it is materially continuous. The rankings of the discrete and continuous are switched in the case of the now. Because it is subjectively one, mirroring in its unity the stability of the mobile, the now may be said to be properly continuous in the sense that by nature, i.e., according to its unvarying subjective identity, the now is continuative of time. The now is only accidentally discrete, i.e., divisive, in the sense that it never actually divides time. The human mind, comparing one now with another, makes a cut in the continuum, a mental division that is incidental to the seamlessness of the time line in nature. From the vantage point of the continuous, the substantially unique now uninterruptedly joins part to part, making past, present, and future homogeneous parts, indistinguishable save relatively along the continuum. From the vantage point of the discrete, the ever-other now punctuates and divides the time line. Yet unlike a fixed point, the now divides only potentially. Avicenna addresses himself to this in assigning two subsenses, one permissible, the other unwarranted, to a potentially divisive now. The first signifies a real possibility of actual division inserted by the mind, and the second a capacity for actual termination by the same now of a lower-order motion. But if in accord with this second subsense the now actually divided cosmic time at various junctures, its continuity would be severed at those points of termination; time, instead of being unbrokenly one, would be splintered into a sequence of

[36] Ibid., p. 323a.

detached time lines, each a time segment but each split from its pre-decessor and successor. The now's unique, unaltered subjectivity that guarantees the oneness and the continuity of cosmic time vetoes divisiveness save in the first subsense of potential. Were the now primarily other, time could no longer be considered, except by logical fiction, as one and the same, and the time continuum would be shredded into tiny strips, each discontinuous and independent from the other, incapable in their sundered state of justifying what we certify beyond cavil as the continuity of one cosmic time.[37]

Properties of and Entities in Time

Space limitations compel us to treat these two themes sketchily under the one heading.

1. We confine ourselves to a summary statement of three of time's properties.

(i) Time is ubiquitous because, looked at absolutely, it stems from the present now which, staying one and the same amid all temporals, is pluralized neither by the plurality of mobiles nor by motions distinguished according to before and after. Time centered in the now, Albert intimates, reveals a kinship to formal number that retains its identity in its multiple application to diverse sets of things numbered.[38]

(ii) As the number of circular motion, time is reiterative or reversible. Its course, illustrated in the cycle of the seasons, again and again traverses the same path. Thus the cyclicity of time proceeds from time as numbered number, for formal number does not return to its point of departure but goes on and on endlessly in a rectilinear manner.[39]

(iii) Time and motion, because quantitatively interchangeable, are reciprocal measures. In formally numbering motion, time essentially measures motion, whereas motion measures time incidentally and *quoad nos*, i.e., as regards our pragmatic convenience.[40]

---

[37] Ibid., c. 12, pp. 331a–332b. *De quatuor coaequaevis*, tr. 2, q. 5, a. 3, ad 1, p. 374a. See Avicenna, *Sufficientia*, II, c. 12, fol. 35A–B. Albert explicitly sets aside the reading of Averroes, *In Phys.*, IV, com. 121D–E (here faithful, Albert remarks, to an Arabic translation that has Aristotle saying that the instant is a point in potency), according to which the instant is divisive in potency because, in contrast to a point, it is ever on the go and therefore cannot be taken twice over as term of the past and principle of the future.

[38] Ibid., c. 9, p. 324a–b.

[39] Ibid., p. 324b.

[40] Ibid., p. 325a–b.

2. After specifying why and how time measures motion, we devote a few words to the scope of time, the sense in which it causes corruption, and the nonnecessity of an infinite time.

(i) All motions submit to time's suzerainty because all these are either faster or slower and stamped as prior and posterior. Taken loosely, i.e., in conjunction with motion, mutation is also measured by time. But viewed strictly, mutation, whether the death of a dog or the sun's illumination of the horizon, cannot abide a third state or interval between the absolute contradictories of nonexistence and existence. Such instantaneous transformations are measured by the now. It is also the now rather than time that measures sublunary substances *qua* mobiles. Because they move locally, celestial bodies surely come under time and the now.[41] As inalterable and incorruptible, however, they slip through the meshes of time and, as absolutely immutable in substance, they are exempt from the governance of the now.

(ii) Time measures a portion of motion, then, replicatively, other portions until the repeated partitive mensuration adds up to measurement of the whole. Moreover, the contention that one motion is commensurate with the whole of time amounts to saying that one super meter stick of indefinite length (inclusive of all ordinary meter sticks) can measure a piece of cloth—an impossibility since only a definite quantity can serve as an instrument of measurement. Time numbers motion part by part and, cumulatively, the whole of a motion. Hence time is wider in compass than any entity measured by it.[42]

(iii) Things at rest, such as a predominantly earthy body, are also measured by time. Oriented toward motion, they fall under the number of motion (a totally immobile body, empty of all real possibility of motion, could not be measured by time), but while things in motion are per se in time, these are only *per accidens* temporalized. Thus whatever is in time is in motion or at rest or, by contrapostion, whatever is neither in motion nor at rest is not in time—a conversion that reinforces the truth that celestial substance is not subsumable under time.[43]

(iv) Past and future entities are encompassed by time also. Substances with repeatable operations, like rising and setting stars and water evaporating to form a cloud, exist in past and future states. Only what are proximately scribed in concrete proper matter and a preordained causal

[41] Ibid., c. 10, p. 326a–b and p. 328a–b; c. 15, p. 337a–338b. The one aeviternal now measures all incorruptible entities (substantially immutable, virtually mutable), such as angels, human souls, and celestial bodies; see *Sum. theol.*, I, tr. 5, q. 23, memb. 2, a. 2, part. 2, p. 183a–b.

[42] Ibid., pp. 327b–328a.

[43] Ibid., c. 11, p. 329a–b.

chain, e.g., an eclipse and human beings already conceived in seed, are truly future entities.[44]

(v) Some ancients hailed time as the wisest of all for the reason that knowledge grows out of experience, but Pythagoras's pithy saying, "Time is unable to learn," seems nearer the mark. The memories of the aged are dilapidated buildings beyond repair; in the relentless rolling on of the years, the old forget more than they recall. Time then per se causes corruption and incidentally causes generation. Not that time properly and directly effects corruption. It is a per se cause indirectly, through its hook-up with the motion it numbers. Motion contributes more to the disintegration than the formation of substance. The substantial change toward which motion disposes only accidentally causes generation, for the new form is impressed by an outside agent. Thus time as such is more responsible for ravage than build-up in nature. Time is indispensable for learning, but new knowledge arises not from the destruction-oriented subject of time but from judicious sifting of experience.[45]

(vi) Averroes elaborates two arguments in support of an endless time. If time were corrupted, its corruption would have to take place in time—an impossible consequent that negates the antecedent. Again, if time came into being with the universe, it did not preexist it. Yet prior to the making of the world, this proposition, "Time will come to be," had to be true; therefore time existed before time—a self-refuting inconvenience annulling the hypothesis that time began. But no one who holds that time can cease, Albert protests, claims that its stoppage occurs in time. Because accidents, motion and time are merely relatively corruptible. Like motion, time can be "corrupted" in its ultimate term, a last now beyond which there is simply no more time. Hence Averroes's first argument turns on an equivocal shuffling of different significations of corruption. Second, before creation the proposition, "Time will come to be," could not be enunciated, since its causal preconditions, ontic directedness and properly disposed matter, along with a mind capable of uttering the proposition, were without actual existence. No doubt the divine mind preexisted the universe, but it is free of temporality and causal composition.[46]

[44] Ibid., pp. 330a–331a.

[45] Ibid., c. 10, p. 328a and c. 14, pp. 336a–337a. De quatuor coaequaevis tr. 2, q. 5, a. 7, pp. 380b–381b.

[46] Ibid., c. 13, pp. 333b–334b. The divine mind (p. 334b) is given more ample consideration in Metaphysica, ed. Bernhard Geyer (Münster Westfalen: Aschendorff, 1964), t. 16 (pt. 2), XI, tr. 2, c. 3, pp. 485a–486b. For Averroes's three arguments (we have cut these down to two by blending the similar first and second reasons), see In phys., IV, com. 121, fol. 197G–K. Albert returns to the problem from a

The overriding truth that it is the number of motion apparently ex-
trudes a time other than essentially psychological. Two ingredients are
constitutive of number: the numerable matter and the operation that
is numbering. The intellectual soul alone is capable of numeration, for
lower animals, while perceiving the quantity of their young, cannot
grasp this through number. But if number has no existence apart from
the soul, then time, not unlike a chimera, is an intentional-construc-
tural entity.[47] According to an alternative approach, apparently espoused by Aristotle and adopted by Averroes, time is potentially present
in the numerable parts, prior and posterior, of motion outside the soul
but, as number, is actually and formally present in the soul.[48] This
mitigated psychological tack unfortunately omits a third, crucial factor
in the texture of number. Besides the numerable matter and the soul
numbering, numeration requires formal number, the source of actual
numbering. Prior to counting there are already ten dogs—the ten that
specifies our counting actually exists outside the soul. So time composed of its form (number itself) and matter (the things numbered)

---

broader perspective, that of the eternity of the world in *Phys.*, VIII, tr. 1, cc. 11–15,
pp. 543–57 (*Super quatuor libros Sententiarum* [revision finished in 1249], vol. 27,
II, d. 1, a. 10, pp. 24ff. and *Sum. theol.*, vol. 32, II, tr. 1, q. 4, a. 5, pt. 3, p. 101,
also bear on this). The first four reasons for an eternal world, he maintains, rest on
two suppositions lacking certitude—that an ingenerable primary matter has to be
beginningless and that time, having no absolutely first now in nature, is eternal.
But a creation produced by pure act makes a primary matter out of nothing at the
first now of the material universe (pp. 552a–554b). In answer to Averroes's objection (*In phys.*, VIII, com. 7, fol. 342M–343D) that a creative act demands an inconceivable passage from potency to act in the unmoved mover, Albert maintains
that not God but things created are affected, i.e., pass from possibility to actuality,
through creation (p. 554b). In this context, by the way, Albert reminds blindly
loyal Aristotelians that Aristotle, a mere mortal making no pretense to be a god,
cannot be revered as infallible. For a more detailed discussion see Anselm Rohner,
O.P., *Das Schöpfungsproblem bei Moses Maimonides, Albertus Magnus und
Thomas von Aquin*, in *Beiträge zur Geschichte der Philosophie des Mittelalters*
(Münster Westfalen: Aschendorff, 1913), vol. 11, no. 5, especially pp. 45–92.

[47] Ibid., c. 16, pp. 339a–b. Technically, the question of the existence of time
is not natural but metaphysical, for submetaphysical disciplines presuppose the
existence of their subject matter. Only metaphysics that deals universally with
being as being propounds questions about the existential status of subject matters
and their attributes. See *Metaphysica*, III, tr. 2, c. 2, pp. 114b–115b, and IV, tr. 1,
c. 1, pp. 161a–162a.

[48] Ibid., p. 339b. For Averroes see *In phys.*, IV, com. 131, fol. 202E, where the
Commentator guardedly disassociates himself from a thoroughgoing psychologized time.

exists as a being of nature independent of the soul. The soul, an agent instead of a formal principle, causes not time but our apprehension of time.[49]

This fresh insight drives from our path six dialectical lions met with earlier.

(i) Albert's lusty realism uncompromisingly retains the full-blown physicality of time in answer to the objection that psychic comparison is necessary to link before and after positions. There is more, not less, in the mobile in motion, and time is nothing other than this incontrovertibly real flow. The implication that time is a continuum marked as prior and posterior dispatches a corollory fallacy, the opinion that time is a series of moments.

(ii) The stance that psychologizes time (because only a soul can number numerables) neglects, we just saw, the formal number in things outside the soul.

(iii) Defining time as the number of the motion of the soul wholly individualizes time, absurdly assigning it residence in one man and not in another.

(iv) The contention that a time seated in the first heaven would demand the simultaneous movement of all its parts merits only short shrift. The right and left parts of the first heaven's motion are not psychically constructed but manifestly exist as phases of one continuous motion.

(v) Galen's subterranean men, we have already established, would grasp heavenly motion effectively, i.e., in other motions caused by the first motion.

(vi) The enclosure of time within the psychic realm because past, present, and future lack physical perdurance is confuted by the distinction appointing not permanent but successive being to time. Consequently, its fleeting parts are physically real because tied to the indivisible ever-flowing now.[50]

[49] Ibid., pp. 339b–340a. Number in nature arises from three causes: material (the dogs numbered), formal (the ten of the dogs), and efficient (the soul actualizing not number but knowledge of a particular number). Averroes's solution, Albert thinks, lumps the latter two principles of number, each an *id quo numeratur*. Elsewhere Albert makes provision for a synoptic view of all duration attainable "through an extension of the soul," but this psychic drawing of the time line from the first to the last now is primarily tied to our conception of eternity. See *Sum. theol.*, I, tr. 5, q. 23, a. 1, part. 2, ad 1, p. 171; part. 2, subpart. 1, sol., p. 175; memb. 3, a. 2, p. 189.

[50] Ibid., p. 340a–b (see n. 16 above and the content it annotates). Albert buttresses argument (iv) by a reference to *De caelo et mundo* (commented on 1248–60), ed. Paulus Hossfeld (Münster Westfalen: Aschendorff, 1971), t. 5 (pt. 1), II,

Here we analytically substantiate notions presupposed as licit throughout. All physical inquiry (including, we may add, current relativity theory) implicitly appeals to worldwide time. Wherever we travel, in fact or in imagination, in the cosmos, we carry with us our time sense attuned to nature's rhythms. Temporal ubiquity is grounded in the universality of motion. Since all things in nature are potentially or actually moved, time, the regular number of motion, is correlatively universal, potentially in things at rest, actually present in things moved.[51]

But is time omnipresent with a general or a numerically one universality? That species of movement other than local motion are enmeshed in time supplies impressive support for a time that indifferently and generally numbers any continuous motion. One outcome, however, deals a death blow to this attractive (and, in our own day, widespread) view: it inescapably leads to a pluralization of time. A time that per se numbers motion has to be as diversified as its many specifically different subjects—the simultaneity of times resulting is of course impossible. Time then is one in meaning and many in application in the likeness of number. Seven is formally unaffected by its application to specifically differentiated dogs and horses; similarly the one number that is time simultaneously terminates specifically diverse motions. Yet time does not measure all motions in the same respect. It is the number of the primary motion, the simplest and most uniform in nature, and, as a consequence, it secondarily, howbeit univocally, measures all other motions. This twofold numbering, however, does not multiply time into times. Subjectified in the primary motion alone, time extrinsically numbers all other motions—only were it intrinsically situated in diverse motions, would it be contradictorily pluralized.[52] Comparison with the generic identity and specific diversity of triangles nails down the same point. Essentially differentiated as triangles, an equilateral and isosceles triangle do not differ as figures. Specific diversity as triangles does not

---

tr. 1, c. 5, pp. 115a–118b. See also *De quatuor coaequaevis*, tr. 2, q. 5, a. 1, pp. 367a–368b.

[51] Ibid., 338b–339a.

[52] Ibid., pp. 340b–342a. On the necessity of the circular character of the primary motion: ibid., VIII, tr. 3, cc. 8–9, pp. 616b–621a. The primary movement is that of the *primum mobile*, the supreme heaven or outermost sphere beyond the fixed stars; *De caelo et mundo*, I, tr. 3, c. 9, p. 74a; II, tr. 3, c. 11, p. 166b. Also, *De quatuor coaequaevis*, tr. 2, q. 5, a. 10, p. 385a. According to *Sum. theol.*, I, tr. 5, q. 23, memb. 3, a. 1, pp. 185b–186a, the ordinary definition of time is proper and that specifying the primary movement as subject is most proper.

disturb their formal identity in genus. So, to repeat, the specific differences among things numbered does not alter the species of a number. Thus the application of time as extrinsic number to specifically different subprimary motions does not undercut its numerical oneness that derives from its residence in the primary motion as a form in its proper subject.[53]

Eternity

All the arguments underpinning the position that confounds eternity with infinite time arbitrarily rule out extra-physical mensuration. We define eternity not through time but through a negation of attributes of time. Whereas time is a measure of motion distributed into parts, eternity is a duration that is partless, unpluralized, and fully indivisible. Albert glosses Boethius's classic definition of eternity ("the whole and all-at-once perfect possession of interminable life") to read: the absolutely fulfilled, stable, unreceived, autonomous, maximal pitch of existence without origin or end. Hence the temporal now, though substantially changeless, is infinitely distant from the eternal now that is subjectively one in being with and only conceptually distinguished from absolutely immutable substance. As the nonhomogeneous exemplary cause of time, eternity is wholly present in, while wholly transcending, the whole of time. God is primarily and essentially eternal. Lower beings sharing in divine unchangeableness or interminability, such as angels, human souls, celestial substances, and simple bodies, may be analogously called eternal. These participative eternals are not truly in eternity but are measured by the *aevum* and time and their respective nows.[54]

Some Difficulties

Time, notoriously slippery at the preanalytical stage, often continues after analysis to balk the hunt for complete perspicuity. Even conceded

[53] Ibid., pp. 342a–343b.

[54] Ibid., tr. 4, cc. 1–5, pp. 344–52. See *Sum. theol.*, I, tr. 5, q. 23, memb. 1, a. 1, part. 1, pp. 166–67; part. 2, pp. 170b–171a; and a. 2, part. 1, pp. 173a–174b, for a richer and presumably more mature reprise of an analysis of Boethius's *authenticum dictum* (*De consolatione philosophiae*, Prosa 6; ML, 63, 858) and the analogous naming of eternals. Also, *De quatuor coaequaevis*, tr. 2, q. 3, a. 2, pp. 342b–350a and a. 4, pp. 354b–356a; *Sent.*, II, d. 8, a. 8, vol. 24, pp. 230a–232b and p. 233a–b. However methodologically gauche, a tractate on a metaphysical measure appended to a strictly physical topic earns a double pedagogical convenience: it forestalls confusion of eternity with endless time and stresses that our concept of eternity is the negative distillate of our notion of time.

the soundness of the Aristotelian definition, it may verge on the unachievable to shape an interpretation so balanced that it does not somehow miscarry. Where practically no over-all solution is invulnerable to strictures, we may be disappointed but should not wonder that Albert's sober exegesis betrays major and minor shortcomings.

1. Albert repeatedly fails to reconcile time as formal number with its status as numbered number, overstresses the unity of the now, proposes a mathematicized basis for time's oneness, and stubbornly clings to the contrary-to-fact stand that time in its very fluency exists as a physical whole.

(i) The upshot of his analysis, if not his intention, is a quasi-mathematical time, essentially formal number applied to motion. Time dephysicalized is time detemporalized; a time not essentially numbered number is not physical time at all.[55]

(ii) A kin error crops up in the inference that time is related to subprimary motions as extrinsic number, i.e., formal number applied to motion. But if subterranean dwellers are truly aware of time, they must cognize time as numbered number, as number enwebbed in motion, effectively no less physical number than that in the primary movement.

(iii) Time as numbered number cyclically recurs, but time as formal number, we are told, is infinite and therefore proceeds irreversibly. But formal number, because abstracted from nature, cannot ground the one-way direction of time. Too, the number series, unlike a continuous unidirectional time, is fixed and discrete.

(iv) If, as is basically true, time is formally discrete, the reverse of what Albert infers results: time has to absolutely number the parts of the continuum dividedly or discretely and only relatively number parts proceeding undividedly.[56]

[55] Albert's basic mistake lies in attempting to think of time as a hybrid of material and formal number: material number in a relative manner, it is mainly the formal number of motion (see n. 26 above and the content to which it refers). But as applied to motion, it cannot be formal number; and to label it the formal number of motion is tantamount to calling it formal-material number, which is no less paradoxical than a strictly rational chimpanzee. This root error springs from his blurring of two senses of measure. First, in virtue of formal number we measure or determine the quantity of a stick as ten units and, second, with the stick (a numbered number) we measure the length of a desk. Unhappily, in Albert's estimation, only a formal number measures; and because time numbers or measures motions, he feels compelled to conceive of time as an (inadmissible) mixed breed, a formal number of motion.

[56] *Phys.*, IV, tr. 3, c. 6, p. 318a–b; see n. 28 above and related matter in the text. Time is formally discrete yet, Albert would have us believe only relatively does it number parts of the continuum emerging discretely or dividedly. At first this disparallel is so jarring as to incline one to surmise that a copyist's lapse has trans-

44

(v) Defining the now as the unit of the mobile runs counter to emphasis on the formal discreteness of time, for the now that makes time is more the number than the unity of the mobile. Furthermore, it seems at loggerheads with the correlation of the now and time to deem the now more continuous than divisive of the continuum. As unceasingly marking diverse time positions, the now of time is unceasingly divisive, clearly more divisive than continuous. Misgivings about the pulverizing of the time line by an actually divisive now misread the analogy between the now and a point. Were no points actual, a line would have no diverse parts, and were the now not actually divisive, past and future would always overlap. The spatial analogue for an arrested and fragmented time is altogether different from a line with actual points: it is the actual severance of the common link between two segments so that a small gap intervenes between the two that were previously linked as two parts of the one continuum.[57]

(vi) Albert overworks the analogy of the unity of time with formal number. To be sure, the one-and-the-sameness of time does partly coincide with formal number unpluralized by application to diverse physical objects. But time as physically one crucially diverges from formal number: not mathematical but physical, not abstracted from but impregnating natural events, it is numbered number effectively dwelling in every nook and cranny of the cosmos.

(vii) Commendable zeal to keep time uncontaminated by a fictionalizing psychologism inclines Albert to turn the blind eye to hazards of a wholly objectivized time. To the telling remonstrance that the mind must be relied on to knit together departed segments with the present, he comes back with the evasive, pointless reply that time is the real flux of the mobile. Indeed obstinate iteration of time's fluency drives home the fatal counterclaim: a successive continuum whose parts coexist without psychic retention is unthinkable. Moreover, formal number, mathematically excerpted from the sensory world, cannot exist as such outside the soul. Without a doubt the ten of dogs exists in nature, but this physical ten serves as the correlate of, without being identified with, the mathematical ten.[58] Time as numbered number cannot be

ferred the modifiers "simpliciter" and "secundum quid," but in fact Albert has once more neglected to pursue rigorously the consequence of designating (correctly, in one major genuine sense) time as formally discrete.

[57] On the necessity of actual indivisibles in the continuum see the shrewd comments of Vincent E. Smith, *The General Science of Nature* (Milwaukee: Bruce, 1958), pp. 350–51.

[58] Perhaps Albert slips into speaking of formal number as a physical formal principle because of his equivocal use of formal number as both nonphysical and physical (time is described as the formal number of motion; see n. 55 above).

denied a fundamental objective physicality, but its parts cannot be wholly objectified; i.e., only the completive activity of the soul can fuse them into one number. Furthermore, in holding fast to the truth that time is no less real than motion, Albert slips into the untruth that motion is wholly objectivized. He misses seeing that time's imitation of motion demands psychic activity to achieve a time line because the fleeting and disappearing parts of motion itself have to be intentionally welded together.[59] Finally, Albert misrepresents Augustine's definition. In essentials, the Augustinist analysis does not rival but complements the Aristotelian approach, since it does not set its arguments in a sheerly physical framework. As other works testify, Augustine never proscribes the physical existence of time. Endeavoring to justify realistic references to past and future, posing questions in a psychological context, the treatise in the *Confessions* is bound to arrive at a psychological answer, that time is a psychic distension—a solution reconcilable with the common Aristotelian posture that time in its totality needs the soul to retain its lapsing parts.[60]

2. Occasionally minor imprecisions and infelicities mar the presentation. Five lesser departures from precision may be listed.

(i) One place runs together continuity caused by the now (subjective unity) with that due to magnitude (quasi-spatial continuity).

(ii) It does not seem entirely accurate to maintain that the now is more knowable to us. In itself the now is more intelligible, but even granted scientific discernment of the cosmic now (inaccessible today and probably for the remote future), most men would go on first grasping time through motion within ordinary experience.

(iii) It appears misleading to hold that the now measures time because it causes time. Since measure is quantitative, the now as number of the mobile would seem to be the foundation for its measurement of time.

(iv) One comment has time measuring motion *secundum essentiam* (according to its formal intelligibility) as well as *secundum esse* (according to its occurrence in magnitude). Motion essentially measured by time is motion in itself continuous—a position Albert elsewhere repudiates.

[59] Preoccupation, at times nearly obsessive, with exorcising the demon of subjectivized time induces Albert to forget the insight that broke the fetters of earlier dialectical puzzlement: time is successive being—therefore its parts cannot coexist except intentionally.

[60] For more details see this writer's *The Concept of Time in St. Augustine* (Rome: *Studia Augustiniana*, 1965).

(v) The remark that animals do not grasp their brood by number seems at least ambiguous. Without formally adding or subtracting, animals sensorily number individuals in a rudimentary way. The sense of time observable in higher animals rests upon perception of number.[61]

Now and then a penchant for terse expression leads to unhappy turns of phrase.

(i) In dismissing the identification of time with the movement of the first sphere, Albert takes pains to insist that time would still be one even if there were two or three first motions—when in fact we can entertain the idea of plural first motions no more than we could acknowledge three papal claimants as all real popes at one and the same time.

(ii) After negating any possibility of simultaneous times, it seems careless to propose as conceivable two coexistent times measured by one now.

(iii) To describe time as continuous number seems inapt. Time may be characterized as a numbered continuum, but no number can be continuous (hence the irremediable oddity of R. Dedekind's continuous system of numbers), for the discontinuum between any two numbers is always unbridgeable.[62]

Lest a critical close savor of disrespect for a great thinker, we may strike at the end one note with which we began: in cursorily entering into Albert's mind, perhaps we discover that, in spite of his speaking an idiom strange to some, he is not a remote figure of a vanished age but an acute compatriot in a joint struggle to let a little more daylight in on the cosmic accident, always easily employable in practice yet frequently exasperatingly baffling in theory, that is physical time.[63]

[61] De Anima (date: circa 1256), ed. Clement Stroick, O.M.I. (Münster Westfalen: Aschendorff, 1968), t. 7 (pt. 1), II, tr. 3, c. 15, p. 103b and tr. 4, c. 6, p. 155a–b list number as one of the five common sensibles.

[62] R. Dedekind, Stetigkeit und irrationale Zahlen (Brunswick, 1872; 5th ed.), sec. 4. Dedekind's theory is lucidly summarized and defended in W. H. Werkmeister, A Philosophy of Science (New York: Harper, 1940), pp. 164–66. However, each irrational number making a cut is a being of reason or construct and therefore cannot be part of a homogeneous series of numbers. Even apart from this anomaly the gap between the numbers cannot be closed: a continuum of numbers is no more thinkable than a line made up of points alone.

[63] An updating of the physical philosophy of time in Albert (and indeed in many medievals) would of course have to probatively disengage its view of unicity from a discredited theory of celestial matter.

The Priority of Soul as Form and Its Proximity to the First Mover: Some Aspects of Albert's Psychology in the First Two Books of His Commentary on Aristotle's *De Anima*

INGRID CRAEMER-RUEGENBERG
University of Cologne

The famous Chapters 4 and 5 of Book Three are not the only parts of Aristotle's *De Anima* that are obscure and difficult. The student of Aristotle's psychology is constantly surprised by discovering unsolved problems, open questions, and extremely terse arguments in this work. But there are some very helpful commentaries on this difficult work, e.g., the commentary of Albertus Magnus. Nearly always, if one is puzzled at a peculiar or obscure thought, Albert's commentary is reliable and helpful. Indeed, Albert generally tries to systematize the often fragmentary thoughts of Aristotle both intensively and extensively. He constructs and defends a consistent 'peripatetic' theory, while using relevant parallel texts from various treatises of the *corpus Aristotelicum*.[1] Although there has been some discussion about the philosophical value of Albert's commentaries,[2] the scholar will at least appreciate Albert's reliability on open questions. It is more and more being recognized nowadays that in these commentaries, faithfully presented by Albert himself as explications of "the Philosopher's" thought, interesting and valuable ideas of Albert's, even an Albertine philosophy, are hidden.[3]

In this paper I intend to show how a typical Albertine analysis is developed in his commentary on the first book of *De Anima*, and how it becomes useful in two ways. First, this analysis concerning the provenience of forms from the First Cause provides a suitable instrument for the interpretation of some difficult passages in the Aristotelian text

[1] In his *De Anima* Albert often cites the *Ethics*, the *De Generatione Animalium*, the *De Sensu et Sensato*, the *Physica*, the *Metereologica*, the *Metaphysica*, and other works by Aristotle.

[2] Cf. Georg Wieland, *Untersuchungen zum Seinsbegriff im Metaphysikkommentar Alberts des Großen*, in *Beiträge zur Geschichte der Philosophie und Theologie des Mittelalters*, NF 7 (Münster, 1972), Introduction, ch. 3–5 and notes, pp. 6–15.

[3] Cf. G. Wieland, op. cit., and *Alberti Magni de Anima*, ed. by C. Stroick, *Opera Omnia*, VII, Pars I (Münster, 1968), Prolegomena XIII.

—a truth which I shall demonstrate by focusing on two instances in the second book of *De Anima*. Second, his theory of forms enables Albert to solve two of the most important problems of thirteenth-century philosophy, the problems of the unity and immortality of the human soul, in a manner which is quite compatible with orthodox Christianity. In this study I shall concentrate on the first two books of Albert's commentary on *De Anima*, with a modest purpose in mind. Certainly, I do not intend to replace or even correct A. Schneider's or L. B. Geiger's profound investigations.[4] Instead, I merely wish to deepen our broad and, in some sense, 'syncretistic' understanding of Albert's ideas on the mind-body problem, by treating and interpreting a few passages of Albert's commentary.[5]

I

1. I shall first deal with the oft-cited Chapter 13 in Book One, Tractate. 2. This chapter refers to Aristotle's refutation of those of his predecessors who believed that the soul was composed of elements. Aristotle suggests in his criticism that those thinkers erroneously explain the faculties of self-movement and sensation in the animal in terms of an alleged homogeneity or analogy of mover and moved thing, i.e., soul and body, as is the case with the sensory faculty and sensible things. Albert is interested in adding further points to this Aristotelian criticism. For this reason he analyzes not only the pre-Aristotelian theories but also two opinions of later philosophers. The first opinion is ascribed to Alexander of Aphrodisias; the second one, called "the opinion of

[4] Arthur Schneider, *Die Psychologie Alberts des Großen nach den Quellen dargestellt*, in *Beiträge zur Geschichte der Philosophie und Theologie des Mittelalters*, IV, Heft 5 (Münster, 1903 and 1906). L. B. Geiger, "La vie, acte essentiel de l'âme —l'esse, acte essentiel de l'essence daprès Albert le Grand," *Arch. Hist. doctr. litt. M.A.*, XVII (Montreal-Paris, 1962), pp. 49–116. Cf. also P. Michaud-Quantin, "La psychologie de l'activité chez Albert le Grand," *Biblioth. Thomiste*, XXXVI (Paris, 1966); E. Gilson, "L'âme rationelle selon Albert le Grand," *Arch. Hist. doctr. litt. M.A.*, VII (1945), pp. 5–72.

[5] Further consideration of studies in the much-better-known questions concerning the complicated Aristotelian theory of the *intellectus agens* would undoubtedly complete this essay. However, there is no urgent necessity here for any additional consideration, since Albert's ideas about the provenience and hierarchy of forms *are* developed in the first two books of *De Anima* and in *De Natura et Origine Animae* (ed. by B. Geyer, *Opera Omnia* XII [Münster 1955], pp. 1–44) — a work which contains many parallels with the relevant chapters of the *De Anima*. As the editors of the *Opera Omnia* note, the *De Natura et Origine Animae* was written later than the *De Anima*. (Cf. Prolegomena IX–X.) In that work Albert himself often cites his commentary on the *De gen. an.* The parallels are noted in the editions.

some of our own confrères (*opinio quorundam nostrorum sociorum*)," has been attributed by A. Schneider to both Alfredus Anglicus and Roger Bacon.[6] While the latter opinion is not important for our purpose, the former leads us to the very center of Albert's view of the psychophysical problem, because there are interesting similarities between Albert's and Alexander's psychological theories, and Alexander's ingenious thoughts seem to have profoundly influenced Albert's own thinking.[7] Albert himself would perhaps interpret this influence as a negative one, insofar as Alexander correctly and acutely pinpoints the problems, but proposes a 'materialistic' solution. For this reason Albert agrees with Alexander on what exactly the problems are, but his solutions tend to be opposed to those of Alexander.

Albert describes Alexander's theory as follows: There is an *incohatio formae* in each matter belonging to a form. Natural bodies are actualized and completed by their forms, and these forms must be habitually and potentially situated in the composition of the elements which constitute natural bodies in varying degrees of complexity. Although the single elements have no formative powers before they are substantially united, their more or less complex combinations govern the characteristic or specific operations of natural bodies. This is why animate beings operate, i.e., exercise their vegetative and sensitive powers, exclusively and completely by means of their organs precisely insofar as their organisms are properly composed. "The substance [=substantial form=]," writes Albert, "which gives existence to the body, and is the perfection of that body, is, first, in the semen of the body formally in potency; and thus, it seems that the soul is [only] in the composition of the elements, whereas the elements themselves are not animate prior to their [substantial] union. And it was Alexander, the Greek Peripatetic [thinker], who expressed this [view]."[8]

Albert seems to be fascinated by the issue itself, but he rejects the above theory—apparently because of its 'materialistic' tendencies. He

[6] A. Schneider, op. cit., p. 431, note 2.

[7] This is an astonishing fact, since Albert's sources of Alexander were not rich. He permanently used the *Commentarium Magnum in De Anima* of Averroes, in which he found numerous doxographical notes referring to Alexander, and may have known also the old Latin version of Alexander's *De sensu et sensato*. However, the other possible sources, viz., the commentaries of Themistius and Johannes Philoponus on the *De Anima* were translated after Albert had finished his *De Anima* and the *De Natura et Origine Animae*.

[8] "Substantia autem, quae dat esse corpori et est perfectio ipsius, primo formali potentia est in semine corporis, et ita videtur, quod sit in commixtione elementorum anima, licet ante commixtionem elementa non sint animatae. Et hoc quidem dixit Alexander Graecus Paripateticus." Loc. cit., p. 52, 70–53, 1.

uses some arguments from authority (taken from Aristotle) and then outlines his own position. The forms of which Alexander is speaking, Albert declares, must be identified with the *formae corporales* which result from the mixture of elements; and consequently, each of them has only one essential operation. Apparently Albert has here in mind the second book of Aristotle's *Physics*, where such forms are shown to cause the 'natural motion' of natural bodies.

Next Albert argues against the opinion of some of his own confères (*Quidam nostrorum sociorum*) and subsequently expounds his own view concerning the provenience of the soul in the body.

First he states the general principle which guides his theory of forms (and souls):

One must realize that every incorporeal agent which impresses its species in the corporeal thing by corporeal means, acts by necessity sometimes in such a way that the species, which it impresses, follows the very subject into which it [the species] is impressed; at other times, it is analogous to the species of the agent; and at again other times, it follows (or is analogous to) both in some way; and this is so because of the diversity of what receives the impression or the form which it induces. By the way, the First Mover is a totally incorporeal agent, which, nevertheless, acts upon matter, which [matter] is [made up] of contraries, and composed of the elements and the qualities of the elements.[9]

What all this means is apparently the following: There are (at least) three realms of being which, in some way, bring about the generation of natural bodies and their functions. To begin with, there is the First Mover (*primus motor*), which is an incorporeal agent (*agens incorporeum*)—an ambiguous phrase in Albert, the ambiguity of which must undoubtedly be derived from the Arabic correlative of *actio* or *energeia*.[10] This First Mover is without any material body (the idea of

[9] "Sciendum igitur, quod omne agens incorporeum quod imprimit speciem suam in rem corpoream et per corporeum instrumentum, oportet, quod agat aliquando sic, quod species, quam imprimit, sequitur magis subiectum, cui imprimitur, et aliquando magis simulatur speciei agentis, et aliquando similatur secundum aliquid utrique; et hoc fit propter diversitatem eius quod suscipit suam impressionem sive formam, quam inducit. Est autem motor primus omnino incorporeum agens, quod tamen agit in materiam, quae est ex contrariis et commixta ex elementis et qualitatibus elementorum." *Loc cit.*, p. 54, 20 ff.

[10] Professor A. Falaturi (University of Cologne) gave me the information that the Greek terms ἐνεργεία ὄν and ποιοῦν often are translated (e.g., in Averroes) by the same Arabic term "*fāʿil*" signifying both, sc., something which is actualized or even mere actuality (the First Mover) and an entity which produces something.

Aristotle); and secondly, he produces *incorporea*, i.e., immaterial entities constituting the second realm of beings. Following Albert, we apparently must assume that these products of the *agens incorporeum* are impressed into material things (*res corporeae*). On the other hand, what is impressed follows either the nature of the material substratum or the *species agentis* or both. How does the First Mover do his work? Albert replies that the First Mover acts through a corporeal instrument in a fourfold manner (*agit per instrumentum corporeum quadrupliciter*). The four instruments at hand are the power that is in celestial bodies (*virtus, quae est in corporibus caelestibus*); the power that is in the descending celestial light (*virtus quae est in luminae caelesti descendente*); the celestial motion (*motus caelestis*) itself; and finally, the first qualities that are in the elements (*qualitates primae quae sunt in elementis*).[11]

These four instruments may be identified as follows: The first of the four, the *virtus, quae est in corporibus caelestibus*, is the power of circular movement in the celestial bodies, on the one hand, and their power of moving other celestial bodies existing in the lower spheres, on the other.[12] We learn something about the second power, the *virtus, quae est in lumine*, in Albert's commentary on *De Anima* (lib. 2 tract. 3 cap. 12). The form which is called *lumen* gives actual visibility to visible things and color to colored things; thus it is the actuality of the transparent as such. Moreover, as coming from the heavenly bodies, this form

> gives life to the living beings, and lends heat and motion to the being of the generables, inasmuch as it is the instrument of the intelligence that, by the motion of lights and by emitting light, brings into being everything that is in nature. . . .[13]

The celestial motion (*motus caelestis*) is immediately caused by the Aristotelian Unmoved Mover, and is the condition of the possibility of the change of movement and rest in the other bodies.[14] The "first

Albert's *agens* seems to be a translation of "*fāʿil*." Averroes, however, proposes another metaphysics of soul; his commentary evidently is *not* the source of Albert's *digressio*.

[11] Loc. cit., p. 54, 31–36.

[12] *Albert, Phys.* VIII (*Opera Omnia*, III), lib. 8 tract. 2 cap. 10 (Paris: Vivès, 1890), pp. 589–592.

[13] "Est autem haec forma quae vocatur lumen vivificativa vivorum et calefactiva et motiva ad esse generabilium, inquantum est instrumentum intelligentiae, quae per motum luminarium lumine emisso movet ad esse omne quod in natura est." Albert, *De Anima*, lib. 2 tract. 3 cap. 12, p. 116, 80–85.

[14] Cf. note 12 above.

qualities that are in the elements" are also mentioned in Aristotle's *Physics* (VIII, 4). There Aristotle endeavors to prove the first premise of his demonstration of the existence of a First or Unmoved Mover, i.e., the principle that whatever is in movement is moved by something else. The seemingly self-moving heavy and light elementary bodies introduce a difficulty here. For this reason Aristotle constructs an ad hoc solution by asserting that things of this kind are moved either by that which *made* them light or heavy or by that which removed the obstacle to their movement.[15] Although the idea that the Unmoved Mover has produced or created the heavy and light things as such is inconsistent with Aristotle's concept of the divine being, Albert (and other commentators) have welcomed it.[16] Thereby, the unmoved moving principle and God as the creator of the world (*creator mundi*) become one in Albert's mind.

All this means that the four instruments produced by the *prima causa* form a system of the necessary conditions of the actual being, movement, and life in the universe. Nevertheless, Albert concedes a certain dependence of most kinds of forms (which form the natural bodies) upon the influence of the specifically structured or composite underlying matter. This is true even of the vegetative and sensory souls. For they are produced "of matter and have their root in matter (*ex materia et radicem habent in materia*)" by virtue of the *agens incorporeum*, which, in turn, is produced by the First Mover (*sive hoc sit intellectus movens stellas sive sit virtus formativa in semine animatorum corporum*).[17] "However," Albert emphasizes, "the root of those souls is not the elementary form or something consequent to the mixture of elements but rather the form impressed by the soul descending into the semen or impressed by the mover of the orbits. This form is educed by the corporeal instruments, which are the light, the power, and the movement of the heavens and the stars, as well as the elementary qualities that contain the powers of the heaven and the soul."[18] Moreover, although there is a certain *incohatio formae* in the mixture of elements, the real formation or actualization is attributed only to the so-called incorporeal agents (*agentia incorporea*). That is why the soul of in-

[15] Aristotle, *Physics*, VIII, 4, 255 b 35–256 a 2; Albert, *Phys.*, lib. 8 tract. 2 cap. 4, pp. 569–74.

[16] Cf. note 15 above.

[17] Albert, *De Anima*, loc. cit.

[18] "Tamen radix istarum animarum non est forma elementalis vel aliquid sequens commixtionem elementorum, sed potius forma impressa ab anima descendente semen vel impressa a motore orbium, sed educta instrumentis corporalibus, quae sunt lumen et virus et motus caelorum et stellarum et qualitates elementales in se habentes caeli et animae virtutes." Ibid.

telligent beings, i.e., the human soul (conceived as the form of the human body), is neither simple nor extraordinary. Forms of this kind are simply higher forms. These forms are far from the "excellence of the contrary elements (*excellentia contrariorum elementalium*)" because they are capable of receiving contraries by thought. They ensure an "equality (*aequalitas*)" similar to that of the heavens, beause they are enlightened by the divine intelligence.[19] As such, intelligent souls are nearer to the first principle than any other forms. Accordingly, they are directly engendered by some higher principle, independently of any material preformation, or, as Albert puts it later on, they are "essentially separated." If they were not so separated in their origin and entity, human intelligence would not be able to operate "separately" (independently) in conceiving, unifying contraries in things, performing abstraction, and considering separate beings.

So much about Albert's views on the origin of souls. I urged at the beginning of this paper that Albert's theory (which I have just sketched) is useful for the interpretation of certain difficult Aristotelian passages. To show this assertion to be true, I shall consider two such passages.

II

There is an open question of some importance in *De Anima* II, 1. Aristotle here makes a fresh start in defining the soul. Recapitulating the elements of the definition already offered he remarks: ". . . the soul is the first grade of actuality of a natural body having life potentially in it. The body so described is a body which is organized."[20] With these words he introduces the following set of questions: (1) Are *only* organized bodies suited to being informed by the kind of form the soul is, or is there a fundamental difference between the forms of unorganized and the forms of organized things? (2) If there is a difference, is it a necessary one, or can souls as well as other forms be indiscriminately distributed to the various classes of 'subjects'? Albert (reliable here as elsewhere) clearly sees this problem (while other commentators ignore it), and provides an answer to it. The answer is based on his above-discussed theory of forms. In his *determinatio* of "what sort of body is that which is said to have life in such possession (*quale sit illud corpus, quod dicimus in tali potestate habere vitam*),"[21] he reminds us of the superior forms and argues as follows: We have seen that there are

[19] Ibid.
[20] Aristotle, *De an.* II, 1, 412 a 15–412 b 1.
[21] Albert, *De an.*, lib. 2 tract. 1 cap. 3, pp. 67, 45–46.

55

generally two kinds of natural forms. There are the simple forms of the elements and of the "mixed bodies (*corpora mixta*)," on the one hand, and forms of higher degree, nearer to the "First Cause acting universally (*causa universaliter agens prima*)," on the other. The lower kind of form comports with the nature of the natural body instead of being superior to it. This simple form of the simple body is dependent on the material qualities of that body and, therefore, determined to perform only one action. For instance, fire can only heat; heavy and light things are capable only of their 'natural motion'; etc. In contrast, the other kind of forms, the higher forms, are in the neighborhood of, i.e., analogous to, the First Cause, which produces all forms. He writes:

> This [higher form] is the incorporeal essence that moves and perfects the body, and has the function of impressing the total nature [on the body] inasmuch as it, in regard to its nature, transcends the nature of every corporeal form; and this [form] is called the soul. And since it receives the power of acting not from the body but from the First Cause, Whose nature it follows [imitates], the soul does not one thing but many things; and each of those acts is proper and essential to it.[22]

All souls, that is, both the subhuman and the human kinds, are situated in greater or lesser proximity to the First Cause; and, taken together, they are all nearer to it than the lower forms of the simple bodies, and analogously follow the nature of the highest principle of being. Moreover, just as the First Cause is productive of all forms (*agens omnes formas*), the souls themselves perform a variety of actions (the different activities of life). Having stated all this, Albert offers his precise answer to the problem he raised:

> [The soul] exercises its essential acts both in and around the body. However, these actions are not done without corporeal instruments. For this reason every body, which habitually possesses the principles of life activities, is necessarily organized, i.e., composed of organs differing in figure and position.[23]

[22] "Et haec est essentia incorporea movens et perficiens corpus, quae habet imprimere in naturam totam, eo quod ordine naturae supra naturam est omnis formae corporeae; et haec vocatur anima. Et quia potestatem agendi non trahit a corpore, sed ex prima causa, cuius naturam sequitur, ideo non agit tantum unum, sed multa, et quodlibet illorum operum est proprium ei et essentiale." Loc. cit., pp. 67, 56–68, 3.

[23] "Actiones autem suas essentiales agit in corpore et circa corpus, quae actiones non fiunt sine intrumentis corporalibus, et ideo omne corpus quod in potestate habituali habet, unde operetur actiones vitae, oportet esse organicum, hoc est ex organis figura et situ differentibus compositum." Loc. cit., p. 68, 4–9.

This truth, in turn, is the reason why only organized beings are capable of being informed by a soul. However, because of a need for some specific form, organized bodies do not have this capability. On the contrary, it is the soul itself that needs a multifunctional body, because the object and the medium of its manifold essential activities is the body.

In lib. 2 tract. 3 cap. 23 of *De Anima* we find another instance of Albert's theory of forms aiding in the explication of Aristotelian ideas. Although the issue here is not as important as the above discussed one, Albert's reliability in resolving it satisfactorily is evident once again. In this text Albert tries to defend a quixotic Aristotelian doctrine:

> While in respect to all the other senses we are inferior to many species of animals, in regard to touch we far excel all other animal species in the exactness of discrimination. That is why man is the most intelligent of all animals. This is confirmed by the fact that it is due to differences in respect to the organ of touch and to nothing else that men differ in their natural endowment. For men whose flesh is hard are ill-endowed by nature; men whose flesh is soft, well-endowed."[24]

In Albert's commentary we find an interesting explanation of this puzzling fact:

> The cause of this [fact] is that the tangible qualities determine the complexion through the way they are mixed. The more remote this complexion is from the excellences, the nearer it is to centrality and equality; and therefore, the more similar to heaven, in which there is absolutely no contrariety. And since the forms are allotted according to the merits of matter, as Plato put it, and since to every combination there corresponds a form, it follows that the noblest form is proper to the more balanced complexion, and the noblest form is the intellective form. . . . Now, some men possess more balanced complexions. . . . For this reason, they are the ones who possess the most perfect touch and are more apt according to the industry of their intellect. . . . And they all have soft and well-endowed bodies.[25]

[24] Aristotle, *De an.* II, 9, 421 a 20–26; English translation by J. A. Smith (Oxford, 1931).

[25] "Causa autem huius est, quia tangibiles qualitates mixtione sua complexionem faciunt, quae complexio, cum magis ab excellentiis recedit, tunc medietati et aequalitati est vicinior et ideo caelo similior, in quo nulla est omnino contrarietas. Et quia secundum merita materiae dantur formae, sicut dixit Plato, et unicuique complexioni propria respondet forma, ideo adaequaliori complexioni debetur anima nobilissima, quae est intellectiva. . . . Inter homines autem quicumque aequaliorem habent complexionem, . . . et ideo illi optimum habent tactum et aptiores sunt secundum industriam intellectus. . . . Et hi omnes sunt mollis et non laxae carnis." Albert, *De Anima*, lib. 2 tract. 3 cap. 23, p. 133, 15–32.

In this view of Albert there is, first of all, an ascending order not only of forms but also of material structures. Secondly and more specifically, the better balanced a mixture of elementary bodies and qualities is the nearer it is to the totally balanced structure of the heavenly bodies. Such an equality of structure (*aequalitas complexionis*) includes also degrees of differences in regard to the "contrarieties" of the simple bodies. Bodies of higher complexity are neither simply hot nor simply cold, neither simply wet nor simply dry, and so on. Yet the sense of touch, as Aristotle says, is based on the organic medium of touch, i.e., flesh, so that an object can be exactly in the middle between the tactile contraries: hot-cold, wet-dry, and so on. Accordingly, Albert declares, the better-balanced organization of a creature causes a better-developed sense of touch. Furthermore, Albert continues, it is precisely this better-balanced mixture and organization that renders a body worthy of being formed "by a very noble form." Among the animals, man has the best-organized body, and men themselves differ from one another in their respective conditions of *aequalitas*. Thus, Albert concludes, some men, viz., those with a better sense of touch and, therefore, with soft flesh, are well endowed by nature to perform acts of intelligence and prudence, while others are less well endowed in that respect.

III

Heretofore we have considered Albert's theory of souls as forms and its explanatory value with regard to some open questions in Aristotle's psychology. Undoubtedly one could easily cite more instances of this value, especially from Book III. Instead, however, let us turn our attention to another value of Albert's theory.

The Albertine theory of the souls as forms, as already indicated, has also considerable systematic value insofar as it prepares the way for a well-founded and reasonable solution of the classic problem of the unity of the human soul. The source of this problem, naturally, is a psychological doctrine of Aristotle, which, in a simplified form, may be described as follows: The different faculties of life and, therefore, of soul, exist more or less separately in the various genera of animate beings. There are animate beings which possess only vegetative powers; others possess also a more or less complete set of sensory faculties; and man, different in his rationality from all other living creatures, possesses, in addition to vegetative and sensory powers, some rational faculties as well. The cooperation of the lower powers alone in a single living being poses such problems as these: Is there any order of unity, ruled by the relatively "highest" faculty, or can two or even more souls work together in an individual organism? Is a unified and individual soul the principle of individuality for living individuals? The problems become especially difficult when extended to the realm of human intelligence.[26]

Intelligence, at least the *intellectus agens* of Aristotle, comes "from without."[27] Albert himself shares this view and expresses it as follows: "The intellectual soul is not educed from matter; instead, it enters from without (*non ex materia dicitur educi, sed potius ab extrinseco ingredi*)." Moreover, Albert continues, the light of the agent intellect is its [the human souls'] root (*radix eius*), in such a way that it [sc. the human soul] is sometimes called by philosophers the result of the divine intellect in the physical body that has life (*resultatio intellectus divini in corpore physico vitam habente*)."[28] Indeed, intelligence seems to be something strange, something divine, that penetrates a certain area of animality. But, in light of this truth, how can there be a union of the lower faculties of the soul with this divine light, in which man, and man alone, participates? Even more important in this context is the question of the immortality of the individual human soul—a doctrine taught by the Koran as well as by the Christian faith. Aristotle and a number of Peripatetic (that is, in Albert's terminology, non-Christian[29]) commentators made a clear distinction: The lower soul and even the passive intellect are destructible, i.e., mortal; whereas the active principle of intelligence alone, separated from the passive intellect and its phantasm, is immortal. However, in its state of separation from the phantasms and the passive intellect, the agent intellect is unable to remember anything.[30] The implication of this position is quite evident: individual immortality is impossible everywhere, and the relation of the power of intelligence to the souls of animate beings is apparently a tenuous one.

In lib. 1 tract. 2 cap. 15, Albert deals with the question of the unity of the human soul. On the basis of Aristotelian terms, he first lists four groups of fundamental faculties of the human soul: (1) the powers of knowing, perceiving, and forming opinions, (2) the generic power of appetite, (3) the power of locomotion, and (4) the power of growth.[31]

26 Cf. Noriko Ushido, *Etude comparative de la psychologie d'Aristote, d'Avicenne et de S. Thomas d'Aquin* (Tokyo, 1968).

27 Aristotle, *De gen. an.* I, 2, 716 b 27–28.

28 Albert, *De an.*, lib. 1 tract. 2 cap. 13, pp. 54, 67ff.

29 Cf. Georg Wieland, op. cit., p. 7, note 13.

30 Aristotle, *De an.* III, 5, 430 a 22–25.

31 (1) "Cognoscere per intellectum et sentire et opinari," (2) "concupiscere . . . et omnino et universaliter appetitus," (3) "movere secundum locum," (4) "augmentatio et detrimentum."

Next, on the basis of this list of human powers, Albert raises a twofold question concerning the principle or principles of the listed powers: Is there only one "essence and power (*essentia et potentia*)" so that we could say such things as "we intellectually know vegetative things" and "we grow through the intellect" (*ita quod possumus dicere, quod vegetative intelligimus et . . . in intellectu augemur . . .*); or are there really distinct and diverse essences and powers (*diversae essentiae et potentiae*), i.e., is there a separate essence and power for each type of action? Albert rejects both extremes and concludes, instead, as follows: "Therefore, there remains only one middle position, that there is one essence that does all these things by diverse natural powers, which [powers] are [all] in that one essence."[32]

Having thus stated his position, Albert commences a long discussion about erroneous ancient and 'modern' theories concerning the question at hand[33] and finally defends his own concept of the unicity of the human soul with its diverse powers (*diversae potentiae*). In doing so he reminds us again of his theory of forms. There are vegetative souls in plants, and they are locally separated from the sensitive souls of animals. But there are vegetative faculties in animals as well. However, it would be wrong to say that, in these cases, a vegetative *soul* is a part of the sensitive soul. Instead, the sensory soul has a vegetative part, but that part is to be described as the "vegetative *power* (*potentia vegetabilis*)" of the sensory soul. In a similar way the sensory power (*potentia sensibilis*) is a part of the intellectual soul. All this becomes evident, Albert continues, when we consider both the special status of souls as forms and the hierarchy of souls. Some souls, as we already know, are nearer to natural bodies and have themselves *incohatio formae* in their bodily structure (although only in an analogous manner), because the lower souls are also impressed by incorporeal agents (*agentia incorporea*). However, other forms are completely the results of the light of intelligence (*omino sunt resultatio luminis intelligentiae*), and that is why there is a hierarchy (as well as a temporal order of development) among the potencies of the individual human soul.[34] That the First Efficient Cause (*causa prima agens*) is the originating principle of every formal determination is, in Albert's thought, a guarantee of the unicity of form (*unitas formae*).

[32] "Remanet igitur unum solum medium quod est: una essentia facere haec omnia per diversas potentias naturales, quae sunt in illa unica essentia." Loc. cit., p. 57, 47–49.

[33] Ibid., pp. 58, 48f. The four "Latin" authors criticized by Albert are: Petrus Hispanus, Adam of Buckfield, Godfridus of Aspall, and Richardus Rufus. Cf. A. Schneider, op. cit., pp. 39–42.

[34] Loc. cit., pp. 60, 66–86.

As to the question of individual immortality or, in Aristotelian terms, of *separatio*, Albert works out a similar line of argument in lib 2 tract. 1 cap. 4.:

> Furthermore, it is manifest not only that the intellectual part [of the human soul] itself becomes separated, but also that the entire intellective soul does so. The necessary reason for this truth is that, since the parts of the soul are the natural powers that flow from it [*sc.* the soul], it is impossible that a separated power should flow from its essence which is united with the body. However, conversely, it is possible that powers operating in the body should flow from that which is essentially separated.[35]

Undoubtedly Albert conceives the role and function of the "intellective part" (*pars intellectiva*) in terms of his own general theory: the incorporeal agents (*agentia incorporea*) act on bodies and even prepare the bodies so that there can be a certain *incohatio formae*. The intelligence of man is to be understood as an excellent instance of an incorporeal agent (*agens incorporeum*) that stands very close to the highest principles. As such, the intelligence is essentially separated and imitates the nature of the First Cause. But intelligence, like each agent of this kind, acts on bodies by means of "instruments" (*instrumenta*), i.e., through the lower faculties of the soul. Therefore, through forming a body by means of the vegetative and sensitive faculties, the "intellectual part (*pars intellectualis*)" causes the unity of the soul. Moreover, since intelligence is separable, the whole human soul is immortal.[36]

Although the reasoning sketched above seems to be typical of Albert and his very own intellectual product, Albert is convinced that he expresses Aristotle's own view. Admittedly, at the end of *De Anima* II, 1, having just determined that souls generally are inseparable from their bodies, while some other parts (whose actuality is not the actuality of the parts of bodies) may well be separable, Aristotle makes a rather agnostic remark: "Further, we have no light on the problem whether the soul may not be the actuality of its body in the sense in which the sailor is the actuality of the ship."[37] Nevertheless, Albert freely uses this statement to support his own reasoning. "The sailor moves a ship," he

---

35 "Amplius autem manifestum est non solum de ipsa parte intellectiva, quod separatur, sed etiam de ipsa tota anima intellectiva, quod separatur. Cuius causa necessaria est, quia cum partes animae sint naturales potestates eius ab ipsa fluentes, impossibile est, quod ab essentia coniuncta cum corpore fluat potestas separata. Sed e converso possibile est, quod ab eo quod est essentialiter separatum, fluant potentiae operantes in corpore." Loc. cit., p. 70, 15–23.

36 Ibid.

37 Aristotle, *De an.* II, 1, 413 a 13–15.

says, "by means of an intellectual species, the 'science of governing (*scientia gubernandi*),' but there is no movement of the ship which is not performed through bodily instruments." Then he adds, "And similarly, if the soul [so] moves the entire body through the control of the intellect, it [*sc.* the soul] is essentially separated (distinct) from the body, even though it has numerous sensory and vegetative powers and operations, which cannot be accounted for without corporeal instruments."[38]

We may summarize briefly. The first two books of Albert's commentary on Aristotle's *De Anima* sufficiently show some of Albert's qualities as a commentator and as a philosopher. Albert believes that he correctly interprets Aristotle's psychological theory. In fact, he faithfully follows Aristotle while discussing and refuting erroneous opinions. On the other hand, in discussing post-Aristotelian theories, Albert has produced a number of treatises which contain interesting thoughts concerning the origin of souls as forms and the hierarchy of the forming powers. Moreover, in his endeavor to solve problems, i.e., to give answers to open and hidden questions, Albert has developed the particular components of his own theory of soul. It is this theory which enables Albert to hold an orthodox, Aristotelian position on the much-debated and still-relevant questions of the unity and immortality of the soul.

[38] "Et similiter, si anima sic movet totum corpus intellectu imperante, ipsa separatur essentialiter a corpore, licet habeat multas vires et operationes sensus et vegetationis, quae non explentur sine instrumentis corporeis." Albert, *De Anima*, lib. 2 tract. 2 cap. 4, p. 70, 56–65.

Part III

Metaphysics

The Meaning of *Esse* in Albert the Great's Texts on Creation in *Summa de Creaturis* and *Scripta Super Sententias*

LEO SWEENEY, S.J.
Loyola University of Chicago

On September 2, 1959, Etienne Gilson wrote a gracious letter to acknowledge a paper, "The Doctrine of Creation in *Liber de Causis*," I had contributed to the volume his North American students published in his honor.[1] In the course of that letter he said:

> One cannot ask a philosopher to conceive creation at a deeper level than that of his own notion of being. If God is the cause of that which being is, then God is a creator and being is a created being. . . . The progress achieved by Thomas Aquinas concerns less the notion of creation than that of being.

Gilson's statements merit serious consideration. If creation causes something to *be* which before *was not* at all, then understanding what an author means by "being" should help disclose how he conceives creation.

In this paper on Albert the Great's texts on creation in two of his early theological writings, I shall investigate what he intends by *ens* or, more precisely, by *esse* so as to discover his stand on *creare*.

Secondary Literature

Consulting bibliographies on Albert reveals that relatively little attention has been given to his doctrine on creation.[2] In 1913 Anselm Rohner

---

[1] C. J. O'Neil, ed., *An Etienne Gilson Tribute Presented by His North American Students* (Milwaukee: Marquette University Press, 1959), pp. 274–89.

[2] See M. H. Laurent and J. Congar, "Essai de bibliographie Albertinienne," *Revue Thomiste* 36 (1931): 422–68; Fernand van Steenberghen, "La littérature albertino-thomiste (1930–1937)," *Revue néoscolastique de philosophie* 41 (1938): 126–61; Francis J. Catania, "A Bibliography of Albert the Great," *Modern Schoolman* 37 (1959–60): 11–28; Roland Houde, "A Bibliography of Albert the Great:

published in *Beiträge zur Geschichte der Philosophie des Mittelalters* a study of the topic in Moses Maimonides, Albert, and Thomas Aquinas.[3] This is mainly concerned with their responses to such questions as: Can one philosophically prove that our universe was created? How does one know it was created in time? How disprove the Peripatetic arguments that the universe is eternal?[4] In a still unpublished Louvain dissertation of 1948, J. R. Losa compared the treatises on creation by Albert, Aquinas, and Bonaventure in their commentaries on Lombard's *Sentences*.[5] Four years later Joseph Hansen's contribution to *Studia Albertina*, a *Festschrift* honoring Bernhard Geyer, focused again on how one knows, according to Albert, the world was created in time.[6] Three years later J. F. Kiley presented a master of art's thesis at St. John's University entitled *The Doctrine of Creation in St. Albert the Great*, which is weakened by Kiley's tendency to read Albert in the light of Aquinas.[7] Finally, William Dunphy touched *passim* upon creation in his valuable paper "St. Albert and the Five Causes,"[8] as is clear from his concluding remarks:

Aristotle and the Peripatetics, proceeding by way of demonstrations *quia* and starting from the world of motion, could not philosophically arrive at an efficient cause that is not in any way a moving cause, namely one that creates everything *ex nihilo*. And what Plato held concerning an efficient cause not related to motion, while resting on merely probable grounds, can now be explained and held by theologians on the strength of principles derived from revelation and the inspiration of the Spirit. [Pp. 20–21]

Some Addenda," *Modern Schoolman* 39 (1961–62): 61–64; M. Schooyans, "Bibliographie philosophique de S. Albert le Grand (1931–1960)," *Revista da Universidade Católica de São Paulo* 21 (1961): 36–88. For studies since 1960 see *Bulletin de théologie ancienne et médiévale, Bulletin Thomiste, Répertoire de Philosophie*, and other bibliographical aids.

[3] *Das Schöpfungsproblem bei Moses Maimonides, Albertus Magnus und Thomas von Aquin*. Band 11, Heft 5 of *Beiträge zur Geschichte der Philosophie des Mittelalters* [hereafter: BGPM] (Münster: Aschendorff, 1913).

[4] The section on Albert is found on pp. 45–92; for a comparison of Albert with Moses Maimonides and Aquinas, see p. 135–38.

[5] "Étude comparée du Traité de la Création dans les *Commentaires des Sentences* de S. Albert, S. Bonaventure et S. Thomas d'Aquin" (Dissertation dactylographiée; Louvain, 1948).

[6] "Zur Frage aufanglosen und zeitlichen Schöpfung bei Albert dem Grossen," *Studia Albertina*, Supplementband 4 of BGPM (1952): 167–88.

[7] "The Doctrine of Creation in St. Albert the Great" (M.A. thesis; New York: St. John's University, 1955).

[8] *Archives d'Histoire Doctrinale et Littéraire du Moyen Âge* 33 (1966); 7–21.

In light of that survey, then, not much secondary literature has been devoted to Albert's doctrine of creation.[9] Have scholars been more concerned with what he said on *esse*? The answer is again somewhat negative. Apart from a few remarks by Peghaire, Pollet, de Solages, and Pelster while treating other topics,[10] only four appear to have studied it in any detail. In his 1926 edition of Aquinas's *De Ente et Essentia*,[11] Roland-Gosselin wrote several chapters on the real distinction between essence and *esse*, one of which concerns the stance Albert took on the problem. In twelve pages (pp. 172–84) Roland-Gosselin presents a sampling of texts from the *Summa de Creaturis, In Sententiarum*, the commentaries on Aristotle's treatises (*Categories, Metaphysics, De Anima, Liber de Causis*), *De Unitate Intellectus*, and *Summa Theologiae*. The passages sampled reveal that "la pensée d'Albert le Grand sur la composition de l'être crée a beaucoup varié" (p. 172) and also that *esse* has several different meanings. For example, it is the *forma totius* or essence taken either concretely (*re* material existents) or abstractly (*re* spiritual existents; pp. 173–75, 181–82); *re* Christ it is aligned, from one point of view, with hypostasis but, from another, with essence or *quod est* and linked with existence (pp. 178–79, 180).[12]

[9] In "Création: La synthèse scolastique," *Dictionnaire de Théologie Catholique* (Paris: Letouzey et Ané, 1938), cols. 2084–2092, H. Pinard mentions Albert only three times, attending mostly to Aquinas and implying that the position of all medieval authors is pretty much the same. In *General Doctrine of Creation in the Thirteenth Century With Special Emphasis on Matthew of Aquasparta* (München: F. Schöningh, 1964), Zachary Hayes gives no extended treatment to Albert's position.

[10] See J. Péghaire, "La causalité du bien selon Albert le Grand," *Études d'Histoire Littéraire et Doctrinale du XIIIᵉ Siècle* (Ottawa: Institut d'Études Médiévales, 1932), pp. 59–89; V.-M. Pollet, "L'union hypostatique d'après S. Albert le Grand," *Revue Thomiste* 38 (1933); 505–32 and 689–724; Bruno de Solages, "La cohérence de la métaphysique de l'âme d'Albert le Grand," *Mélanges Cavallera* (Toulouse: Bibliothèque de l'Institut Catholique, 1948), pp. 367–400; F. Pelster, "Die *Quaestio* Alberts des Grossen über das Ein Sein in Christus nach Cod. Vat. Lat. 4245; Ein Beitrag zur Geschichte des Problems," *Divus Thomas* (Fribourg) 26 (1948); 3–25. Also see E. Gilson, *History of Christian Philosophy in the Middle Ages* [hereafter: *HCP*] (New York: Random House, 1955), p. 669, n. 5.

[11] M.-D. Roland-Gosselin, *Le "De Ente et Essentia" de S. Thomas d'Aquin* (Kain: Le Saulchoir, 1926; 2d ed., 1948).

[12] In *ibid.*, pp. 180–83, Roland-Gosselin notes that in the *Summa Theologiae* Albert uses *id quod est* and *esse* equivocally. His attempts on pp. 183–84 to eliminate that equivocation terminates thus: "Il semble plus conforme à la vérité historique de laisser à la pensée d'Albert le Grand l'indétermination que nous avons constatée. . . . Albert le Grand semble avoir été de ces esprits vastes, ouverts à toutes les influences, d'une mémoire tenance, incapables d'oublier ou d'abandonner une idée, et qui se trouvent empêchés par leur étendue même, et leur fidélité, d'unifier leur

Four decades later Léonard Ducharme published an important article, "*Esse* chez saint Albert la Grand. Introduction à la métaphysique de ses premiers écrits," the subtitle of which indicates its restriction to the two early treatises: *Summa de Creaturis* and *In Sententiarum*.[13] In them Albert at times does use *esse* (as Ducharme establishes) to express "existence" as the situation in which things find themselves when efficiently caused by external agents (p. 4). Existence thus understood has to do with the *fact* that various things *are* and *are caused* by God or (say) a carpenter, and Albert uses *esse* in stating that fact. But the fact that things exist is never considered by him to be a perfection, let alone their supreme perfection, and hence *esse* never designates existence as an ontological constituent and perfection of anything (p. 8; also see pp. 11–12, 16, 37). Rather, *esse* most frequently and properly signifies essence or specific nature—namely, the *quo est* by which a *quod est* is that which it specifically is, the reality and definition which the *forma totius* gives to whatever is (pp. 11–13, 18–19). In the phrases "esse essentiae" or "esse ut actus essentiae," the first noun points to the very effect and reality which an essence causes within its concrete subject (pp. 24 sqq. and 32 sqq.).[14]

Five years after Ducharme's publication there appeared Geiger's long study in the Canadian annual *Études d'histoire littéraire et doctrinale* entitled "La vie, acte essential de l'âme [et] l'*esse*, acte de l'essence d'après Albert-le-Grand."[15] Basically agreeing with Ducharme's interpretation that *esse* is linked chiefly with essence,[16] Geiger parallels the relationship of essence to *esse* with that of soul to life. Life is the formal effect of the soul within the living body. *Vivere* is the animation or vivification effected by the soul's presence within matter: it is what the soul formally causes as an intrinsic constituent of a living existent. It emanates from the soul as the latter's essential and continuous act and is, thereby, a sort of intermediary between soul and body (see pp. 56–97, especially pp. 59–62, 85–87, and the résumé on pp. 92–97). Similarly, *esse* is the formal effect of a concrete essence within a being. It is the specification of matter by the *forma totius*. It is the

---

pensée." A. Hufnagel's solution is to question whether the *Summa Theologiae* is rightly attributed to Albert as author—see "Zur Echtheitsfrage der *Summa Theologiae* Alberts des Grossen," *Theologische Quartalschrift* 146 (1966); 8–39. Also see E. Gilson, *HCP*, p. 671, n. 12.

[13] *Revue de l'Université d'Ottawa* 27 (1957); 1–44.

[14] See *ibid.*, p. 33: "*l'esse* est l'effet de l'essence dans le sujet concret."

[15] *Études histoire littéraire et doctrinale*, 17 (1962): 49–116.

[16] Geiger also grants (with Ducharme) that *esse* on occasion does point to existence as a fact but not as a perfection—see *ibid.*, pp. 62, 104, 106.

essentialization, the essential determination effected by the presence of a definite nature within an individual *quod est*. It is the act emanating from essence; it is diffused (*diffunditur*) by the form. It is a quasi-intermediary between the principle (the essence or *quo est*) and the recipient (the *quod est* or matter; see pp. 97–111, especially pp. 97–98, 100–108, 110–11).

Even the tightly abridged and simplified version of Geiger's reading just presented shows it to be profound and helpful. But one negative comment on his methodology seems called for. On page 50, note 9, he states that

> Albert presents the same doctrine, often expressed in the same terms, in his first as well as his last treatises, both philosophical and theological in nature. Hence, one may abstract from questions of chronology and from the distinction between philosophical and theological writings.

That statement makes me uneasy. One can know that the same position on *esse* is presented in philosophical or theological treatises from different temporal periods of Albert's career only if one has first arranged and then read them in the chronological order they were written. But if they are read in that fashion, why not present the results of that reading in a chronological order?

The fourth and final study of *esse* is Georg Wieland's *Untersuchungen zum Seinsbegriff im Metaphysikkommentar Alberts des Grossen.*[17] He accepts Geiger's exegesis of *esse* as act of form or essence but complements it with *esse* as the *primum creatum* from Albert's *De Causis et Processu Universitatis.*[18] Let us speak briefly on those two points.

Form or essence gives *esse*, which is in fact the "diffusio formae." In that phrase "forma" stands for "forma totius" and not "forma partis"[19] because the latter, even though the act of matter, is potential with respect to *esse*, which issues into the individual thing from form-and-matter as its act and completion and which accordingly needs as source the form (= *forma totius*), which is, to some extent, over and beyond that composite of matter/form. In support of that interpretation Wie-

[17] Münster: Aschendorff, 1972. Wieland first submitted this as a doctoral dissertation in 1969 to Ruhr-Universität Bochum. It now appears as Band VII in the new series of *BGPM*.

[18] This is Albert's commentary on the *Liber de Causis*, which is neoplatonic in its philosophical positions (see below, n. 20) but was considered by Albert as belonging to the Aristotelian *Metaphysics*. Hence, Wieland justly includes it in his study of Albert's commentary on the *Metaphysics*.

[19] This phrase Wieland believes (see pp. 72–90, especially pp. 75–76) Geiger left ambiguous and hence seeks to dispel the ambiguity. On "forma totius," see pp. 28 sqq., 39.

land quotes these lines from Albert's *Metaphysica*, I, tr. 4, c. 9 (Geyer edition, p. 60, lines 27–30 and 33–35):

> Forma est quasi foris manens dicta, et quanto plus manet foras materiam substantia et esse et operatione, verius habet nomen formae. . . . Illae autem formae quae in materia sunt imagines vocantur, eo quod sunt formarum verarum resultationes et imitationes, quantum permittunt materiae, ut dicit Plato.

Hence the form, the diffusion of which is *esse*, the form which has *esse* as its essential and proper act, is the *forma totius*—namely, "forma, quae est totum esse et est species" (*Meta.*, II, c. 9; p. 100, ll. 77 sq.; quoted by Wieland on p. 67, n. 4, and *passim*). Consequently, *esse* is the formal effect of the essence or form which makes a being be *what it is* (p. 93). It is the intermediary between essence and the individual (pp. 90, 103), which it also makes one, intelligible, definable and nameable (pp. 94 sqq.). Just as accidents are products of substance, so *esse* is the product of essence (p. 70), from which however it is only virtually distinct through a "distinctio rationis rationcinatae cum fundamento in re" (p. 93, n. 136).

As so conceived, *esse* belongs to the Aristotelian dimension of Albert's thought and answers the question *quid sit res*. But one must, Wieland continues, ask also *an sit res*, the answer to which Albert finds in Prop. IV of the Neoplatonic treatise, *Liber de Causis*: "Prima rerum creatarum est esse, et non est ante ipsum creatum aliud."[20] Considered

[20] The treatise is Neoplatonic in its philosophy (basically, that of Plotinus and Proclus), but whether its author is Arabian, Jewish, or Christian is still not clear. For surveys of authorship, see H. Bédoret, "L'auteur et la traducteur du *Liber de Causis*," *Revue néoscolastique de philosophie* 41 (1938): 519–33; H. D. Saffrey, *Sancti Thomae de Aquino Super Librum de Causis Expositio* (Fribourg: Société Philosophique Louvain, 1954), pp. xv sqq.; G. C. Anawati, "Prolégomènes à une nouvelle édition du *De Causis* arabe," *Mélanges L. Massignon* (Paris: A. Maisonneuve, 1957), pp. 73–85 (he favors a ninth-century Arabian Neoplatonist as author); L. Sweeney, S.J., "Research Difficulties in the *Liber de Causis*," *Modern Schoolman* 36 (1958–59): 109–10; H.-D. Saffrey, "L'état actuel des recherches sur le *Liber de Causis* comme source de la métaphysique au moyen âge" in P. Wilpert, ed., *Miscellanea Mediaevalia* (Berlin: Walter de Gruyter, 1963), 2:267–81 (see especially p. 274: "Il nous est impossible de décider si le *Liber* a été compilé par un ancien philosophe arabe, ou si déjà avant lui un original grec ou syriaque existait, qu'il se serait contenté de traduire"); A. Pattin, "Le *Liber de Causis*," *Tijdschrift voor Filosofie* 28 (1966): 90–98; A. Badawi, *La transmission de la philosophie grecque au monde arabe* (Paris: J. Vrin, 1968), pp. 60–72. I shall use the Latin text as found in Otto Bardenhewer, *Die pseudo-aristotelische Schrift Ueber das reine Gute bekannt unter dem Namen Liber de Causis* (Freiburg im Breisgau: Herder, 1882), pp. 163 sqq.; for a German translation of the Arabic text, see *ibid.*, pp. 58–118.

as *primum creatum, esse* pertains to the relationship that all created existents have to the first cause: in each of these *esse* is His effect and allows one to say that the thing *is, exists* (pp. 108–109). It is the "prima effluxio dei" and, thus, involves an "Aktivität von einem vorgeordneten Prinzip," just as "esse ut actus essentiae" entails an activity from a principle too—the form which "dat esse" (p. 109). *Esse* as *primum creatum* and as act of form has, then, two distinct sources, but the relationship between the two conceptions of *esse* and between its two principles is not clearly set forth by Albert.[21] Despite that lack of clarity, though, his grafting a Neoplatonist version of creation (wherein *esse* is *primum creatum*) upon an Aristotelian theory of *ousia* (within which *esse* is *actus essentiae*) to answer the double question of *an sit res* and *quid sit res* discloses Albert's commentaries on Aristotle to be no mere compilations of disjointed materials but a genuine contribution to medieval philosophy and theology (pp. 111–12).

Obviously Wieland's rather spectacular conclusions are directly relevant to this paper on *esse* in Albert's texts on creation. Undoubtedly, too, they are attractive. Whether or not they are valid cannot be decided until one has independently studied Albert, especially his *De Causis et de Processu Universitatis*. But one negative note can be sounded now on his methodology. On occasion Wieland tends to excerpt short portions (sometimes a single sentence) of the same text and to repeat them in connection with various topics throughout his book.[22] This tendency can lead one to assess an excerpt apart from its context and also to impart to his interpretation a higher degree of textual strength than merited.

The previous survey of the attempts four scholars made to cope with *esse* in Albert's writings is helpful by illustrating procedural flaws to be avoided and, second, by stressing questions which need reflection. We should read Albert's treatises in a chronological order (vs. Geiger) and, also, study key-texts in them not piecemeal but each in its entirety within its context (*vs.* Wieland). Among questions meriting attention within the two general areas of *esse* and creation are whether *esse* is linked with existence (if so, as a mere fact or as a perfection?) or only with essence; what essence means: whether it is synonymous with form and, if so, in what sense; how *esse* fits into the Boethian scheme of *quo est/quod est*; what connection *esse* has with prime matter; whether and

21 Wieland also finds a similar lack of clarity in whether creation is a necessary or a free act—see *op. cit.*, p. 60, n. 67. But see below, n. 46.

22 One such is: "forma, quae est totum esse et est species" (*Meta.*, II, c. 9) quoted by Wieland on p. 67, n. 4, and referred to on pp. 74, 76, 78 and *passim.*

how it is the *primum creatum*; whether God creates freely; what creation strictly taken entails.[23]

Let us now reflect upon such questions in Albert's own treatises, chronologically ordered.

Text A: Summa de Creaturis, Pars I, Tr. 1, q. 2, a. 1:
"*An materia sit*," ad 1 and ad 2

The first key-text is from his *Summa de Creaturis*,[24] which (in the Jammy edition and for our purposes) consists of two parts. The second of these is "De homine"; the first is "De coaequaevis": the four *creata* which God made simultaneously and which are all equal inasmuch as each is a principle of further creation: matter, the "caelum empyreum,"

---

[23] On this last question see L. Sweeney, "Doctrine of Creation in the *Liber de Causis*," p. 288, quoted below in the portion of this paper corresponding to n. 45.

[24] Written between 1240 and 1243 in the judgment of F. J. Catania, "Divine Infinity According to Albert the Great's Commentary on the *Sentences*" (Ph.D. dissertation; St. Louis University, 1959), p. 9, who gives a helpful survey of the views of Lottin, Doucet and Brady (*ibid.*, pp. 8–10). Also see J. A. Weisheipl, "Life and Works of Albert the Great," *Albertus Magnus and the Sciences: Commemorative Essays* (Toronto: Pontifical Institute of Mediavel Studies, 1980): *Summa Parisiensis*, of which the *Summa de Creaturis* is a section, was composed at Paris before his commentary on the *Sentences* and apparently as a result of his disputations as master. For A. Maurer, *Medieval Philosophy* (New York: Random House, 1962), p. 403, n. 1, it was composed 1236–43; for Etienne Gilson (with M. H. Laurent), 1228–33—see HCP, p. 668, n. 2. This much seems clear: the *Summa* is among Albert's earliest works and is earlier than *In Sententiarum*.

On the plan of the complete *Summa*, see P. G. Meersseman, *Introductio in Opera Omnia B. Alberti Magni* (Brugis Apud Carolum Beyaert, 1932), pp. 107–10: the *Summa* consists of four books, each with subdivisions—*De Deo Uno et Trino*; *De Creatione et Creaturis*; *De Bono et de Virtutibus*; *De Incarnatione, Sacramentis, Resurrectione*. "De Coaequaevis" is the first part of Book Two. For a different and chronological arrangement, see B. Geyer, *Alberti Magni Opera Omnia*, Tomus XXVIII: *De Bono* (Monasterii Westfalorum in Aedibus Aschendorff, 1951), "Prolegomena," p. XIX: (1) *De Sacramentis*, (2) *De Incarnatione*, (3) *De Resurrectione*, (4) *De IV coaequaevis*, (5) *De Homine*, (6) *De Bono*.

Vol. XXVII of the Cologne critical edition, which will contain "De IV Coaequaevis," has not yet been published (only Vol. XXVI [1958], which contains *De Sacramentis, De Incarnatione, De Resurrectione*, and Vol. XXVIII, cited above and containing *De Bono*, have so far appeared). Consequently, my references to the "De IV Coaequaevis" portion of the *Summa* are to the seventeenth-century edition: Petrus Jammy, *Opera B. Alberti Magni* (Lugduni Sumptibus Claudii Prost, 1651), Vol. XIX: *Summa de Creaturis Divisa in Duas Partes*. Its Latin text I accept without change except for occasional simplification of punctuation and modernized spelling, as well as a few corrections required to make sense of a passage (which however are always indicated). Also, references in the "Index Tractatuum . . ." of the volume are occasionally inaccurate and have been corrected.

angelic nature and time (Pars I, Tr. 4, c. 69, *solutio*; XIX, 215A). Our text concerns the first of these *coaequaeva*—matter—in a *quaestio* which comes after Albert had in an initial question of eight articles discussed creation itself ("an creatio sit; quid sit; cuius sit proprius actus creare; utrum creatio sit communicabilis alii; utrum sit opus naturae vel voluntatis; utrum creatio sit actus separatus ab opere naturae et propositi; utrum actus creationis plus sit ostensivus potentiae vel sapientiae vel bonitatis; utrum actus creationis sit naturalis vel miraculosus"). In the first article of question 2, "De Materia," Albert asks whether prime matter exists ("an materia sit") and answers through the familiar technique of four *videtur quod non's*, five *sed contra's* (drawn from *Glossa super Genesim*, Augustine's *Confessions*, XII, and Aristotle's *Physics*), a *solutio* (which consists of two words *re* those *sed contra's*: "Quod concedimus") and, finally, replies to the four *videtur quod non's* (Pars I, Tr. 1, q. 2; XIX, 7C–8C).

Let us turn to the first of those replies, which confronts this endeavor to show that prime matter does not exist. Since form gives *esse*, since to lack *esse* is to be nothing, since prime matter entirely lacks form, matter is entirely without *esse* and thus, precisely as prime matter, is nothing [and, hence, does not exist].

> Forma dat esse; ergo quod caret omni forma caret omni esse; sed materia prima secundum rationem primae materiae accepta caret omni forma; ergo caret omni esse; et quicquid caret omni esse nihil est; ergo materia prima nihil est secundum rationem materiae primae accepta, quia caret omni forma; ergo caret omni esse. [*Ibid., videtur quod non* 1; p. 7D]

Albert's reply to that argumentation is indeed interesting but puzzling. Although prime matter has of itself the *esse* which properly belongs to what is a subject and potency, this is *esse secundum quid* and not *esse simpliciter*, which however form gives to matter; [hence, prime matter does exist].

> Dicentes ad primum quod forma dat esse; materia autem habet esse subjecti et potentiae, et hoc habet a seipsa, et hoc non est esse simpliciter sed secundum quid. [*Ibid.,* ad 1; p. 8B]

Puzzlement issues from several sources. In the sentence just quoted, the *esse* which "forma dat" is no doubt "esse simpliciter," which amounts to "existence" in light of the problem at hand: whether or not prime matter exists. But if so, how can both Geiger and Wieland so confidently refer the clause to the formal causality form or essence exercises within an existent—the diffusion of the form, the specification by which a form makes the existent be *what he is* and not *be* simply?[25] Second, must not the first noun in the clause "forma dat esse" stand for "forma partis" rather than "forma totius" since the form at issue is the counterpart of prime matter? If this should be the case, though, what of Wieland's claim that "forma" in this formula is "forma totius"?[26] Third, the "esse subjecti et potentiae," which prime matter has of itself, is "esse secundum quid" and pertains to *what* matter is, to its very nature.[27] But if (with Geiger and Wieland; see above, n. 25) the *esse* which form is responsible for as an intrinsic cause is the specific determination of the existent, might not the *esse* which matter has by reason of its very status as subject and potency be the effect it exercises in that existent as intrinsic cause and, thus, be the limitation and individuation of the individual existent?[28] But no matter what one's re-

[25] On Geiger, see *art. cit.*, pp. 103–105 and 108 sqq. (where he attends mainly to *De Anima* and *De Unitate Intellectus*); on Wieland see *op. cit.*, pp. 26–27 and 72 sqq. (where he attends solely to *Meta.*). Also see the previous portions of my paper corresponding to footnotes 15–16 and 17–21.

[26] On "forma" *re* "materia" as "forma substantialis" and, hence, "forma partis," see *ibid.*, a. 2 ("Quid sit Materia"), ad 1 (p. 9D): "prima potentia materiae est ad formam substantialem"; *ibid.*, ad [3] (p. 10A): "Et primum dicit etiam ante quod nihil est: potentia enim materiae primo est ad substantialem formam et ad alias per accidens, scilicet propter illam"; *ibid., ad illud quod objicitur contra quartam* [*definitionem materiae*] (p. 11A): "Inter materiam autem primam et formam substantialem non est medium." For Wieland's position see above, n. 19.

[27] On the essence of matter as subject and potency see also *ibid.*, a. 1, ad 4 (p. 8C): "Unumquodque dicitur perfectum quando est in debito statu sui esse; et ideo materia perfecta est, quando habet rationem subjecti ad formas generabilium et corruptibilium"; *ibid.*, a. 2, *solutio* (p. 9C): "substantia et entitas materiae in se considerata non est intelligibilis proprio intellectu sed intelligitur secundum privationem, scilicet quod hoc est materia quod praeter formas accidentales et substantiales invenitur in ente"; *ibid.*, a. 3, ad 3 (p. 11D): "materia prima in ratione materiae accepta non potest abstrahi a ratione potentiae, quia ipsa secundum seipsam habet rationem potentiae: secundum seipsam enim subjectum est, et ratio potentiae et ratio subjecti in ipsa sunt idem, et sic habet formam quandam rationis."

Question: what link, if any, is there between the "esse seundum quid" which matter has of itself (see key-text A, under discussion) and "incohatio formae" in matter? On this last see Geiger, *art. cit.*, pp. 23–25, 105–107, esp. p. 105 and n. 214; G. Wieland, *op. cit.*, pp. 84–87 with notes.

[28] On matter as the principle of individuation in sensible existents, see *ibid.*, a. 5, *solutio* (p. 15C): "Dicendum quemadmodum dicit Aristoteles in primo *de caelo et mundo* quod cum dico hoc caelum, dico materiam; sed cum dico caelum, dico formam"; *ibid.*, Tr. 4, q. 28, a. 1, *solutio* (p. 97D): "Notandum quod quoddam facit personam et aliquid ostendit eam esse discretam. Hoc autem facit personam quod facit per se unam eam; nihil autem facit eam per se unam nisi particulatio formae super hanc materiam. . . . Individuantia autem ostendunt personam distinctam esse et in materialibus quidem materialiter sunt individuantia,

action is to that, this seems obvious: the *esse* in the single sentence which constitutes Albert's *ad primum* has a twofold meaning: existence (the *esse simpliciter* which "forma dat") and nature or essence (the *esse secundum quid* which matter has on its own).

What information does Albert give on those (and other) points in *ad secundum*, which concludes our Text A and in which Albert answers this *videtur quod non? Esse* is what is created first (as Aristotle says in *Liber de Causis*) and nothing else is created before it; accordingly, whatever is prior to *esse* is not created; but whatever is prior to form is also prior to *esse*; hence, whatever is prior to form is not created; but prime matter is prior to form and, thus, is not created; but whatever is not created is nothing; therefore, prime matter is nothing [and, accordingly, does not exist].[29]

> Dicit Philosophus in *libro de causis* quod prima rerum creatarum est esse, et non est ante ipsum creatum aliud. Ergo quod est ante esse non est de numero creatorum; sed quicquid est ante formam est ante esse; ergo quod est ante formam non est de numero creatorum; materia autem prima est ante formam; ergo non est de numero creatorum; et quicquid non est de numero creatorum, nihil est; ergo materia prima nihil est. [*Ibid., videtur quod non* 2; p. 7D]

Albert's response to that impressive line of argumentation is equally impressive but not without problems, as will be evident from this paraphrase.

When *esse* is said in the *Liber de Causis* to be the first of created things, *esse* stands for *ens* (as the one commenting there on Proposition 4 and Blessed Dionysius both make clear)[30] and "first" by nature refers to that which is not [entirely] convertible with subsequent subsistents. In this sense *ens* is absolutely first. Why so? Because the process of resolving what is posterior to what is prior comes to a halt in *ens*. Consequently, "first" here has to do with a principle of cognition. But when

in intellectualibus spiritualter." See Roland-Gosselin, *op. cit.*, pp. 89–103, especially pp. 89–94 for exegesis and texts from *Summa de Creaturis* and *In Sententiarum*.

29 I omit in my paraphrase and Latin quotation the two proofs why what is before *esse* is what is before form because Albert is silent in *ad secundum* on those proofs, which also are not directly relevant to our topic. But see below, n. 33.

30 See Dionysius, *De Divinis Nominibus*, ch. 5, #266 of the Latin translation found in C. Pera, *Thomae Aquinatis in Librum Beati Dionysii de Divinis Nominibus Expositio* (Turin: Marietti, 1950), p. 230: "Et ante alias ipsius participationes esse propositum est"; *ibid.*, #267: "Et quidem principia existentium omnia esse participant et sunt et principia sunt et primum sunt, postea principia sunt. . . . Per se participationes invenies ipso esse primum illas participantes et ipso esse quidem primum existentes, postea huius aut huius principia existentes et participare esse et existentes et participatas."

matter is said to be "first," "principle" is understood with respect to generation and time. Obviously, then, "first" is used equivocally, because when applied to *ens* it is a principle of cognition with reference to what can be fitted into predicaments, but when applied to matter it is a principle of generation with respect to the existents generated.

Ad aliud dicendum quod cum dicitur prima rerum creatarum est esse, ponitur esse pro ente, sicut dicit ibi Commentator in expositione illius propositionis. Et idem dicit beatus Dionysius in *libro de divinis nominibus*, cap. 5 de ente. Et dicitur ibi primum natura a quo non convertitur consequentia subsistendi, et sic ens est absolute primum, quia in ipso stat resolutio posteriorum in prius. Et ibidem hoc primum ponit principium cognitionis. Cum autem dicitur materia prima, ponitur principium secundum rationem generationis et temporis. Et sic patet quod primum hinc inde ponitur aequivoce, quia cum dicitur de ente est principium cognitionis respectu eorum quae ordinabilia sunt in praedicamento. Cum autem dicitur de materia, est principium generationis respectu generatorum. [*Ibid.*, *ad secundum*; p. 8B]

Where are the problem areas of which we spoke in that important reply? One consists in how to translate and interpret the sentence, "Et dicitur ibi primum natura a quo non convertitur consequentia subsistendi, et sic ens est absolute primum, quia in ipso stat resolutio posteriorum in prius." My paraphrase reads: "*first* by nature refers to that which is not [fully] convertible with subsequent subsistents. In this sense *ens* is absolutely first. Why so? Because the process of resolving what is posterior to what is prior comes to a halt in *ens*." That is an endeavor to make Albert intelligible and not to translate the precise wording of his Latin. But what data is elsewhere provided to ground that endeavor? The author of the *Liber de Causis*, Prop. 1, states: "Quando removes virtutem rationalem ab homine, non remanet homo, et remanet vivum, spirans, sensibile. Et quando removes ab eo vivum, non remanet vivum, et remanet esse, quoniam esse non removetur ab eo sed removetur vivum. . . . Remanet ergo homo esse. Cum ergo non est individuum homo, est animal, et si non est animal, est esse tantum." The process thus described could be what Albert intends by "in ipso [*ente or esse*] stat resolutio posteriorum in prius," since he had already referred in the *Summa de Creaturis* (q. 1, a. 1, arg. 3; p. 1D sq.) to Prop. 1.[31] Second, in a portion of our next key-text (*In II Sent.*, d. 1,

[31] On "resolutio" see *In I Sent.*, d. 8, a. 24 ad 1 (Jammy ed., XIV, 155D–156A): "Quod objicitur de ente dicendum quod id in quo stat resolutio nostri intellectus est simplex secundum quid et simpliciter compositum. Intellectus enim

76

a. 1, ad "id quod objicitur de tertia expositione"; XIV, p. 5A), we read: "Secundum rationem formae et simplicitatis nihil est ante esse, quia omnia aliquo modo se habent ex additione ad ens, etiam unum et verum et bonum." These last three "convertuntur cum ente," which nonetheless retains its prior status as that to which the others are added. Accordingly, it makes some sense to understand Albert as meaning: *ens* or *esse* is first as that at which stops the resolution of humanity, animality and life, and as that to which *bonum* and the other convertibles are added. Hence, my paraphrase: "*esse* or *ens* as 'first' refers to that which is not [fully] convertible with subsequent subsistents. In this sense *ens* is absolutely first. Why so? Because the process of resolving what is posterior to what is prior comes to a halt in *ens*."

But Albert's *ad secundum* contains another and more serious difficulty. The *videtur quod non* which it is answering is explicitly directed at showing that prime matter does not exist since it is (to reverse the order of points made there) nothing, not created, prior to form, prior to *esse*. But in his reply Albert explicitly sets down only why *esse* (= *ens*) and matter are "first" in an equivocal sense and leaves the reader to infer that the priority of *esse* neither excludes that of matter nor prevents matter from existing because *esse* can also mean "existere." More fully stated: the priority of *esse* in the *Liber de Causis* has to do with cognition, whereas that of prime matter has to do with generation and time: it is prior to form inasmuch as of itself it is not form but the potency to receive form; accordingly, prime matter precedes form and yet *is*—because the *esse* spoken of in the *Liber* pertains directly to knowledge and not to the temporal world where generation and other changes occur and where *esse* as "existence" is operative—and is created.

If our reading of *ad secundum* is accurate, then, Albert applies *esse*

resolvens abstrahit universale a particulari et ulterius magis universale a minus universali, et ideo non aufert nisi differentias coarctantes, et verum est quod secundum ablationem illarum differentiarum ens simplex est et ideo stat in ipso resolutio." To date the only information found in the *Summa de Creaturis* on "subsistere" comes from *ibid.*, tr. 1, q. 2, a. 2, *ad id quod objicitur contra tertiam definitionem* (XIX, 10C–D): "Sic se habet informe et materia ad substantiam et hoc aliquid et quod est. Et intelligit per informe rationem privationis in materia, per materiam autem naturam subjecti, per substantiam autem intelligit formam, per hoc aliquid determinatam ac compositam substantiam: hoc aliquid enim est forma contracta per materiam. Per hoc quod est intelligit rationem subsistentiae, quam habet composita substantia a compositione materiae et formae. Unde quod est idem quod nunc est apud naturam. Per formam autem intelligitur materia secundum quod accipit esse a forma: secundum Philosophum enim in 7 *metaphysicae*, idem est esse subjecti et formae in composito, quia subjectum non habet esse nisi a forma."

explicitly to the intramental world, where *ens* is contrasted with such other conceptions as *verum*, *unum* and *bonum* or, again, with "man," "animal," and "life" (as in *Liber de Causis*) or, again, with the predicaments. Implicitly, though, he applies *esse* to the extramental world of actual existents, where prime matter is an ingredient in their coming to be through generation but itself exists as that "quod praeter formas accidentales et substantiales invenitur in ente" (*ibid.*, a. 2, *solutio*; XIX, p. 9D) through divine creation.[32]

And if these results (i.e., *esse* points to *ens* as concept and to existence as fact) are joined with those attained earlier in our exegesis of *ad primum*, we have a third meaning for *esse*, which matter has of itself: its nature as subject and potency, which is *esse secundum quid*. Nowhere (at least in the portions of *Summa de Creaturis* so far studied) does *esse* point to the form itself or its essential act.[33] In *ad primum*, in fact, "forma dat esse" appears to link existence with form.

But perhaps the picture will change in the key-text we now take up.

Text B: In II Sent., *d. 1, a. 1*, ad objectionem
de tertia explicatione[34]

The passage at hand is occasioned by Lombard's quotation from *Genesis*, 1, 1: "In principio creavit Deus caelum et terram," and, more exactly, by his triple explanation of that verse, the first two of which concentrate on "principium" (which is taken to refer to the Son and, secondly, to time; XV, pp. 3D–4A), the third on "caelum et terram"

---

[32] On matter as created see *ibid.*, a. 3, *solutio* (p. 11C), which consists in Albert's saying, "Quod concedimus," where *quod* refers to this *sed contra* (p. 11B–C): "Augustinus in 12 *confessionum*: Tu Domine fecisti mundum de materia informi, quam fecisti de nulla re pene nulla [*read*: nullam] rem. Item, Augustinus in libro *de trinitate* dicit quod omne ens est ab ente primo quod est Deus. Materia prima est ens. Ergo est ab ente primo, et non nisi per creatum; ergo est creata." Also see below, n. 47.

[33] One comes closest to this in the first of two proofs in *videtur quod non* 2 of a. 1 ("An materia sit") why whatever is prior to form is also prior to esse: "Quod autem hoc sit ante esse quod est ante formam patet ex hoc quod esse non est nisi individui vel speciei vel generis vel principii, et omne tale est a forma; ergo omne tale est a forma individui vel speciei vel generis vel principii" (p. 7D). But, as noted above (n. 29), Albert in *ad secundum* takes no notice of that proof.

[34] Albert's *Scripta Super IV Libros Sententiarum* (to give its full title—see P. G. Meersseman, *op. cit.*, p. 106) is to be dated after the *Summa de Creaturis* (1249 is its *terminus ad quem*): see F. J. Catania, *op. cit.*, p. 9. According to W. Kübel, *Alberti Magni Opera Omnia*, Tomus XXVI: *De Sacramentis . . .* (1958), "Prolegomena," p. X, it is almost certain that Albert was writing *In II Sent.*, in 1246. Since the Cologne critical edition is not yet published, we shall use the Jammy edition (see above, n. 24, last paragraph), Vol. XV.

78

(which stands for "angelicam naturam et materiam quatuor elementorum"; *ibid.*, p. 4C). The key-text is Albert's reply to this objection
against the third interpretation. According to Aristotle, *esse* is what is
created first, and no other creature is created before it; therefore, the
angelic nature and prime matter are not first.

> Objicitur autem: sicut dicit Philosophus prima rerum creatarum est
> esse et non est ante ipsum creatura alia; ergo angelica natura et
> materia prima non sunt prima, ut videtur. [*Ibid.*, p. 4C]

What is Albert's response? The objection is solved (he comments) inasmuch as "first" is used with reference either to the intelligibility of
form and simplicity or to the order substance has in *esse*. According to
the intelligibility of form and simplicity nothing is prior to *esse* because
everything—even *unum*, *verum* and *bonum*, as was established above
(*In I Sent.*, d. 46)—is in some sense an addition to *ens*. But according to
the order of substance in nature and *esse* all philosophers hold that the
first intelligence is what the creator of the universe created first. What
they call "intelligences" we call "angels." Thus, the explanation that
"in the beginning God created the angelic nature first" holds because
creation has to do with *esse* rather than with simplicity, which comes
about by abstraction through the intellect.

> Ad id quod objicitur de tertia [expositione] dicendum quod soluta
> est objectio, quia primum dicitur duobus modis, scilicet secundum
> rationem formae et simplicitatis, et secundum ordinem substantiae
> in essendo. Secundum rationem formae et simplicitatis nihil est ante
> esse, quia omnia aliquo modo se habent ex additione ad ens, etiam
> unum et verum et bonum, ut in penultima distinctione primi libri
> est ostensum. Sed secundum ordinem substantiae in natura et esse
> opinio omnium philosophorum est quod intelligentia prima sit
> primum causatum a creatore universitatis. Quod autem illi intelli-
> gentias nos vocamus angelos; et tunc stat expositio illa quia creatio
> potius respicit esse quam ordinem simplicitatis. In abstractione
> autem fit per intellectum. [*Ibid.*, *ad objectionem* . . .; p. 5A]

In the objection Judaeo-Christianity confronts pagan Aristotelianism
(Neoplatonism, actually) on what God created first. According to the
Old Testament, as interpreted by Lombard, it was angels and prime
matter; for the author of the *Liber de Causis* it was *esse*. In his reply
Albert tries (unsuccessfully, I would say) to defuse the explosive situation by distinguishing two levels on which "first" is applicable. One of
them has to do with actual substances or natures: intelligences [human

souls, animals, plants]. Here "first" pertains to the existents which are highest hierarchically: intelligences or angels. These *Genesis*, 1, 1, described as created first, since creation concerns *esse* or existence.[35] The other level consists of intelligibilities, forms, quiddities achieved through intellectual abstraction, and here one intelligibility is prior to another if it is more simple. Which intelligibility is first, then? *Ens* because it is less complex than *verum*, *unum*, and *bonum*, which are additions to it: for example, *verum* is "being-as-*related-to-intellect*."[36]

Such is Albert's explicit message, which at first hearing seems sound enough. Why, then, is it deficient? Because he has not directly faced the objection that God first created *esse* and not the angelic nature. In his answer he removes the *esse* of the *Liber de Causis*, Prop. 4, from the actual universe, in which alone creation takes place, by reducing it to an intelligibility (*ens*). Because of simplicity in its content or comprehension this may have priority over other intelligibilities (true, good, one), but it is not something capable of being created: no concept can, strictly speaking, be created, but only thought of, analyzed, reflected upon. Yet Prop. 4 of the *Liber* reads: "Prima *rerum creatarum* est esse." Despite his clear acknowledgment that *esse* can signify existence in creationist contexts, then, Albert apparently excludes that meaning from Prop. 4, where it stands rather for the intelligibility or *ratio* of "ens" with only a conceptual priority.

Perhaps, though, the reference he gives in his reply to his commentary on d. 46 of Lombard's *Sentences*, Book One, will remedy the situation. Beginning with article 11 of d. 46, his remarks there concern truth (for example, "quid sit; quot modis dicatur veritas; de conversione ipsius cum bono et ente et uno; secundum quem ordinem habent se

---

[35] *Ibid.*, ". . . creatio potius respicit esse quam ordinem simpliciatis."

In his defense here of the third explanation Albert has so far said nothing of the last word in the phrase: "angelica natura et materia." But see the subsequent two paragraphs ("Si autem" and "Ad aliud"), the pertinent lines of which are these: "Etiam secundum philosophos materia ponitur primo antequam aliquid fiat ex ipsa. . . . [Deus] intelligit omnia simul in materia creata et non in formis distinctis."

[36] See *In I Sent.*, d. 46, a. 14 [*solutio*] (XIV, p. 669B): "Verum autem dicit relationem ad formam ad minus exemplarem per quam habet rationem manifestationis; et ideo dicit Hilarius quod verum est declarativum entis: oportet enim in quolibet esse principium intellgendi aliquod per quod ordinetur ad intellectum. Bonitas autem et bonum dicunt respectum ad finem extra a quo est et ad quem est, quia enim bonus est sumus, et inquantum sumus boni sumus." On abstraction see *ibid.*, d. 8, a. 18 ad 4 (p. 153A); *ibid.*, a. 24, ad 1 (p. 155D), quoted in n. 31 above; U. Dähnert, *Die Erkenntnislehre des Albertus Magnus gemessen an den Stufen der "abstractio"* (Leipzig: G. Gerhardt, 1933); E. Gilson, *HCP*, pp. 286–87 and p. 671, n. 11; H. Johnston, "Intellectual Abstraction in St. Albert," *Philosophical Studies* 10 (1960): 204–12.

adinvicem unum, verum, bonum et ens") and contain two relevant passages, each entailing a discussion of *Liber de Causis*, Prop. 4.

In the first he takes issue with this objection against Augustine's statement "verum est id quod est": If the true is that which is, then truth is a thing's entity and, thus, its *esse* and *quod est* are the same— an identity found only in God; therefore, any truth would be God—a conclusion which is false, and, hence, Augustine's definition is null and void.

> Verum est id quod est; ergo a conjugatis veritas est rei entitas; ergo esse suum et quod est idem habet; ergo ipsum est quod habet; et hoc non convenit nisi Deo; ergo omnis veritas esset Deus, quod falsum est; ergo diffinitio est nulla. [*In I Sent.*, d. 46, a. 11; XIV, p. 665A]

Albert begins to defend Augustine by distinguishing between a thing's "entitas vel id quod est" as in itself and as found in a concrete nature or subject.[37] Grant that distinction, and it is not always accurate to say that "a thing's truth is its entity" or "the true is that which is." Why so? If "entity" is understood precisely as such and in itself [and if "truth" is affirmed to be "entity" in this sense], then truth (because entity) would be (*esset*) the first creature, according to Aristotle's statement, "*esse* is what is created first and nothing else is created before it"; also "that which is" will be described (*dicetur*) as "that which has *esse*," which then is the act of entity or essence so understood. [In this case one should not define a thing's truth as its entity or the true as that which is.] But if one takes "entity" and "that which is" in their concrete natures ("supposita natura quaedam"), he views them with reference to determinate species ("secundum modum determinationis ad speciem"), and thereby truth is the entity by which something or other truly is and "true" is that which truly is, as exemplified in the phrases, true gold, true color, true body, true science. Yet one should note that the determination of "that which is" to a nature is not properly to a species as such [because "being" transcends species, genus and other predicaments]. But conceding that, one may say "that which is" is "that which truly is in nature" and, thus, that the "true" equals "that which is." Consequently, neither truth and entity nor the true and what-is are entirely identical, as will be clearer later.

> Ad id quod quaeritur de diffinitione Augustini, dicendum quod rei entitas vel id quod est accipitur dupliciter, scilicet in se vel ut sup-

[37] A difficulty in interpreting Albert's response lies in the fact that he simultaneously distinguishes "entitas" and "id quod est" each in two ways: "in se vel ut supposita natura quaedam." Once one is aware of that fact, what he says is comparatively clear.

posita natura quaedam; et sic, ut opinor, non bene diceretur veritas rei entitas esse vel verum esse id quod est. Accipitur etiam [read: enim] entitas secundum modum determinationis ad speciem, et sic veritas est entitas qua res vere est et verum est id quod vere est. Si vero entitas accipiatur prout supponitur per nomen entitatis, tunc in veritate entitas esset prima creatura, secundum quod dicit Philosophus quod prima rerum creatarum est esse, et non est ante ipsam creatum aliud; et id quod est dicetur id quod habet esse, quod est actus sic intellectae entitatis vel essentiae. Si autem accipiatur id quod est prout dicit quandam determinationem circa esse, tunc non trahitur ad speciem, et tunc vere est quia unumquodque tunc vere est quando trahitur ad speciem sibi propriam ex natura determinata, sicut dicimus verum aurum et verum colorem et verum corpus et veram scientiam. Et hoc sonare videtur id quod est, quia id quod est est id quod vere est in natura. Et sic patet quod non omnino idem sunt veritas et entitas. Et hoc infra magis patebit. [*Ibid., ad objectionem de definitione Augustini*; p. 665C]

Despite the demands Albert makes upon one's intelligence and patience because of his elliptical and disjointed Latin, a couple of relevant points are clear. Unlike his silence in *In II Sent.*, d. 1, a. 1, *ad objectionem de tertia explicatione* (which we are still trying to cope with) on creation with respect to *Liber de Causis*, Prop. 4, and unlike his taking *esse* there as the concept of *ens* rather than as "existence," Albert talks about creation (truth if entity would be the first creature) and, secondly, he explicates *esse* as the act of entity or of essence taken as such and in itself ("id quod est dicetur id quod habet esse, quod est actus sic intellectae entitatis vel essentiae"). As "act of entity or essence," would not *esse* be (as Geiger and Wieland wish) the act which essence or entity gives to an *id quod est*? If so, it is neither a mere intelligibility nor existence but a third and, literally, essential factor in a created existent. But if Albert is already aware of *esse* in this sense, he is in the passage from *In II Sent.* no less silent on it than he is on existence. Before returning to *In II Sent.*, though, let us study another discussion on truth where he utilizes *Liber de Causis*, Prop. 4.

That utilization is found in the *solutio* of *In I Sent.*, d. 46, a. 13: "Utrum verum convertatur cum ente, uno et bono." One may (he acknowledges) grant their convertibility in direct predication if *ens, verum, bonum,* and *unum* are taken concretely; thus, one may say that "a being is good, true and one." But considered abstractly, they are not convertible or directly predicable except of God, and in creatures it is wrong to say that essence *is* truth or goodness or unity.[38] Nor should one affirm that essence is true, truth is being or goodness is true. But it is even more improper to say that "essence is being or good" than to say that "truth is being and one." Whence the impropriety? From the fact that *esse* or essence is what is created first, according to Aristotle's *Liber de Causis*, Prop. 4, and no other creature is prior. Consequently, essence has nothing to serve as its foundation or subject,[39] of which it would in turn serve as form; the result is that essence as essence cannot be in nature unless created from nothing. Everything other than essence comes about, as one reads there in the commentary on Prop. 4, through formation of essence—for instance, in the order of nature the good presupposes the concept of essence as that in which it is. Therefore, the intelligibility of essence is based upon [no substrate but upon] nothingness and thereby is prior to all else. Hence, too, one will not say that essence "*is* truth" but "entails truth" as predicable of it; similarly, not: "essence *is* goodness" but "entails goodness."[40] But someone may in-

[38] "Concretive sumpta" and "abstractive sumpta" correspond to "supposita natura quaedam" and "in se" of the previous text (a. 11, *ad objectionem de definitione Augustini*; p. 665C), which ended up with: "infra magis patebit."

In the third sentence of the current text (*ibid.*, a. 13, *solutio*) *ens* is not a noun but an adjective so as to be parallel with *verum, bonum,* and *unum*—for example, "veritas est *ens* . . . essentia est *ens* vel bona . . . veritas est *ens* vel veritas est una" (italics added).

[39] *Ibid.*, a. 14 [solutio] (p. 669B) makes "substrate" be a synonym for "foundation" and "subject": "Sic generaliter considerando ista [ens, unum, verum, bonum] ut consideraverunt Sancti, dicemus quod inter ista essentia et ens est primum natura, circa quod ut substratum sibi ponuntur alia." From the fact *esse* or *ens* or *essentia* serves as substrate, foundation, subject for subsequent determinations or "forms" one may infer that it is like matter (intelligible or spiritual). See E. Gilson, *HCP*, pp. 279–80.

[40] In the Latin text Albert promises to touch on unity later ("De unitate autem est alia ratio, quae infra patebit"), a promise which he kept in the final paragraph of the *solutio* and which contains this relevant information: unity, truth and so on add to essence not another nature but a relationship to the First Cause—"Si autem tu quaeras utrum unum se habeat ex additione ad alterum, dico quod si intelligatur additio alterius naturae, sicut forma et materia sunt alterius naturae et substantia et accidens sunt alterius naturae, tunc unum non addit super alterum. Si autem intelligatur additio secundum rationem respectus ad attributum causae primae, tunc unum addit super alterum rationem respectus, quia tunc essentia dicetur fluens ab essentia prima, veritas fluens a sapientia et bonitas fluens a bonitate; et ideo omne ens est verum et unum et bonum (p. 668A).

In those lines note the frequency of "fluens" as a description of divine causality, which incidentally separates the position of the "sancti" in *ibid.*, a. 14, from Aristotle's: "Si autem quaeritur secundum quem ordinem se habeant adinvicem unum, verum, bonum, et ens, dicendum quod secundum Philosophum ante omnia sunt ens et unum. Philosophus enim non ponit quod verum et bonum sint dispositiones

quire why essence cannot be termed "true" and "good" if truth and goodness can be predicable of it. The answer is that essence as such is not conceivable as formed upon any other or prior *ratio*; this is in line with Boethius: "that-which-is involves something over and beyond itself but *esse* has no such addition." Again, one properly says not that "truth *is* essence" but "entails essence." Nonetheless, essence, truth, goodness and unity are convertible when taken concretely because everything is being, true, good and one.

> Solutio. Ad hoc sine praejudicio potest dici quod ista quatuor convertuntur concretive sumpta, scilicet ens, unum, verum, bonum, in recto, scilicet quod ens est bonum et verum et unum, et sic de omnibus. Si autem sumantur abstractive, non credo quod [convertuntur] secundum rectam praedicationem nisi in Deo; in creaturis autem non, quia non credo quod haec sit vera: essentia est veritas vel bonitas vel unitas. Hoc autem est impropria: essentia est vera et veritas est ens et bonitas vera; tamen haec est magis impropria: essentia est ens vel bona, quam haec: veritas est ens vel veritas est una. Cuius ratio sic patet per Philosophum in *libro causarum*, qui dicit quod prima rerum creatarum est esse vel essentia et non est ante ipsum creatura alia; ergo non est in quo fundetur essentia sicut id circa quod sit ut forma subjecti alicuius; et ideo etiam secundum ordinem naturae non potest essentia in ratione essentiae esse nisi creata de nihilo. Omnia autem alia, ut dicit Commentator ibidem, sunt per informationem circa essentiam; et dat exemplum de bono quod secundum ordinem naturae praemittit sibi intellectum essentiae in qua est; ergo patet quod essentia dicit intellectum suum super nihil fundatum, et in omnibus priorem. Unde loquendo sic de essentia non dicetur veritas sed veritatis, quia veritas ponitur circa ipsam; et non dicetur bonitas sed bonitatis. . . .
>
> Si autem tu quaeras quare non dicatur vera et bona, ex quo veritas et bonitas ponuntur circa ipsam, dico quod loquendo de simplici essentia non potest dici quod illa non intelligitur [*read*: illa intelligitur] informata secundum rationem. Unde Boetius in *libro de*

---

generaliter concomitantes ens; nec divisio entis secundum quod est ens est per verum et bonum, quia Philosophus non considerat ens secundum quod fluit ab ente primo et uno et sapiente et bono, sed ipse considerat ens secundum quod stat in ipso intellectus resolvens posterius in prius et compositum in simplex et secundum quod ipsum per prius et posterius colligit omnia; et ideo de vero et bono non determinat per hunc modum, sed de bono quod est finis ad quem est motus" (669B; Albert immediately thereafter contrasts Aristotle's view with that of the "sancti" in the sentence already quoted in note 39 above).

hebdomadibus: quod est habet aliquid praeter id quod ipsum est, esse vero nihil habet admixtum. Eodem modo veritas non dicetur essentia sed essentiae proprie loquendo. Eodem modo est de bonitate. Tamen secundum supposita concretive dicta convertuntur, quia quodlibet est ens, verum, bonum, et unum. [*Ibid.*, a. 13, *solutio*; pp. 667D–668A].

In that long paraphrase and quotation what interests us is how Albert explains the excerpt from the *Liber*. One is inaccurate (so his comments run) in stating that essence "is truth" or "is true"[41] because such statements might incline us to think that the awareness of essence comes after that of truth, that essence is based upon and received in truth as a form in a subject or substrate. But as Aristotle makes clear in Prop. 4 of the *Liber*, *esse* or essence is what is first created and no other creature (*sic*) comes before it. Consequently, essence as essence cannot *be* unless it is created from nothing, which alone (except for God as creator) precedes it ("secundum ordinem naturae non potest essentia in ratione essentiae esse nisi creata de nihilo"). Everything else (e.g., truth, goodness, unity) comes about as a form or determination or addition[42] received in essence as in its subject ("omnia autem alia . . . fiunt per informationem circa essentiam") and, thereby, is subsequent to essence.

Several points are noteworthy in Albert's explanation. On one occasion *esse* apparently means existence and this with reference to creation; "secundum ordinem naturae non potest essentia in ratione essentiae *esse* nisi creata de nihilo." Second, *esse* in Prop. 4 of the *Liber* is nonetheless viewed as *essentia*: ("prima rerum creatarum est esse vel essentia"), as also in Boethius' *De Hebdomadibus*: "Esse vero nihil habet admixtum. Eodem modo veritas non dicetur *essentia sed essentiae*." Third, the essence which God creates from nothing and thereby causes to exist serves as the basis, subject, substrate of subsequent realities, which function as its forms or determinations. Finally, essence, truth, goodness and unity involve concepts, intelligibilities, *rationes* also: "[bonum] praemittit sibi *intellectum* essentiae in qua est; ergo . . . essentia dicit *intellectum suum* super nihil fundatum et

---

[41] For convenience I shall illustrate Albert's point through truth solely. Also, my paraphrase omits what he believes is the worst statement of all, since I suspect the accuracy of the italicized word: "Essentia est *ens* vel bona." Why could not *ens* be predicated of *essentia*? Perhaps, we should read: "Essentia est una vel bona"—not "vera," which appeared earlier in the sentence.

[42] On "addition," see *ibid.*, final paragraph of *solutio*, which is quoted in n. 40 above (first paragraph) and which explains that what is added is not a second nature but a relationship to the First Cause.

in omnibus priorem. . . . [Simplex essentia] non potest dici quod . . . *intelligitur* informata secundum *rationem.*" That is, we are *aware of* essence before goodness and the others; again, the very intelligibility of goodness rests upon and presupposes that of essence, the intelligibility of which however presupposes nothing.

Summary

From *In II Sent.*, d. 1, a. 1, we moved back to *In I Sent.*, d. 46, articles 11 and 13, in the hope that these might unloosen the knot Albert had tied in the former: even though Prop. 4 of the *Liber de Causis* has plainly to do with creation ("prima rerum *creatarum* est esse") and, presumably, with existence, he transferred *esse* (= *ens*) from the actual world of creatures to that of intelligibilities, where *ens* precedes *verum*, *bonum* and *unum* in virtue of its greater simplicity. That hope is fulfilled somewhat. In article 11 (*ad objectionem* . . .) of *In I Sent.*, d. 46, Prop. 4 is discussed in the light of creation (truth if entity would be the first creature), and, also, *esse* is explicated as the act of entity or essence and no longer as solely the intelligibility of *ens*. In *ibid.*, a. 13 (*solutio*), he again places the *esse* of Prop. 4 within a creationist setting, where it is linked again with essence ("prima rerum creatarum est esse *vel essentia*), which however exists because created from nothing (hence, *esse* means "existere" also) and which receives all subsequent determinations as their subject. But there is another and intramental dimension to *esse* or essence, as well as to truth, goodness and unity: the fact that they are intelligible and predicable. And article 13 inquires precisely into the sort of intelligibility and predicability *ens*, *verum*, and so on entail: whether they are synonyms, whether they are convertible with one another, which of them comes first in our awareness, how the others are added to it.

This dimension it is which Albert in Text B (*In II Sent.*, d. 1, a. 1, *ad objectionem* . . .) isolated in view of the problem at hand: did God first create angelic nature and prime matter, as Lombard interprets *Genesis*, or was it *esse*, as we read in the *Liber*? Confronted with different questions, as in *In I Sent.*, d. 46, he gave other and complementary exegeses of the *Liber*, Prop. 4.

Conclusions

But we are mainly interested in what *esse* means in Albert's texts on creation. In the key passages so far studied, it turns out to be a many-splendored thing. *Esse* is entity, as in *In I Sent.*, d. 46, a. 11, *ad ob-*

jectionem . . .: "in veritate entitas esset prima creatura, secundum quod dicit Philosophus quod prima creatarum est esse." It is essence, as in *ibid.*, a. 13, *solutio*: "esse vel essentia." Once it is even designated as the act of essence or entity—*ibid.*, a. 11, *ad objectionem* . . .: "esse quod est actus sic intellectae entitatis vel essentiae."[43] It is the nature of matter as subject and potency—*Summa de Creaturis*, Pars I, Tr. 1, q. 2, a. 1, ad 1: "Materia autem habet esse subjecti et potentiae, . . . et hoc [est esse] secundum quid." It is the intelligibility, *ens* (*ibid.*, ad 2), which functions as the principle of our cognition of the predicaments (*ibid.*: "cum [primum] dicitur de ente, est principium cognitionis respectu eorum quae ordinabilia sunt in praedicamento"); that at which the resolution of posterior to prior intelligibilities stops (*ibid.*: "in ipso [ente] stat resolutio posteriorum in prius"); that to which subsequent *rationes* are added that also arise through intellectual abstraction (*ibid.*: "[ens] a quo non convertitur consequentia subsistendi, et sic ens est absolute primum"; also *In II Sent.*, d. 1, a. 1, *ad objectionem* . . .: "secundum rationem formae et simplicitatis [*vs.* secundum ordinem substantiae in essendo] nihil est ante esse, quia omnia aliquo modo se habent ex additione ad ens, etiam unum et verum et bonum . . . [ordo simplicitatis qui] in abstractione autem fit per intellectum"); that which if taken precisely *qua* abstract is not convertible with good, true and one *re* creatures since the concept of (say) "good" presupposes the concept of "essence," which however presupposes no prior *ratio* (*In I Sent.*, d. 46, a. 13, solutio: "Si autem [ens, unum, verum, bonum] sumantur abstractive, non credo quod [convertuntur] secundum rectam praedicationem . . . in creaturis . . .; [bonum] secundum ordinem naturae praemittit sibi intellectum essentiae in qua est . . . essentia dicit intellectum suum super nihil fundatum et in omnibus priorem").

Finally, *esse* also expresses existence when it is the *esse simpliciter* which a *forma partis* gives to prime matter and which makes it exist (*Summa de Creaturis*, Pars I, tr. 1, q. 2, a. 1, ad 1); the *esse* which pertains to the temporal world where generation brings about existents (implied in *ibid.*, ad 2); the *esse* which creation results in (*In II Sent.*, d. 1, a. 1, *ad objectionem* . . .: "creatio potius respicit esse quam ordinem simplicitatis"); the *esse* by which an essence as essence *is* inasmuch as it is created from nothing (*In I Sent.*, d. 46, a. 13, *solutio*: "secundum ordinem naturae non potest essentia in ratione essentiae esse nisi creata de nihilo").

---

[43] See also *ibid.*, a. 16 ("An veritas est simplex et incommutabilis?"), *solutio* (p. 672B): "Non credo aliquam illarum [veritatis, bonitatis, unitatis, entitatis] esse compositam ex quo est et esse, secundum quod [id quod] est dicit aliquid ens in se, in quo diffunditur esse quod est actus assentiae."

This last signification of *esse* as *existere* helps guarantee that *creatio* even in these early treatises of Albert has an authentic ring.[44] In order to realize this, let us first describe "creation" in its authentic and technical sense. Put more precisely: what factors does a genuine doctrine of creation necessarily entail? These appear to be three. The producer himself must undergo

> . . . no change in the act of producing, neither losing nor acquiring any perfection, and the implication is that he is both all-perfect and entirely free. Next, what is produced must be really distinct from the producer and, finally, must be *wholly* produced. For the causality ascribed by an author to his First Principle to be authentically creationist, it must include all those factors. Obviously, that inclusion need only be implicit, provided the writer somehow indicates his mind. For example, one can be sure that the product is *wholly* produced if the author states that God made it from nothing or that He produced even its prime matter or that He does not cause the item merely to be such and such but actually to exist. Obviously, too, the clear presence of one factor can imply another. For instance, if divine causality makes something actually exist which before was not, one can infer that such an effect is really distinct from its cause.[45]

If those factors are applied to Albert's doctrine, how does he fare? Very well. God is (he explicitly notes) immutable, all-perfect, and entirely free and, thus, He undergoes no change in creating.[46] Also,

[44] But *esse* signifies *existere* only as expressing the *fact that* things exist and not as an act or component by which they exist, as L. Ducharme has convincingly argued (see the paragraph above which corresponds to footnotes 13 and 14; *re* Geiger, see n. 16).

[45] L. Sweeney, "Doctrine of Creation in *Liber de Causis*," p. 288. This conception of creation is based upon statements from the Fourth Lateran Council (H. Denzinger, *Enchiridion Symbolorum* [32d edition; Friburgi Brisg.: Herder, 1963], no. 800) and the Vatican Council (*ibid.*, nos. 3024 sq.). For an analysis of these statements, see Pinard, "Création," cols. 2081 and 2181–95.

Interestingly enough, creation was not explicated in conciliar documents as a production *ex nihilo* until the Lateran Council of 1215: "[Deus] qui sua omnipotenti virtute simul ab initio temporis utramque de nihilo condidit creaturam, spiritualem et corporalem" (Denzinger, *op. cit.*, no. 800). That explicit description had, though, been given much earlier by such authors as Hermas (whose *The Shepherd* is dated ca. 140 A.D.), Origen, Chrysostom, Leo, Tertullian, Lactantius and Augustine. For references and discussion see A. Solignac, *Les Confessions*, Vol. 14 of *Oeuvres de S. Augustin* (Paris: Desclée de Brouwer, 1962), pp. 603–606.

[46] On God as immutable, see *In I Sent.*, d. 8, a. 16 (pp. 150 sqq.); as all-perfect, see *ibid.*, d. 34, a. 4 solutio (p. 498D); *Super Dionysium de Divinis Nominibus,*

every creature is really distinct from the Creator because he makes that which before was not now actually exist. Moreover, what is created is, as such, wholly produced by God, since He not only makes it from nothing and produces even its prime matter but also causes it actually to be.[47]

But granted that Albert's position on creation is sound and that his viewing *esse* as existence helps to account for that soundness (to create is to cause something to exist which before was in no way), still his God does not *properly* cause existence if to be real is for him (as Ducharme, Geiger and Wieland suggest) to be essence rather than to exist.[48] And if to create is to cause things to exist, then to create is not an exercise of proper causality for God, Who properly causes what things are and not that they are.[49]

c. 13: "Utrum hoc nomen 'perfectum' deo conveniat" (Cologne critical edition, XXXVII, pp. 433, 1. 32-p. 435, l. 42; as free, see *In I Sent.*, d. 30, a. 3 solutio (p. 448D); *ibid.*, d. 45, a. 1 ("An in Deo sit volutas"; pp. 640–41); *In II Sent.*, d. 1, a. 2 ad [6] (p. 6B); *ibid.*, a 3 ad [3] and ad [4] (p. 7B); *ibid.*, a. 5, *ad hoc quod quaeritur* (p. 10D); *ibid.*, a. 6 *solutio* (p. 11C). For Wieland's comments on divine freedom in creating, see above, n. 21.

[47] On prime matter as divinely created, see above, n. 32; *In II Sent.*, d. 1, a. 3 in entirety (XIV, pp. 6C sq.). On creation as causing something to exist by making it from nothing, see *ibid.*, ad 1 (p. 7A): "creatio non dicit actum vel passionem quae media sit inter Deum agentem et id quod educitur de non esse, sed potius relationem consequentem ipsum quod nunc primo de nihilo est et ante non fuit. . . . Et huius haec est ratio, quia perfecti agentis est agere non actione media, in qua res prius sit in fieri quam in esse. . . . Vere creantis nihil aliud est quam quod esse faciat rem postquam non fuit sine mutatione media"; *ibid.*, ad 4 (p. 7B): "Materia non est ante omne fieri si fieri dicatur actio creantis, quia cum illa nihil sit nisi facere ex imperio suo rem nunc esse postquam non fuit de ea aliquid nec potentia nec actu, illud fieri non praesupponit sibi potentiam aliquam, quia nec est proprie fieri." Also see *Summa de Creaturis*, Pars I, Tr. 1, q. 1, a. 2, *argumentum* 1 (XIX, p. 2D); *ibid.*, a. 3, *argumenta* 2 and 3 (p. 3D); *ibid.*, ad *sed contra* 4 (p. 4B); *ibid.*, a. 4, *sed contra* 1 (p. 4C); *ibid.*, a. 5, *solutio* (p. 5A); *ibid.*, a. 7, ad *sed contra* (p. 6D); *In II Sent.*, d. 1, a. 3 ad 1 (XIV, p. 7A); *ibid.*, ad 4 (p. 7B); *ibid.*, a. 6, ad 2 (p. 11D); *ibid.*, a. 7, *sed contra* 2 (p. 12A); *ibid.*, d. 3, a. 7, [*solutio*] (p. 58D); *ibid.*, d. 30, a. 1, ad 1 (p. 446D); *ibid.*, a. 2, *solutio* and ad 1 (p. 447D).

[48] That reality for Albert is not existence, see above, n. 44 with its references. That reality is some or other essence follows from the fact which Ducharme, Geiger, and Wieland have stressed (see discussion above in the paper corresponding to footnotes 13–21) that *esse* is *actus essentiae—In I Sent.*, d. 46, a. 11, *ad objectionem* . . . (p. 665C): "Esse quod est actus sic intellectae entitatis vel essentiae"; *ibid.*, a. 16, *solutio* (p. 672B): [id quod est dicitur] aliquid ens in se, in quo diffunditur esse quod est actus essentiae" (quoted above, n. 43).

[49] At least not "proper causality" in the sense Thomas Aquinas gives to the phrase—see next paragraph with texts cited in note 50. But Albert has his own understanding of the phrase, as will be clear below, last two paragraphs.

Let me explain by speaking first of a "proper *effect*" without direct reference to creation and God.

Whenever a single effect is produced by two or more different agents (for example, by principal and instrumental causes), *each agent makes a unique contribution to that effect* because each acts according to what it is if it is to act at all, and what each is makes it unique and diverse from everything else. *The unique contribution which an agent makes by acting according to what it is is called its "proper effect."* No matter what other effects it may have, then, *every agent has a proper effect, since an agent always acts according to what it is.*

By way of example, consider a teacher using a piece of red chalk to write "dog" upon the blackboard. The effect produced is composite and yet one. It is composite inasmuch as it is a symbol which is both meaningful and colored. It is one insofar as it is a single symbol where the color expresses the meaning, which in turn determines the precise position of chalk particles on the board. That effect is wholly caused by both the principal and instrumental agents, since each causes both meaning and color, but differently. The teacher causes the color through the chalk, but the meaning directly and of himself; the chalk causes the meaning only as moved by the teacher, and the color directly in virtue of its own nature. By directly causing the meaning, then, the teacher also causes the color; by directly causing the color, the instrument also causes the meaning. What is the *proper effect* of each cause? For the teacher it is the meaning, because by nature he is an intelligent being and agent. For the chalk it is the color, because by nature it is a piece of red chalk.

Whatever an agent causes in virtue of what it itself is, then, is its proper effect.[50]

---

[50] L. Sweeney, S.J., *A Metaphysics of Authentic Existentialism* (Englewood Cliffs, N.J.: Prentice-Hall, 1965; Ann Arbor: University Microfilms "Books on Demand," 1977), pp. 234–35. See Aquinas, S.T., I, 8, 1 resp.: "Cum autem Deus sit ipsum esse per suam essentiam, oportet quod esse creatum sit proprius effectus eius; sicut ignire est proprius effectus ignis"; *ibid.*, I, 45, 5, resp.: "Creare non potest esse propria actio nisi solius Dei. Oportet enim universaliores effectus in universaliores et priores causas reducere. Inter omnes autem effectus universalissimum est ipsum esse. Unde oportet quod sit proprius effectus primae et universalissimae causae, quae est Deus. . . . Producere autem esse absolute, non inquantum est hoc vel tale, pertinet ad rationem creationis. Unde manifestum est quod creatio est propria actio ipsius Dei. . . . Videmus quod securis scindendo lignum quod habet ex proprietate suae formae producit scamni formam, quae est effectus proprius principalis agentis. Illud autem quod est proprius effectus Dei creantis est illud quod

To state the same from the point of view of "proper cause": the agent properly causes that in the effect which corresponds to what he is, to his nature.

Now, if God's very nature is existence (as it is for Aquinas), then He properly causes all things to exist; but to cause something to exist which before was not at all is to create; therefore, a God who *is* existence properly creates: creation is (so to speak) merely an exercise of proper causality for Him, through which an existent universe replaces nothingness and by which beings are produced *precisely as beings* since "being" here is "that which actually exists." Gilson's words quoted above describe Aquinas's position so well they merit repetition:

> One cannot ask a philosopher to conceive creation at a deeper level than that of his own notion of being. If God is the cause of that which being is, then God is a creator and being is a created being. . . . The progress achieved by Thomas Aquinas concerns less the notion of creation than that of being.

Thomas conceived creation on the very level of being itself, since God properly causes *being* in all beings. Thus the achievement of this student of Albert was first to have modified the notion of being, which then harmonized perfectly with that of creation.

That harmony seems lacking in the texts of his teacher. For if God's very nature is not existence but some or other essence—for instance, immutability, as Augustine holds—,[51] then He properly causes things

praesupponitur omnibus aliis, scilicet esse absolute." Also see *ibid.*, I, 105, 5 resp.; S.C.G, III, c. 68, "Adhuc."

[51] See *Confessions* VII, c. 11, #17 (John K. Ryan [transl.], *The Confessions of St. Augustine* [New York: Doubleday Image Books, 1960], p. 171): "That truly is which endures unchangeably. . . . [God] abides in himself" (Skutella Latin text: "Id enim vere est quod inconmutabiliter manet. . . . Ille autem in se manens innovat omnia"); *ibid.*, c. 17, #23 (Ryan trans., pp. 175–76), where his awareness that to be real is to be immutable leads him to realize that God is and is immutability, truth, eternity (these last two are so closely linked with immutability as to be interchangeable with it): "[From reflecting upon sound judgments I had made,] I found that immutable, true, and eternal Truth which exists above my changeable mind." Moving from bodies to within the soul and its multiple powers, all of which are variable, Augustine finds the light which enables his soul to assent that "beyond all doubt the immutable must be preferred to the mutable. Hence it might come to know this immutable being, for unless it could know it in some way, it could in no wise have set it with certainty above the mutable. Thus in a flash of its trembling sight it came to That Which Is" (Skutella edition: "Hoc ergo quaerens unde iudicarem cum ita judicarem, inveneram inconmutabilem et veram veritatis aeternitatem supra mentem meam conmutabilem. . . . ut inveniret quo lumine aspargeretur cum sine ulla dubitatione clamaret inconmutabile praeferendum esse

to be immutable, whereas secondary agents (parents, carpenters, etc.) properly cause them to exist. But in order that there *be* secondary agents, God must cause them to exist—i.e., He must create them. This He does but not properly: even in creating them He properly causes them not to exist but to be immutable. If Albert is an essentialist (as Ducharme, Geiger, and Wieland intimate),[52] then to be real is for him to be essence of some sort or other, and, second, God's reality is Essence. Accordingly, his God in creating properly causes a thing not to exist but to be essence. That is, creation is not an exercise of proper causality (see above, n. 49). Creation does not account for the very being of beings. It is not aligned fully and directly with being itself.

Significantly enough, this distinction between nonproperly causing something to *be* and properly causing it to be *what it is* helps one understand why creation is difficult for an essentialist to cope with and, also, why in Neoplatonism production of existents occurs in two moments or stages: procession and reversion. In the first the primal cause overflows, and thereby the existence of the effect is accounted for; in the second that which has overflown and now exists (e.g., Plotinus calls it intelligible matter, otherness, *dynamis*) turns back to the cause, contemplates it, completes itself, and thereby becomes what it is. A Neoplatonist who believes in creation (e.g., the author of the *Liber de Causis*) retains those two stages but interprets them thus.[53] In the first creation replaces emanation: the Creator causes intelligible matter (the author of the *Liber* calls this *esse* in Prop. 4) to exist, which in the second moment and under continued divine, but noncreational influence is completed and perfected through information so as to be what it is. The Creator properly causes the creature thereby to be what it is but not that it is, because the Creator is not existence but the One or the One-Good or some other Essence.

Here, though, a question arises: can the One or the One-Good rightly be called "Essence"? Yes, provided the word is not restricted to the level of being (as it usually is) but is taken to mean whatever can serve as a predicate in a sentence. "One," "good" and "true" can be predicated of an existent and, thus, are "essences," no less than are "immutable," "eternal," "simple" and so on. Hence, if the Creator for a theologian or philosopher is the One or the One-Good or Im-

---

mutabili, unde nosset ipsum inconmutabile—quod nisi aliquo modo nosset, nullo modo illud mutabili certa praeponeret—et pervenit ad id quod est in ictu trepidantis aspectus").

[52] See above, n. 48.

[53] See L. Sweeney, "Doctrine of Creation in *Liber de Causis*," pp. 282–85.

mutability or Eternity or (as perhaps is the case with Albert) Simplicity,[54] then He properly causes creatures to be one or good or immutable or eternal or simple but not to exist. Only He Who *is* Existence properly causes them to exist.

In this connection it is intriguing to note that Albert computes the perfection of a cause not from *what* it causes (properly or otherwise) but from its *manner of causing*:

> Ad aliud dicendum quod haec propositio est falsa: causatum primae causae verius est ens quam causatum secundae causae. Et si quis probet eam sic: sicut se habet causa prima ad secundam, ita causatum primae causae ad causatum secundae causae, dicendum quod propositio falsa est. Si ergo quaeritur in quo attenditur nobilitas causae primae respectu secundae, dicendum quod in modo causandi, quia causa prima causat per seipsam et non causa secunda, sed secunda causa non causat nisi supposita prima.[55]

This computation results in Albert's using "proper effect" or "proper cause" differently than was explained above, as is disclosed in these lines from his commentary on the *Liber de Causis*:

> Primae autem causae quae causat non causante quodam alio proprius actus causare [*read*: creare] est. Qui enim causat non causante quodam alio ante se, ex nihilo facit omne quod facit. Si autem praesupponeret aliud ante se causans, non ex nihilo faceret, sed id quod jam est formaret id quod facit et causat. Actus ergo primae causae proprie creatio est quo res est; primum est quod ante nihil

---

[54] See E. Gilson, *HCP*, pp. 291–92. These texts on simplicity from Albert should be taken into account: *In I Sent.*, d. 8, a. 4 *solutio* (XIV, pp. 138D–139B); *ibid.*, a. 15, *solutio* (p. 149B); *ibid.*, a. 22, ad 1 and ad 2 (p. 155A); *ibid.*, a. 24, *solutio* and *ad ultimum* (pp. 155D and 156D); *ibid.*, a. 28, [*solutio*] (p. 161A); *ibid.*, d. 34, a. 1 *solutio* (p. 495B). Also *S.T.*, Pars I, Tr. 4, q. 19, membrum 1, solutio (Vol. XVII, p. 68C); *ibid.*, q. 20, membra 1–5 (pp. 73–80); *Liber de Causis et Processu Universitatis*, Bk. I, tr. 2, c. 5 (Borgnet ed., Vol. X, p. 395a); *ibid.*, tr. 3, c. 1, p. 401d; *ibid.*, tr. 4, c. 1, p. 411d; *ibid.*, tr. 4, c. 3, p. 414d; *ibid.*, Bk. II, tr. 1, c. 17, p. 462a; *ibid.*, c. 18, p. 463d; *ibid.*, tr. 4, c. 11, p. 584d; *ibid.*, tr. 5, c. 12, p. 604a.

[55] *Summa de Creaturis*, Pars I, Tr. 1, q. 2, a. 3 ad 2; p. 11D. In the text quoted Albert is answering this argumentation that matter is not created: "Item, causatum causae primae verius est ens quam causatum causae secundae; sed creatum est causatum causae primae; ergo [creatum] verius erit ens quam causatum causae secundae. Inde ulterius: effectus formae verius est ens quam materia; sed effectus primae causae, ut habitum est, verius est ens quam effectus secundae; ergo materia non erit effectus primae causae; sed creatum est effectus primae causae, ut probatum est in primo syllogismo; ergo materia non est creatum" (*ibid., videtur quod non* 2; p. 11B).

93

praesupponit; esse igitur in omnibus quae sunt primae causae proprius effectus est.[56]

God properly causes *esse* because as the absolutely First Cause He causes solely through and of Himself: such is His unique manner of causing. The causality exercised by every other agent is subsequent to His, based upon His, presupposes His because He is supreme and primal. Therefore, He properly creates, and *esse* is His proper effect, which secondary agents then form and determine.

Can anyone conceive how greater similarity in language can be combined with greater diversity in meaning than that one finds in Albert's theory on *esse* and creation when compared with that of his star pupil, Aquinas?[57] For the latter *esse* is God's proper effect because His very nature is to exist, and, thus, existence in an effect is that which corresponds directly to what He is. It is that which He causes by acting in accord with what He Himself essentially is. It is the perfection *par excellence* of an existent, the intrinsic source of its other perfections, the actuation of its forms and, in general, of its essence.[58] But for Albert *esse* is the proper effect of God because He alone causes it: no other agent precedes Him, the activity of all other agents presupposes His. They determine and complete the *esse* which He creates and which then serves as universal substrate and subject for the perfections which they add.[59]

[56] *De Causis et Processu Universitatis,* Liber II, Tr. 1, c. 13 (Bornet ed., X, 454); also see *ibid.,* tr. 2, c. 17, p. 403D. But see *ibid.,* tr. 3, c. 10, p. 559a.

[57] On Aquinas see texts listed in n. 50 above and the portions of this paper corresponding to notes 48–50.

[58] *De Potentia,* q. 7, a. 2 ad 9 (Marietti ed., p. 192): "Hoc quod dico esse est actualitas omnium actuum, et propter hoc est perfectio omnium perfectionum"; *S.C.G.,* I, c. 28 (Leonine Manual ed., p. 29d): "Omnis enim nobilitas cuiuscumque rei est sibi secundum suum esse. . . . Sic ergo secundum modum quo res habet esse est suus modus in nobilitate"; *S.T.,* I, 3, 4 resp. (Leonine Manual ed., p. 17b): "Esse est actualitas omnis formae vel naturae"; *ibid.,* I, 4, 1, ad 3 (p. 21d): "Ipsum esse est perfectissimum omnium: comparatur enim ad omnia ut actus. Nihil enim habet actualitatem nisi inquantum est; unde ipsum esse est actualitas omnium rerum et etiam ipsarum formarum. Unde non comparatur ad alia sicut recipiens ad receptum; sed magis sicut receptum ad recipiens. Cum enim dico esse hominis vel equi vel cuiuscumque alterius, ipsum esse consideratur ut formale et receptum"; *ibid.,* I, 8, 1 resp. (p. 36c): "Esse autem est illud quod est magis intimum cuilibet et quod profundius omnibus inest, cum sit formale respectu omnium quae in re sunt."

[59] Yet *esse* is not potency but act—in fact, the act which contains *vivere* and other acts and from which they emerge. At least, such is Albert's position in his commentary (written between 1265 and 1272) on the *Liber de Causis.* See Leo Sweeney, S.J., "*Esse Primum Creatum* in Albert the Great's *Liber de Causis et Processu Universitatis,*" *Thomist,* 44 (1980).

94

At the beginning of a book on Alfred North Whitehead "which includes destructive criticism of Whitehead," Nathaniel Lawrence nonetheless claimed that his "major indebtedness is to Whitehead himself." He admitted that "there may seem to be an irony in [that] claim." But Whitehead himself

> summarized his critique of Einstein with the remark that "the worst homage we can pay to genius is to accept uncritically formulations of truths which we owe to it." A student who does not differ from his teacher has learned little from him.[60]

The differences which set Aquinas's position so widely apart from Albert's show how much he had learned from him. Judged by Lawrence's criterion, Albert must have been a superb teacher, as well as excellent scholar and impressive thinker.

[60] *Whitehead's Philosophical Development* (New York: Greenwood Press, 1968), p. ix.

"Knowable" and "Namable" in Albert the Great's Commentary on the *Divine Names*

FRANCIS J. CATANIA
Loyola University of Chicago

The recent edition of Albert the Great's Commentary on the *Divine Names*[1] may be of interest not only to scholars working in Albert but also to those interested in the Thomistic doctrines of analogy,[2] as well as to philosophers of religion whose concern is "religious language."[3] Probably because *DN* existed only in manuscript form prior to this edition, there is little published work on this important treatise apart from the writings of Francis Ruello.[4] His 1963 study, while concerned with the same general topic, differs from this article in several respects:

1. Ruello's study of *DN* was based upon the precritical availability of manuscripts; it appears appropriate to conduct a fresh study with a critical text.[5]

2. Ruello's focus is *ratio,* which he approaches metaphysically as providing a bridge to a knowledge of God as He is in Himself and not

---

[1] Alberti Magni, *Opera Omnia.* Tomus XXXVII, pars 1: Super Dionysium De Divinis Nominibus. Primum edidit Paulus Simon. Monasterii Westfalorum, Aschendorff, 1972. Hereafter I will refer to the text as *DN.* References will include Chapter number, page number of this edition, and line numbers. Simon dates *DN* around 1250. *DN,* Prol., VI–VII.

[2] C. Vansteenkiste, O.P., makes this observation in "Il decimo volume del nuovo Alberto Magno," *Angelicum* (1974) 51: 122–23.

[3] See, for example, David Burrell, C.S.C., *Analogy and Philosophical Language* (New Haven: Yale University Press, 1973). I do not wish to enter the discussion of the accuracy/adequacy of Burrell's treatment of Thomas Aquinas on analogy, but it is striking to discover the similarity between his interpretation of Aquinas and the position of Albert in *DN.*

[4] Of particular interest to this study is his *Les "Noms Divins" et Leurs "Raisons" selon Saint Albert Le Grand Commentateur du "De Divinis Nominibus* (Paris: J. Vrin, 1963).

[5] Ruello used the Codex Parisinus Mazarinianus (Paris: Bibliothèque Mazarine, 873; Ruello, *op. cit.,* p. 7). This was one of several manuscripts employed by Simon, who argued for the primacy of Codex Neapolitanus (Napoli, Biblioteca Nazionale I.B. 54) *DN,* Prolegomena, pp. xii–xvii.

simply in His causality;[6] the approach taken here is epistemological and linguistic and casts some doubt about whether Albert's treatment can support any claim to reach a knowledge of God as He is in Himself.

3. Ruello seems to assume that somewhere at the heart of analogous causality, there is the element of univocal causality;[7] I do not think Albert's texts can support such a reading.

On the whole, however, I do not regard my approach as contradicting that of Ruello's so much as offering an additional perspective on the problems of knowing and naming.

Some limits must be placed on the analysis of the understanding and use of "knowable" and "namable" in *DN*. First, I will limit this discussion to the characteristics of knowing and naming as exhibited in the claims to know and to name God. Second, the issues are formulated in Albert's response to the text of *DN*; this means that his position is developed by addressing a certain set of questions: it is context-dependent. A study which compared the position revealed here with the position in the Commentary on the *Sentences* and/or the *Summa Theologiae* would reveal the significance of that context; but such a study is left for another time.[8] Third, one of the consequences of *DN*

[6] Ruello, *op. cit.*, p. 96: Si notre interprétation est exacte, nous à une triple conclusion: avant d'être unie à Dieu et de le connaitre *per ablationem omnium* ou *per ignorantiam*, l'âme sait que Dieu, cause univoque des créatures, possède en soi les raisons qui lui permettent de les produire et elle atteint ces raisons elles-mêmes; mais puisque, par elles-mêmes, ces raisons ne sont pas participées, l'âme qui les connait sans les comprendre sait que Dieu est en lui-même (*quia est*) quelque chose comme être, vie ou sagesse. Seul le mode de signification des noms qu'elle utilise pour nommer Dieu ne s'appliqué pas à Dieu. Dans l'état d'union, la connaissance de Dieu *per causam* ne s'évanouit pas: l'âme atteint toujours Dieu en ses raisons puisqu'elle atteint Dieu qui est ces raisons, mais elle atteint Dieu en une telle transcendance qu'à son sujet il est plus vrai de nier d'affirmer. Enfin il apparait que si Dieu est connu *per causam* ou *per ablationem omnium* il ne l'est pas *ut causa*. Le terme de notre connaissance de Dieu n'est pas sa causalité, il est Dieu en lui-même, ou selon sa substance.

[7] Ruello, *op. cit.*, pp. 95–96: Mais la connaissance *per ablationem omnium* n'exclut pas de soi la connaissance *per causam* puisque s'il est vrai qu'en un sens Dieu n'est pas cause univoque, il est vrai, en un autre, qu'il le soit. Le problème serait donc de savoir si dans l'état d'union l'âme qui connait Dieu *per ablationem omnium* le connait également *per causam*. A défaut d'expérience, peut-être doit-on noter que l'idée d'une causalité non-univoque de Dieu suppose celle d'une causalité univoque de ce même Dieu.

[8] Ruello, *op. cit.*, has in part approached such a study by including the notion of *ratio* as it appears in Albert's earlier Commentary on the *Sentences*. I know of no comparable study of the later *Summa Theologiae*. My own previous work on divine infinity has also included some elements of such an approach. (See my "Divine Infinity in Albert the Great's Commentary on the *Sentences* of Peter

being a Commentary is the need to raise questions about the extent to which Albert is "merely" explaining the text or also giving his own position or even presenting his own reasoned views on issues suggested by the text.[9] My approach here is to focus on the issues which are raised and Albert's responses to those issues; the other concerns will be addressed as necessary to that primary focus.

Van Steenkiste's general survey of the new edition both as to its technical adequacy[10] and to its content[11] confirms the importance of continued study of Albert's texts both as a contribution to the history of theological development and also to the perspective he brings to particular philosophical and theological issues.

I. The Context

In Chapter Seven, Albert follows the inquiry, raised in the text, concerning how it is that we can claim to have knowledge of God. The reason why the text raises a question is as follows: All human knowledge concerns things that are either sensible or intelligible[12] and that also are existing.[13] But God does not belong to the class of existing things since all such are included in one of the predicamental genera, and God is not in any genus. God is not intelligible because He is above every intellect; he is not sensible because he is entirely immaterial. If sensibility or intelligibility and existence are conditions of the possibility of knowledge, then an authentic philosophical issue is raised: is it appropriate, after all, to use the word "knowable" when referring to any of the aspects of our relationships with God (Utrum Deus sit cognoscibilis a nobis)?

One of the intriguing questions of this text is, Why does Albert wait until Chapter Seven to raise a question seemingly implied in and even foundational to the preceding six chapters? An obvious response is that

Lombard," *Medieval Studies* 22 [1960]: 27–42; and "Albert the Great, Boethius, and Divine Infinity," *Recherches de Théologie ancienne et médiévale* 28 [1961]: 97–114.)

9 Ruello has addressed this question in an appendix to the study mentioned earlier (Ruello, *op. cit.*, pp. 185–89) without resolving the issue, although he tends to regard Albert more as a commentator than as an original author.

10. Van Steenkiste, *op. cit.*, p. 113: "L'edizione del testo è veramente esemplare." To the very few questions he raises about the accurary of the readings or, perhaps (?) merely printing errors (pp. 113–15), I must add one (printing?) error of importance: p. 13, line 56, 'quid' should read 'quia.' See note # 37.

11 Van Steenkiste, *op. cit.*, p. 119: "Il commento di Alberto è assai interessante dal punto di visa dottrinale, sia per la filosofia che per la teologia."

12 DN VII, 355.40: Omnes cognitiones in has duas reducantur.

13 DN VII, 355.41: Cum non sit cognitio nisi de ente.

he is simply following the text and the order in which it raises issues. Formally, the question "whether God is knowable by us" is viewed as part of the general question of knowledge:

> Having resolved the issues concerning active divine knowledge [sapientia] whereby God knows things, now [Dionysius] resolves the question of passive divine knowledge [cognitio], that is, [the knowledge] whereby we know him.[14]

So, even though the position developed in Chapter Seven has been operative throughout the treatise, the orderly progression of topics characteristic of DN relegates formal treatment to this text.

But a second response is possible. In the first chapter there is continuous but undeveloped reference to the problems of claiming to have knowledge of God,[15] because Albert is interested in establishing some aspects of the relationships between "naming" and "knowing" within a discussion whose primary focus is "names." In fact, the major theme running throughout DN is expressed by Albert in his gloss on the phrase "ineffabilibus et ignotis." This phrase, says Albert, refers to divinity

> which is "speakable" and "known" only in an extended sense of those words [secundum quid], that is, by knowing in an undefined way that [God is]. But [God] is "unspeakable" and "unknown" in the ordinary sense of those words [simpliciter] because we don't know [of Him] what He is or on account of what He is.[16]

Accordingly, Albert realizes that to discuss the divine names is to raise at the same time one issue after the other which bears upon a claim to know the divine;[17] but his own order of proceeding, reflecting the text of DN, includes postponing formal treatment of "knowable" until after a discussion of "names." But why begin with names? Because the religious experience out of which this theology arises begins in

---

[14] DN VII, 355.29–32: Determinato de sapientia divina activa, id est qua ipse cognoscit res, determinat de cognitione ipsius passiva, idest qualiter nos cognoscimus ipsum.

[15] DN I, 2.51–52: deus et simpliciter non notus nobis, secundum quid vero notus; I, 39.51–52: modus essendi eius remanet nobis ignotus, scientes tamen 'quia est' confuse.

[16] DN I, 5.12–16: Ineffabilibus et ignotis, scilicet divinis, quae sunt effabilia et nota secundum quid, scilicet coquoscendo 'quia' indeterminate, et ineffabilia et ignota simpliciter, quia nescitur de eis 'quid' et 'propter quid'; et haec expositio currit per totum hunc librum.

[17] DN I, 25.55–57: Non enim significatur res a nobis, nisi secundum quod cognoscitur.

hearing the divine names especially as handed on in and through the sacred scriptures.[18] Members of the [Christian] community *use* the divine names before reflecting upon the philosophical problems generated by the claim "to name." It is this use that Albert begins with and to which he continually refers as he attempts an exposition of what that use reveals about the basic relationship between man and God. For Albert, the fact of *using* divine names does imply a relationship between man and God, even though we may not understand the terms of that relationship[19] and may even be mistaken in calling it "knowledge."[20] Accordingly, although the logical reconstruction of Albert's position would begin with an inquiry into the meaning of and evidence for any claimed relationship between man and God (including both the extent to which we could *know* such a relationship and whether such a relationship would itself involve any activity that can be recognized as *knowledge*), Albert's own exposition begins by simply recognizing, on the authority of Scripture, that men in fact use the name "God" to refer[21] and also use other names to amplify the image/notion of that to which the name "God" refers.[22] This usage implies some sort of relationship of man to the One which man addresses,[23] and Albert notes that we move naturally to claim knowledge of that which we so easily name.[24] He then begins, reflectively, to recognize the limits which such knowledge claims must include[25] so that the appropriateness of claim-

[18] DN I, 4.34–35: Hic ostendit, quo significatur deus his nominibus, quia per sacram scripturam.

[19] DN I, 5.17–21: Modus quidem iste quo deo coniungimur per cognitionem, et notus est et dici potest ex illa parte qua in nobis est, sed ex parte obiecti, quod est infinitum, secundum quod scilicet deo *coniungimur*, ineffabilis et ignotus est . . . . Also: DN I, 40.2–4: . . . nec est inconveniens, ut deus, secundum quod est in se, sit supra se, secundum quod est in cognitione nostra.

[20] Hence, the *inquiry*: Utrum deus sit cognoscibilis nobis?

[21] The opening line of Albert's Commentary is a quotation from Psalm 8: "Admirable is your name on the whole of the earth." The Psalmist here is *addressing* the Lord.

[22] The purpose of DN is to explore the range of names which are appropriately used of God.

[23] Albert understands the words of Jeremiah "Nomen tuum invocatum est super nos" as expressing a relationship to God that is like a relationship to a univocal cause. See DN I, 1.32–35.

[24] DN I, 25.55–57: Non enim significatur res a nobis, nisi secundum quod cognoscitur.

[25] Near the beginning of Chapter I, Albert, following the lead of the text which refers to its own treatment De hac . . . *supersubstantiali et occulta deitate*, raises two central issues: "Whether the divine substance can be seen by any created intellect" and "If the divine substance is, in any way at all, visible, is it able to be comprehended" (DN I, 9.65–68). His approach to these issues is repeated and amplified in Chapter 7 and will be treated in conjunction with that text.

ing *knowledge* appears as an inquiry to be sustained rather than as a simple assertion.

What Albert reveals is that he does have a philosophy of knowledge the terms of which are derived from our "ordinary" encounter with the physical world. While God is not Himself an object of that sort of encounter,[26] Albert is at pains to show that whatever knowledge-claims we can make with respect to God are continuous with those ordinary encounters. Three moves bolster this account of the continuity of Albert's knowledge-claim about God with his general philosophy of knowing.

1. It is the *use* of the divine names (grounded in the sacred scriptures, preaching, prayer) that creates the sense of meaningfulness which verges on or even, perhaps, crosses over into a knowledge claim. Albert could have espoused a fideism. And, in fact, there are aspects of his position that could support such a judgment in the end.[27] But if Albert's position is fideistic after all, it is a fideism which is held off as long as possible as he returns again and again to those aspects of our ordinary processes of knowing that seem to be open to the sorts of extension that are necessary with the unique object, God.

2. The right sorts of distinctions must be made even within the context of our knowledge of the physical world. Such distinctions as

   a. *Quia est, quid est* (passim)
   b. *Attingere, pertransire totum* (I, 10–11)
   c. *Abstractio per resolutionem, abstractio intentionis* (VII, 356)
   d. *Res significata, modum significationis* (I, 32; VII, 358; VII, 349)
   e. *Objectum, ipse se obicit* (I, 33; I, 11)

are Albert's vehicles for exploiting the language characteristics that enable him to develop a rational theology. These characteristics reveal that our use of language in many ordinary situations already includes dimensions that open that language to transcendent usage without creating any special rules for that purpose. Although the particular use of each of the above distinctions is explored in what follows, we may note here, as an example, that if we reflect upon our use of a word such as "wise" we find that it ranges over a diverse set of contexts. We may, for example, speak of a "wise judge" or a "wise farmer." In each case, although it is quite appropriate to use the same word, we have to say

[26] DN VII, 355.38–42: Quicquid cognoscitur a nobis est sensibile vel intelligibile . . . et existens . . . sed deus nullum horum est.

[27] The strict limits on "philosophy" (note 32); the initiative on God's part in a knowledge of Him (note 30); the emphasis on negative knowledge; the limits on affirmation (*passim*).

that what it means for a judge to be wise is simply not the same as what it means for a farmer to be wise. What we intend by saying "wise" (*res significata*) is not really separable in any given case from the way we express what we intend (*modus significationis*) *in that particular case*; what is striking about "wise" is that the *res significata* is nòt limited to any particular *modus significationis* (although there always must be some *modus*), so that it is not meaningless[28] to affirm "God is wise" even when we do not know the *modus* in His case, since for such a name no one *modus* is more appropriate than others.[29]

3. There is also an aspect of experience itself which appears to be foundational to any knowledge-claim with respect to God. It is the experience of *intellectual reflection*, perhaps most obviously as practiced by "philosophers." When Albert is comparing the mode of natural knowledge (*philosophicus*) to that mode which is rooted in faith (*divinus*),[30] his intent is to show that the strength and limit of *philosophicus* is that it owes its character to being caused by things inferior to our intellect even when the object of knowledge is not itself inferior to our intellect. Understanding rooted in faith (*divinus*), however, arises when that which is above our intellect endows us with him-

[28] The question here is the meaningfulness and not directly the truth of such statements as "God is wise." Of course, such a claim would have to be justified on appropriate grounds. For a treatment of these general issues in Aquinas, see Burrell, *op. cit.*, pp. 119–93, as well as his "Aquinas' Articulating Transcendence," in *Exercises in Religious Understanding* (Notre Dame: University of Notre Dame Press, 1974).

[29] Such names are "transcendentals" inasmuch as they are not restricted to particular classes or genera and in this respect differ radically from such names as *red* or *heavy*. Albert's constant position is that God is not in a genus (not only in *DN*, but also in his Commentary on the *Sentences*; see my "Albert the Great, Boethius, and Divine Infinity" in *loc. cit.*). The position is worked out in a doctrine of *perfection* (generally following Anselm; *DN* VII, 348.33–36: Sed omnia huiusmodi quae simpliciter et melius est esse quam non esse, secundum regulam Anselmi dicuntur analogice de deo et creaturis et primo inveniuntur in deo.) and in using the soul as a *model* (*DN* VII, 337.1–10: Determinato de divinis nominibus, quae nominant essentiam vel naturam, incipit hic determinare de nominibus, quae secundum rationem nominis nominant id quod assequitur naturam. Et dividitur in duas; quaedam enim assequuntur naturam sicut perfectiones potentiarum in anima nostra, quaedam vero naturam ipsius animae per se, vel quaedam assequuntur partes animae, quaedam totam essentiam animae). But following out these arguments is beyond the scope of this paper.

[30] *DN* VII, 348.55–66: Sciendum est autem ad evidentiam huius, quod duplex modus est, quo accipimus cognitionem de rebus, unus philosophicus et alter divinus. Philosophicus quidem modus est, secundum quod scientia nostra causatur ab entibus, quae subsunt nostro intellectui, vel quantum ad modum accipiendi scientiam. . . . Modum autem divinus est, secundum quod accipimus cognitionem ab eo quod est supra intellectum nostrum, inquantum illud immittit se nobis.

self.[31] But when Albert describes the philosophers' own approach, he notes a reflective, perhaps a doubly reflective moment:

We have to say that "philosophers" have not arrived at God through reason by means of any sort of intellectual analysis. For there are two sorts of intellectual analysis [resolutio intellectus]: the analysis of composite intelligibilities into their simple components (as everything can be resolved into 'being') or the tracing back of caused-things to their causes. For the first sort of analysis, it is necessary that there be an end of the analysis which is a principle [and element] of the composite intelligibility. But God does not enter into composition with anything else. For the second sort of analysis it is necessary to presume some sort of proportion between caused and cause (otherwise, something-caused would not lead us to one cause rather than to another). But God is not the sort of cause which is proportioned to any effect. Therefore, since there is no way that God can be the conclusion of a rational analysis, philosophers have not known God in that way. But by beginning with the conclusions of such analyses, to some extent they have come to some sort of knowledge of God because they saw that

    a. that simple element which enters into composition [with other elements] is not the ultimate of simplicity;
    b. that cause which is proportioned (to its effects) is not the universal cause of the whole of being. Accordingly, philosophers have made many errors about God because they could not, by philosophical reasonings, arrive directly at a knowledge of him.[32]

---

[31] It should be noted that the *modus divinus* does not result in any intuition of the divine essence. DN VII, 348.68–73: Et ideo quando venit in illud [quod est supra intellectum nostrum], non figitur in ipso tamquam in aliquo determinato cuius fines vel essentiae vel virtutis vel operationis vel proprietatum inspiciat, sed sicut in quodam pelago infinito, in quo verius cognoscit quid non est, quam quid est.

[32] DN I, 8.54–75: Et dicendum, quod Philosophi non pervenerunt per rationem in deum sicut in id in quo stat resolutio intellectus, quia intellectus vel resolvit intentiones compositas in simplas, sicut omnia in ens, aut causata in causam. Et secundum primam resolutionem oportet esse terminum resolutionis, quod est principium compositionis; deus autem non est componibile alteri. Secundum vero secundam resolutionem oportet procedere supposita proportione causati ad causam; alias causatum non magis duceret in causam unam quam in aliam. Deus autem non est causa proportionata alicui effectui, et ideo nullo modo potest esse terminus resolutionis, quae est per rationem. Et ideo philosophi non cognoverunt ipsum sicut terminum resolutionis suae, sed ex termino suae resolutionis aliqualiter devenerunt in cognitionem eius, quia viderunt simplex, quod est componibile, non esse in fine simplicitatis et causam proportionantam non esse universalem causam totius entis. Et propter hoc in multis erraverunt de deo, quia non

So it is precisely in doing the sorts of analytical inquiries that are the stock in trade of natural philosophy that we become aware that inquiry is not satisfied by those analyses and thereby may become open to questions of ultimate grounding and universal causality.

Our approach to this topic centers around two key texts of DN. Since, however, Albert's own approach to the issues includes the logical priority of "knowable" over "namable,"[33] even though the two themes can be discussed only in relation to each other, we will discuss the two texts in reverse order with respect to their location in DN:

Text A: Whether God is knowable by us? (DN, VII, pp. 355–59)

Text B: The *solutio* to the question, What is the subject of this book? (DN, I, p. 2, lines 23–49)

II. *Text A: Whether God Is Knowable by Us*

There are problems with a claim that God is knowable by us; Albert collects six of the general issues under "quod non videtur" and then adds several qualifiers to his own account. The six general issues are:

1. There is no proportion between God and our knowing power, as there must be between a knower and what is knowable.

2. The process of human understanding involves an abstraction from the thing to be known; but no abstraction from God is possible.

3. Scripture says, "No one has ever seen God." The "seeing" to which it refers is "understanding."

4. Whatever we know we know either as conditioned (*principiatum*) or as a condition for others (*principium*). But God is not conditioned (since He has no origin), nor is He a condition (because "conditions" are known with the greatest certainty).

5. Whatever is infinite in every way cannot be received by our intellect.

6. That which is simple is completely present in whatever it is present, since it has no parts some of which might fall within and others without. But to be "completely within" is to be "comprehended." Now God both is simple and also is not comprehended. Therefore, He is entirely unknown to us.

These issues are countered by references to Damascene and Boethius, who claim that "knowledge of God is naturally implanted in us."

potuerunt per rationes philosophicas directe in cognitionem eius devenire. Et per hoc patent solutio ad obiecta.

[33] See note 17.

Having outlined this dialectic by the use of arguments and authorities, Albert presents his own *solutio*:

Avicenna points out that some things cannot be understood perfectly *either* because of the *eminence* of their perfection (as is the case with God) about which Aristotle says that the most evident of things is related to our intellect (the way the light of the sun is related to an owl's eye); *or* because of a *deficiency* of perfection (as is the case with "the potential," like matter, or with those things that are always involved with "potential" such as motion and time). Neither of these two cases can be understood perfectly because we know of such things only 'that it is' and not 'what it is.' But regardless of how it is in the other cases, it is surely true that of God we do not know 'what He is.' We only know 'that he is' and even that we know in an unclear way (*confuse*) because our intellect doesn't reach the defining point of His being (*terminum eius*).[34]

Albert's use of the six general issues, his reference to "natural knowledge of God," and the opening of his own *solutio* are all quite in line with the usual Medieval approach to this question.[35] His treatment begins to become distinctive as he uses the adverb *confuse* to describe the way in which we know of God 'that he is' and as he develops his position by reference to the way he regards the processes associated with definition. Our treatment of this text, accordingly, will address first (1) the adverb *confuse*, next (2) issues connected with definition, and finally (3) the consequences of these two issues for Albert's doctrine of "knowable."

1. *Quia est, et hoc etiam confuse.*

The earliest approach to the problem of *confuse* in DN appears to be supported, if not inspired, by the text from Saint Paul (1 Cor.) wherein he says: "We see now in a hidden way by means of a mirror; but then

[34] DN VII, 356.32–45: Solutio: Dicendum, quod quaedam non possunt intelligi perfecto intellectu, ut dicit Avicenna, duplici ratione: aut propter eminentiam suae perfectionis, sicut deus, de quo dicit Philosophus, quod manifestissima rerum se habent ad intellectum nostrum sicut lumen solis ad oculum noctuae, aut propter defectum a perfectione, sicut potentia, ut materia et ea quae sunt semper admixta potentiae, ut motus et tempus. Et haec quidem dicuntur non comprehendi perfecto intellectu, quia cognoscimus de ipsis tantum 'quia est' et non 'quid est'; sed quicquid sit de aliis, de deo certum est, quod non cognoscimus de ipso 'quid est', sed tantum 'quia est', et hoc etiam confuse, quia intellectus noster non tangit terminum eius.

[35] As examples, Saint Thomas Aquinas, *Summa Theologiae* I, 12, 1; Saint Bonaventure, *In I Sent.*, d.III, p. 1, a.u.

we will see face to face."[36] Albert sees two issues here: how is knowledge of God *in via* distinguished from that *in patria*; and, even *in patria*, does knowledge of God mean intellectual comprehension of God? His answer to both questions is summed up in the text:

> We have to say to the next points that our knowledge will be perfected [in heaven] not by a different *sort* of knowledge that would bear upon 'what' [God is] or 'on account of what' [God is]. Rather, our knowledge will be perfected by another *manner* of knowing; for, we will see that [God is] directly; [this is a knowledge] we now see in a hidden way and veiled by a mirror-like approach.[37]

Not even the Blessed in heaven will know 'what' God is. Their knowledge is a perfect mode of our (imperfect) knowledge. Our knowledge is imperfect, first, because it is mediated (through causality) and, second, because the sort of causality at issue is not the same as our ordinary causal knowledge.

> [God] is knowable by us only in a confused understanding [*confuso intellectu*] because we do not comprehend 'what' God is but only 'that' He is, and even this we know in an unclear way [*confuse*] because we do not know Him through an effect that is univocal to him, and immediate and essential.[38]

Nowhere in *DN* does Albert attempt to provide arguments in support of the claim that "God exists"; as indicated above, *DN* begins with assuming a relationship between God and man and labels that relationship "causal."[39] The precise problem of *DN* is to make sense of this claim, not to support its truth with arguments. This concern is funda-

36 Within the question, "Whether the divine substance can be seen by any created intellect?" *DN* I, 10.59–63: Item, I Cor. XII (12): Videmus nunc per speculum in aenigmate, tunc autem facie ad faciem; videre autem facie ad faciem est videre sine medio, ut dicit Augustinus; ergo videbimus substantiam eius immediate. On the medieval theologians' treatment of *in patria* in the light of official church teaching, see Leo Sweeney, "Bonaventure and Aquinas on the Divine Being as Infinite," *Southwestern Journal of Philosophy* 5 (1974): n. 9.

37 *DN* I, 13.53–57: Ad id quod sequitur, dicendum, quod cognitio nostra perficietur non alia cognitione 'quid' vel 'propter quid', sed alio modo cognoscendi, quia videbimus 'quia'* sine medio, quod nunc in aenigmate et speculo velatum videmus. (*The printed text has 'quid', but 'quia' is the proper reading as the context and other texts make clear.)

38 *DN* I, 32.12–16: A nobis tamen non est cognoscibilis nisi confuso intellectu, quia non comprehendimus de deo, 'quid' est, sed tantum 'quia', et hoc confuse, cum non cognoscamus ipsum per effectum univocum sibi et immediatum et essentialem.

39 See notes 23 and 32.

mental to the whole of a theology, since the unclear, uncertain character of the knowledge 'that God is' affects all other claims about God, the knowledge of which depends upon that one claim.[40] To make sense of such a causal claim is to show how the claim that "God is cause of all" fits in with our ordinary understanding of cause.

First, Albert raises a doubt about whether the claim that God is cause of all can support any sort of affirming theology. Things that agree in a name must also agree in the possession of a property signified by that name. But there is a doubt that God has anything in common with any creature. Therefore, there is doubt that even claiming that 'God is cause of all' can support an affirming theology. The reason for doubting any communality between God and creatures is rooted in the doctrine that 'x agrees with y' can occur in one of three ways: univocally, equivocally, analogously. Since 'equivocally' is reducible to 'univocally' and since Albert agrees that there is no univocal communality between God and creatures, the issue becomes: how do we understand "analogous communality?"[41]

Second, to raise a question about "analogous communality" [convenientia secundum analogiam] is relevant to an understanding of confuse since it is precisely as not having an effect which is univocal to God upon which to ground our knowledge that leads Albert to describe our knowledge 'quia' as confuse.[42]

Third, he is careful to note that the analogous communality that is claimed between God and creatures does not consist in God sharing per prius that very same property which creatures share per posterius. This sort of analogy would rank God first in a certain class and would have the advantage of dissipating much agnosticism inasmuch as we could claim to know (the content of) that very quality which would be

[40] DN I, 39.51–54: . . . scientes tamen 'quia est' confuse, et propter incertitudinem eius remanent omnia alia nobis ignota, quorum cognito ab ipso dependent.

[41] DN I, 35.17–35: Sed videtur, quod hoc quod sit causa rerum, non sit sufficiens ratio, quare nominetur affirmationibus omnium. Quorumcumque est convenientia in nomine, oportet esse convenientiam in proprietate significata per nomen; sed deus non habet convenientiam cum aliqua creatura in natura significata per aliquod nomen; ergo non convenit cum eis in nomine. Probatio mediae: Omnis convenientia aut est secundum aequivocationem aut secundum univocationem aut secundum analogiam. Non potest autem esse convenientia secundum univocationem, quia nihil est univocum deo et creaturae; nec iterum secundum aequivocationem quia omne aequivocum reducitur ad aliquod univocum, et sic redit eadem ratio; nec iterum secundum analogiam, quia oporteret aliquid inesse pluribus secundum prius et posterius, quod esset simplicius et prius eis, sicut ens prius est substantia et accidente; deo autem nihil est prius; ergo non potest esse aliqua convenientia ipsius ad creaturas.

[42] See note 38.

found both in God and in creatures. But this would bring God within the bounds of our usual subject-predicate grammar with its basis in the structure of composite being; and God is not composite. Therefore, Albert concludes that the sort of analogous communality that binds God and creatures in a knowledge act is one in which God is claimed to be substantially that which creatures are by participation. This different way of being-something is enough to locate God outside any class, even though we are not in a position to say just what 'to be x substantially' means.[43]

Next Albert amplifies our not being in such a cognitive position by pointing to the difference between 'knowing that' God is and 'knowing the being' which is God. Although we have an unclear knowledge 'that God is' (*quia est*), the foremost name[44] among the other names of God is *Qui est*. But we have no way to arrive at a knowledge of the meaning of this name, since ordinary intellectual analyses, as we saw earlier,[45] end up with some being[46] or some cause which is not God. In this text the meaning of *confuse* as describing our knowledge *quia* is exemplified by noting that the being which is God is not reached through an analysis of a composite being into its simple elements nor through an analysis of a caused being to its cause, since God is not proportioned to any caused being.[47] Consequently, we remain in ignorance of God's manner

[43] DN I, 35.45–56: Solutio: Dicimus, quod haec ratio est sufficiens, ut deus possit nominari ab omnibus causatis, quia est causa omnium; et bene concedimus, quod habet convenientiam cum causatis non univocationis, sed analogiae, non tamen talis analogiae, quod aliquid idem participetur a deo per prius et a causatis per posterius, quia sic esset aliquid simplicius et prius deo, sed quia deus est secundum substantiam aliquid ut vita vel sapientia vel huiusmodi non per participationem et alia participant illud accedendo ad primum, quantum possunt, sicut est convenientia exemplatorum ad exemplar.

[44] DN I, 39.42–43: "... prius aliis secundum rationem."

[45] See note 32.

[46] It is part of the very meaning of being [*ens*] as we understand it in our ordinary knowledge that 'being' involve composition. The reason is that all of our ideas carry as part of their content the manner in which that intelligible content is found in creatures. The best we can do is deny that that intelligible content is found in God in the way it is found in creatures without, however, being in a position to say just how it is found in God. See DN I, 32.29–33: "Ad primum . . . . Si autem dicimus ipsum ens, significatur duo, essentia scilicet et habens essentiam, et sic deficit nomen a simplicitate dei, in quo non est aliud essentia et habens essentiam." See also "Ad quartum dicendum, quod res significatae per talia nomina per prius et verissime sibi conveniunt; quia tamen significant illas res per modum quo sunt in creaturis, quia aliter non innotescunt nobis, ideo per talia nomina non comprehendimus de ipso 'quid' est, sed tantum 'quia' per causatum."

[47] Albert notes that there is a way in which God is proportioned to our intellect: the 'quia est' of any being, at least in an unclear way, is so proportioned but not so as to generate knowledge of essence. DN VII, 356.60–66: Secundum hoc ergo

of being (*modus essendi*), an ignorance which, as we saw earlier, affects every claim to know something about God.[48]

Finally, Albert points out that, far from being an unacceptable agnosticism, it is most appropriate that we are not in a position to say what manner of being is God's: "Nor is it inappropriate that God, as He is in Himself, be beyond [God] as He appears within our knowledge."[49] This ignorance of God's *modus essendi* becomes involved with issues of definition and brings us to the second main point of the text.

2. *Intellectus noster non tangit terminum eius.*

Earlier I translated this phrase as: "Our intellect does not reach the defining point of His being." I think this meaning is justified not only by the context as worked out above but especially by the very next sentence in the text which raises a problem with the position Albert has been arguing:

> Someone might say: not to know 'what it is' in the case of God is not to miss out on any authentic knowledge, because 'what is it' is an appropriate question only for those things which have a definition. Everything which has a definition is composite. But God is simple and so in his case [the question] 'what is it' is misplaced.[50]

The sense of the problem raised here is logically on a par with issues Albert has raised earlier: just as our ordinary processes of intellectual

---

dicendum ad primum, quod 'quia est' cuiuslibet rei et etiam dei proportionatum quaedam confusa cognitio de re, et hoc cognoscimus de ipso; sed 'quid est' ipsius improportionatum est omni intellectui creato, et ideo hoc de ipso cognoscere non possumus.

[48] DN I, 39.37–54: Solutio: Dicendum, quod intentio Dionysii est dicere, quod deus secundum omne nomen est innominabilis a nobis perfecte et secundum id quod est, licet nominemus ipsum per huiusmodi nomina, 'quia est,' et hoc confuse, sicut SUPRA habitum est. Interalia tamen eius nomina unum est quod est prius aliis secundum rationem, scilicet 'qui est,' ut INFRA dicet Dionysius. Et ideo est magis remotum a cognitione nostra, cum non possimus in illud, neque per resolutionem compositi in simplex, eo quod illud ens quod est deus, non est terminus resolutionis, cum non veniat ad compositionem alicuius, nec iterum per resolutionem causati in causam vel posterioris in prius, cum non sit proportionatum alicui causato. Et ideo modus essendi eius ramanet nobis ignotus, scientes tamen 'quia est' confuse, et propter incertitudinem eius remanent omnia alia nobis ignota, quarum cognitio ab ipso dependet.

[49] DN I, 40.2–4: . . . nec est inconveniens, ut deus, secundum quod est in se, sit supra se, secundum quod est in cognitione nostra.

[50] DN VII, 356.45–50: Et si dicatur, quod 'quid est' non invenitur nisi in his quae habent diffinitionem, quae omnia sunt composita, deus autem simplex est et ita non habet 'quid est' et ita ignorantes 'quid est' ipsius nihil ipsius ignoramus, . . .

analysis fail in the case of God, just as our use of "cause" with reference to God forces us to speak of a "cause not proportioned to any effect," so our attempt to describe how we can claim knowledge 'that God is' without, as is usually the case, implying some knowledge of 'what it is' forces us to rethink what is involved in claiming to know a thing. Instead, however, of locating God beyond 'things with an essence' in order to avoid the implicit character of composition which seems to belong to all those things which have definitions, Albert proposes a different model:

We must say that we do not have 'what it is'-type knowledge only of those things we can define and which have an essence which is explicated by means of a definition. We also have 'what it is'-type knowledge of the defining [elements that enter into those definitions]. Each of these has an essence as well; such elements-of-definitions are, however, entirely included within and received by our intellect. God, too, does not have an essence in the manner of a composite being; but in his case, he is not included within nor received by our intellect; and that is why we do not know 'what he is.'[51]

One part of Albert's response, then, is to propose that we need not think of God's essence as involving a definition after the manner of genus/difference or some other sort of composite structure. We are already aware of essence-type knowledge which we have of the elements of genus/difference definitions; these elements need not themselves be composite in the way ordinary definitions are composite. This reflective understanding of essence-type knowledge opens us to the possibility of a noncomposite essence with an intelligibility which, unlike the above "elements," is not exhausted by our intellectual knowledge of it.

To understand Albert's position here, it is useful to return to his treatment of the question of whether the Blessed in heaven see the substance of God, remembering that the knowledge of God which the Blessed have is not different from ours on earth in *kind* but only in the perfection of its *manner* of knowing.[52]

---

51 DN VII, 50–59: . . . dicendum, quod non solum de diffinitis scimus 'quid est,' quae habent quiditatem, quae explicatur per diffinitionem, sed etiam de quolibet diffinientium, quorum unumquodque est quiditas ipsa, quae tamen tota clauditur et accipitur per intellectum nostrum. Similiter et deus est quiditas et essentia quaedam, quamvis non habeat quiditatem per modum compositorum; tamen quiditas eius non clauditur nec accipitur in intellectu nostro, et ideo dicitur, quod nescimus de ipso 'quid est.'

52 See note 37.

The main text is as follows:

All the Blessed will see the substance of God, 'that it is;' but no created intellect can see 'what' [God is]. For, since knowledge of 'what it is' is the basis of all causal knowledge, to know of a thing what-it-is is to include in a glance the outer limits of its essence. In this way the whole of its being would be enclosed within a created intellect. Since whatever encloses another is greater than what is enclosed therein, this would make the created intellect greater than God: this is absurd.[53]

Albert's account touches on several basic issues: (a) the meaning of "to see God"; (b) the relation of knowledge of God to abstraction; (c) some understanding of the infiniteness and finiteness of God; (d) measure and definiteness.

a) "To see" has two meanings: "to attain the thing seen" and "to encompass the whole of what is seen." Only the former is possible to a created intellect; it is not possible for such an intellect to encompass the whole of God's being, even if it were to do so by knowing one attribute after the other.[54] The Blessed "attain" God in a perfected way because they see Him directly (*sine medio*),[55] whereas we on earth can know "that God is" only reflectively and by means of the knowledge of creatures.[56]

[53] DN I, 10.64–72: Solutio: Dicimus, quod substantiam dei, 'quia est,' omnes beati videbunt; 'quid' autem sit, nullus intellectus creatus videre potest. Cum enim cognitio 'quid est' sit principalis causarum, oporteret, si cognosceretur 'quid est,' ut circumspicerentur termini essentiae eius. Et sic totum esse eius clauderetur in intellectu creato; et ita intellectus creatus esset maior deo, cum omne claudens sit maius eo quod clauditur: quod absurdum est.

[54] DN I, 10.73–11.7: Ad primum ergo dicendum, quod videre est attingere ad rem visam; et sic non intelligit evangelista neque Chrysostomus, quod deus non videatur. Est etiam videre visu rem pertransire, quia sicut probat Euclides, omne quod videtur, videtur sub angulo cuiusdam trianguli cuius angulus est in oculo et basis ad rem visam, sive visus fiat extra mittendo sive per immutationem ab exteriori. Videtur autem res per lineam dividentem triangulum, et ideo non videtur tota simul, sed sub discursu de uno in aliud; et quando tota res pertransitur, dicitur tota videri. Sic autem videri non potest deus pertranseundo totum quod est.

[55] DN I, 11.8–12: Ad rationem vero ipsius primam dicendum, quod increabile non potest videri a creabili sic, quod pertranseatur ab ipso, sed ita, quod attingat ipsam substantiam sine medio. Et propter hoc non removetur, quin creatum sit semper sub increato.
See also "objection 6" (p. 12) and its response (p. 13).

[56] Albert likens the general way in which we come to know God to the way in which Philosophers have come to speak of our knowledge of the agent intellect. In fact, he notes, the presence of God in us is in some sense like a light, perhaps better, like a light dawning, as he noted in discussing the reflective understanding that can

b) The expansion of this point involves some understanding of the relation of that which is knowable to the one knowing, a relation that is sometimes named "abstraction." "The way in which a knowable is knowable" (*modus cognoscibilis*) has two meanings: one refers to its essence or nature; the other refers to the way it becomes an object of the intellect.[57] To know something *secundum suam quidditatem* is to know all of which that essence is the intelligible ground (*ratio*). In God's case, this would be to know all things. Albert notes that God *would* be for us such a principle of knowing things if we *were* able to know him in this way.[58] But neither we nor the Blessed have that sort of knowledge. Rather, God becomes an object of our intellect when our intellect grasps (*accipit*) him under one or another limited intelligibility (*ratio*). Here Albert plays on the Latin word *obiectum*: the second way in which a knowable is knowable is insofar as it becomes an object (*obiectum*) of our intellect; it is in this "second way" that God "presents Himself" (*obicit se*) to our intellect. A "knowable" becomes an object for our intellect insofar as we grasp (*accipit*) it under a particular, definite intelligibility (*ratio*); God presents Himself to our intellect under a particular, definite intelligibility. At stake here is the extent to which God is active in our knowing Him. Albert is quite clear in the case of the Blessed; they need a special "illumination" by which they

occur when we realize that a cause proportioned to its effect is not the universal cause of all being (see note 32). *DN* VII, 356.67-74: Ad secundum dicendum, quod deus est per essentiam in anima, non tamen ut natura quaedam animae, sed ut lux quaedam intellectus, et hoc sufficit ad hoc quod cognoscatur per intellectum; immo quod sic est in anima, cognoscitur sub specie cuiuslibet intelligibilis, sicut dicunt PHILOSOPHI de intellectu agente. Et similiter de deo cognoscimus, 'quia est,' per cognitionem cuiuslibet creaturae.

[57] *DN* I, 11.36-58: Ad aliud dicendum, quod modus cognoscibilis duplex est: unus secundum suam quiditatem, et secundum istum modum non videtur deus nisi a se. Alius modus rei est, secundum quod est obiectum intellectus, qui accipit ipsum in tali vel tali ratione. Quamvis enim rationes uniantur in re ipsa, intellectus tamen potest accipere unam sine alia, sicut quamvis punctus sit unus, tamen secundum quod est principium infinitarum linearum exeuntium a centro ad circumferentiam, habet plures rationes, et ita quamvis intellectus accipiat ipsum secundum aliquam sui rationem, non oportet, quod accipiat omnia quorum est principium, quia non est necesse, quod accipiat ipsum in omnibus suis rationibus. Similiter cum intellectus accipiat deum, non comprehendendo quidditatem eius, quo modo solum esset necessarium, ut cognosceret omnia quorum est ratio, sed secundum quod obicit se ei secundum hanc vel illam rationem, non oportet, quod cognoscat omnia quorum est ratio, et tamen cognoscit ipsum per modum sui, quia uterque modus est modus eius, secundum quod est; et non differt in ipso secundum rem, sed diversitas est ex parte accipientis.

[58] See also *DN* VII, 357.53-55: ". . . similiter deus esset principium nobis ad alia cognoscenda, si ipsum perfecte cognoscere possemus."

become "proportioned" to knowing God.[59] But this need for a "theophany" is involved in the fact that the Blessed see *sine medio*. As far as knowledge of God *in via*, we note the following:

i) the mode of understanding rooted in faith (*divinus*) involves a movement from God to us;[60]

ii) distinct from faith is the *modus philosophicus* which, although liable to error, is a distinctive understanding which can yield knowledge *quia* based upon our reflective understanding of the limits of ordinary causal knowledge;[61]

iii) Albert's explicit reference to abstraction in the texts we are considering has two moves. First, he distinguishes the sort of abstraction that occurs when we analyze a complex thing into its component parts from the only sort of abstraction that is necessary for an act of understanding: the abstraction of an intelligible meaning (*abstractio intentionis*). This latter is the sort which is relevant to a knowledge of God. Second, Albert describes this abstraction not as grasping one part of a thing which has parts, but as grasping (*accipitur*) through an activity of the intellect itself (*per actionem intellectus*) one definite intelligible aspect of a thing (*ratio quaedam rei*).[62]

This discussion appears to bear upon Ruello's treatment (mentioned above) of *ratio* as providing a bridge to a knowledge of God as He is in Himself. First, Ruello recognizes that Albert continually denies that we ever have knowledge of God *quid est*. I believe it would be an erroneous reading of the text to equate such *quid est* knowledge with *comprehensive* knowledge of God, even though both are denied of the Blessed as well as of those still on earth (the argument for this claim is made throughout the paper).

Second, in discussing *quia est* knowledge, Albert makes a sharp distinction between the *manner* in which the Blessed know God and that in which those on earth know God. The Blessed know by means of

[59] *DN* I, 11.28-35: Ad illud autem quod obicitur per rationem, dicendum, quod intellectus creatus secundum naturalia sua non habet proportionem ad cognoscendum deum, secundum tamen quod iuvatur per illuminationes sive theophanias descendentes a deo, efficitur proportionatus, non quidem ad videndum, quid est deus, sed ad videndum ipsum attingendo substantiam eius, secundum quod ipse se obicit sub tali vel tali ratione.

[60] See note 30.

[61] See note 32.

[62] *DN* VII, 356.74-82: Id tamen quod obicitur, quod a simplicissimo non potest fieri abstractio, nihil valet, quia hoc est verum de abstractione, quae fit per resolutionem rei in sua componentia, quae non requiritur ad intelligendum, sed tantum abstractio intentionis, quae potest abstrahi etiam a simplicissimo secundum esse, sicut a puncto. Non enim est aliqua pars rei, sed tantum accipitur per actionem intellectus ut ratio quaedam rei.

114

an illumination which allows them to reach God's substance insofar as He presents Himself to them *sub tali vel tali ratione*.[63] This illumination is just like the illumination involved in angelic knowledge[64] and is authenticated as being of God Himself (as well as of other things through such knowledge)[65] because of coming immediately (*sine medio*) from God Himself. For the Blessed, then, the *rationes* do give access to the *substantia* of God. But no such guarantee is found on earth. The *rationes* by which we represent God are not of God *sine medio*. They are derived from the world and, retaining that worldliness, cannot be claimed to give access to the *substantia* of God (as is the case with the Blessed) unless we presuppose what we wish to prove: namely, that a *ratio* abstracted from things is identical with the *ratio* as *idea* in God. I do not find Albert making such a presupposition; I find his basic argument in *DN* to be in the opposite direction. It is, of course, clear that such a presupposition would be in line with the Neoplatonic inspiration not only of the Dionysian texts but of the *Liber de Causis* as well as of Albert's admitted debt to the theological treatises of Boethius. These sources make even more remarkable Albert's caution in the claims he makes to knowledge of God.

This conclusion is supported, to some extent, by the further distinction made between "faith" and "philosophy." In addition to the observations made earlier, Albert appears to accept the description of the way faith works in us as "moving after the manner of nature" rather than "after the manner of reason."[66] To the extent that faith is more like virtue than like knowledge, for someone to believe is not for him to have acquired an additional *ratio*, but for him to *accept* the revelatory power of the names sanctified by the sacred scriptures.

[63] See note 59.

[64] DN IV, 170.73–171.22: . . . et ideo dicimus, quod angeli, qui illuminantur a deo, habent cognitionem de rebus ex speciebus essentialium principiorum rei propriorum, quae sunt in causa prima sicut in causa propria. . . . Has autem proprias rationes rerum quae sunt in primo sicut in principio operativo et cognoscitivo, influit ipsum primum sicut ad esse in naturam, ita ad cognitionem in mentes angelicas; et ideo accipiunt propriam cognitionem de rebus, ac si acciperent per abstractionem ab ipsis rebus; . . . Et eadem est ratio de cognitione animae separatae.

[65] See notes 64 and 58.

[66] DN IV, 170.18–26: (2) Ad idem: in hoc differt cognitio fidei a cognitione illuminatorum a deo de aliquo cognoscibili, quod fides movet per modum naturae informando conscientiam sicut virtus, ut dicit TULLIUS, non autem movet per modum rationis, quia credens nescit rationam eius quod credit. Unde dicitur, quod 'credere non potest quis nisi volens'. Si autem moveret fides per modum rationis, possit cogi, sicut quis cogitur demonstratione.

Although this statement appears in the dialectic of arguments that *precedes* Albert's *solutio*, he does not indicate any problem with the account of faith in his *solutio* or in his "answers to arguments."

Thirdly, Ruello notes a distinction between the starting point and the term of our knowledge of God: while the former can only be the causality of God, the latter is God Himself.[67] Our analysis does not support this reading of the text. Part of the difficulty lies in determining how it is that knowledge *quia est* becomes intelligible to us and in what does such intelligibility consist. Ruello here employs his discussion of *ratio* to answer these questions. Presumably, to know *quia est* of God under *tali vel tali ratione* is to know that "Divine Wisdom exists" or that "Divine Goodness exists" and to know the difference between them *as rationes* while assenting to their real identity as God. Apart from the possibility of the Illuminated Blessed, I find Albert's argument amounts to this: By understanding that a cause proportioned to its effect is not the cause of the whole of being, we come to see that the very meaning of cause is open to use in the inquiry into the universal ground of all beings; similarly, those perfections (such as wisdom, goodness) which range over, while not limited to, particular genera can be used in an equally transcendent manner, and thereby to be available for transcendent reference. It is true that "Divine Wisdom" does not mean "wisdom as found to be caused"; it does *refer* to that unknown whatever-it-is which we affirm as divine reality such that it could be a source of wisdom. But we are misled if we think that by so affirming we know what Divine Wisdom means.[68]

[67] Ruello, *op. cit.*, p. 127: A la première, difficulté, nous répondons que si saint Albert crut pouvoir maintenir l'idée qu'un nom divin exprimait Dieu en lui-même (dans l'ordre du *quia est*, ainsi qu'il a été précisé) et non pas en sa causalité, c'est qu'il distingue soigneusement le point de départ de notre connaissance de Dieu et son point d'arrivée. Il est équivoque de dire: nous ne connaissons Dieu que par ses participations. Il faut accorder à cette proposition toute sa vérité, s'il s'agit de dire quel est le principe de notre connaissance, mais s'il faut préciser le terme de celle-ci, la remarque est inexacte. Nous connaissons ce que les créatures participent des perfections divines et nous en venons à connaître la Sagesse divine ou telle autre noblesse de Dieu qui, par elle-même, n'est pas participée et que Dieu est substantiellement.

[68] DN II, 80.61–70: Solutio: Dicendum, quod nullum divinorum nominum potest humana ratione reserari, 'quid est', et hoc concludunt rationes. Sed de quibusdam divinis nominibus potest perfecte manifestari, 'quia est', sicut quod est bonus et sapiens et huiusmodi, quamvis quid sit bonitas et sapientia eius, maneat nobis occultum; de quibusdam vero nec etiam 'quia' per rationem potest manifestari, sicut ea maxime, quae pertinent ad discretionem personarum; et haec est intentio litterae. It is in the light of a text such as this, that the following lines from Albert should be understood. DN II, 81.30–40: Cognoscentes enim ea quae participant creaturae de nobilitatibus divinis, venimus in cognitionem ipsius sapientiae divinae, quia est, secundum quod est in ipso, non participata, sicut omnis nostra cognitio incipit a sensu, non tamen oportet, quod nihil cognoscamus ultra sensibile, sed ex sensibilibus devenimus in intelligibilia. Similiter ex causato devenimus in causam,

Accordingly, there are three knowledges: the Blessed in heaven see that God exists immediately and because God reveals Himself to them; those who have faith know that God exists through the mediation of the Scriptures and preaching which are instruments whereby God endows them with Himself; a less trustworthy approach is the knowledge that God exists mediated through the (philosopher's) reflective understanding of the limited applicability of the ordinary concepts of being and causality.

c) Albert's claim that no created intellect can know what God is, is bound up with his treatment of God as infinite. It might be possible to say that God as infinite is the ontological side of the epistemological claim about the extent of our knowledge of God. But there is a hedge on that statement because of the tension Albert feels in describing God as infinite. The source of that tension is his intent to safeguard the transcendence of God for both metaphysical[69] and epistemological[70] reasons and at the same time not give up the claim that God is "determinate" and "particular" being.[71] The tension is explained in part[72] by Albert's concept of "infinite" as a negation of some sort of extrinsic boundary[73]: by reference to that possible boundary, God is unbounded or infinite. Albert quotes Damascene that God is not bounded (*non finitur*) by time (because He always is) nor

de qua causa per rationis inquisitionem intelligimus condiciones quasdam quae non sunt in effectu; et per hoc patet solutio ad primum.
Albert surely confuses the issue by saying both "secundum quod est in ipso" and also "quamvis quid sit bonitas et sapientia eius, maneat nobis occultum."

[69] *DN* I, 8.71–72: ". . . causam proportionatam non esse universalem causam totius entis."

[70] *DN* I, 11.: "Sic autem videri non potest deus pertranscundo totum quod est."

[71] *DN* V, 315.49–57: Non potest autem dici, quod materia sit principium determinans, quia sic in rebus immaterialibus, sicut est angelus et deus, non esset determinatio, et sic non essent hoc aliquid; nec aliquae operationes horum essent, quia 'operationes particularium sunt.' Unde oportet dicere 'quod est' principium determinationis; hoc enim invenitur in omnibus determinatis et in deo, quamvis secundum rem in ipso 'quod est' et 'quo est' non differant.

[72] For an extensive treatment of Albert's use of infinite in his Commentary on the *Sentences*, see my "Divine Infinity," *loc. cit.*

[73] Albert begins by noting two meanings of infinite, one "by privation," the other "by negation." *DN* VII, 357.8–20: ". . . quod deus non dicitur infinitus privative, quia sic esset imperfectissimum, et quod sic infinitum est, numquam cognoscitur, secundum quod est infinitum, quia secundum quod infinitum est, semper est extra intellectum; quod autem ipsius est intra intellectum, est finitum, sicut dicitur in PHYSICIS, quod 'infinitum est, cuius quantitatem accipientibus semper est aliquid extra sumere.' Sed deus dicitur infinitus negative, quia, sicut dicit DAMASCENUS, non finitur tempore, quia semper est, nec loco, quia ubique est, nec intellectu, quia non contingit terminos cognoscendo 'quid' ipsius, sed attingit aliqualiter ipsum, cognoscendo, quia est."

by place (because He is everywhere) nor by intellect (because intellect does not reach a knowledge of what He is).

In the earlier text (Chapter I) Albert explains his preference for the term *non-finitus*, which highlights the negative meaning as distinct from the privative (which means 'lacking an end one *ought* to have') and also allows him to address the question of whether God, since He is an end (*finis*) is not thereby *finitus*. Albert quotes "the Philosopher" to say that "an end is neither finite nor infinite."[74] There are two sorts of end, one internal and the other external. An internal end, such as a point with reference to a line, is embraced by that of which it is the end. So here is an end which is "comprehended" but is not thereby described as *finitus*. The "point" is Albert's model of how it is that one can say that God is comprehended (by Himself) but is not thereby *finitus* with reference to Himself.[75]

There is another sort of end which is external to that of which it is the end; the example is "place." This sort of end exceeds what it terminates and is more properly said to comprehend it than to be comprehended by it. By reflecting on the function of such an end, we can move to the notion of an end external of any bounded being, which end would embrace and exceed that bounded being. From this notion we may hypothesize an end of the whole of being which would embrace and transcend all bounded beings. This allows Albert to introduce some expansion of the concept of God, without losing sight of the negative approach he is taking.[76]

[74] *DN* I, 12.50–59: Solutio: Dicendum, quod infinitum dicitur dupliciter: privative et negative. Privative infinitum esse imperfectum est; est enim carens fine, natum habere, a quo res perfecta est; et sic deus non potest dici infinitus. Nec etiam dicitur finitus, cum sit finis; et finis, ut dicit PHILOSOPHUS, neque finitus neque infinitus est. Sed negative potest dici infinitus, idest nonfinitus, sicut dicit DAMASCENUS, quia dicitur infinitus, eo quod non finitur comprehensione intellectus vel loco vel tempore vel diffinitione.

[75] *DN* I, 12.59–71: "Nec tamen est dicendum, sicut QUIDAM dicunt, quod est non finitus nobis, finitus sibi, eo quod se capit. Haec enim determinatio 'mihi,' cum dicitur 'non finitus mihi,' non trahit ab eo quod est simpliciter; unde si simpliciter esset finitus, et mihi esset finitus. Et cum hoc sit falsum, simpliciter non est finitus et ita nulli finitus, nec sibi nec alii. Sed est non finitus, sicut nec punctus, quamvis nihil sui sit extra ipsum, non dicitur finitus, nec sibi nec alii, sed finis. Est autem duplex finis: unus intra, et hic comprehenditur eo cuius est finis; nihil enim de puncto est extra lineam nec aliquid lineae extra superficien." But see *DN* VII, 357.30–33, where Albert says: ". . . et sic quodammodo est finitus sibi, non autem nobis, quia illud perquod sic mensuramus ipsum, etiam est nobis infinitum." Here, however, Albert is addressing another topic, namely, whether God can be said to be "measured" by anything, and not whether he is *finitus* by reason of his comprehending himself.

[76] *DN* I, 12.71–13.4: Est autem alius finis extra, sicut locus, et hic quidem

d) In order to complete his response to the objection that God is in every way infinite, Albert adds to his position that God is most properly described as *non-finitus* by admitting that there is a way in which he could be said to be *finitus sibi*. That way has something to do with procedures of "measuring" as occasioned by the use of such language as: "God's power is as extensive as His being" or "The Father is equal to the Son" or "God's strength matches His ability." Albert balks at trying to conceive of an infinite being compared to an infinite. An infinite is that which always has some point beyond the point you have reached; as such, one infinite would be simply incommensurable with another. But Albert's religious tradition does use the language of comparison and measure; consequently, Albert proceeds to account for this use, only taking care to point the measuring process in the right direction. The model for the discussion is taken from the use we make of hands and fingers to measure something. The idea is that the standard which is used to measure other things is not itself measured by *those* things but may be conceived as "measuring itself" by regarding one and the same reality now from one point of view and now from another.[77] In a similar way God is not measured nor made finite by any creature, but can be conceived as being the measure of Himself. Even in that case, however, although in some sense God could be said to be *finitus sibi*, that which we regard as the measure (e.g., *quantus filius*) is just as infinite to us as that which we regard as being measured (e.g., *tantus pater*).[78]

Probably the basis of Albert's move here, although it remains undeveloped in *DN*, is his concern that "being infinite" does not quite protect the definiteness and particularity which must characterize being. In another context where he seeks the source of definiteness (*principium determinans*) in the structure of being he notes:

We cannot say that matter is the source of definiteness because then in immaterial things, such as angel and God, there would be no

finis excedit id cuius est finis, et comprehendit magis quam comprehendatur. Unde si sit finis alicuius entis determinati, comprehendet illud et excedet; et si sit finis universi, excedet omnia. Tale autem est deus, et ideo omnia excedit nec aliquo comprehenditur, neque loco neque intellectu.

77 DN VII, 357.20–27: Sed sicut secunda mensura mensuratur per primam, prima autem non mensuratur per secundam, sed per designationem suae quantitatis supra ipsam, sicut palmus mensuratur per digitum, digitus autem mensuratur per suam quantitatem in alia ratione acceptam, sicut dicimus, quod tantus est digitus quanta est latitudo extensa inter duos tales terminos.

78 *Ibid.*: . . . ita etiam, quamvis deus non mensuretur neque finiature per aliquid creatum, mensuratur tamen per seipsum, sicut dicimus, quod tanta est virtus sua, quanta potentia sua, et sic quodammodo est finitus sibi, non autem nobis, quia illud per quod sic mensuramus ipsum, etiam est nobis infinitum.

definiteness (*determinatio*), and then they would not be individual (*hoc aliquid*). Nor would they thereby have any activities, because "activities belong to particular beings." So we have to say that "what a thing is" (*quod est*) is the source of definiteness: this applies to all definite things, even God; although in God there is no difference between "*quod est*" and "*quo est*."[79]

The reference to Boethius's doctrine of *quod est* and *quo est* merely emphasizes how basic *simplicitas* is to his doctrine of God.[80] The point here, however, is that it is important to Albert to extend the notion of "definite being" to God, and hence his hedging on the doctrine of infinity.

3. In ablatione omnium, in excessu, in omnium causa.[81]

The outcome of Albert's treatment of the "knowableness" of God in Chapter VII is a summary statement of *DN*'s threefold way by which we come to a knowledge of God from creatures. All three ways share in the same caveat which Albert announces as built into the structure of our language. In fact, the three ways themselves are argued by Albert as the logical consequences of attempting to put language to a use other than that provided for by its origins. The sixth objection asks the general question, How did you come up with these three ways?[82] Albert's response (in the body of the text) is intended to show that three and only three ways are possible because of the structure of language itself. First he expresses a general principle of language usage:

> Beginning with the last point (6), as was noted before, we use names according to the way the thing meant [by the name] is found among those things which come within the range of our intellect. For, that is how we generate scientific knowledge. Consequently, there is a difference between the way a thing of this sort is found in those things which transcend our intellect and the way a name is able to express meaning.[83]

[79] *DN* V, 315.49–57; see note 70.
[80] See my "Albert the Great, Boethius, and Divine Infinity," *loc. cit.*
[81] *DN* VII, 358.34–42: Modi ergo tres, quos ponit, sunt isti: quia ex creaturis in deum ascendimus *in ablatione omnium,* idest omnia negando ab ipso, *et in excessu,* idest ea quae sunt in creaturis, excedenter ponendo in ipso, *et in omnium causa,* idest ponendo eum causam omnium quae sunt in creaturis, ut si invenian sapientiam in creaturis, dicam, quod deus non est talis sapientia, sed est causa huius sapientiae et est eminenter habens sapientiam.
[82] *DN* VII, 358.70–71: (6) Praeterea quaeritur, penes quid accipiantur isti modi.
[83] *DN* VII, 358.72–78: Solutio: (6) Dicendum primo ad hoc ultimum, quod,

It is important to note that Albert does not argue that we somehow can disengage the *res significata* from its *modus* and supply it with a mode proper to the divine. What he does argue is that every use of a name must recall that the way it expresses meaning is reflective of its natural home within the context of physical reality. For we do not know the manner of God's being; we simply know that it is not our manner of being. Put another way: the names we use derive their meaning from their context which is the physical world. We have no way to discern what that name means in a divine context.[84] What we can do is recognize that some names are open to use beyond the context from which they are derived and, in such a use, be ready to negate the applicability of the original context to the extended use.[85] Albert's text goes on to specify the three possibilities:

Accordingly, the "thing meant by a name" can be considered in two ways: either insofar as the thing meant goes beyond the meaning of the name itself (and this is the approach *per excessum*), or insofar as the thing meant is signified by that name. In this case, however, there are two possibilities: either insofar as the thing meant is in [what is] an effect (and this is the approach *per causam*), or insofar as the thing meant is [named as belonging to] a cause which transcends the [physical] mode (and this approach is *per omnium ablationem*).[86]

sicut SUPRA dictum est, nos imponimus nomina secundum illum modum quo invenitur res significata in rebus, quae sunt sub intellectu nostro, ex quibus accipimus scientias, et ideo alius est modus quo huiusmodi res invenitur in his quae sunt supra intellectum nostrum, et alius est modus, quo significat nomen.

84 We have no intuitive access to decontextualized "meanings" and could not know meanings except as provided by the context of the physical world. DN I, 32.44–49: "Ad quartum dicendum, quod res significatae per talia nomina per prius et verissime sibi conveniunt; quia tamen significant illas res per modum, quo sunt in creaturis, quia aliter non innotescunt nobis, ideo per talia nomina non comprehendimus de ipso 'quid' est, sed tantum 'quia' per causatum."

85 Albert reinforces the claim of the text that *negation* is the truest sort of approach. The reason is that affirmations are not totally true, since they are not true with respect to the (built-in) way of expressing meaning which is proper to such a name. DN VII, 359.42–47: "Dicit ergo, quod *divinissima*, idest perfectissima et verissima, *dei cognitio est per ignorantiam*, idest per omnium ablationem, quia simpliciter verum est, secundum quod significatur per nomen; affirmationes autem non sunt verae de ipso secundum modum significandi per nomen."

86 DN VII, 358.79–86: Unde res significata per nomen potest dupliciter considerari: aut secundum quod excedit significationem nominis, et sic est modus, qui est per excessum, aut secundum quod significatur per nomen, et hoc dupliciter: vel secundum quod est in effectu, et sic est modus, qui est per causam, aut secundum quod est in causa, quae est extra istum modum, et sic modus per omnium ablationem.

Albert is particularly defensive of the third approach, by negation. An objection points out that negation tells us nothing for sure and so cannot really be a help toward knowledge of God.[87] Negations can help, Albert replies, if they affirm *something* even in denying something else. For example, to deny that the soul is a material substance involves affirming that it is a substance in some sense. In some cases we can continue to move in the direction of clearing up our knowledge until we arrive at the proper being of a thing. While we cannot arrive at the proper being of God, knowledge *quia*, which we have *confuse*, is moved in one direction rather than another by appropriate negations.[88]

In the *Mystical Theology*, Albert is especially graphic in describing the approach *per ablationem*:

Just as when rocks are cut away, we find remaining on the surface of the stone, things which were hidden by parts which are now removed: certain images of things like bulls or lions or dogs—which images are not the things themselves; so, similarly, by removing things from God we come upon something *like* the divine nature which, however, is not the divine nature itself but manifests it. When, for example, we remove from [God] "not-living" it remains that [He is] living; since, however, "life," insofar as the name itself has a meaning, means "the process of life" this does not express [the manner of] the divine nature, but acts as a manifestation of it, just as a likeness [would do].[89]

[87] *DN* VII, 358.43–47: Dubitatur autem hic de istis modis. Negatio enim nihil certificat; quod autem non certificat, non potest esse nobis via ad aliquid cognoscendum; ergo in deum non possumus ascendere omnium ablatione vel negatione.

[88] *DN* VII, 358.87–359.5: Ad primum ergo dicendum, quod negatio, quae nihil relinquit, nihil certificat, sed per negationes, quae aliquid relinquunt, determinatur confusio intellectus ad aliquid certum, et utimur eis loco differentiarum in his quorum propter sui simplicitatem differentias positivas accipere non possumus; sicut si dicam, quod anima non est substantia corporea, relinquendo, quod sit substantia, determino animam ad aliquid, et sic deinceps, quousque deveniatur ad esse proprium rei. Et similiter, ut dicit RABBI MOYSES, per nagationes determinatur aliquo modo confusio intellectus nostri circa deum, quamvis numquam deveniamus ad esse proprium ipsius.

[89] *Beati Alberti Magni . . . Commentarii in D. Dionysium*, R. A. P. F. Petrum Jammy, *Operum*, Tomus XIII (Lugdieni, 1651), p. 128: ". . . sicut quando saxa abscinduntur, remanent in superficie lapidis quae prius erat tecta alia parte, per remotionem illius partis, quaedam rerum imagines, puta tauri vel leonis vel canis aut aliquid simile, quae tamen non sunt res illae: ita per remotiones rerum a Deo, invenimus aliquid simile divinae naturae, quae tamen non est divina natura in se, sed manifestat eam: sicut per hoc quod removemus ab eo non viventia, relinquitur quod sit vivens, cum tamen vita secundum quod nomine significatur, significet

This illustration of the outcome of *ablatione* should not lead us to forget that this negative process is concerned with a *cause* which is affirmed to be transcendent to ordinary categories. The approach *per causam* is concerned with the same causal relation but now from the perspective of what is discoverable in that which is caused. In Chapter I, while explaining why the text refers to God as "better than any account that can be given of Him" Albert notes the reason:

> ... since He is not known except through what He causes, He is not named except through the name of what He causes (especially of what He causes first). Therefore He exceeds every name we give Him.[90]

Thus, *per excessum* is also linked to causality. In reflecting on Albert's account of this threefold way, it is very difficult to specify the real differences among the three. I would rather regard them as three perspectives on one complex procedure. In trying to account for their three-ness Albert seems more involved in saving the text than in demonstrating a position.

III. *Text B: The* Solutio *to the Question, What Is the Subject of This Book?*

As we have suggested earlier, the interrelationships of knowing and naming have occasioned raising all of the major issues of Text B while discussing "knowable" as treated in Text A. Rather than simply repeat parts of that discussion, we will use this section to focus Albert's position on two interrelated themes: analogy and the concept of univocal causality, as these themes are operative in our claims to know and to name God.

The very first question Albert raises in *DN* is, What is the subject matter of the book?

> We say that the subject matter of this book is the Divine Name— not, however, in general, but in a certain restricted sense. For we are not here talking about symbolic names (these are not said properly of God but only through metaphorical language); rather, we are treating those names which name God in a proper sense [*proprie*] as a cause, focusing on those attributes by which things

vita processionem, quae non est divina natura, sed aliquid manifestans ipsam sicut sua similitudo."

[90] *DN* I, 29.40–43: . . . cum non cognoscatur nisi per suum causatum, non nominatur nisi per nomen causati sui, primi maxime, et ideo omne nomen sibi datum a nobis excedit.

come forth from Him as from a univocal cause. [This approach is possible because] those things participate (in a secondary way) that very thing which is in Him truly and absolutely as far as what we intend by using that name [*res significata*] is concerned; although it is true that the way we express what we intend [*modus significandi*] falls short of representing that meaning *as* it is found in God. In fact, it leaves that meaning [*as* it is found in God] in a state of hidden-ness. The reason for this is that such a name carries its meaning according to the way we express what we intend [*modus significationis*] and that "way" reflects how that meaning [*res*] exists in *us* from whom the name comes to be used. That is why the mystical [names] also are said to be "hidden" in a certain sense.[91]

The operative terms in this part of the text are *proprie* and *res significata/modus significandi*. In the light of our earlier discussion, I contend that Albert refers to "univocal cause" because he wishes to distinguish those names which are said of God *proprie* from those which are only "symbolic" (which he understands to be "metaphorical"). The *res significata/modus significandi* distinction serves to highlight the strangeness of this sort of univocity, since it emphasizes that the very *res* which ought to be open to us on the basis of a univocal relationship is, in fact, hidden (*occulta*) in God because we can do no more than say that the way we express what we intend (taken as it is from ourselves) does not (*per ablationem*) apply to God. If we concentrate on the process *per ablationem*, we are developing a theology of "what can we say about the intended meaning as it is found in God": this is a theology of the unknown; if we concentrate on the presence of the intended meaning (*ratio*) in, say, ourselves whom we come to understand as caused, and *therefore* as possessing that *ratio* in a derived and secondary sense, we may affirm God as source of that *ratio* but, again, do not know what that *ratio* means in God Himself.[92]

[91] *DN* I, 2.23–37: Solutio: (1–4) Dicimus, quod nomen divinum secundum suam communitatem non est subiectum huius libri, sed aliquo modo restrictum. Non enim hic agitur de nominibus symbolicis, quae non proprie dicuntur de deo, sed per quandam similitudinem, sed de illis quae proprie nominant ipsum, secundum quod est causa, quantum ad attributa, quibus emanant res ab ipso sicut a causa univoca, participantes per posterius illud ipsum quod in eo est vere et absolute, quantum ad rem significatam per nomen, quamvis modus significandi deficiat a repraesentatione eius, secundum quod est in deo, relinquens illud in occulto propter hoc quod significat secundum modum, quo illa res est in nobis, a quibus est impositum nomen. Unde et mystica dicuntur quasi occulta.

[92] *DN* I, 2.37–49: Haec autem nomina possunt dupliciter considerari: aut secundum effluxum causatorum a causa, participantium rationem nominis per posterius, et sic agitur de eis in libro isto, aut secundum quod ex resolutione causa-

Right from the start Albert recognizes the strangeness of this univocal causality and specifies it as a "univocity of analogy."[93] His interest is primarily to distinguish the mode of divine causality from equivocation (since this would immediately be agnosticism); but even more properly he wishes to deny that God is not a univocal cause, this double negative being the best approximation to the truth.[94] The reason for hesitating is that we do not know (and thus cannot name) God through an effect that is univocal to Him.[95]

On the other hand, when specifying the meaning of analogy as applicable to a causal relation, Albert wishes to distinguish the analogy he has in mind from that usually employed by "philosophers." But this wish carries with it some ambiguities. "Analagous causality" is only one member of the set of analagous relationships. The set is illustrated by such examples as:

1. Being (*ens*) as said of that which actually exists and that which is in potency to exist;[96]

2. Being (*ens*) as prior to substance and accidents;[97]

3. Being (*ens*) as in substance and in accident;[98]

torum in causam relinquitur ignotum significatum nominis, prout est in causa, propter modum eminentem ipsius causae, et sic agitur de ipsis in libro DE MYSTICA THEOLOGIA. Unde subiectum proprium istius libri est nomen divinum, quod facit notitiam causae secundum attributa, inquantum exeunt ab eo causata in participatione attributorum; et in hoc uniuntur omnia nomina de quibus hic agitur.

[93] DN I, 1.27-32: De attributis enim causae sciendum, quod non aequivoce, sed univoce dicuntur de causatis, sed tali univocatione qualis potest esse ibi, quae est analogiae, secundum quod dicit ORIGENES, quod deus dicitur sciens et intelligens, quia scientia et intellectu nos implet.
But see also DN IV, 184.52-56: "Non autem intelligendum est, quod dicatur de deo pulchritudo, tantum quia facit pulchritudinem, sed quia facit per essentiam suam sicut causa univoca. Unde sequitur, quod sua essentia, quae est ipse, sit summa pulchritudo et prima."

[94] DN I, 32.16-22: Et ideo non possumus ipsum affirmative nominare secundum quod 'quid' est, sed tantum per ea quae sunt in effectibus, quibus ipsum cognoscimus, quae verius per modum illum removentur a causa non univoca, quam insint, et ideo negative maxime et proprie nominatur a nobis.

[95] DN I, 32.12-16: A nobis tamen non est cognoscibilis nisi confuso intellectu, quia non comprehendimus de deo, 'quid' est, sed tantum 'quia' et hoc confuse, cum non cognoscamus ipsum per effectum univocum sibi et immediatum et essentialem.

[96] DN V, 308.48-51: "Sicut vere-ens dicitur de actu existente et non-vere-ens de eo quod est in potentia, de quibus dicitur ens analogice."

[97] DN I, 35.31-34: "Secundum analogiam . . . aliquid inesse pluribus secundum prius et posterius . . . sicut ens prius est substantia et accidente . . . ."

[98] DN XIII, 445.56-58: ". . . in communitate autem analogiae est aliquid unum in pluribus diversis modis, sicut ens in substantia et accidente et sanum in homine et urina."

4. That which a (physical) cause possesses *per prius* and its caused objects *per posterius*;[99]

5. Created being (*ens creatum*) which is found in some things in a way closer to the origin of all things (*per prius*) than in others (*per posterius*);[100]

6. Health as said of man and of urine;[101]

7. In general, the likeness between an exemplar and those things modeled after it;[102]

8. God who is, say, wisdom substantially in comparison to wise men who participate in wisdom by coming near to God's.[103]

Numbers 1, 2, 3, 5, and 6 are analogous but not causal relationships (it may be argued that they are founded on a causal relationship, but then everything can be viewed in that way). The point is that when we wish to link a single name with two entities we must do so on the basis of a communality between them. To conceive of the two as sharing in some third thing which is not simply the same as either of them is to exercise the analogous mode of thinking and naming which is properly philosophical, that is, which involves the two sorts of analysis discussed earlier.[104] This analogous communality is "philosophical" because we are able to specify not only the *res significata* (whereby there is communality) but also the different *modi significandi* (whereby there is analogous knowledge) appropriate to each member. But God becomes involved in our knowledge claims only *after* we have recognized analogous communality among caused things proportioned to their causes and *after* we have seen the simplicity of created being exemplified in a variety of concrete existents.[105] In the case of God, however, although we may have grounds for affirming certain transcendental names, we do not know how the supposed communality is exemplified in Him, hence Albert's hesitancy in clearly

[99] *DN* I, 35.49–51: "Non tamen analogiae, quod aliquid idem participetur a deo per prius et a causatis per posterius, quia sic esset aliquid simplicius et prius deo." Although Albert is here denying this sort of analogy of God, clearly he recognizes that it can exist in causal relations other than with God.

[100] *DN* V, 308.62–66: "Ista analogia est quae consideratur in philosophia, secundum quam accipitur ens creatum, quod intrat substantiam rerum, in quibusdam existens per prius et in quibusdam per posterius."

[101] See note 98.

[102] *DN* I, 35.55–56.

[103] *DN* I, 35. See note 43.

[104] See note 32.

[105] *DN* V, 304.57–60: Cognoscitur tamen ut terminus resolutionis, secundum quod invenimus ipsum post omnia causata et post omnem simplicitatem creaturarum.

naming the relationship "analogous." For there really cannot be anything strictly "one" which God has in common with anything else; otherwise, the simplicity of God would be negated.[106]

IV. *Tentative Conclusions*

Our reading of *DN* from the viewpoint of "knowable" and "namable" has succeeded mostly in raising questions for future study. Tentative positions I have explored above include:

1. That Albert is much more "agnostic" in his claims to knowledge of God than the work of Ruello, for example, appears to have discovered;

2. That the reason for the "agnosticism" is not a fideism but a close attention to the structure of the language we must employ if we wish to speak at all;

3. That the language he attends to is the actual use of the sacred scriptures in addressing that which we call God;

4. That Albert's position does not rest upon a theory of illumination or of intuition of essences, otherwise he would make much more of a claim of insight into, say, Divine Wisdom than simply, as he does, *that* there is such a thing;

5. That his description of the knowledge which the Blessed in heaven enjoy is continuous with his description of either the "philosophic" or the "divine" mode of knowing here on earth;

6. That the *res significata/modus significandi* distinction dominates his *account* of naming God; while

7. The rule of *simplicity* as primary in our statements about God is operative throughout, but not fully developed.

Other areas of further investigation should include:

1. A comparison of *DN* with his own *Summa Theologiae* as well as with the work of Saint Thomas Aquinas;

2. An analysis of perfection and the transcendentals as particularly suited for divine names;

---

[106] DN XIII, 445.58–66: Sed non potest aliquid unum esse in deo et in quodam altero, quia oporteret, quod contraheretur in utroque, et sic deus esset compositus et esset in ipso universale et particulare; et ideo non est in deo aliqua dictarum communitatum ad aliquid aliud; sed est tamen aliquis modus analogiae ipsius ad creaturas, non quod idem sit in utroque, sed quia similitudo eius quod est in deo, invenitur in creaturis secundum suam virtutem.

3. The role of the soul as a model and source of appropriate names; and

4. That moment in properly philosophical reflection which, by exposing the inadequacy of causes which are proportioned to their effects to account for the whole of causality, open inquiry out on to God.

Part IV

Physics and Metaphysics

The Individual Human Being in Saint Albert's Earlier Writings

LÉONARD DUCHARME, O.M.I.
University of Ottawa

The self-standing value of individual beings often appears as holding little interest for philosophers and metaphysicians. Since they are mainly preoccupied with the universal and the necessary, they grant scant recognition to the singular and the contingent and often seem to explain it away. Yet uneasiness pervades many of their theories. Our thinking and our language maintain uncanny links with the modest individual things, and philosophy has never succeeded in ignoring those links for a very long period without giving rise to a reaction. In the twelfth century, the outcry shared by all opponents of "exaggerated realism" was: *Nihil est praeter individuum.* None of the lofty universals, "man," "animal," enjoys the undisputed resilience of the humble individual thing, a result of the unchallengeable fact of its being here and now, and no trick of scientific legerdemain can really obliterate that unique privilege, even in the eyes of philosophy.

Medieval authors had extra reasons to pay attention to individual material beings, and particularly to individual human persons. Because of their religious belief, they had to see every singular thing as the result of God's creation, and various accommodations of the theory of participation could not satisfy many of them, when they attempted to account for the authenticity of the individual. Still more, they had to find a way of saying how every individual human soul is immortal and how every individual human body is to resurrect. Moreover, they needed clear notions of "person" and of "individual," in order to express two dogmas of their faith, namely the Trinity of Persons in God and the union of the human and divine natures in one individual being, Christ. They also had to outline an unequivocal distinction between God's unique identity and the unquestionable identity of individual men and Angels. One can discover a medieval's vision of the individual being within those various theological contexts or within outwardly philosophical contexts (e.g. Is matter simple?), where those theological preoccupations are present.

The present essay will try to do just that, about Albert's earlier writings, his *Summa de Creaturis*, and his *Commentary on the Sentences*.[1]

Terminology and General Description

A general presentation of the individual being is given twice in the *Commentary*, first, when Albert deals with Trinity and, second, when he considers Christ. In both instances the immediate subject of interest is found in the quest for a precise vocabulary that could be used in theology. Without being repetitious, both texts have practically the same content, and they will be summed up together.

About earthly things (*in inferioribus*) we use different words when speaking of an individual being. We say "natural thing" (*res naturae, res naturalis*), and that expression designates the individual as a well-identified thing in nature (*hoc aliquid*); first intended by nature in generation, it is also the ultimate fruit of that generation. That natural thing is a composite of matter and form, or of *quod est* and *quo est*. The word "supposit" (*suppositum*) adds to that original meaning, since it says that a natural thing stands under (*supponitur*) a common nature as incommunicable (while the common nature is communicable). Further, the natural thing, a complete being in itself, provides the accidents with the support they need to be; it is a "subject" (*subjectum*). As such it is called "substance" (*substantia*), or, in Greek, *hypostasis*. On the other hand, a given sum total of accidents can be found together only in one natural thing and identifies it among all others. So recognizable, the natural thing is called "individual" (*individuum*). Ultimately, the human individual being is called "person" (*persona*), in order to stress the fact of its absolute incommunicability; it is permeable only to the "composition" of the intellect in an affirmative proposition. There is more in that enumeration than a mere multiplicity of words; it reveals the many facets on the individual being. Al-

---

[1] This article should be read as a chapter following the study I published years ago: "*Esse*" *chez saint Albert le Grand. Introduction à la métaphysique de ses premiers écrits*. In *Revue de l'Université d'Ottawa*, t. 27 (1957), *Section spéciale*, pp. 209*–252*. As in the first article, only texts from the *Summa de Creaturis* and the *Commentary on the Sentences* are used here. The rationale behind that limitation, as explained p. 210* of my first article, still appears to me as valid. My approach to Saint Albert, indeed to the whole history of philosophy, has changed as years go by. The original redaction of the present study has been entirely rewritten. References to my first article will be identified as follows: L. Ducharme, "*Esse*" ... p. Translations are mine.

bert sees an order among those terms: "natural thing" is first, and the others "add" to its meaning.[2]

The natural thing is described as a composite of matter and form, or of *quod est* and *quo est*. The analysis of those two compositions will lead us to the comprehension of Albert's doctrine about the individual being. But two previous points must be noted. First, only the composite is truly a "something" (*hoc aliquid*); the human soul is not.[3] The nature, common to many individuals, is not either, even if it can be called a "substance," in a secondary sense of that word; only the "natural thing" is a "first substance."[4] Second, Albert, with many others, considered that God alone is absolutely simple, that absolute simplicity being the guaranty of his uniqueness. All created beings consist of a plurality, at least of a duality.[5]

The compositions of matter and form and of *quod est* and *quo est* are compared with each other in a text dealing with universal hylemorphism. "Is there one matter for all creatures?" Albert says that some do admit such a common matter, and he explains how their position can be understood. Then he proceeds to propose what is evidently his personal opinion:

> If one would rather speak differently, one would say that there is not one matter for all substances, just what is said in the text quoted from Aristotle; and, according to that view, substances' composition is twofold; in some substances there is a composition of matter and form, as is the case in substances subject to generation and corruption, in which neither [matter nor form] is predicated of the composed substance. The composite, indeed, is neither matter nor form; therefore, in such [substances], the universal which is predicated of the composite is not found in the form of the matter, but in the form of the united whole (*forma totius conjuncti*). In some [substances], on the other hand, there is no such composition, but [a composition] of *quo est* and *quod est* as Boethius says; and the *quo est* is the form of the whole, *quod est* signifies the very whole, whose form the *forma totius* is. That composition is found in substances not subject to generation and corruption, and, in them, the *forma totius* does not differ from the form of the matter, since such [substance] does not have matter. Therefore, the very whole, which is

[2] 1 *Sent.*, d. 26, art. 4, sol. 3 *Sent.*, d. 6, art. 2, sol. Generation intends the production of the subject for the sake of the form. L. Ducharme, "*Esse*" . . . p. 225. n. 59.

[3] 2 *Sent.*, d. 17, art. 2, ad 2.

[4] *Summa* I, tr. 4, q. 29, *art. unic*, ad 1.

[5] Ducharme, "*Esse*" . . ., pp. 213–16; 218.

expressed by *quod est*, is not made distinct [individually] by matter, because of the same reason [viz., it does not have matter]. And, this is true mainly of spiritual substances, in which one is not to admit any other composition than that of the supposit and of the nature whose supposit it is.[6]

The text is self-explanatory. Two preoccupations are present all through Albert's writings: to ensure that all created things are composed, God alone being simple, and, second, to maintain the possibility of universal predication. The hylemorphic composition, proper to earthly substances, answers both preoccupations, thanks to the addition of the *forma totius* to the couple matter and form. The composition of *quod est* and *quo est*, found principally (*praecipue*) in spiritual substances, performs the same functions. (The heavenly bodies, while ungenerated and incorruptible, are in a special situation.) As is often the case with medieval writers, the opposition between the two compositions, given here as radical, does not indicate that they cannot be found together in the same being, and Albert superimposes them in some of his texts; that is suggested by the "principally." Little, if anything, will be added, in the following pages, to that vision of the individual being. It is a composite, and it contains an element which makes universal predication possible. Nevertheless, the separate analysis of both compositions should help toward a better understanding of that basic idea.

Matter and Form

According to Albert's doctrine concerning the distinction between various sciences, the consideration of matter belongs to the natural philosopher, at least when matter is seen as the principle of motion. But the metaphysician is also interested in matter; metaphysics considers the first predicaments of being, and mainly the very first, substance; it will, therefore, consider matter and form as parts of substance, and of being.[7]

Albert's version of hylemorphism is rather standard Aristotelianism, at least in the expression of its major pronouncements.[8] Yet some elements of it sound somewhat foreign to what is still largely considered as authentic "Aristotelian" tradition. Reasons for that are well known. Aristotle had just been discovered; he had come to the School together

[6] *Summa* I, tr. 1, q. 2, art. 5, sol.

[7] *Summa* II, tr. 1, q. 58, art. 1, sol.

[8] The main elements of that version of hylemorphism have been summed up by L. De Raeymaeker, in "Albert le Grand philosophe. Les lignes fondamentales de son système métaphysique," *Revue néoscolastique*, t. 35 (1933), p. 20–24.

with commentaries and texts using him in a Neoplatonic context, and he had met with a trend of thought which was strongly influenced by Augustine, and by the Pseudo-Denis. Accommodations were unavoidable, which would, at times, modify the Philosopher's very inspiration. Aristotle's thought had its own difficulties. Some of them resulted from the extension of hylemorphism to man. Aristotle himself had changed his view of intellectual knowledge, and of the personal immortality of the human soul, after he had made that extension.[9] While the medievals were unaware of that evolution, some of them were ill at ease with the idea of a spiritual soul being the form of a material body. The controversies about the unity or plurality of forms, about the unity of the human intellect, and about the personal immortality of the soul were looming on the horizon. On the other hand, Augustine's idea of the soul being a spiritual substance in itself, governing a body, was widely admitted, and the soul thus appeared as the true reality of man. Adopting Aristotle's vocabulary, and calling that soul the substantial form of a body did not immediately alter the "traditional" understanding of man. Since many of Albert's general affirmations about form are found in contexts where he deals immediately with the human soul, accommodations were again unavoidable, even if he affirms that the soul is not a completely independent substance.[10]

Another difficulty arises from the fact that Albert has adopted, from Avicenna by his own recognition, a distinction between *forma partis* and *forma totius*, between the form of matter, a part of the composite with matter itself, and the form of the whole as such.

Albert's doctrine about matter has been found wanting by some historians, in comparison with what was considered as "stock Aristotelianism." For instance, the fact that he does not see matter as "pure potency" but as an incipient form, has been judged as a weakness of his hylemorphic theory.[11] That could be true, but texts supporting that vision of matter, when explained, seem natural within Albert's general way of thinking. God alone is absolutely simple, and a matter that would be pure potency could hardly be seen as a composite.[12] Along

[9] Cf. R. A. Gauthier, "Introduction," in R. A. Gauthier et J. Y. Jolif, *L'Éthique à Nicomaque* 2d ed. (Louvain, Publications universitaires, 1970), t. 1, pp. 58 sqq. Gauthier records what first was a surprise to many, when Aristotle was found to be not quite "Aristotelian."

[10] Quite a few of Aristotle's own affirmations can be understood as meaning that the form is the whole of the significant reality of things. There again, Aristotle may not have been thoroughly "Aristotelian."

[11] A. Delorme, "La morphogénèse d'Albert le Grand dans l'embryologie scolastique," *Revue thomiste*, t. 14 (1931), p. 358.

[12] *Summa* I, tr. 1, q. 2, art. 4, sol.

the same line of thinking, Albert would not say that matter, in its very substance, is totally relative to form. The only entities that have no other reality besides their very referral to another are the divine persons within Trinity, and no such entirely relative entity can be found among created things. But, Albert hastens to assure, that matter is united to form immediately, without the intervention of an intermediary link.[13] When the theological inspiration of those accommodations is recognized, one might still be right in seeing them as "weaknesses," in reference to another approach, but Albert's conception, as a whole, is coherent and reasonably faithful to "Aristotelianism." Standard affirmations to that effect are numerous. Thus matter is not intelligible in itself, but it can be known only through its very reference to form. If one would attempt to know it as not actually united with form, one would then see it as "privation," that is, in relation to a form of which it would appear deprived. Since forms are acquired through change, matter is given as the basic substratum of the primary type of change: generation and corruption. The subject, constituted by the union of matter and form, will be the substratum of all other changes, but because of its matter.[14] Matter is the "principle of individuation" of material beings.[15] Other elements of Albert's idea of matter belong to natural philosophy rather than to metaphysics.

In his description of the earthly substances Albert mentioned two forms: the form of the matter (*forma partis*) and the form of the whole (*Forma totius*). The form of the matter is the source of all the perfections that are present in the matter and in the composite, giving them their *esse*. It gives them *esse* and *rationem*.[16] Still more, the form is said to "be" the *ratio* of the common nature.[17] *Ratio* cannot be translated; it can, at best, be explained.[18] In this context, and in others similar

13 1 *Sent.*, d. 26, art. 6, ad 8.
14 *Summa* I, tr. 1, q. 2, art. 2, ad 5.
15 Among many texts, 1 *Sent.*, d. 2, art. 20, sol.
16 Ducharme, "*Esse*" . . ., pp. 220–31.
17 1 *Sent.*, d. 15, art. 10, ad 3.
18 *Ratio* is a problem word, and not only for historians of medieval philosophy. Cf. A. Yon, Ratio et les mots de la famille reor. [. . .] (Paris, Champion, 1933). Simplistic understanding and translations of it in medieval texts have led to many errors. My own renditions of it in "*Esse*" . . . now appear to me as quite horrendous, e.g. "qualité," p. 123*, "concept," p. 229*. Excuses could probably be made for them, but I much rather confess past blissful ignorance. We need a very serious historical study of the various meanings of the word; from that study a basic meaning might emerge, which would clarify derived meanings. Until that study has been made, we have to grope for a decently precise signification, almost in every case. The fact that *ratio* was used to translate the Greek *logos*, did not help; *logos* is a problem word itself. Neither does the fact that *ratio* can mean the knowing power,

to it, *ratio* can be understood as meaning the ultimate core of the reality of whatever it is said to be the *ratio*, not as isolated in itself, that would be its *esse*, but as the mind's interlocutor, mostly but not exclusively, in the epistemic dialogue; the *ratio* is the mind's objective partner, in the exchange medievals understood knowledge, and science, to be. The form gives the composite to be of a distinct nature (*esse*), and within the composite, it confers, upon matter and upon the composite itself, the capacity it possesses of its own, to be the objective associates of the mind in the knowledge undertaking (*ratio*). That interpretation seems to account for the texts where Albert says that form "gives" *esse* and *rationem*. It may appear to be wanting in reference to affirmations where form is said to "be" the *ratio* of the common nature. Those texts could be understood as stating that form, alone and by itself, provides all that is worth knowing in a thing, at least when scientific knowledge is concerned. Such an interpretation would probably be too narrow, particularly when reading Albert, not always a master of precision in his use of words. Descriptions of the manner in which form gives *esse* might provide a better insight into his vision. Form is the giver of *esse* by "producing" itself in the whole (*facit se in formato*) and, still better, its "giving" is a diffusion of itself in the whole (*suum dare est diffusio sui in formato*).[19] Form is certainly the main element of the reality (*esse*), and of the knowability (*ratio*), but it radiates both over matter and over the composite, by the very diffusion of itself within the whole. It "is" the *ratio* of the common nature, just by being itself within the composite. One last character of the form is rather standard: it is the act of matter, and the first act of the whole.[20]

Another affirmation needs more explaining. It has been said above that Albert considers matter to be the "principle of individuation" of the common nature, among material individual beings. According to him, form also has an influence on that distinction.

Strictly speaking, diversity opposes identity, and identity has no other source but a substantial element, therefore, no diversity can

the reason, since reason has been understood in so many different ways, with varied functions and prerogatives. Historians of scholastic philosophy know how the controversy about the distinction between essence and existence, whether that distinction is a "real" distinction, or a distinction "of reason" (*ratione, secundum rationem*), has muddled up the meaning of *ratio*. In many a medieval text, it is quite apparent that a distinction *secundum rationem* is quite "real," and not only the result of "reason's" frolics, no matter how scientifically inspired those frolics might be.

19 Ducharme, "*Esse*" . . ., p. 227. "Producing" is the best translation I can find for *facit*, although it may sound too strong. Cf. *infra*, p. 20, n. 40.

20 Ducharme, "*Esse*" . . . pp. 227–31.

be found anywhere but where there is a distinction (*divisio*) according to substantial forms, distinct [from one another] according to *esse* [i.e., actual conditions of realization]; division (*divisio*) occurs through matter's separation.[21]

In earthly things, there is the substantial form of each thing, whose act is to bound the thing to itself, and to separate it from others in which there is not actually the same numerical form; the act of that form therefore, which is to bound and separate from others, makes the thing one in itself, and is its unity.[22]

Albert is faithful to himself. Form is the source of all perfections in a thing. Self-identity and unity are perfections, even at the level of numerically multiple beings, united under a common species; therefore, form must, in some way, be their source. In earthly substances forms are multiplied numerically because of the separation of matter into distinct portions, but, within an individual being, form is the principle of unity and cohesion, of identity, and it gives the being to be what it is, sealing in perfection, so to speak, a separation which, of itself, it would not have produced. The distinction (*divisio*) is a result of matter, but the diversity (*diversitas*) of distinct identities is attributed to form.[23] Earthly individual beings are true beings, and their diversity is not a screen which would hide a more basic identity. Their diversity and their unity have a substantial source, their form, which is part of them and gives them unity, just as it gives them *esse* and *ratio*. The metaphysical authenticity of the individual earthly "natural thing" is unquestionable, and its root is found in the substantial form. Even if that form is submitted to the laws of matter; it assumes them and elevates them to perfection. Nothing is, but the individual, and it truly is, thanks to its form. With this said, and well said, the problem of the "universals" remains untouched. Albert will solve it through his theory of abstraction.[24]

Here is a text that gives the essentials of Albert's theory of abstraction. It is the *solutio* of an article dealing with the intelligibility of the "intelligible species":

[21] 1 *Sent.*, d. 23, art. 8, sol. Same idea: 1 *Sent.*, d. 24, art. 1, sol.

[22] 1 *Sent.*, d. 19, art. 12, ad 3. Same idea: 1 *Sent.*, d. 19, art. 17, sol.

[23] The text illustrates Albert's freedom in his use of "is." The form is said to "make the thing one," and to "be" its unity. At this point of our analysis, I think it is better to consider this as "freedom." It will appear that it is more than that.

[24] Albert's theory of knowledge has been examined in details by many historians. Only the elements of that theory relevant to our study will be touched here. For a more nearly complete study of his theory of abstraction, one can see U. Dähnert, *Die Erkenntnislehre des Albertus Magnus, gemessen an den Stufen der "Abstractio"* [...] (Leipzig, 1934).

138

All that is intelligible, according to its being intelligible, has that simplicity which is produced through disentanglement (*resolutionem*) from matter, and from matter's sequels (*appendicitiis*). But matter is twofold (*duplex*), viz, subject to movement, and standing under the universal (*substans universali*). Matter which is subject to movement is not what the thing is, and it is in potency to a form which is a part of the thing and is not its whole, and, because of that, such a form is not predicated of the thing. Matter, on the other hand, which is standing under the universal, is what the thing is, because it is that particular being which is pointed to (*hoc aliquid*), and its form is the form of the whole (*forma totius*), and not the form of a part [of the same whole] (*forma partis*), and, because of that, such a form is predicated of the thing in its totality. Sequels of that [second] matter are properties and accidents, restricting and individualizing the form which is universal, [molding] that form on matter, which is particular. And, when it is said that the intellect abstracts from matter, it is understood about matter that is particular. That is evident: the intellect does not indeed abstract "man" but from this and that man, and it does not abstract "man" from the [initial] semen, nor from the [complete] body. And, in like manner, the intellect abstracts "angel" from this and that Angel, and "soul" from this and that soul, and likewise for others.[25]

The immediate meaning of the text is simple. Abstraction has one purpose: to reach a universal content of knowledge that can be predicated of things. The substantial form, as a part of the whole, cannot be that predicable universal, even if it is a human spiritual soul; since it is individual, isolating it from its body would not result in universality. Universality is found in another form, the *forma totius*, disengaged from all individual restrictions. (Even the universal "angel" is reached through a similar process. Angels are purely spiritual beings, devoid of all matter, yet "angel" must abstract from this and that Angel, who do appear as some "second matter".[26]) That understanding is rather common among various proponents of abstraction. What is less common is the distinction between two matters and two forms, even if Albert says that he borrowed the distinction between *forma partis* and *forma totius* from Avicenna, and is sure that it is present in Averroes, and even if, according to him, Aristotle "seems" to mention it. Those two levels of signification, in the use of the hylemorphic vocabulary, are not unrelated in Albert's mind. The matter which is part of the

[25] *Summa* II, tr. 1, q. 58, art. 1, sol.
[26] More will be said about that in the analysis of the *quod est–quo est* duality.

whole is the principle of individuation for the whole; it is easy to understand that the individual subject should be called "matter," precisely
when it is considered as individual. Albert also says that the subject
owes its potentiality, an attribute of materiality, to its matter.[27]

The meaning of the distinction between the *forma partis* and the
forma totius is less apparent and demands more explanation. Approaching the question "is *the* soul *a* substance?" Albert meets with an objection saying that if *the* soul is *a* substance, the human soul will fall
under the subdivision of "incorporeal substance," while man would
come under "corporeal substance." Now species coming under a subalternate genus are further apart than species coming under a proximate
genus; therefore, there would be a greater distance between a man and
his soul than between a man and a donkey. The context is evidently
logical, and "substance" is primarily used as a genus, with species
under it. Here is Albert's answer:

> When "substance" is divided into corporeal and incorporeal, *the*
> soul is not considered in any way as constituted by a "difference"
> that would be "incorporeal," because it would then be considered as
> a species; but, rather, when "body" is divided into "besouled" and
> "unbesouled," "soul" is used as the "difference" within that division
> of "body," and *the* soul [of a living being] differs from that differ-
> ence only in that, that under the word "soul," it is given as a natural
> form, which is the form of a part, namely matter, a form which is
> not predicated either of that part or of the whole, while, under
> "besouled," it is understood as a form which can be predicated of
> the whole; nevertheless, that form which is "difference" is abstracted
> from the whole, according to the potency which is in one of its parts,
> that is in *the* soul.[28]

Albert adds that those considerations are logical, but he finally draws
from them a conclusion that is no longer logical and brings us back to
the problem of the two forms. In "besouled," a species, the difference
"soul" determines the genus "body," as any specific difference does,
but Albert adds that it so appears as a *forma totius*. We must then
understand that a *forma totius* is the expression of a species according

[27] Again, that view is related to the theories about the Angels, and the *quod est–
quo est* duality.

[28] *Summa* II, tr. 1, q. 2, art. 1, ad 3. Much of the difficulty of the Latin text
comes from the fact that Latin has no articles. In my translation I have added *the*
and *a* where English asks for them, to the best of my understanding of the Latin
text. The whole question of whether the human soul is a substance by itself is
present in the text. I find it more advisable to read it only inasmuch as it casts light
on the problem of the two forms.

to its difference, and that, when predicated, it signifies the species. We must also understand that the difference "soul" is abstracted from the whole, "according to the potency that is in one of its parts, that is in the soul." The *forma partis* is the source of the *forma totius*. The soul is consistently given as an act by Albert; here, he describes it as "potency"; that is an extension. Since matter is together the source of individuation and of potentiality, whatever is individual can be called a "potency," even a form; being individual, it is not actually intelligible, and must undergo abstraction.

While the question "Is *the* soul *a* substance?" was general, the objection was raised in reference to the human soul. Here is another text where the problem of the two forms reappears about the human being. In it Albert compares the "composition" of the human and divine natures in Christ, which he calls an "improper composition," with another "composition," which he considers as first, and properly called "composition":

> The first composition, properly called composition, is that of soul and body, soul which I say to be the act of an organic physical body, having life in potency. And to that composition follows the *forma totius*, which is "man", or "humanity", if one may speak about it abstractedly; and that form is the species in this particular individual. Indeed, form is twofold [or: there are two forms (*est duplex forma*)], namely the form of the matter, or form of a part, or of potency, and that form is the end of generation in nature, and it is a part of the thing, and such a form, the soul, is in man. There is another form, which is the *ratio* of the thing, and its whole *esse* according to the *ratio* (*secundum rationem*); and that form follows the composition of the natural form and of the natural potency, which is matter. And the Lord Jesus did have that consecutive form, because of the natural composition thanks to which he is a true man, and one *suppositum* in the human species.[29]

The first composition of natural matter, or potency, and of natural form gives a being to be of a definite specific nature, and makes it a supposit in a species. We know that the giver is the form, radiating itself within the composite. Another form follows (*sequitur*) that first composition, the *forma totius*. That second form is "the species in this particular individual" (*species in hoc individuo particulari*), it is its *ratio* and "its whole *esse* according to [for the?] *the ratio*" (*secundum rationem*). The first *ratio* means again "the core of the reality of the thing." The second, in *secundum rationem*, is more intricate. It could

[29] 3 *Sent.*, d. 2, art. 5, sol.

have the same meaning and only stress the fact that what gives *esse* gives *rationem* also; but it could explicitate that the *forma totius* stands out as the whole meaning of a thing, when that thing confronts the knowing power, the reason. One thing though is clear, the *forma totius* is "the species in this particular individual" (*species in hoc individuo particulari*). The formula recalls Avicenna's distinction between nature in (of) itself (*natura secundum se*), universal nature (*natura ut universalis*), and nature as found in individuals (*natura ut in individuis*). Albert has not adopted Avicenna's theories about the "absolute essence" (*essentia absoluta*), but something of it can be found in his writings. "Species in this particular individual" is an example of that. The *forma totius* follows the first composition, because of the form of the matter, and it gives *esse* and *ratio* both to the matter and to the composite; that *esse* is called, at times, the *esse* of the essence (*esse essentiae*).[30] Since Christ is composed of a body and of a human soul, he is a true man and a supposit in the human species; that was Albert's immediate preoccupation. But we must find in the whole text an account of Albert's vision of the individual being: it is a supposit to the specific nature. Within a particular individual, the specific nature is evidently not in a situation of universality, and abstraction will have to bring it to the state of simplicity which is proper to intelligibles, so that its latent universality be unveiled.[31] But, following the coming of the *forma partis*, the *forma totius*, the species is present within the individual.

Two more questions deserve attention about that theory. One refers to the better wording to be used, when speaking of the *forma totius*; should one say "man" or "humanity"? In this text Albert hesitates about "humanity": "if one may talk about it abstractedly" (*si licet*). Another can arise about the relationship between the two forms. Here Albert says only that the *forma totius* "follows" the first composition of matter and form. Both questions reappear in another text, the second more explicitly.

Albert wants to establish that a resurrected man is numerically identical with the man he was before he died. One of the objections against that identity reads as follows:

[30] Ducharme, "*Esse*" . . ., pp. 330 sqq.

[31] That is why some texts seem to be conflicting about the *forma totius* being universal or not. Avicenna's distinction between the *natura ut in individuis* and the *natura universalis* is felt again. The common nature *ut in individuis* is not universal; its latent universality will have to be unveiled by abstraction, before the *natura universalis* is reached. Most of the texts where that conflict appears refer to the *quo est*, the parallel of the *forma totius*, in the *quod est—quo est* duality. I shall quote them later on. Cf. *infra*, n. 64.

Those whose substantial form is not numerically identical are not numerically identical; but, the substantial form of a dying man, and the substantial form of that man when he resurrects are not numerically one. [. . .] The substantial form is "humanity" which perishes with death, since a dead man is no man, and a form that disappears into nothingness does not return numerically identical; as the Philosopher says, "morning's health is not evening's health."

Here is Albert's answer:

There are two ways in which this can be answered. If we say with Avicenna that the *forma totius* is other than (*alia quam*) the *forma partis* which is the soul, since the *forma totius* is predicable, like "man" and "animal" of this and that man, then that form is signified abstractedly, even if improperly, when I say "humanity," and that form does not remain otherwise than potentially after death, in the elements of the whole, whose form it is. And, because of that form (*ratione illius formae*), the individual does not have numerical identity, but only the species [remains identical], which [species] is indifferent toward numerical identity or diversity. But from that soul completing that matter, and from that matter, it does possess numerical identity. Therefore, it does not follow that, not having the same *forma totius*, be that form the form of species, genus or *esse*, it is not numerically identical. Furthermore, it is the same species, even if its *esse* is not identical in that given individual, before and after death. [The resurrected man] is therefore numerically identical in the species with the first man, and the species is not destroyed by death but accidentally, according to the *esse* it has, following its situation in this individual.

But if we think, with Averroes and Aristotle, that the *forma totius* is the form of the matter, distinct from it *ratione* (*ratione tamen differens*), as he [Aristotle] seems to admit it, in the seventh [book] of the First Philosophy, then it is clear that a resurrected man is numerically identical [with the previously living man] and that the form is not destroyed, [neither] in itself nor according to its *esse*, but only according to the *ratio* of its predication of the composite, since that composite is dissolved.[32]

It is easy to understand why Albert prefers the concrete "man" over the abstract "humanity," as an expression of the *forma totius*. The *forma totius* must be predicable, and "man" predicates easily; "humanity"

---

[32] 4 *Sent.*, d. 44, art. 11, arg. 2 and ad 2. That "indifferent" species could be a remnant of the theory of "indifference" about "universals."

does not. Albert accepts "humanity" from the objection, but he considers that the expression is not proper.

The wording of the text does not help seeing Albert's position about the relationship between the two forms. The *forma totius* is given as being possibly the form of a species, of a genus, and even of *esse*. In almost all other texts it is the simple equivalent of species; here it appears as if any predicable universal can be considered as a *forma totius*, e.g., genus; the *forma totius* of *esse* could then be *ens*, which is predicable. But even in this text, out of that unique sentence, the *forma totius* is always the species; and *esse*, in all its other appearances, means the concrete manner in which the specific nature is realized: before death, after death, after resurrection.[33] *Ratio* is given a very weak meaning in "according to the *ratio* of its predication" (*quoad rationem praedicationis de composito*), and could be translated by "point of view." The only change that befalls the *forma totius* after death is that it can no longer be predicated of the composite, since the composite is dissolved. In *"ratione illius formae,"* *ratione* means because, but that "because" is strong, it is the very *ratio* of the form that makes the consequence necessary.

It would be useless to analyze the reasoning through which Albert shows how the resurrected man is identical with the man who had died; it does not belong to our purpose. But the two opinions about the relationships between the two forms will hold our attention. According to Albert, Avicenna says that the *forma totius* is "other" than the *forma partis*, while Averroes and Aristotle say that it is the *forma partis*, differing from it *ratione*. He could seem to lean toward that second view, for motives of theological expediency, since it offers an easier solution for his immediate problem. But, most of the time, he admits readily that he has borrowed the distinction between the two forms from Avicenna, and even here he manages to salvage the numerical identity of the resurrected man, while thinking within the Avicennian context. It would be a mistake to find in our text an opposition between a "real distinction" and a "distinction of reason," if one is to consider Albert's own position, and even Avicenna's position as Albert understands it.[34] That this could be the immediate meaning of our text might provide the subject of a spirited debate, spirited and useless. It will be more profitable to forgo that chance and read the text together with all the others that deal with the two forms. The *forma totius* is reached by abstraction from the individualizing conditions, in which the species is found in a natural thing, and abstraction finds it in the form of the

33 Ducharme, *"Esse"* . . ., pp. 246–48.
34 Which is exactly what I found in that text, years ago!

matter, seen as "potency." The two forms are "others," just as the universal is "other" than the singular, while giving it its *esse* and its *ratio*. Anybody is free to argue that such a difference is "real" or "of reason," Albert may have done it, even if this is not the way I read the text, but little benefit would derive from that argument. There is more here than an academic discussion about the difference between the two forms, with an explanation of universal knowledge as its background, together with the solution of a theological problem. Albert is dealing with immortality and resurrection, and the form he has in mind is a spiritual human soul. That a spiritual soul is the substantial form of a body does raise very special problems no other forms would evoke. Final resurrection is an object of faith; immortality is not necessarily; but, because of Albert's view of the theological expression of faith, a whole philosophy of man is involved here, with its own difficulties. That philosophy is important in our present study. Another text will bring us back to the heart of that philosophy, since it deals directly with the conditions of an embodied spiritual soul. Again, the immediate question is theological: "Is Christ's soul submitted to suffering in its totality?"

I say that the soul is completely subject to suffering in the body. [. . .] But one must understand that two [points] are to be considered about the soul, namely that it is the nature of man, and [that it is] the principle of human activities. From the first point of view, it is considered in three ways. Some [characteristics] belong to it as substantial form, some as soul, some as it is the nature of man, precisely as man. According to its being a substantial form, it is itself the perfection of the human body. [Albert then explains that the balance (*temperamentum*) it produces in the human body between the various "elements" is superior to the balance obtained in other bodies because of their forms. Because of that, as a substantial form, it resembles the forms of heavenly bodies]. Therefore, the *ratio* of form and act in it is the highest of all (*nobilissima*). As soul, it is the act of a body, which is not only the fruit of such a balanced composition, but also having life; that is found in all organic [things], and thus it belongs to the soul to radiate various energies (*vires*) in various parts of the body. That again, the human soul possesses in the highest way. [To Albert, this is evident because of the superior beauty of human bodies, as compared with other living bodies]. Third, [the soul is considered] according to its being the nature of man as man (*ut homo est*), nature, I say, giving a man the *esse* and *rationem* of man (according to what the Philosopher says in II *De Anima*, that the soul is substance according to the *rationem*, because it gives *esse* and *rationem* to the besouled body). And so, the rational soul, considered as [the] nature [of man], must necessarily have something more than a [mere] form, and more than a [mere] soul. And that is what a certain philosopher says: that it must have, flowing from it, some energies that are linked to organs, because it is a form giving *esse* as a nature [does], and other [energies] that are not linked [to organs]; these [last energies] are related to energies that are linked [to organs], inasmuch as they receive their species from them, and they are related to separate substances, inasmuch as they participate of their light. And that is what the Philosopher says: the noble soul has three operations, viz., divine, animal, and intellectual. So considered, the whole of a soul united [to a body] shares into the sufferings [of its body]. Soul is also to be considered as being the principle of human activities, and seen as such, it is not necessary that it shares in its totality, the [body's] suffering, because some of its energies may be [occupied] in the contemplation of eternals, and some others submitted to passivities proper to bodies.[35]

The immediate question is theological, and it touches the reality of Incarnation. Is Christ a true man, and, during his Passion, did he suffer as completely as any other human being would have? The question was debated, and, at the beginning of his *solutio*, Albert recalls that a certain abbot had said, in a sermon, that Christ's soul had not suffered in its "superior part"; but the Parisian university of Masters had condemned him as heretical. Albert's argumentation comes to this: Christ has suffered, just like any other man would have. But, in all men, the human soul is capable of a "divine" activity, the contemplations of "eternals"; that contemplation is not hampered, even if the soul shares completely in the body's torture, and the beatitude that follows that contemplation does not oppose total human suffering. That idea of the soul owes nothing to faith, since it is found in Aristotle.

In order to establish that, Albert sums up his whole philosophy of the human soul. That soul is a true substantial form; it is even superior to all other forms; it is also an authentic soul, the act of a body; again, it is superior to all other souls. But it is also the "nature" of man as man; it gives a man the *esse* and the *ratio* of man; and, so considered, it appears as man's very "substance." Now, since it is rational, it is more than a mere form, and more than a mere soul. Albert, quoting an unnamed philosopher, goes on to say that, while some of that soul's resources of activity are linked to an organic support, others are not. The latter are indeed related to the former, since they receive their "species" from

[35] 3 *Sent.*, d. 15, art. 3, sol.

146

them, but they are also akin to separate substances and share some of the light which is proper to them. And so, the human soul, in most of its activities, is entirely involved with its body, but, its "divine" activity, the contemplation of eternals, is not impeded because of that involvement: its species may come from functions that are bound to a bodily organ, but its "light" is of a different order.

All that leads to the conclusion that Albert sees the human soul as enjoying a certain degree of freedom toward its body. The human soul does perform all its functions as a form and as a soul; it even does it better than other forms and other souls, but it is more than a mere form or soul. In his answer to an objection, Albert uses the vocabulary of the argument and calls the soul an "intelligence," an obvious reference to the "intelligences" of Neoplatonism; as an "intelligence," it is very close to separate substances, and its "divine" activity is not engulfed in its body.

That immediate solution of a theological problem concurs with Albert's general philosophy of man. A rigid application of the hylemorphic theory to man raises serious difficulties, and not only for a Christian believer. Aristotle had changed his mind about the immortality of the soul, and about intellectual knowledge, after he had extended that theory to human beings. Albert went the other way, and softened the hylemorphic theory, by introducing into it, with Avicenna, elements of Neoplatonism.[36] He does see the soul as a form, but the idea of "perfec-

---

[36] That has been well illustrated by E. Gilson, "L'âme raisonnable chez Albert le Grand." *AHDLMA*, t. 18 (1943), pp. 3–72. Mr. Gilson follows the *Summa theologiae* as a guide, but he also quotes from the earlier writings. It would be useless to repeat that masterly study. Here and there, the far more explicit expressions of the *Summa theologiae* do reflect their very affirmative character over more subdued formulas found in the earlier writings. Gilson insists that Albert considered the human soul as a substance. There is no doubt about the fact that Albert considered that the human soul comes under the predicament "substance," since it can not be seen as an accident. But the earlier writings reveal a hesitation about calling the soul "a substance," without any qualification. Since Latin has no articles, some texts are open to more than one interpretation. "*Anima est substantia*" can mean "the soul is a substance," or "[the] soul is substance," and the choice between the two translations is not always easy. Less questionable formulas can help. For instance, Albert says openly in the *Summa theologiae* that the soul is a "*hoc aliquid*" (Gilson, p. 44). He had denied it in the *Commentary*, and his denial is so emphatic that it can not be explained away, which Mr. Gilson almost does (p. 26, n. 3). Here is the text: "That the soul be a *hoc aliquid* has been said by Masters, not by Philosophers nor by Saints; and I think that that saying is false (*puto quod est dictum falsum*). My reason is that in the beginning of the second [book] of the *De Anima*, it is found that matter is not *hoc aliquid*, nor form, that even the soul is not *hoc aliquid*. But I do well concede that the soul is a composed substance; but it is not composed as *hoc aliquid*, because, according to its nature (*secundum naturam*), it depends

147

tion" attracts him, and comparing the soul to a "pilot" appears as appropriate: the soul is a perfection in itself, besides, and even before, being the form of a body.[37] By some of its "parts," the two intellects, which are not attached to organic parts of the body, it is one of the "intelligences," the separate substances.[38] And again, those accommodations are not to be attributed exclusively to Albert's theological preoccupations, even if those preoccupations should not be disregarded. Albert really sees man in this manner. It is then natural that he should consider the soul as the "substance," the "nature" of man.

---

on its body (*dependentiam habet*) even if it could be without it. But I well concede that the soul's perfection is not altogether (*omnino*) complete without its body" (2 Sent., d. 17, art. 2, ad 2). "*Puto quod est dictum falsum*" is so strong that it can not be attentuated. At least on that point Albert's "evolution" can be expressed just one way: he changed his mind about it. And, there may be more to it than the mere acceptation of a formula that had first been rejected. I think that the *Summa theologiae*, as studied by Gilson, bears witness to a hardening of Albert's position about the "substantiality" of the human soul. In his first writings, he, at times, calls it a substance, as we have just read: "*est substantia composita*"; while saying that the soul is a true substantial form, he also sees it as a "motor," a "pilot"; he even prefers "perfection" and "act" over "form," in order to stress the soul's value in itself. But if that autonomous value of the soul is overstressed, its union to the body could seem "accidental," and Albert rejects that view. When he compares the soul to Angels, he writes: *Anima inclinatur ad corpus ut actus, Angelus autem non. Et ideo substantiale dicimus animae esse quod sit actus corporis* (*Summa* II, tr. 1, q. 4, art. 1, sol.). We have read above, in the text denying that the soul is *hoc aliquid*, that that inclination results in a *dependentia* of such strength that the soul's perfection is not altogether complete when it is without its body. Because of that, it is certainly preferable not to extend to the human soul what Albert says about Angels, unless he does it himself. Albert seems to warn against unwarranted comparisons of that kind. I have quoted above a text from an article of the *Summa*, where Albert asks explicitly: "Is *the* soul *a* substance?" (p. 10ª, n. 27). Albert insists on the fact that speaking about the soul in terms of "genus" and "specie" is "logical" and "transcendent," and that such vocabulary is not used in natural philosophy nor in first philosophy. Nevertheless, answering an objection, he writes: "If one would say that soul is a species, and that it divides, the way a subalternate genus does, into vegetative, sensitive, and rational, one would then speak only in comparison with self-subsisting species (*species per se existentes*); and it is evident that soul is no species in that manner. Therefore, that understanding of *the* soul is an error, even if we would then be speaking logically about it" (*Summa* II, tr. 1, q. 2, art. 1, ad 1.). Albert, with many others, considers Angels to be self-existing "species"; souls are not. Very often, texts seem to suggest that Albert should conclude unequivocally that the human soul is "a substance." When he draws that conclusion, he qualifies it immediately. Quotations from the *Summa theologiae* found in Gilson's article indicate that Albert had become far more affirmative toward the end of his career, about that question. The earlier writings are less articulate, and it is better to leave them to their own undetermination.

[37] *Summa* II, tr. 1, q. 4, *passim*; particularly, art. 1.

[38] *Summa* II, tr. 1, q. 1, art. 1, ad 4.

Within that general perspective some points of Albert's doctrine find a very natural meaning. For instance, the human soul is a true *forma partis*, but it possesses some of the attributes of the *forma totius*, or better, the *forma totius* owes all that it is to the soul. Being just a part, the soul cannot be predicated of the whole, and, as such, it is "other" than the predicable *forma totius*. But abstraction will reach the *forma totius* just by disengaging the human soul, the "nature," the "substance" of man, from the individuating conditions it would not have caused by itself, even if it consecrates them in perfection and unity. Individualized or universal, the *ratio* of man is always the same, and ultimately, the soul "is" the *ratio* of the common nature, of the "species in this particular individual," it gives it its *esse*.[39] While analyzing the texts, one after the other, discretion seemed to be imperative on that matter.[40] The over-all impression that remains, after they have all been read, is clear. The human soul "is" the *ratio* of the human nature.

Yet Albert tries to maintain a balance between two extremes. The soul is the *ratio* of the human nature in the individual man, but Albert is very consistent in his affirmations about it being only a part of the living composite. The human soul is independent from its body, it will subsist after its dissolution in death, but that independence is not total, and Albert refuses to see the soul as a concrete being, a *hoc aliquid*. "In its very nature (*secundum naturam*) it depends on its body, even if it could be without it. But I do well concede that its [the soul's] perfection is not altogether (*omino*) complete without its body."[41] Even Albert's

---

[39] L. B. Geiger, "La vie acte essentiel de l'âme—l'*esse*, acte de l'essence d'après Albert le Grand." That study is F. Geiger's contribution to a collective publication: *Etudes d'histoire littéraire et doctrinale* (Montréal-Paris: Institut d'Etudes médiévales—J. Vrin, 1962), pp. 49–116. It is an excellent account of Albert's philosophy of the soul, from that point of view. F. Geiger uses mostly Albert's *De Anima*, but he also quotes the *Summa de Creaturis* and the *Commentary*. His analyses show that, according to Albert, the soul possesses life in itself, and gives the body a life which is somewhat different from its own. One must agree with F. Geiger that such a vision appears as a form of dualism; Albert maintains that view even in the case of the vegetative and sensitive souls (p. 66). In his conclusion Geiger uses the word "syncretism" (p. 111), and that could well give its true meaning to Albert's "evolution." That evolution consists mostly of a change in the balance between the same two elements intertwined in that syncretism: "Aristotelian" hylemorphism and Neoplatonism. Geiger also points out that Albert's affirmation about the soul giving *esse* by a radiation of itself over the composite (*suum dare est diffusio sui in formato*) is borrowed from the "metaphysics of light" (p. 70). That is very obvious, but it had escaped me in 1957. Ducharme, "*Esse*" . . ., p. 227. I now acknowledge my debt to him. Cf. *supra*, n. 20.

[40] Cf. *supra*, p. 7–8.

[41] 2 Sent., d. 17, art. 2, ad 2.

most fervent admirers must admit that his philosophy of man is ambiguous.

His philosophy of the individual being is also puzzling. The individual being is extolled: it alone is a "natural thing," a "something," a "substance" in the complete sense of the word; the soul is not, and the common nature is not either. But the individual being is declared unintelligible. Intelligibility is reached together with simplicity, and abstraction will have to disengage a universal *forma totius* from the complexity of individuating elements in order to reach intelligibility. So that the unique individual being appears as the "Great Unknown" in Albert's philosophy. The *forma totius* is the "species in that particular individual," and Albert often repeats: "The species is the whole *esse* of individual things" (*species est totum esse individuorum*).[42] The individual thing is the Great Unknown, because, in its very individuality, it is uninteresting; its whole meaningful reality is found in the species present in it, as in a container.

The manner in which Albert's philosophy of the individual being is both ambiguous and puzzling, is typically medieval; the fact that it be both is not.

Quod Est–Quo Est (Esse)

The first description we have read of the "natural thing" said that it is composed of matter and form, or of *quod est* and *quo est*, the latter composition being found principally in spiritual substances.[43] Throughout Albert's earlier writings that is the first meaning of that composition. (It does happen, though, that the material subject, composed of matter and form, is called a *quod est* while the *forma totius* is given as a *quo est*.[44]) Albert did not admit universal hylemorphism. In the text from the *Summa*, where the description of the individual being is found, he first presents the opinion of those who do admit it and gives the reasons why they do. He then adds: "If one would rather speak differently," and offers what is evidently his own opinion. The *Commentary* is more affirmative.

> It has always been my opinion that Angels are composed of essential parts, but not of matter and form. I do not say that matter is the first principle of composition of substance as such, but of mobile substances, so that, where there is no potency to movement, I do not say

[42] Ducharme, "*Esse*" . . ., p. 220. E.g., 3 *Sent.*, d. 10, art. 1, *quaestiuncula* 2, *sed contra* 2 and *resp*.

[43] Cf. *supra* p. 3–4.

[44] E.g. *Summa* I, tr. 4, q., 21, art. 1, sol.

that there is matter, unless "matter" is given a very broad and improper meaning.

His main reason is that "philosophers do not speak of matter, unless they refer to the subject of a privation." Further in the text he repeats that, according to Boethius and "all philosophers," the *ratio* of potency is not identical in the potential element present in spiritual substances, and in matter. But there is potency in spiritual substances, and that explains "unless 'matter' is given a very broad and improper meaning." Besides potency, created substances also have other common characteristics, e.g., to stand under a form and to support it. It is necessary, therefore, to find a "substance" common to all of them. But that "substance" should be called *fundamentum* rather than matter, since, because of the *ratio* of potency, "matter" would be said equivocally of them all.[45] Albert might be more lenient toward "material." In the *Summa*, already facing the fact that there is potentiality in spiritual substances, he would concede that their potency could be called "material," since "material" says less (*minus dicit*) than "matter." Potency, in spiritual substances, has some of the properties found in matter: it "receives," it "does not reduce itself to act, but is reduced to act by another"; that potency, in spiritual substances, has its source in the *quod est*. He adds: "therefore in matter," a concession he will reject in the *Commentary*.[46] I do not believe that this is sufficient to admit an evolution about that question. Matter is often given as the prototype of all "potencies," and that is enough to explain what looks like a concession, in the answer to an objection, particularly in an article whose *solutio* begins with a presentation of the opinion held by the supporters of universal hylemorphism. Albert did understand their stand, but we may accept as an expression of his true mind, even in the *Summa*, the affirmation of the *Commentary*: "It has always been my opinion that Angels are composed of essential parts, but not of matter and form." Albert's leniency in the *Summa*, as compared with his more uncompromising stand in the *Commentary*, may have come from a different understanding of the "philosophers." In the *Commentary* he simply rejects the word "matter" when he speaks about Angels, because Boethius and all philosophers do not speak of matter unless they want to explain "privation," and the *ratio* of potency is different in spiritual substances from what it is in material beings. While writing the *Summa*, he had read them differently:

Philosophers give "matter" and "form" a broad meaning. And that

45 2 *Sent.*, d. 3, art. 4, sol.
46 *Summa* I, tr. 1, q. 2, art. 5, ad 2.

is apparent in the 3rd [book] of the *De Anima,* where the Philosopher says: Because, as in any nature, other is the matter in each genus, which is potency in all of them, and other is the cause, the efficient [agent] [...].[47]

Albert then explains that this is the reason why philosophers do admit a passive and an active potencies in spiritual beings. But he adds that, even if some philosophers use the hylemorphic vocabulary, strictly speaking *(proprie)*, *quod est* and *esse* are better than "matter" and "form."

Albert had inherited the vocabulary of *quod est* and *quo est* from Boethius, as he acknowledges it himself. Boethius said *esse* rather than *quo est,* and Albert does the same at times, as in the text just quoted above, but, very often, he says *quo est,* a practice widely followed by *Doctores,* according to him.[48] The origin of that vocabulary is well known. *Quod est* had long been the only available Latin translation for the Greek *to on,* before the Latins, reluctantly indeed, coined and accepted *ens.*[49] *Esse* translated *einai,* and, in Boethius, it had all the nuances of Aristotle's *einai.*[50] That vocabulary was to be used, later on, within the context of the controversy about the distinction between essence and existence. Albert himself was to yield to that usage in the *Summa theologiae.*[51] No texts from the *Summa de Creaturis* or from the *Commentary* can be understood as referring to that controversy; Albert does not yet even think about it. He follows Boethius. Later on, under Avicenna's influence, he will change his views, and modify the meaning of his vocabulary.[52]

The general meaning of *quod est* is presented early in the *Summa.* Albert, in order to justify one of Aristotle's definitions of matter, explains some elements of the Philosopher's vocabulary. Here is how he understood *quod est,* as he had probably found it where *quod est* translated *to on:*

> By *hoc quod est,* he [Aristotle] understands the *ratio* of subsistence (*rationem subsistentiae*) a composed substance has from the compo-

[47] *Summa* I., tr. 4, q. 21, art. 1, ad 4.

[48] 1 Sent., d. 3, art. 33, sol.

[49] E. Gilson, "Notes sur le vocabulaire de l'être," *L'être et l'essence,* 2d ed. (Paris; Vrin, 1962), pp. 335–39.

[50] M. D. Roland-Gosselin, *Le "De Ente et Essentia" de S. Thomas D'Aquin* ... (Paris: Vrin, 1948), pp. 142–45.

[51] E.g., *Summa theologiae* II, q. 3, *membrum* 3, art. 3. Cf. G. Meerseman, *Geschichte des Albertismus* ... (Paris, 1933), t. 1, p. 58.

[52] M. D. Roland-Gosselin, *op. cit.,* pp. 172–84.

sition of matter and form. Thus, *quod est* is identical with "what is being now" (*quod nunc est*) in nature.[53]

Quod est means "what is being now," the actual, individual being. Albert himself explains the "ratio of subsistence." It is the *ratio* of actual presence in nature a substance has, from the composition of matter and form: *quod est* is the equivalent of "what is now in nature," a being, being now.[54]

That general meaning has been given a more specific use in the duality of *quod est* and *quo est*, in order to explain how created spiritual substances are composed, even if they do not consist of matter and form. In that specific usage, *quod est* is the concrete subject, and *quo est* is the equivalent of the *forma totius* of the material substances. But the original general meaning is not entirely lost, and Albert often writes "in the thing that is [now]" (*in eo quod est*). That general meaning of the duality of *quod est* and *quo est* is known to us, and we have already read it in the text where the "natural thing" was described. Here is another text where it is further explained. Albert uses the *quod est* and *quo est* duality more frequently when he speaks of Angels. He also advocates it when he wants to establish that the human soul is not simple. That is the question here: "Is the soul composed in its substance (*secundum substantiam*)?"

> I agree—that the soul is essentially composed, but not [that it is composed] of matter and form.

He then repeats the reasons why he does not admit universal hylemorphism. He goes on:

> But Doctors say that it is composed of *quod est* and *quo est*; and, then, *quod est* differs from matter, like a supposit from its potency to the form under which it is (*cui supponitur*). That *quod est* is a "something" that can be predicated of the thing that is (*de eo quod est*). *Quo est*, on the other hand, is not found in our Author, Boethius says *esse*. That is the essence, according to the act it has in the thing

53 *Summa* I, tr. 1, q. 2, art. 2, ad 1. I would not dare translate the wonderful *rationem* in *rationem subsistentiae*. It illustrates the exquisite volatility of *ratio*. That *ratio* of subsistence, coming to a substance from its composition of matter and form, is really what makes it an actual being. Of course, that *ratio* can be known, and "concept" comes to the mind. But Gilson's scintillating, even if not quite convincing, rebuttal-confession about the inconceivability of "to be" should prevent anybody from using "concept." E. Gilson, *Being and Some Philosophers*, 2d ed. (Toronto: Pontifical Institute of Mediaeval Studies, 1952), pp. 216–32.

54 English, because of its use of "being" both as a noun and as a participle, allows the repetition with no danger of redundance.

that is (*in eo quod est*), that is in "this something" (*hoc aliquid*), or in this "supposit." So that, in such [substances], the individuation of *esse* comes from the properties following the *quod est* itself, inasmuch as it is something revealing itself here and now to the intellect. I say that the soul is composed of those [two elements], and so are Angels.

Because of that, *quo est* differs from *a* form, since *a* form is separable, and it is the form of a part (*forma partis*) which is matter; but *quo est* or *esse* is not separated from what is (*eo quod est*), and it is a *forma totius*, that says the whole *esse* of the *quod est*, by way of a formal *esse*, the *esse* of the species in this individual, in conformity with what Boethius says: the species is the whole *esse* of individuals. Whatever is after the species is part of the individuating [elements].[55]

The general meaning of the text is clear, even if it is intricately woven. Doctors who do not admit universal hylemorphism follow Boethius and substitute *quod est* and *quo est* (*esse*) to matter and form, in order to explain the soul's composition. But that substitution is not to be understood as a mere duplication; it is a parallel, and just that. All that can be said of matter cannot be repeated about the *quod est*, nor what is said of the form, be said of the *quo est*.

The *quod est* differs from matter as does the subject from its potentiality to its form. The "like" is to be understood as denoting a parallel, not a similarity. In material things the subject owes its potentiality to its matter, and it is different from that matter, which in turns differs from its potentiality. Not having matter, the spiritual supposits owe to themselves a potentiality from which they differ.[56] The *quod est* can be predicated of the very thing that is; matter cannot. (Another text will help make this clearer.)

The *quo est*, the *esse* is the essence, according to the act it has in the *quod est*. Essence appears here openly as "beingness," giving *esse*, being, to the thing that is.[57]

Spiritual substances, having no matter (Albert thinks of the Angels he is about to mention, not of the human souls he is presently discussing), must be individuated by themselves. Human souls are individually multiplied under the human species, because of their bodies. Angels are distinct from one another, as subsisting species under a

[55] 1 *Sent.*, d. 3, art. 33, sol.

[56] That is in line with Albert's view of the difference between matter and its potentiality to form.

[57] Ducharme, "*Esse*" . . . pp. 240–46. Since I was writing in French, I had no equivalent of "beingness" at my disposal. See also Geiger, *op. cit.*

genus; each of them is a personal being. Here Albert admits ignorance: the differences causing that multiplicity are hidden from us.[58]

The duality of *quod est* and *quo est* fulfils one primary function. It expresses that all created substances are composed, even spiritual substances devoid of matter. God only is absolutely simple. Albert presents that composition in a comparison with the composition of matter and form but insists that this comparison expresses a parallelism, not an absolute identity. Such is the unvarying meaning of the composition of *quod est* and *quo est* throughout his earlier writings.[59] Piling up more texts where that view is repeated, even with minor variations, would be no more than a very scholarly exercise in futility.

Some particular points may be of interest. The parallel between the two compositions helps understand the distinction between the soul's two "parts," the active and the passive intellects:

> The active intellect is a part of the soul. We have said above that the diversity of properties and potencies of the soul flow from the diversity of the principles entering the composition of the soul, which are *quod est* and *quo est*, or act and potency if those [last two] terms are understood in a broadened way. And, because of that, we say that the active intellect is a part of the soul, flowing from that through which [the soul] is (*quo est*), or act, the passive intellect is a part of the soul, flowing from what the soul is (*quod est*), or potency.[60]

Albert takes advantage of the grammatical flexibility of the expressions *quod est* and *quo est*, and, doing this, he reveals the ultimate meaning of that "composition," the composition of an individual subject with its common nature. His *quod est* must, very often, be translated by

---

[58] *Summa* I, tr. 4, q. 28, art. 2, ad 1.

[59] Some historians are sure that they have detected an evolution on that question from the *Summa* to the *Commentary*. Albert would have relinquished the *quod est–quo est* duality in the *Commentary*, or, at least, he would have changed its meaning. E.g., O. Lottin, "La composition hylemorphique des substances spirituelles. Les débuts de la controverse," *Revue néoscolastique* . . ., t. 34 (1932), p. 34, n. 2; M. D. Roland-Gosselin, *op. cit.*, p. 176. I spare my readers the tedious details of the painstaking analyses that have convinced me no such evolution can be proved. Albert does at times oppose God's simplicity to all creatures' composition, by other means. He does it in the *Summa* as well as in the *Commentary*. E.g., he will say that all creatures have relations to God, that those relations are not "nothing" in them, and they compose with what the creatures are (1 *Sent.*, d. 2, art. 13, sol.–1 *Sent.*, d. 8, art. 15, *ad aliud.*). But his favorite explanation is the *quod est–quo est* duality, particularly when he refers specifically to human souls and to Angels, and not to creatures in general.

[60] *Summa* I., tr. 1, q. 55, art. 4.

"the" *quod est*, and his *quo est* by "the" *quo est*, since they are given as two parts of a composition. *Quod est* really means "something that is" [what it is], thanks to the *esse* giving it to be [what it is]. That *esse* is primarily formal, essential.[61] But since matter and form, the matter and the substantial form of earthly beings, are the first instances of "act" and "potency," Albert finds it necessary to guard against too close a comparison, and he points out that the meaning of the two words must be broadened, when they are used to describe the *quo est* and the *quod est* as parts of a spiritual substance.

There is another point which it is important to remember: the parallel between the two compositions is to be understood just as that, a parallel. Matter is not predicable of the supposit; *quod est* is:

> If one asks how that [composition] must be "worded" (*significari*), it is to be said, following what Aristotle says in the first [book] of the *De coelo et mundo*: "When I say 'this heaven,' I say matter, when I say 'heaven,' I say form." Similarly, when I say "this Angel" or "that soul," I say the supposit, when I say "Angel" or "soul," I say the nature whose [that Angel or that soul] is the supposit. And, therefore, in these, and *quod est* and *quo est* are predicated of the supposit.[62]

Again Albert refers primarily to the immediate meaning of *quod est* in *id quod est*; that is why I have omitted "the" before *quod est* and *quo est*. *Id quod est* means "what it is." Albert just wants to salvage predicative propositions like "Sortes is what he is," and "Raphael is what he is" (*est id quod est*). What is truly predicable is the expression *id quod est*, not "the" *quod est*, the individual supposit. We know that, as far as predication is concerned, the *quo est* and the *forma partis* are in the same situation. They are predicable, provided one uses a concrete term, such as "man," rather than an abstract term, such as "humanity."[63]

[61] Ducharme, "*Esse*" . . ., *passim*. Also Geiger, *op. cit.*

[62] *Summa* I., tr. 1, q. 2, art. 5, sol.

[63] Albert varies on that. Both the *forma totius* and the *quo est* are "the species in this particular individual." His variations are the result of the distinction between "nature in itself"—"nature as universal"—"nature as in the individuals." The *quo est* and the *forma totius* are the "species as in the individuals," as such, having *esse* in individuals, the nature is not universal, and is not predicable. Abstraction will be necessary before universality is reached. So Albert denies more frequently that the *forma totius* or the *quo est* are universal. E.g., "I do not understand that the *forma totius* is identical with the universal, since it has *esse* in the composite; but it is the form through which something "is" *esse*, as the Philosopher says. And from it, through knowledge (*per intentionem*), the uni-

One last text will hold our attention. It sums up most of what we have read about the *quod est–quo est* duality, and it will bring us back to the conclusion we had reached, after studying the hylemorphic composition of the individual being. The question is: "Is truth (*veritas*) simple, and unchangeable (*incommutabilis*)"?

> Truth is a form that is first in its genus, just as goodness, unity and entity, even though there is an order among those as has already been said, and, therefore, I do not believe that any of those [first forms] are composed of *quod est* and *quo est*, inasmuch as *quod est* expresses something being in itself (*aliquid ens in se*), in which *esse* is diffused, which [*esse*] is the act of the essence. But I do well concede that truth contains in itself many elements of intellection (*plures intellectus*), because it contains indirectly (*oblique*) the understanding of essence (*intellectum essentiae*), as [the understanding] of that to which a form belongs (*ut cujus est*), and [besides that] it has its own proper understanding (*intellectum*). And therefore, it does not equal God's simplicity. And, I believe similarly, that the same must be said about any form that is first in its genus.[64]

Whenever the problem of simplicity arises, Albert's first preoccupation is to ensure that anything, even a notion, is seen as consisting of a duality, God alone being absolutely simple. So he finds a duality of understanding within the meaning of "truth," which, later on, he will list among the "first notions" (*primae intentiones*). Those first notions are no equals; there is an order among them: "essence" is first, and it stands as an exception. When it is used as meaning the pure and simple understanding of being, it signifies "simple essence," and *Qui est*, as a name, is proper to God.[65] "Truth" is not absolutely simple in its significative content; it means "essence," adding to it its own proper "form." Within that complex signification "essence" appears as some sort of a "subject" having the quality expressed by "truth" (*ut cujus est*). But Albert does not believe (*non credo*) that that duality can be considered as one of *quod est* and *quo est*, because of the meaning of *quod est*. A *quod est* is a subject, and a true subject is a "something that is." "Essence" may appear as the subject of the form signified in "truth," but "essence" is an abstract term; it designates a form, not a

---

versal is abstracted." *Summa* I, q. 21, art. 1, sol. Same thing about the *quo est*: 2 *Sent.*, d. 31, art. 1, ad 1. Sometimes Albert overlooks that nicety and identifies *quod est* with "particular" and *quo est* with "universal." E.g., 1 *Sent.*, d. 9, art. 8, ad 2.–1 *Sent.*, d. 19, art. 15, *sed contra* 1.

64 1 *Sent.*, d. 46, art. 16, sol.

65 Ducharme, "*Esse*" . . ., pp. 213–14.

"something." The "understanding of essence" (*intellectus essentiae*) is found, as designating a subject, in "being" (*ens*), a concrete term, and not in the abstract "essence" (*essentia*).

Later on in the same article Albert refuses to accept one of Augustine's affirmations, according to which one could say: "truth is true"— "goodness is good," etc. The detailed argumentation is rather intricate, and would add nothing to what we already know about the duality of *quod est* and *quo est*. It comes to this: Albert does not admit, even at the level of the first notions, that a concrete predicate can be attributed to an abstract subject (*concretum ponitur de abstracto*). Even as an adjective "true" means "something having truth," and "truth," not signifying "something," cannot be said to be "having truth." Augustine's authority notwithstanding, "oneness" (*unitas*) does not signify a "something" but a form, a form giving a subject to be one, to have unity.[66] Albert prefers the concrete "man" over the abstract "humanity" as an expression of the *forma totius*, because it can be predicated of the concrete subject. But only because of that reason. Strictly speaking, "truth is true" means nothing more than "truth is truth."[67] Brought down to its basic meaning, the concrete term means only the form expressed by the abstract word.

And here we find the ultimate meaning of Albert's frequent affirmation: "The species is the whole reality of individuals" (*Species est totum esse individuorum*). That meaning is absolute. The concrete term "man" may well be a more suitable predicate than the abstract "humanity," but, even if it designates a concrete subject more appropriately than its equivalent abstract "humanity," it does not mean more than the species, which is signified directly by "humanity"; individual characters are left unsaid by the concrete, just as completely as they are by the abstract term. This is why "truth is true" means nothing more than the tautological "truth is truth." "Truth" is a form, and it is the form that gives something having it, being its subject, to be true, and to be knowable as "true." "Essence" is a form; "humanity" is a form. It is the form that gives *esse* and *rationem*, because the form (*forma totius, quo est*) is the "species in the individual," and the species is the whole reality of individuals. Albert prefers the concrete terms for the sake of sound predication, not because they would reveal the secrets of individuality more completely than the abstract words.

[66] 1 *Sent.*, d. 46, art. 16, sol. That is the best interpretation I could reach of that intricate discussion.
[67] *Ibid.*

From a historian's point of view, Albert's philosophy of the individual human being appears as thoroughly medieval. It evolves within the boundaries set by the Christian faith; it borrows from Aristotle, from Doctors of the Church, and from Neoplatonism. It stands on guard for God's simplicity, it compares individual human beings and human souls with Angels and with celestial bodies, in the perspectives created by the simultaneous admission of hylemorphism and of the hierarchy of "separate intelligences."[68] It is also typical of the first part of the thirteenth century, when it had become apparent that official prohibitions, even backed up by threats of excommunication, would not stop Aristotle's invasion of the School, not only at the Faculty of Arts, but also at the Faculty of Theology. Albert belonged to the group of Masters who were aware not only that Aristotle would not be avoided but also that he was offering theologians an admirable philosophical instrument. As Gilson has demonstrated, Albert did not see clearly that Avicenna's Aristotelianism was quite different from Aristotle's doctrine. He read the Philosopher with Avicenna's eyes, but he wanted to make the Philosopher readable for all. But, at the end of this essay, I feel very free to say that one must be interested in medieval thought to read a detailed presentation of Albert's philosophy of the individual being.

Yet all historians and all philosophers must learn a lesson from Albert. Philosophical thinking had developed and flourished within very concrete historical conditions before Albert, it did the same in Albert's time, and it has continued to do the same since the thirteenth century. That period had characteristics of its own; they have disappeared. Other periods have offered philosophy other resources, and they have also tried to keep it within their own frontiers. Historians must record it, and philosophers should be aware of it and fear any orthodoxy. Philosophers cannot be foreign to their times, but they must try to keep philosophy reasonably free from incidental restrictions that would become too stringent. Some of the philosophical "dogmas" of the thirteenth century were legacies from pagan antiquity, they have been handed down to philosophers of following ages, and they have remained "dogmas" long after religious dogmas lost their dominion over philosophy.

Saving God's simplicity is not our main preoccupation any longer;

68 I have omitted references to Albert's theories about celestial bodies. They are only accommodations, common at that time, of the hylemorphic theory, since each of the celestial bodies was considered as a subsisting species under the same genus. I do not believe that, in doing so, I have betrayed his vision of the individual human being, and it has helped keep this essay reasonably readable.

we leave Angels to theologians, and space science has mercifully relieved us of any concern about "celestial bodies." Individual human beings are still a part of our lot, and I think that they should constitute the main part of it. We should pay more than tepid lip service to them. Albert had adopted the very ancient idea that philosophy, being a science, had to deal with the universal, the species, in individuals, of course, but mainly in itself. Philosophers all through the ages have cherished that view of philosophy as the most precious gem of their collective heritage. The history of philosophy knows of many blazing holocausts offered before the altar of universality. Philosophy must salvage its universal scientific character with the same obstinacy Albert displayed in his defense of God's simplicity and of the personal immortality of human souls. What cannot be universal and necessary we should forget, or entrust to belief. Philosophy can be a science only if it is universal and deals in necessity, and philosophy will be a science, or it will be no longer.

Seldom, in long whiles, timid efforts were made in order to recognize the unique value of individual beings, and to say it philosophically. The Middle Ages have witnessed some of those efforts, other periods have, and our own does too. But, very often, those undertakings come to the same conclusion: the individual being is unique and admirable, but it is philosophically unexpressible. Confronted with that dead end, philosophy either turns back to the more manageable universals or it admits its defeat, and philosophers have written thousands of admirable pages lamenting the tragically heroic fate of philosophy, the sighing, sobbing, "impossible science."[69]

We might possibly do better. We could leave "science" to the specialists of various sciences, and while listening to them, since we are far away from Albert's four elements, philosophize, trying to lend the voice of reason to human beings and to the unexpressible individual human being. Reason is not necessarily "scientific." Our philosophical congresses would never attract half the attention the media keep for terrorist attacks, wars, sex scandals, or sports events. But they might be more lively, and human beings might listen to us, if we, as philosophers, would speak in defense of the innocent individual victims of senseless violence, in defense of the individual human beings, distorted into zombies in our sex shows and in our boxing rings. The shortcomings in Albert's philosophy of the individual human being do not set him apart among philosophers; having read about them might help us recognize our own shortcomings and loathe them.

[69] The presently widespread view of philosophy as being only "formal logic," appears to me just as the expression of a more radical "unconditional surrender."

The Enduring Question of Action at a Distance in Saint Albert the Great

FRANCIS J. KOVACH
University of Oklahoma

Saint Albert, the great son of Swabia, who died in Cologne seven hundred years ago, November 15, 1280, is universally recognized as one of the four greatest philosopher-theologians of high scholasticism and certainly the most outstanding and most respected scientist of his century. Nevertheless, Saint Thomas Aquinas and Duns Scotus, as well as Saint Bonaventure, have received more attention from the historians than Saint Albert has. In his works there are numerous doctrines, theories, and views pertaining to the three generic fields of his excellence, which are little known, if known at all. For this reason it is appropriate that a commemorative study should deal with one of those many neglected objects of Saint Albert's thought—a topic which is naturally of great interest to all the three areas of Albert's scholarship: philosophy, theology, and science. Accordingly, the subject of this essay is Saint Albert's treatment of one of the enduring questions of human thought—action at a distance.

Here I shall discuss this topic in three main parts. The first will attempt to show the truly enduring character of the question of action at a distance, by listing in the form of a logical division the various treatments this question has received throughout history. In the second and central part of the paper I will attempt to determine what Saint Albert has to say about this intriguing question, and how his view on it may be classified in light of the categories listed in Part One. In the third and concluding part I will consider the related issues of the originality and influence of Saint Albert's theory and treatment of action at a distance.

I. *The Enduring Character of the Question of Action at a Distance*

In the majority of cases ordinary experience seems to show that one body acts on another by touch (contact), whereas the same experience seems also to point to some instances in which the agent acts on a distant body and does so *without* the use of a medium. This twofold experience gives rise to the question, Is contact a necessary condition of causation, or is action at a distance also possible? Since causation by contact is apparently experienced more often than causation seemingly without contact, it is proper to call the question at hand a continguist question.

A question is rightly called an enduring question if, throughout history, it has received some treatment from authorities in the field or fields to which the question is naturally related and, more significantly, if the question has received numerous more or less different treatments or answers from the proper authorities.

Granting these two criteria, the chronological and the doctrinal, of the enduringness of any question, it can be shown that action at a distance is undoubtedly an enduring question—at least in philosophy and science. For with regard to the first or chronological criterion, some treatment of the contiguist question can be found in some fashion in ancient Greek philosophy, beginning with the Presocratics, and also in the patristic, the medieval, especially the high scholastic, and the Renaissance literatures, as well as in the writings of modern and contemporary philosophers and scientists.

To utilize the second, or doctrinal, criterion of enduring questions, one must first of all realize that, as history shows, there are two possible reactions to the contiguist question *before* any answer is attempted or given: "The question is unreasonable or meaningless" and "The question is reasonable or meaningful." The former view may be termed contiguist irrationalism; the latter, contiguist rationalism.

1. *Contiguist irrationalism* has been expressed in two generic ways: implicitly and explicitly. The former version implies, while the latter version formally states, that the contiguist question is meaningless for some reason.

Implicit contiguist irrationalism, from the logical point of view, is either indirect or direct, according to whether the irrationalist implication at hand follows from some explicit doctrine either immediately or only through an intermediate premise.

The *indirect* version of implicit contiguist irrationalism has two forms, as it may rest on a more or a less radical denial of the components of reality. The more radical denial at hand is that nothing exists (Gorgias of Leontini[1]). The less radical denial is that there is

[1] In my article "The Question of the Eternity of the World in St. Bonaventure and S. Thomas—A Critical Analysis," *Southwestern Journal of Philosophy* 5

neither multitude nor change in reality, which reality is beginningless or "eternal" (Parmenides, Zeno). Both doctrines evidently imply that there are no efficient causes and effects and, hence, that any question concerning the *modus operandi* of causes is unreasonable.

The *direct* version of implicit contiguist irrationalism holds that causes do not exist, and it holds this view in a more or less radical manner. The more radical view is that causes do not exist because they cannot—being mere mental relations (Pyrrhonists). The less radical position is that, as a matter of fact, there are no causes; instead, "cause" (as well as "change" or "activity") is a mere "superstition" or an "unintelligible" or "contradictory" concept (F. Zöllner [1878],[2] F. Nietzsche [1882], E. Mach [1883], F. H. Bradley [1893], A. Einstein [1915], L. Wittgenstein [1921], M. Schlick [1949], et al.).

The *explicit* contiguist irrationalism formally states the irrationality of the question whether causal contact is necessary or, instead, action at a distance is possible. This position has a pure and a mixed form. The former (K. Pearson [1892], B. Russell [1912]) does not contain any element of contiguist rationalism; the latter does—such as explicit metaphysical and physical contiguism (Peter Aureolus [1312–19]) or physical anticontiguism (Fernand Renoirte [1923]).

2. In contrast to the first generic position of contiguist irrationalism, *contiguist rationalism* maintains that the contiguist question is reasonable and answers it in one of two generic manners: that of contiguist agnosticism or that of contiguist realism.

In view of the *contiguist agnosticism* the answer to the contiguist question is unknown. This position may be expressed implicitly or explicitly, and the implicit version either generically or specifically.

Representatives of *generic implicit* agnosticism imply their position

(Summer, 1974): 141–72, reprinted in *Bonaventure and Aquinas*, Robert W. Shahan and Francis J. Kovach, eds. (Norman: University of Oklahoma Press, 1976), pp. 155–86, I gave the text references to all the representatives of the various views I listed on that enduring question (pp. 142–48 and 156–62, respectively). Owing to the much greater diversity of views on action at a distance, I cannot do the same in this essay because of space limitations. Instead, after referring to an author, I shall give the year of the first publication of the first work expressing the view of that author on our topic, or, in cases of premodern and early modern authors, the date of the composition of the first such work by the author, if the date is known.

2 The name of Zöllner, as well as of Sextus Empiricus, is listed in two radically different categories of views, because these two authors incorporate heterogeneous elements in their total views or reports of views on action at a distance. A few other names, like those of Suárez and Leibniz, appear twice because the views of those authors are characteristic from two different points of view.

by teaching that all things are unknowable or that knowledge in general is impossible (Pyrrho, Timon of Phlius, Arcesilaus, Carneades, et al.). Those representing the *specific* version of implicit contiguist agnosticism hold that efficient causes are unknown to us, and unknown either empirically (Aenesidimus, Sextus Empiricus, Algazel, I. Newton [1717], A. Comte [1830], J. S. Mill [1843], H. Spencer [1864], John O'Neill [1923], Herbert Feigl [1955], et al.) or because their existence is *a priori* indemonstrable (John of Mirecourt, Nicholas of Autrecourt).

Explicit contiguist agnosticism is partly moderate, partly immoderate, as it formally teaches that the answer to the contiguist question is unknowable either personally to the holder of the view (John Peter Olivi [ca. 1296]) or to man in general (G. Vásquez [1598], F. M. A. Voltaire [1728], P. Coffey [1914], J. Donat [before 1936],[3] W. A. McGrea [1952], Mario Bunger [1959], et al.).

Causal contiguism is physical, metaphysical, or both physical and metaphysical, according to whether the necessity of causal contact is applied by the advocates of this generic position to corporeal agents only or to agent in general or to both corporeal agent in general and agent in general.

3. *Physical* causal contiguism is either implicit or explicit according to whether the necessity of contact for causation is merely implied or formally stated.

Implicit physical contiguism is represented in three forms: as descriptive, as interpretive, or as both descriptive and interpretive physical contiguism. The *descriptive* version consistently describes alleged or factual activities in terms of causal contact (Anaxagoras, Giambatista Beccaria [1753]). The interpretive version postulates either causal contact (Johannes Philoponus) or some medium in order to account for apparent instances of corporeal action at a distance. The combined version both describes certain activities in terms of causal contact and postulates some medium in accounting for certain activities (Empedocles, Leucippus, Democritus).

The purely *interpretive* form of implicit physical contiguism may postulate either a dynamic medium, i.e., some effluvium moving from the agent to the distant patient, or some static, i.e., interjacent, medium transmitting the power from the agent to the patient or else both

---

[3] A phrase within parentheses such as "before 1936" means in connection with modern and contemporary authors that the work referred to was published, but *not* for the *first* time, in the listed year. In the case of some Renaissance authors, the year given in such phrase is the one in which the author died.

effluvia and interjacent media. Representatives of the first version include Epicurus, Lucretius, Marsilius Ficinus, Descartes (1644), Thomas Brown (1646), Sir Kenelm Digby (1657), Robert Boyle (1672), W. Watson (1746), B. Franklin (1747), J. A. Nollet (1749), P. S. Laplace (1808), et al.

Those postulating some interjacent medium to account for apparent corporeal actions at a distance may conceive that medium, according to the place where it acts as a medium, as being either particular (transmitting some specific influence of certain corporeal agents only) or universal, commonly called aether (conceived as filling all interstellar spaces as well as the interstices of all bodies). Thus, for all alleged benumbing effect of the torpedo fish ($\nu\alpha\rho\kappa\acute{\eta}$) upon the fisherman's hand touching only the net which caught the torpedo fish or a rod that killed the fish, Simplicius, Themistius, Johannes Philoponus, Olympiodorus, and Averroes all postulate the net or the rod to be the medium, whereas Descartes (1644), Robert Hook (1655), G. W. Leibniz (1714), John Bernoulli, Jr. (1736), J. MacCullagh (1837), Sir G. G. Stokes (1845), Joseph Boussinesq (1868), et al., postulate aether.

Among the advocates of the aether theory, some conceive the aether as a one-role medium (H. Cavendish [1771], Thomas Young [1800], A. Fresnel [1866]); others, as a two-role medium (L. Euler [1746], Sir W. Herschel [1800], George Green [1828]); and again others, as a three-role medium (B. Riemann [1867], Sir J. Larmou [1895]).

Explicit physical contiguism formally expresses the necessity of causal contact or the impossibility of a corporeal action at a distance. This generic view is either postulatory or argumentative.

The postulatory version takes for granted either the need for causal contact (Proclus, Roger Marston, John Buridan [d. 1358], Crysostom Iavelli [d. 1645], M. A. Zimara [1556], Dr. Samuel Clarke [1715], F. X. Meehan [1940]) or the existence and presence of a medium (Peter Gassendi [1658], Georgorius De Rhodes [1671]). The *argumentative* version employs either empirical arguments (Aristotle, Ludovicus De San [1881], S. Reinstadler [1901], K. Dougherty [1952]) or *a priori* arguments (Jacobus de Viterbo [1292], Thomas Hobbes [1655], Christian Wolff [1754], J. F. Herbart [1837], Ernst Haeckel [1899], R. G. Collingwood [1940]) or both types of arguments (Hieronymus Fracastorius [1574], Pseudo-Aegidius [sixteenth century?], H. Haan [1848], Albert Stöckl [1892], S. De Backer [1899], et al.).

4. *Metaphysical* contiguism maintains the necessity of contact and the impossibility of action at a distance with regard not only to all

corporeal but also to all incorporeal agents. According to the way it is expressed, this position on the contiguist issue is either implicit or explicit.

Implicit metaphysical contiguism indicates the impossibility of any action at distance in one of at least three ways: by concluding from the devil's acting everywhere to the devil's omnipresence (Pseudo-Athanasius) or from God's acting everywhere to divine ubiquity (Cyrillus Alexandrinus, Saint Anselm, Hugh of Saint Victor, Peter Lombard (1146–50), Gandulphus Bononiensis, Alan de Lille, William of Auxerre, Richard of Middleton (after 1224), F. Toletus [ca. 1573], Louis Cardinal Billot [before 1931], Arnold J. Benedetto [1963], et al.) or else from God's acting everywhere and the angel's acting in different place to divine omnipresence and angelic presence or angelic movement, respectively (John Damascene, Thomas of Argentina).

Explicit metaphysical contiguism formally expresses the universal necessity of direct or indirect contact and is either *postulatory* or *argumentative*. The former takes for granted the necessity of causal contact with regard to all agents as a probable truth (Durandus de S. Porciano [1317]) or as a certain truth (Jean de Paris [1284], Jacob of Therines [d. 1321], Dionysius Cartusianus, Joannes Capreolus [d. 1444], Franciscus Sylvius [before 1698], F. J. B. Gonet [1798], C. R. Billuart [1847], A. Tanquerei [1894], Valentino Zubizaretta [1937], J. P. Mulles [1961], et al.). The latter, or argumentative, version argues either at the physical level, with empirical arguments only (F. T. M. Zigliara [1876], Joseph Kleutgen [1881], or at the metaphysical level alone (Joannes de Janduno [d. 1328], Cajetan [1525], D. Banez [written ca. 1590], S. Tongiorgi [1867], Michael de Maria [before 1904], B. Boedder [before 1911], Arthur Little [1946], et al.) or else at both levels (D. Soto [1545], F. Suárez [1579], L. Molina [1622], M. Liberatore [before 1875], S. Schiffini [1886], J. Van der Aa [1888], et al.).

Probably the largest and most influential group of schoolmen maintain both *physical* and *metaphysical* contiguism in one of two forms. One is explicit at both levels and then held as a probably true position (A. C. Cotter [1931], Henry Van Läer [1953]) or as a certainly true position (Thomas Aquinas [1252], Ioannes de Neapoli [d. ca. 1315], Franciscus de Sylvester = Ferrariensis [d. 1528], F. Toletus [1573], F. Suárez [1579], A. Boucat Biturico [1736], V. L. Gotti [1753], T. Pesch [1883], J. Hontheim [1893], J. Gredt [1899], S. A. Lortie [before 1921], E. Hugon [before 1922], C. Boyer [1937], et al.). The other form is explicit at the physical level and implicit at the metaphysical level (Giles of Rome [written 1275–90], Emanuel Maignan [1652], et al.).

166

5. The generic counterpart of causal contiguism is *causal anti-contiguism*—the position that action at a distance is possible. It has been advocated at the physical, at the metaphysical, and also at both levels.

Physical anticontiguism considers corporeal action at a distance possible and does so either implicitly or explicitly.

Implicit physical anticontiguism is either empirical or doctrinal. Representatives of the *empirical* version simply speak of alleged or real facts which, *prima facie* at least, seem to be possible only if corporeal action at a distance is possible. Thus authors speaking of the torpedo fish as acting at a distance include Theophrastus, Plinius Secundus, Plutarch, C. Aelianus, C. I. Solinus, Alexander of Aphrodisias, Plotinus, Isidore of Seville, Petrus Pomponatius (1567);[4] those mentioning acts of magic, like casting spells on distant persons, effects of an "evil eye," acts of "sympathy," lunar influences, magnetism, etc., include Pseudo-Aristotle (with regard to the *Problemata* and *De mirabilibus ausculta-tionibus*), Theophrastus, Theocritus, Vergil, Plinius Secundus, C. Aelianus, C. I. Solinus, Plotinus, Ambrosius, Isidore of Seville, Petrus Pomponatius, Francis Bacon (1627), Sylvester Maurus (1658), George de Rhodes (1671), et al.

Representatives of the *doctrinal* version of implicit physical anti-contiguism generally state certain doctrines which may or do imply the possibility of corporeal action at a distance (Hero of Alexandria, Plotinus, Avicenna, Joannes a S. Amando, Giordano Bruno [1591], Daniel Bernoulli [1728], Gowin Knight [1754], C. A. Coulomb [1784], S. D. Poisson [1811], H. C. Oersted [1820], K. Neumann [1832], W. Weber [1846], B. Riemann [1876], et al.).

Explicit physical anticontiguism is advocated in a moderate and an immoderate form. Advocates of the *moderate* position formally teach that corporeal action at a distance is possible; advocates of the immoderate view maintain that corporeal action at a distance is not only possible but also the only possible, i.e., the necessary, form of corporeal action, as corporeal action by contact is impossible. The moderate version is either *empirical* or doctrinal. The former explicitly states the possibility of corporeal action at a distance on the basis of alleged or true instances of such action (Alexander of Aphrodisias, Francis Bacon [1627], John Locke [1700], W. R. Browne [1881]. The latter, or

---

4 For text references on ancient literature concerning the torpedo fish, see F. J. Kovach, "Action at a Distance in Duns Scotus and Modern Science," *Regnum Hominis et Regnum Dei, Acta Quarti Congressus Scotistici Internationalis* (*Studia Scholatico-Scotistica*, 6), tom. I, C. Bérubé, ed. (Romae: Societas Internationalis Scotistica, 1978), pp. 482–83, n. 23.

doctrinal, form of moderate explicit physical anticontiguism formally postulates the possibility of corporeal action at a distance as the principle of certain scientific or philosophic theories and postulates it either as a certain truth (Paul DuBois-Reymond [1890], Sir W. Thomson = Lord Kelvin [1893]) or as a probable truth (Wilhelm Wundt [1889]).

Immoderate physical anticontiguism considers the necessity of corporeal action at a distance and the impossibility of action by contact as being either certainly true (Sextus Empiricus, R. J. Boskovich [1758], and I. Kant [1768], B. Bolzano [1827], F. Zöllner [1878]) or probably true (Hermann Lotze [1879], Charles Renouvier [1897], Joseph Schwertschlager [1922]).

6. Corresponding to physical anticontiguism is *metaphysical anticontiguism* in either an implicit or an explicit form.

Implicit metaphysical anticontiguism maintains by implication that God can act where He is not (Hebrews: "God resides in the temple of Jerusalem"; A. Steuco [before 1603], C. Vorstius and Faustus Socinus: "God resides in heaven"; D. Erasmus: "God is not present in filthy places"; William J. Brossnan [1928]; G. Esser [1952]).

Explicit metaphysical anticontiguism is the position formally holding that divine action at a distance is possible. It is generally found in connection with certain compromise positions,[5] and may also be advocated together with explicit physical anticontiguism (Bartholomaeus Mastrius [before 1698]).

7. Besides the genera of causal contiguism and anticontiguism, there is a combination of these two generic positions, which may be called *compromise* positions. According to the level at which the compromise between contiguism and anticontiguism is made by the various authors, there are one-level and two-level compromises.

One-level compromise is either physical or metaphysical, while two-level compromise is both physical and metaphysical. In addition to this twofold division, the compromise positions may be either implicit or explicit.

Implicit physical one-level compromise views imply either that corporeal action is always by contact, but psychic action at a distance is or may be possible (Plato); or that, generally, physical acts are by contact, but some corporeal, including psychic, acts at a distance are possible (Plutarch); or that, generally, physical action is by contact, but gravity seems to be an action at a distance (Michael Faraday [1846]); or else that physical action at a distance may not be im-

[5] See Sections 7–9 below in this historical analysis.

possible, but causal contiguism is more probably true (Rudolf Clausius [1875], Heinrich Hertz [1892]).

Explicit physical compromises include the explicit doctrines that (1) "material" and "active" causation are by contact, but "transnatural" causation takes place at a distance (Tommaso Campanella [d. 1639]); (2) corporeal action is naturally by contact, but corporeal action at a distance is possible either by divine substitution (John of Saint Thomas [1637]; George de Rhodes [1671]) or by "divine miracle" (G. W. Leibniz [1714], L. Euler [1760–61]) or else by an "immaterial power" (William Gilbert [1600], Johannes Kepler [1618]); (3) corporeal action at a distance is physically impossible, but its "metaphysical" impossibility has not been demonstrated (David Cardinal Mercier); (4) corporeal action at a distance without the immediacy of power is impossible, but without the immediacy of substance possible (Konstatin Gutberlet [1879]); (5) there *is* no corporeal action at a distance, but metaphysically such action is possible (J. de la Vaissière [1912]); (6) action at a distance is impossible or factually an open question if the terms "matter" and "size" are taken in the traditional sense, but such an action is a necessity if the same terms are taken in the dynamist sense (E. von Hartmann [1902]); and (7) action at a distance must be said to be possible or impossible according to the meanings of the term "boundary" or of several related terms (James Tallarico [1962]).

8. *Metaphysical one-level compromises* make some concession to causal anticontiguism at the cost of causal contiguism with regard to divine causation.

One form of such a compromise implies the truth of causal contiguism and explicitly states a conceivable exception to it with regard to God (John de Ripa [1354]). A second version explicitly states that God could act at a distance if He were not immense (Leonard Lessius [1619], D. Palmieri [1875]). A third version asserts that the impossibility of action at a distance in general is well founded but not apodictically proved (Joseph Hellin [1952]).

9. *Metaphysical two-level* compromises treat separately the possibility of action at a distance at the physical and at the metaphysical levels. These compromise views are either partly or completely explicit.

In one *partly explicit* two-level compromise view, God is actually and the soul is necessarily present to the thing acted upon; yet the possibility of some apparent actions at a distance (that of psychic phenomena) is recognized (Saint Augustine, Laurentius Janssens [1900]). In another such view, divine action at a distance is possible, while corporeal contact is necessary, although not by absolute necessity (Gregorius de Valentia [1603]). In a third such view, divine action at a distance is absolutely impossible, whereas corporeal action at a distance is impossible "at least naturally," but not if God intervenes (J. J. Urràburu [1899]). In a fourth such view, God is omnipresent but not because He acts on all creatures (thus implying that divine action at a distance is absolutely speaking possible), whereas corporeal actions are generally by contact, although not always (thus implying that some corporeal action at a distance is possible) (William Ockham).

Completely explicit two-level metaphysical compromises may be partly ambiguous (at least apparently) or completely unambiguous.

One *partly ambiguous* two-level metaphysical compromise position is this: God is necessarily present to what He acts upon, but for the creature action at a distance is possible and nobler than action by contact—leaving open the question whether such action at a distance occurs with or without the use of a medium (Alexander of Hales). Another such view is this: Primarily by virtue of His immensity, God is actually present to the creature on which He acts; corporeal action is generally by contact, yet only contact by power, not contact by substance, is required—possibly meaning corporeal action at a distance with or without a medium (Saint Bonaventure?).

The *completely unambiguous* and completely explicit two-level metaphysical compromises include numerous partly different versions, which can be divided into three groups: compromises which are composite only at the physical level, compromises which are composite only at the metaphysical level, and compromises which are composite at both the physical and the metaphysical level.

Completely unambiguous compromises which are *composite only at the physical level* include the following theories: (1) Spiritual action is by presence; corporeal action at a distance is naturally impossible, but by divine power possible (Thomas of Sutton [before 1316]); and (2) divine action at a distance is possible; most corporeal actions are naturally by contact, but some corporeal actions at a distance are possible (Joannes de Bassolis [d. 1347?]).

Composite at the metaphysical level only are the following completely unambiguous compromises: (1) God could, but does not, act at a distance, and angelic locution is an action at a distance; corporeal action at a distance is possible (Francis of Meyronnes [d. 1328]); (2) physical contiguism is true; but metaphysical contiguism with regard to God is at least questionable—meaning that God does, as a fact,

act by presence, but He could act at a distance (Peter of Navarra [written: 1318–23]); (3) God could, even if He does not, act at a distance; contact is not necessary for any kind of action (Gabriel Biel [1495]); (4) in fact, God is omnipresent, and acts as such, but He may act at a distance; however, corporeal action at a distance is naturally impossible (Alexander Crombie [1829]).

Finally, the following completely unambiguous theories are *composite at both the physical and the metaphysical level*: (1) Divine action at a distance is absolutely possible; yet, in fact, God is necessarily present (except in creation) to the creature acted upon; angelic action at a distance is possible; contact for corporeal action is generally necessary, while some corporeal actions at a distance are possible (at least if another power of the same corporeal agent predisposes the body for an action at a distance) (Duns Scotus). (2) Divine action at a distance is possible, but not a fact, by reason of infinity; corporeal action is generally by contact, but some inanimate and intelligent actions at a distance are possible (Peter of Aquila [before 1334]). (3) Absolutely, divine action at a distance is possible, but actually God is present to the creature on which He acts; on the other hand, corporeal action at a distance is possible, but only within a limited sphere (Peter Fonseca [1597]). (4) Both divine and corporeal actions at a distance are impossible; but even if the latter were possible, the former would still be impossible—meaning that divine action at a distance is absolutely impossible, whereas its corporeal counterpart is only relatively impossible (Richard Tabarella [1962]).

In the light of all these divergent opinions of ancient, medieval, modern, and contemporary authors on the possibility or impossibility of action at a distance, there can be no doubt about the enduring character of the question of action at a distance; and it would be quite surprising if Albert had nothing to say about this issue. However, what specifically Albert said about this topic, and to which of the above-listed categories his position belongs are questions to be answered in the next and main part of this study.

II. *Albert's Position on Action at a Distance*

Two methodological principles will be used in this investigation of the position Albert has taken on the question of action at a distance. One is that two separate sets of texts will be considered successively: one contiguistic; one *prima facie* anticontiguistic. The second principle is that the contiguistic texts will be considered in their chronological order—so far as that order is known to us,[6] whereas the seemingly anticontiguistic texts will be analyzed in a partly logical and a partly chronological order.

1. Contiguist Texts

There are at least sixteen texts in eight works that demand our initial attention in attempting to determine the position Albert has taken on action at a distance, viz., two in the *Summa de Creaturis*; three in the *Commentary on the Sentences*; three in the *Physica*; three in the *De caelo mundo*; one each in the *De Natura Locorum*, the *De Animalibus*, and the *Metaphysica*; and two in the *Summa Theologiae*.

a) Summa de Creaturis Texts (1245–50)

(1) Summa de Creaturis, I, tr. 4, q. 60 a. 2 (Borgnet edition, 34, 634–38)

In this article Albert raises the question of the mode or manner in which angels speak to each other: *Quo sermone loquantur Angeli?*

In the *solutio* of the article Albert compares two angels engaged in talking with two mutually distant sources of physical light which reach each other. In doing so, he lists three conditions necessary for the meeting of the two lights. The first is that there be no medium interfering with the propagation of the two lights. The second is that each light be turned directly toward the other. The third is that there be a proportion between their powers of propagating light and their mutual distance. Albert explains the third condition by remarking that if two lights are too far apart obviously their rays cannot meet, "as a light in England does not meet a light in Italy."[7]

The third of these three conditions is the chronologically first statement relevant to Albert's position on action at a distance. For when Albert declares that there must be proportion between the distance of the two light sources and their powers of emitting rays, he obviously

---

[6] As a concrete guideline I shall use the chronology of the works by Albert as it is to be found on pp. 257b–258a of J. A. Weisheipl, "Albert the Great (Albertus Magnus), St.," *New Catholic Encyclopedia* (San Francisco, Toronto, Sydney: McGraw Hill, 1967), I, 254b–258a.

[7] "Ad hoc enim, quod lumen coniungatur lumine nihil exigitur amplius, quam quod non sit medium impediens coniunctionem illam, et quod sit unum directe ordinatum contra alterum in situ, et quod sit distantia proportionata potentiae immutandi ipsorum luminum: quia si distarent ultra quam possent diffundere radios, tunc non coniungerentur, sicut lumen in Anglia non coniungitur lumini in Italia . . . ." *Summa de Creat.*, I, tr. 4 q. 60 a. 2, solutio (Borgnet, 34, 636a).

means that unless a source of light is powerful enough to emit light rays a certain distance the light source will not be able to affect a distant object, such as another light source. This, in turn, implies that a source of light cannot act as an agent upon a distant object unless its rays traverse the whole distance between the source of light and the distant object; and this latter premise, in turn, evidently rests on the universal principle that no corporeal agent can act at a distance without a medium transfering the power from that agent to the distant body.

The last implication of the theory of physical light clearly shows that, in this early work at least, Albert maintains the position of physical contiguism, i.e., that no material agent can act at a distance without a medium.

(2) *Summa de Creaturis*, II, q. 45 a. 4 (Borgnet, 35, 417b)

The context in which Albert refers to the Aristotelian story about the bloody mirrors is the discussion of the question whether the sense organs are only passive in receiving the images ("species") from the perceived object or else they are also active. The Aristotelian story is used here by Albert as an argument for the *active* character of the perceiving sense organs, and it is stated as follows:

Aristotle seems to prove this [sc. view]: A menstruating woman, upon looking into a new mirror, sends a cloud of blood to that mirror—a fact the reason of which has been given above. Therefore, it seems that the eye acts upon the visible as much as it is acted upon by it.[8]

Albert refers in this passage to Aristotle, *De insomniis*, cap. 2, which reads as follows:

If a woman looks into a highly polished mirror during the menstrual period, the surface of the mirror becomes clouded with a blood-red colour (νεφέλη αἱματόδης) (and if the mirror is a new one the stain is not easy to remove, but if it is an old one there is less difficulty).[9]

The significance of the Aristotelian argument lies in the explanation Albert offers for this story in the *solutio* of the article adopting Aris-

[8] "Hoc enim videtur Aristoteles probare: menstruosa enim inspiciente speculum novum, accidit speculo nubes sanguinea: cuius ratio supra est consignata. Ergo videtur oculus agere in visibile, sicut patitur ab ipso." *Summa de Creat.*, II, q. 45 a. 4, obi. unica (Borgnet, 35, 417b).

[9] Aristotle, *De insomniis*, c. 2, 459b 27–33. Trans. by W. S. Hett in the Loeb edition of Aristotle, *Parva Naturalia* (Cambridge, Mass.: Harvard University Press, 1957), p. 357. Aristotle's original model for this theory is probably Empedocles. (Cf. Aetius, *Placita* A 88.)

totle's own interpretation of the alleged fact at hand. Albert points out that the sense organs are per se passive in receiving the images but *per accidens* they can also be active in so far as "warm vapors" and "subtle spirits" (*spiritus subtiles*) are released from the sense organ and "infect" (*inficiunt*) the neighboring object. More specifically, the distilled menstrual blood "runs out" all veins, including the veins in the eyes, and thus the vapors escaping from the veins of the eyes become infected with that blood; and the vapors, in turn, infect the mirror and other bodies in the vicinity (although the infection on other bodies is not so apparent as on the mirror). This process of infection, adds Albert, is similar to that in which wine or oil become affected by neighboring odors transmitted to the wine and oil through odoriferous vapors.[10]

What this Aristotelian explanation adopted by Albert reveals about Albert's position on the question of action at a distance is that rendering a distant object bloody merely by looking into the object is by no means an actual instance of action at a distance. For, although neither Aristotle nor Albert asserts that the transmission of bloody vapors is empirically observable, both of these great thinkers postulate the collection of menstrual blood in the eyes of the woman, the outpouring of the bloody vapor from the eyes, and the traversing of that vapor from the eyes of the woman to the surface of the mirror; and they postulate all this evidently for one reason, viz., to show that the infection of the mirror's surface by the menstrual blood is not the result of a corporeal action at a distance.[11] Indeed, certain words in the Aristotelian texts,

[10] "Solutio. Concedendo ultimas rationes, dicendum organa sensuum tantum pati in sentiendo et nihil agere nisi per accidens, scilicet in quantum vapores calidi et spiritus subtiles resolvuntur ab organis et inficiunt vicina sibi: in distillatione enim sanguinis menstrui sanguis decurrit ab omnibus venis: et cum venae sanguinis sint in oculo ut spiritus, vapores qui egrediuntur ab oculo, inficiuntur illo sanguine et inficiunt speculum, . . . et alia corpora vicina inficiunt, licet infectio non ita apparet: sicut etiam vinum vel oleum inficitur ex odoribus vicinis prout odorabiles vapores transeunt in vinum vel oleum, etc." *Summa de Creat.*, II, q. 45 a. 4 (Borgnet, 35, 417b–518b).

[11] Cf. the corresponding passage in Aristotle: "The reason for this [*sc.* the collection of blood on the mirror, as described in 459b 27–33] is that, as we have said, the organ of sight not only is acted upon by the air, but also sets up an active process, just as bright objects do; for the organ of sight is itself a bright object possessing colour. Now it is reasonable to suppose (εὐλόγως) that at the menstrual periods the eyes are in the same state as any other part of the body and there is the additional fact that they are naturally full of blood vessels. Thus, when menstruation takes place, as the result of a feverish disorder of the blood, the difference of condition in the eyes, though invisible to us (ἄδηλος), is none the less real (for the nature of the menses and of the semen is the same); and the eyes set up a movement in the air (ὁ δ'ἀὴρ κινεῖται ὑπ' αὐτῶν). This imparts a certain quality to the layer of air extending over the mirror (τὸν ἐπὶ τῶν κατόπτρων ἀέρα συνεχῆ ὄντα

174

like ἄδηλος and εὐλόγως, make it unquestionably clear that Aristotle is postulating the transmission of the bloody vapor without any empirical evidence; and it is equally obvious that the only reason for this postulation is *avoiding* the implication that there is any corporeal action at a distance involved in the story of bloody mirrors. In so far, then, as Albert adopts and approves of this contiguist explanation, evidently he too implies that no corporeal action at a distance is involved in the story in question.

There is also a significant implication in the first and empirical reason Albert uses in the *sed contra* of the same article against the view that the sense organs are *as* active as passive in their functioning. He points to our self-consciousness which reveals that when we see or, generally, perceive things, we are receptive by "taking in" (*intu suscipientes*) information, but we do not send out anything (*nihil extra mittentes*). Then he continues the argument as follows:

> But whatever sends nothing out and, instead, takes only in, does not act. Consequently the organs do not act at all; they are merely acted upon and receive [*sc.* action].[12]

One cannot help noticing in this argumentation the implications of the premise, "Whatever sends nothing out . . . does not act." For in the previous lines action was connected with a spatially distant object, the mirror; and considering the term *emittere*, the premise in question is true especially in case of a distance between corporeal agent and corporeal patient. Therefore, what Albert indicates here is that there cannot be a body that is affected by a distant corporeal agent unless that agent transmits its action through a medium to the recipient. Thus this argument contains an additional implication of Albert's position that direct or indirect contact between a corporeal agent and its recipient is necessary for causation.

ποιόν τινα ποιεῖ καὶ τοιοῦτον οἷον αὐτὸς πάσχει) and assimilates it to itself; and this layer affects the surface of the mirror." (*De insomniis*, c.2, 459b 33–460a 13; tr. cit. p. 357.) ". . . This conclusion is further supported by what occurs with wines and with the preparation of perfumes. For oil which has been prepared quickly takes on the scent of what is near it, and wines are affected the same way; for they acquire the smell not merely of what is put into them, or mixed in small quantities with them, but even of that which is placed or grows near (πλησίον) the vessels which contain them." (*Ibid.* 460a 27–33; tr. cit. p. 359.)

12 "Sed contra hoc obiicitur: quia 1. Supra probatum est, quod videmus et generaliter sentimus intus suscipientes et nihil extra mittentes: sed quidquid nihil extra mittit, sed tantum intus suscipit, nihil agit: ergo organa nihil agunt, sed tantum patiuntur et suscipiuntur." (Albert, *Summa de Creat.*, II, q. 45, a. 4, sed contra, p. 417b.)

b) Commentary on the Sentences Texts (ca. 1245–49)

(1) In. I. Sent. d. 9, I, a. 13, sol. (Borgnet, 25, 293b)

In this article Albert raises again the question whether the angels talk. In the *solutio*, Albert answers this question affirmatively by adding that, in order to determine how they talk, one must presuppose an analogy —that of two mutually distant physical lights.[13] One can immediately see that Albert is about to use the analogy between physical lights and angels, known from the *Summa de Creaturis*. Indeed, in the subsequent sentences he lists the three necessary physical conditions of two mutually distant lights meeting each other and the corresponding immaterial conditions of angelic locution—the former three being identical with the three conditions noted in the *Summa de Creaturis*, although they are listed in a partly different sequence: The first is the directedness of one light toward the other; the second, the absence of all interfering obstacles between the two lights; and the third, a distance between the lights, which is proportionate to the power of diffusion, "because a light that is in Paris does not reach a light which is in Rome."[14]

By reason of the third material condition, Albert implies here the impossibility of physical action at a distance, just as he did, as shown above, in his previous work. For this reason no explanation of this text is needed here.

(2) In. I. Sent. d. 37, A, a. 1 (Borgnet, 26, 228–31)

This article deals with the problem of divine omnipresence. First, Albert lists no fewer than nine arguments for the ubiquity of God, four of which are significant from the point of view of the contiguist question.

The first of these four objections, the very first among the nine, is stated quite simply this way: "There is a world; therefore God is everywhere conserving the world" (*Mundus est: ergo Deus est ubique conservans mundum*). The detailed proof of the conclusion reads as follows: The world, meaning the totality of creatures, is being conserved

---

13 "Concedo, quod Angeli loquuntur et qualiter loquuntur, secundum quod opinor, ad hoc videndum oportet praesupponere quoddam simile. Ponamus duo lumina distantia a se . . . ." *In I. Sent.* d. 9, I, a. 13, sol. (Borgnet, 25, 293b).

14 "(Ad) hoc quod unum illorum luminum penetret aliud non exiguntur nisi tria, quorum unum est quod unum directe ordinetur contra aliud in situ, et quod nullum medium prohibens et claudens unum ab alio sit interpositum, et quod sit distantia proportionata potentiae immutandi, quia lumen Parisiis existens, non immutabit usque ad lumen quod est Romae." (*Ibid.*)

in existence; therefore, there is a being conserving it. That which conserves is related to the conserved, as the cause is to its effect. Since cause and effect are not identical, the being conserving it is not the world or any part of the world. On the other hand, the world is being conserved everywhere. Consequently the conserver of the world is also everywhere. Nothing but God is this conserver. Therefore God is everywhere.[15]

Simple reflection reveals that the premise, "The world is conserved everywhere," leads to the conclusion, "The conserver of the world is everywhere," *only if* it is necessarily and universally true that the agent must be present to its patient either by its substance (essence) or by its power transmitted through a medium to the patient; and if, in God's case, divine power and divine substance (essence) are really identical. Thus it is evident that Albert implicitly postulates these two principles or premises, the first of which is no other than the contiguist principle, i.e., the view of causal contiguism, postulated to apply not only to the finite and material agents but also to the infinite and immaterial agent —God. Consequently, in this first argument for divine omnipresence Albert implies not merely physical contiguism, as in the *Summa de Creaturis* and in the above-discussed article of the *Sentences* commentary, but also *metaphysical* contiguism. For this reason this argument not only is relevant to Albert's position on the contiguist issue but also represents a very important extension of his causal contiguism from the level of corporeal agents (discussed in the previous texts) to the metaphysical level of all agents.

Three additional arguments contain contiguist implications. One of them, the third for divine ubiquity, reads as follows: According to Gregory, all things are made out of nothing, and would (as such) tend toward nothingness if the hands of the Omnipotent did not contain them. All things are made out of nothing. Therefore their container must be present everywhere (*ubique oportet adesse continentem*); and consequently, the container himself is everywhere.[16] Evidently the intermediate conclusion, that the container or conserver of the world must be present everywhere, follows from the stated premise only if the principle of causal contact applies analogously even to God, the omnipotent agent.

Albert's fifth argument for divine omnipresence also has contiguist implications: The self-conserving power represents a power that needs

15 "(Conservatur) autem ubique: ergo conservans mundum quod nec mundus est, nec de mundo, erit ubique: hoc autem non est nisi Deus: ergo Deus erit ubique." *In I. Sent.* d. 37, A. a. 1, arg. 1 (Borgnet, 6, 228a).

16 *Art. cit.*, arg. 3, p. 228b.

no other being, and as such it belongs only to God. On the other hand, since every other being is by another, and thus needs that by which it exists, the power of self-conservation cannot be ascribed to any created being, neither to any place nor to any part of the world. Consequently, every created being is immediately by God. From this it follows that God is everywhere conserving the world (*ergo Deus est ubique mundum conservans*).[17] The implied premise here again is that every agent is necessarily where it acts.

The conclusion of the analysis of these three arguments for divine omnipresence is thus clear: In all three arguments Albert goes beyond the implicit physical contiguism of the previous texts and implies instead metaphysical contiguism—a transition analogous to that which Aristotle apparently makes from *Physics*, VII, 2 (dealing with corporeal changes and agents) to *Physics*, VIII, 10, 267b 6–9 (asserting that the immaterial First Mover must be present at the circumference of the first heaven, which it directly moves eternally). Thus the only possible further development on the part of Albert would be an *explicit* affirmation of the contiguist principle. This affirmation may be expected to come somewhere in the article at hand, for the simple reason that Albert must sooner or later explicitly state the very principle on which, as their metaphysical foundation, four of his arguments of the thesis of the article, the omnipresence of God, rest. This is exactly what Albert does, and does appropriately, in the sixth ubiquity argument, which is the fourth and last argument employing the contiguist principle.

The text at hand, as it stands, in the Borgnet edition, reads as follows:

> Even if it is supposed that God grants the world the power of self-conservation, it is still necessary that the world receive that habitual power from God. But between every receiver and received there is some essential contract (*sed inter omne accipiens et acceptum est contractus quidam essentialis*), unless the receiver is [a receiver] through an influence which is transmitted [to it] by some medium (*nisi sit recipiens per influentiam quae deferatur per medium aliquid*). Therefore it is necessary that everywhere [every] conserved part of the world spiritually touch God, or else that there be some medium (*ergo necesse est, quod ubique pars mundi conservata spiritualiter attingat Deum, vel aliquod medium erit*). Therefore, it is necessary that God be present everywhere.[18]

17 Art. cit., arg. 5, p. 229a.
18 Art. cit., arg. 6, *item*, p. 229b.

Before we consider the contiguist significance of this text, two difficulties need to be discussed here. One is that the Latin text contains the term *contractus* rather than the term *contactus*. The other is that the second sentence reads, in part, "between every receiver and received."

The first difficulty disappears if one realizes that *contractus* in medieval Latin is a variant of *contactus*.[19] In fact, no other known meaning of *contractus* fits into the context, since the listed second alternative speaks of reception through a medium, to which only reception by *contact* is opposed. The second difficulty is more serious. For the context requires an "essential" contact (contact by substance) not between "every receiver and received" (for the corporeal substance and its power cannot be side by side, i.e., in contact; instead, the former must contain the latter as the substrate does its accident) but between every *giver* and receiver. Thus, the phrase in question must be considered some kind of error and should read *inter omne dans et accipiens*.

With these two corrections in mind it is easy to see that, in the text in hand, Albert formally endorses the Aristotelian doctrine of causal contiguism in its metaphysical universality, i.e., that no causal influence is possible without either a contact between agent and patient or an interjacent medium transmitting the influence from the agent to the patient. This, in turn, is to say that in this fourth omnipresence argument Albert finally formulates his position of metaphysical contiguism explicitly and unequivocally and, through it, the absolute impossibility of action at a distance.

As far as the seven objections to divine omnipotence are concerned, only two of them are relevant to the contiguist issue, the fifth and the seventh. To grasp the doctrinal significance of the fifth objection, one must first realize that celestial influence on terrestrial beings is *prima facie* an instance of physical action at a distance. However, while the counterargument at hand serves to show the nonubiquity of God, Albert formulates it so as to leave no doubt that he does not consider celestial influences anticontiguistically. For he remarks, "The celestial powers, which are most efficacious, do not conserve or act immediately [that is, by way of action at a distance] but rather through the mediation of the elements."[20] Albert aims to show through this premise of the counterargument that acting through intermediaries is ignoble and as such cannot apply to God, but repeats his view of the mediacy of celes-

[19] Cf. "*Contractus* 1: Territorium, regio, tractus. 2: pro Contactus. 3: mancus, membris captus. 4: commercium." *Glossarium Mediae et Infimae Latinitatis*, tom. II. Du Cange, Carpenterius, Henschel, & Favre, eds. (Londre: D. Nutt, 1883), p. 537a.
[20] *Art. cit.* in contrarium 5, p. 230a.

tial influence with its contiguist implication in the reply to this argument.[21]

In the seventh counterargument Albert points out that only the "essential," i.e., the material and formal, causes are in the secondary causes in a threefold manner—by essence, by presence, and by power; whereas the efficient cause is present in the secondary causes only by power (*per potentiam tantum*). Consequently, Albert reasons, this truth must apply to God also, as He is only the efficient but neither the material nor the formal cause of the creatures.[22] In his reply Albert explicitly concedes the assertion about the efficient causes by saying, "they do not touch each other, except through the influence which one exerts over the other" (*causae efficientes . . . non tangunt se nisi per influentiam quam habet una super aliam*). Then he adds, the presence of the created efficient causes to their patients by power is a sign of imperfection on their part; and thus, the presence of God to the creatures upon which He acts cannot be limited to presence by power only.[23] The first part of this reply is unquestionably an additional implicit affirmation of Albert's casual contiguism.

Summing up the analysis, in this article Albert both implicitly and explicitly endorses causal contiguism as valid at the physical as well as the metaphysical level.

(3) *In I. Sent.* d. 37, L, a. 22 (Borgnet, 26, 257–62)

This article deals with angelic locomotion. Albert lines up first no fewer than nine arguments against the fact or the possibility of angelic locomotion. The last of these objections is of indirect importance to us, inasmuch as Albert states in it that the natural place of the angels is the highest, shining, supraempirical heaven (*caelum empyreum*).[24] The relevance of this doctrine to the contiguist question is shown in the subsequent parts of the article.

Next, three arguments of angelic locomotion are listed, the third of which is not numbered in the Borgnet edition. The first of the three employs a quotation from Saint John Damascene: The angel moves readily and speedily from one place to another, his speed being com-

[21] "Ad aliud dicendum, quod virtutes coelestes movent secundum diversitatem sui situs ad diversa: et ideo habent motus declinationum, ascensionum, et descensionum, et occultationum et praeventionum, et oppositionum, et similia: et ideo oportuit ipsas elongari a materia generabilium et corruptibilium, ut totam sic diversimode posset movere." (*Art. cit.* in contarium 5um, p. 231a.)

[22] *Art. cit.*, in contrarium 7um, p. 230b.

[23] *Art. cit.*, ad 7, p. 231ab.

[24] *In I. Sent.* d. 37, L, a. 22, obi. 2a (Borgnet, 26, 258b). Cf. *Summa Theol.* II, tr. 3 q. 12 m. 1 (Borgnet, 32, 149–51).

mensurate to his nature; and he is said to operate in diverse places.[25] Damascene here connects angelic movement with angelic operation obviously on contiguist grounds, implying that the angel must move from one place to another because he can act only where he is. This argument is significant because, evidently, Albert agrees with Damascene on this implicitly contiguist argument.

Albert's agreement with Damascene on the contiguist implication at hand is obvious from the second argument, which is Albert's own:

No thing that lacks power which is multiplicable in any way in a medium, and that does not exist by essence everywhere can operate, except where it is itself (*Nihil . . . operari potest nisi ubi ipsum est*). The angel is such a substance. Therefore he does not operate, except where he is (*ergo non operatur nisi ubi ipse est*).[26]

This argument is of great importance for three reasons. One is that it explicitly predicates of all beings except God the need for causal contact. The second reason is that this text, unlike the sixth argument in the previously analyzed article of the same work, is free from confusing and misleading terms and errors. The third reason is that this text explicitly extends the validity of the contiguist principle to angelic operation upon material beings.

The applicability of the need for causal contact to angelic operation is reaffirmed in the third and unnumbered argument:

The angel has the power of intellectual substance; the medium located between heaven and earth is unable to come to share in this power, because it [*sc.* this medium] is an inanimate body. From this [premise] one can proceed [arguing] as follows: The angel does not operate, except where he is (*Angelus non operatur nisi ubi est*); but he operates in diverse places successively rather than simultaneously, and that means [*sc.* for the angel] moving through space or local motion as a consequent. Therefore, the angel has locomotion.[27]

By virtue of the major premise ("Nothing . . . can operate, except where it is itself"), the premise "the angel does not operate, except where he is" explicitly extends the contiguist principle to spiritual agents acting upon bodies. With this statement Albert completes the expression of the metaphysical universality of causal contiguism, for he

[25] Damascenus, *De fide orthodoxa*, II, 3 (Migne, *Patrologia Graeca* [henceforth: *PG*] 94, 869a–c).

[26] Albert, *art. cit.*, sed contra 2a, p. 259a.

[27] *In I. Sent.* d. 37, L, a. 22, item, p. 259a.

applies here the principle of contact to finite spiritual agents, after he applied it to corporeal agents as well as to the infinite spiritual agent.

c) *Physica* Texts (ca. 1245–48)

(1) *Physica*, III, tr. 1 c. 7 (Borgnet, 3, 196b–97b)

The topic of this chapter is the second or quasi-material definition of change (*motus*). In discussing this issue, Albert writes two statements relevant to our interest.

The first contiguist remark concerns the fact that some changes terminate in rest: "[The agent] does not lead [the thing moved] to rest, except by contact" (*nisi per contactum*). This is a clear but non-universal expression of physical contiguism.

The second statement, in contrast to the first, is evidently universal: "Motion (change) does not occur in the moved, except by the act of the mover; and by reason of physical contact it is necessary that the mover be together [with the moved] or be moved [by the moved] when it causes motion" (*per rationem tactus physici oportet quod movens simul sit vel moveatur cum movet*).

(2) *Physica*, VII, tr. 1 c. 3 (Borgnet, 3, 489–92b)

(*a*) Albert commences this chapter by observing that the demonstration presented in the previous chapter (that there is no infinite regress in the movers and the things moved) postulated that all movers and moved things become one. However, he goes on, this postulate cannot be true, unless the mover and the moved are directly present (*nisi immediata sint motor et id quod movetur*) in such a way that, between them, there is neither a plenum nor a vacuum (*inter ea nec plenum sit, nec vacuum*). For this reason, Albert declares, it is necessary that it be demonstrated that, between the mover and that which is moved by it, there is no medium in case of any kind of change (*oportet nos hic determinare, quod inter motorem et id quod movetur ab ipso, nihil sit medium secundum omnem motum in genere*).

The demonstration at hand begins with the categorical assertion that "evidently, there is no medium between the generator and the directly generated (*manifestum est, quod inter generans et generatum et* [*sic!*] *proximum nihil est medium*), because the formative power, which is the proximate generator, is in the semen." For this reason (writes Albert), the contiguist thesis needs to be demonstrated only in regard to those genera of change in which the contact between the agent and the patient is not so obvious (*occultum*). This declaration is followed by a detailed argumentation for causal contiguism with regard to the four known empirical genera of locomotion (*pulsio, tractio, vectio,* and *vertigo*), more or less paraphrasing Aristotle's *Physics,* VII, 2, in the present chapter; and with regard to alteration and augmentation (i.e., qualitative and quantitative changes) in the subsequent fourth chapter.

The argumentation in these two chapters is patently inductive—empirical, like Aristotle's own in the *Physics,* so as to render Albert's physical contiguism inductively demonstrative (rather than postulatory).

(*b*) In addition to the over-all argumentation, two specific topics within the lengthy argumentation of Chapter Three deserve special mention.

One of these topics is contained in the demonstration for the particular thesis that there is no medium between the mover and the spatially moved in case of throwing (*expulsio*). Albert argues for the contact between the thrower's hand and the stone thrown (*et in hoc motu* [*sc. lapidis a manu proiecti*] *etiam movens immediate coniungitur ei, quod movetur*) as follows: The air in which the thrown stone moves is the natural place of the stone, and the power of throwing is in it [*sc.* the air] (*virtus proiieciens est in ipso*). Evidently this Albertine account of the locomotion of the thrown stone is Aristotle's theory of missiles, which, like the Platonic theory of *periosis,* is contiguistic.[28]

The second specific topic of interest is brought up by Albert in connection with the discussion of traction (*tractio*):

Not all things which are pulled in some manner are said to be moved by the movement of traction. Instead, things are sometimes moved more by the natural movement of that which is drawn (*plus motu naturali eius quod trahitur*).

This principle holds true, Albert continues, for the food that reaches the various parts of the body and for the falling bodies as well as for the magnet. With regard to the last instance Albert makes the following statement at this point:

The magnet also moves in this fashion toward the iron, because of the similarity of form the magnet has to iron (*magnes movetur ad ferrum propter similitudinem formae quam habet cum ferro*). And for this reason the iron is its [natural] place. This is also the reason why, when the power of this similarity is hindered [by something], the iron does not move toward the magnet, nor does the magnet toward the iron. . . . And this movement, too, is such that the mover is conjoined with the mobile being that it moves (*et*

28 Aristotle, *De caelo,* III, 2, 301b 26–28. Cf. Aristotle, *Phys.* IV, 7, 214a 29–31; VIII, 10, 266b 27–267a 18; *De insomniis,* 2,459a 28–b 1. Cf. Plato, *Tim.* 58e, 80bc.

iste motus est etiam sic, quod movens coniunctum est suo mobili quod movetur ab ipso). For the power of the stone is diffused in the medium to the iron, and vice versa; and this power that touches [the other stone] is the direct mover (*virtus lapidis diffunditur in medio usque ad ferrum, et e converso: et haec virtus tangens est movens immediatum*).

Albert winds up this theory of attraction by adding that similarity is the case with the attraction of *kakabre* and a number of precious stones.[29] The contiguistic character of Albert's theory of magnetism (and electric atraction), like his theory of missiles, is, thus, indisputable.

(3) *Physica*, VIII, tr. 4 c. 6 (Borgnet, 3, 631b).

The Aristotelian topic of this chapter is the place of the First Mover with regard to heaven. Aristotle's line of reasoning is the following: Since the First Mover originally causes the circular motion of heaven, it must be at some point or area of heaven—a doctrine implying that even the divine agent must be where He acts. There are only two such possible places: the center and the circumference of the universe, since "these are the first principles from which a sphere is derived. But the things nearest the movement are those whose motion is quickest and in this case it is the motion of the circumference [that is, the first heaven or sphere] that is the quickest: therefore the movement occupies the circumference.[30]

Basically following Aristotle's argument, Albert reasons in this chapter as follows: If the First Mover were a power situated in the body and the (first) act of the body, it would undoubtedly be in the very center of the body, around which the motion goes on; for the First Mover is immobile. However, since it is a separate power and a substance uninfused into a body, the First Mover must be where its effect, which is motion, is greater (*oportet ipsum esse ubi major est effectus eius, qui est motus*). Therefore it is located at the circumference, inasmuch as it influences the motion of the circumference of the universe, so that this influence is equal in every part of the circumference. This holds true above all for the First Mover and the first moved (*sc.* the first heaven), because the motion of the first heaven is both the fastest and the one in which all inferior celestial motions participate.

[29] Albert, *Phys.* VII, tr. 1 c. 3 (Borgnet, 3, 491b).
[30] Aristotle, *Phys.* VII, 10, 267b 6–8. R. P. Hardie and R. K. Gaye, trs., in *The Basic Works of Aristotle*, R. McKeon, ed. (New York: Random House, 1941), p. 393.

It is obvious that the premise, The First Mover must be where the motion it causes is greatest, is true only if it is true that the agent must be where it acts and that the closer a place is to where the agent moves, the greater is there the effect of the agent. But the former of these two *implied* premises is the contiguist principle; and the latter implied premise is a consequent of the contiguist principle, viz., that the effect of every agent is continuously spreading through some medium to the last body affected by the operation of the agent. Thus, as he does in some previously analyzed texts, Albert here applies the implied principle of contact to the divine Agent, and in doing so reveals again, and most clearly, his metaphysical contiguism.

d) *De Caelo et Mundo* Texts (c. 1248–60)

(1) *De caelo et mundo*, I, tr. 3 c. 2 (Geyer, 5, pars 1, pp. 57–58)

In this chapter Albert discusses a specific cosmological view, which he finds unacceptable; and in stating that view, he uses (as did Averroes before him)[31] the magnet as an analogy. The magnet, Albert observes, attracts the iron which is nearby (*attrahit ferrum sibi propinquum*), but does not attract a remote piece of iron, because "the power of the attracting stone does not reach it [*sc.* that piece of iron]" (*ad illud non pervenit virtus lapidis attrahentis*).[32]

In this text Albert terms the theory of the adversaries unreasonable (*extra normam rationis*); however, since he does not object to the analogy of magnetic attraction, the view expressed on magnetic attraction may be considered as one conforming to Albert's own idea of magnetism. This much being granted, we have here a specific and analogous application of one of the three conditions repeatedly expressed by Albert before, viz., that, while the effect of the corporeal agent travels through a medium to its distant recipient, the distance to be traversed is limited by the power of the corporeal agent. Both of these principles, as shown in connection with the spread of physical light, reveal Albert's adherence to the principle of causal contact.

(2) *De Caelo et Mundo*, II, tr. 3 c. 2 (Geyer 5, pars 1, pp. 144–46a)

The topic of this chapter is the cause of heat in the region of air. Albert commences the discussion by adopting the Aristotelian doctrine[33] that

[31] ". . . sicut motus ferri ad magnetem." Averroes, *In I. De caelo*, comm. 81 (fol. 54M).

[32] Albert, *De caelo et mundo*, I, tr. 3 c. 2 (Geyer, tom. 5, parts 1, pp. 57b–58a).

[33] Aristotle, *Meteor.* I, 4, 341b 36–342a 3. Cf. Averroes, *In II. De caelo*, comm. 42 (fol. 125).

the heat in the air undoubtedly (*absque dubio*) comes "from the stars, light, and locomotion."[34] Albert explains the role of locomotion in the causation of celestial heat, as Aristotle did originally, by friction, which, as observation shows, can warm up and even ignite solid bodies. Thus, he goes on, it is understandable that the circular motion of the very large celestial bodies should induce the form of fire in the neighboring material elements, and warm up the air neighboring those material elements. Thus the heat in the air is originally caused by the stars, even though the stars do not move in the air; instead, only the effect of their locomotion extends or reaches down to the region of air (*motus earum effectum suum extendit ad aerem*).[35] Needless to say, this theory is patently contiguistic, and conforms to the thinking of Aristotle as well as to the contiguism Albert displays in the texts heretofore considered.

Next, having attempted to explain in what sense the stars may be said to be ignited despite their being of the immutable fifth element rather than of the changeable terrestrial elements, Albert takes up an objection to his Aristotelian theory—an objection originally raised by Alexander of Aphrodisias. The basis of Alexander's objection is Aristotle's almost casual remark in the *De caelo*[36] that "the heat and light which they emit are engendered as the air is chafed by their [*sc.* the stars'] movement (ὑπὸ τῆς ἐκείνων φορᾶς)."[37] Alexander argues against this remark (relates Albert) on the basis of the principle of contiguism pronounced by Aristotle himself in the *De Generatione Animalium*:[38] Everything that acts touches (*omne quod agit, tangit*), that is, has an extreme which is together with the extreme of the body touched (*ultimum suum habet simul cum ultimo tacti*). Since then that which changes another by heat or motion acts and, consequently, touches, the stars must touch the air. However, this is not the case. For, again according to Aristotle, between the celestial sphere and the air there is the region of fire.[39] Alexander replies to his own objections (Albert continues reporting) that it is not always true that the thing which acts touches in such a way that its extreme and the extreme of the thing acted upon are together (*non semper est verum, quod omne*

[34] Albert, *De caelo et mundo*, II, tr. 3 c. 2 (Geyer, tom. 5, pars 1, p. 144, 36–40). Cf. *ibid.*, cap. 1, p. 143, 27–28.

[35] *Ibid.*, p. 144b 64.

[36] Aristotle, *De caelo*, II, 7, 289a 20–22.

[37] English translation from the Loeb edition, p. 179.

[38] Aristotle, *De gen. an.* II, i, 734a 3–4. Cf. Albert, *De animalibus*, XVI, tr. 1 c. 2 (Borgnet, 12, 136b), to be discussed below.

[39] Aristotle, *De caelo*, I, 2, 269b 14–17; *Meteor.* I, 3, 339b 16–19; 341a 3–4.

quod agit tangit ita, quod ultimum eius sit cum ultimo eius in quod agit). In support of this view (Albert concludes his report) Alexander brings up the fish called the stupifier (*stupefactor*). For when this fish is in a net, it does not touch the hand of the fisherman, nor is it itself in stupor; and yet it numbs the hand of the fisherman (*quando ille est in reti, non quidem tangit manum piscatoris nec etiam ipse est stupidus et tamen stupefacit manum piscatoris*).[40]

In the next part of this historical account Albert relates that the above solution of Alexander, apparently amounting to the admission of the factuality and possibility of some corporeal action at a distance, did not please (*non placet*) either Themistius or Averroes. They maintained that the benumbing fish *does* act on the net (*piscis stupefactor agit in rete*), although it does not numb the net, as the net has no senses; instead, the fish causes the net to receive some influence (*agit in rete actionem passionis alicuius*) which, in turn, numbs the hand of the fisherman (*quae stupefacit manum piscatoris*), and would numb also the net if the net had any senses.[41] Correspondingly, both Themistius and Averroes rejected the application of Alexander's theory of the torpedo fish to the stars, by their denying that the stars cause heat in the distant air. Instead, they reasoned, it is not necessary that the agent always touch the recipient directly, as it suffices for it to do so through a medium (*non oportet, quod immediate semper tangat id quod agit, sed sufficit, quod per medium tangat*).[42] Accordingly, the movement of the stars affects both the fire and the air, although differently. For the same action affects the one directly affected differently from the one affected through a medium.

Having outlined the theory of Alexander and that of Themistius and Averroes, as he understands them, Albert declares that he approves, with some qualification, of Alexander's (*Nos autem Alexandri solutionem secundum aliquid approbamus*) rather than of Themistius's and Averroes's solution of the question of stellar heat. In his opinion, Albert explains, the stars do possess the properties of the terrestrial elements (which are capable of alteration), although the stars are made of matter incapable of alteration; but the stars possess those qualities not in the sense that they are modified by them but rather in the sense

[40] Alexander, *Meteor.* A 3, p. 18, 21–24. However, Albert relates all this about Alexander as well as the subsequent part of the controversy involving Themistius and Averroes, from Averroes, *In II. De caelo*, comm. 42 (fol. 125A–127C). For the numbing effect of the torpedo fish, described as being caused by direct contact, see also Albert, *De animalibus*, VIII, tr. 3, cap. un. (Borgnet, 11, 455b).

[41] Albert, *De caelo*, II, tr. 3 c.2, *ed. cit.*, p. 145, 45–58.

[42] *Ibid.*, p. 145, 76–78.

that the stars cause those qualities in the matter that is susceptible of a contrariety of qualities. This is to say, the stars actually impart heat to the inferior bodies even though the stars themselves are not formally hot.[43] What Albert seems to mean by this theory is that the stars act on the lower bodies in a manner somewhat similar to that of the torpedo fish and the net or rod touching that fish; for while neither the torpedo fish nor the net or rod is numbed, through the unnumbed net or rod the fish can cause numbness in the hand which touches the net or rod.[44]

In this complex discussion two things are relevant to our topic. One is that Albert's solution of the problem of stellar heat is contiguistic, but contiguistic in a refined, sophisticated fashion, partly utilizing and partly going beyond Alexander's view. Causation, Albert holds, always necessitates and involves contact, but the causal contact may be either direct or indirect—the latter alternative meaning contact through a medium. On the other hand, the medium, if it is interjacent rather than an effluvium of the agent, transmits the power of the agent to the distant patient by possessing that power formally or virtually. Thus, the stars and the region of fire posses stellar heat virtually; and a net or a rod, one part of which touches a torpedo fish while another part touches a hand, contains the power of numbing *virtually*. With this theory Albert rejects what he considers to be the view of Themistius and Averroes, viz., that the interjacent medium is affected by the agent the same way as the patient is—formally. At the same time, he partly changes and improves on the theory of Alexander, who did not make the distinction between formal and virtual possession of the power transmitted by the agent.

In light of these details, this *De caelo* text offers an insight into some details of Albert's theory of physical contiguism, which details cannot be found in any text heretofore analyzed.

[43] *Ibid.*, p. 145, 94–146, 7.

[44] Incidentally, Albert mentions this fish in other works too. The brief 125th article of *De animalibus*, XXIV, entitled *"De torpedine"* (the name most commonly used in ancient, mediaeval, and even Renaissance and early modern literature for this kind of fish), is confined in a scientifically professional fashion to a description of the numbing power of the torpedo, a description which closely resembles that of Aristotle's in *De historia animalium*, IX, 37, 620b 19–29, and does not make clear whether the numbing occurs at a distance: "Torpedo piscis est," writes Albert, "quem stupifactorem in praehibitis libris nominavimus. Hic in limo occultatus pisces *accedentes* corripit et devorat, et tangentem quantumcumque celeriter retrahit, stupefacit, ita quod unus de sociis nostris extremitate digiti tantum pungens, tetigit eum, et infra dimidium annum loturis calidis et unguentis vix a brachio sensum refecit." *De animal.* XXIV, tr. un. n. 125 (Borgnet, 12, p. 536b). Cf. also Albert, *De animal.* VIII, tr. 3 cap. un. (Borgnet, 11, 455b), as well as Aristotle, *De historia animalium*, IX, 37, 620b 19–29.

(3) *De Caelo et Mundo*, II, tr. 3 c. 3 (Geyer, 5, pars 1, pp. 146–48)

In this chapter Albert discusses the question whether all stars or only some stars cause stellar heat on earth. Following Avicenna,[45] Albert denies the former alternative on the empirical grounds that, unlike the sun, the entire heaven does not shine (*non micat*) and that which does not shine does not emit light and, thus, cannot cause heat. Instead, Albert continues, it is the sun that emits light and is the sole cause of celestial heat reaching the earth. He lists five reasons for this unique solar role: the size and density of the sun; the intensity of its light; the purity of solar matter, which allows light to emanate more easily from it, and the *natural* role of solar light to move the celestial fire (*movere ignem*). It is because of this natural role of solar light that some philosophers, like Avicenna,[46] maintained that the light ray, as such (*radius solis in eo quod radius*), does not produce heat; instead, heat is "the property of fire, which is moved by the solar rays as the iron is by magnet" (*calor est a properietate ignis, qui movetur a radiis eius sicut ferrum a magnete*), and this heat is brought down to earth by rays of the sun (*adducitur cum radiis eius*).[47]

It is this analogy which Albert draws between solar light rays carrying the heat and the magnet attracting iron that interests us here. The first thing that is obvious about this alleged analogy is that it is not made clear by Albert. For what Albert seems to hold, under Arabic influence, about sun rays is that they carry the heat along from the upper region of fire down to earth whereas, according to observation, the magnet seems to pull to itself the distant iron. This is to say, the motion of heat caused by solar rays is an instance of pushing on the part of the light rays, and accidental motion on the part of the heat (this motion being itself an instance of pushing in regard to the sun);[48] whereas the action exerted upon the iron by the magnet is an apparent instance of pulling. Where, then, does the similarity Albert has in mind lie?

One may suggest that Albert had in mind sorts of magnetic rays corresponding to the light rays of the sun, with both kinds of rays *somehow* causing the locomotion of something else—the heat and the iron, respectively. This interpretation (confirmed by *Phys.* VII, tr. 1 c. 3) means that, despite the lack of any empirical evidence, Albert postulates a magnetic medium of the dynamic or effluent type which,

[45] Avicenna, *De caelo et mundo*, c. 14 (fol. 41v–42r).

[46] Avicenna, *op. cit.*, c. 16 (fol. 42rv).

[47] Albert, *De caelo et mundo*, II, tr. 3 c. 3 (Geyer, V, 1, p. 147a 45–48).

[48] Aristotle, *Phys.* VII, 2, 243b 15–244a 2.

upon reaching the distant iron, so affects that iron that it will begin to move *toward* the magnet by way on an inclination. Now, evidently, the only conceivable reason why Albert, the great and empirically minded philosopher of science, should postulate a medium to account for a natural phenomenon without any empirical evidence is that he refused to see in magnetic attraction an instance of action at a distance; and thus he preferred to work out a *contiguist* model for magnetic attraction. Granting all this, Albert is obviously as dogmatic about physical contiguism in regard to magnetism as he is, as seen, about solar heat and the numbing action of the torpedo fish.

e) *De Natura Locorum*, tr. 1 c. 5 (Borgnet, 9, 536–37) (before 1259)

(1) In this chapter Albert discusses the common properties of the places of the bodies composed of the four terrestrial elements. During the discussion he expresses four doctrines. One is that there is no point in the places to be found in the water, the air, and the earth which does not have special properties of its own, i.e., special powers which inform the things located in those places. The second is that all these special properties or powers stem from the powers of the stars (*a virtute stellarum*). The third doctrine is that the stars determine the special properties of each and every place and give special powers to every body located in those places—mostly by means of the rays emitted by the lights of the stars (*compertum est coelum diffundere virtutes formativas in omne quod est: maxime autem diffundit eas per radios emissos a luminibus stellarum*).[49] Finally, the fourth doctrine is that the various configurations and angles of the light rays cause different powers in the terrestrial things so that as the configurations and angles of the light rays change with the circular motion of heaven, the light rays inform the bodies in the respective places with more or less different properties. That is why, remarks Albert, no two generated beings on earth are completely similar to each other, although generally there is a similarity of properties in things located in neighboring places.[50]

The third of these views is quite significant for our purpose here. That doctrine shows that the stellar influence on earthly beings (by the unqualified assertion of which Albert gives strong support to contemporary believers in astrology) may perhaps *seem* to be, although *it is not*, an instance of action at a distance in the material universe. This view receives added relevance to our subject by reason of the fact that Albert applies it to the empirical fact of magnetism.

49 Albert, *De nat. loc.* tr. 1 c. 5 (Borgnet, 9, 537a).
50 *Ibid.*, p. 537a–b.

2) Albert introduces this topic of magnetism as the logical continuation of the fourth doctrine. The similarity and dissimilarity of places and of the formative powers in the various places can well be observed in a certain kind of magnet which, at one angle, turns away from the iron and, at another, attracts it (*in quodam magnetis genere, qui uno angulo fugit ferrum, et in alio attrahit ipsum*). For since one angle does not differ from another by a large portion of place, reasons Albert, it is only natural that the very near places should have diverse and contrary powers. The reason for this is obvious: the contrariety of powers at hand cannot be due to matter, for matter is not the cause of power and form; thus it must be due to the place informed by the given configuration of the light rays of the stars (*oportet igitur quod sit ex loco informato a figuratione radiorum stellarum*).[51]

The doctrinal significance of this passage lies in the fact that Albert attributes the polarity of magnetic forces to the distant stars, since they determine the specific qualities or powers of the magnet with regard to the smallest places by their own formative powers transmitted to the magnet through the stellar light rays.

Adding this view to the doctrine expressed in the above-considered third *De caelo* text,[52] we come to recognize the *twofold* contiguist character of Albert's theory of magnetism. On the one hand, the magnet's attractive and repulsive powers affecting the iron stem from the distant stars, which *transmit* these powers to the magnet through their light rays used as a medium. On the other hand, the attraction (as well as, presumably, the repulsion) the magnet exerts upon the distant iron is itself conceived contiguistically in terms of some emanating medium, so that neither the possession nor the exercise of magnetic power involves any action at a distance.

f) De Animalibus, XVI, tr. 1 c. 2 (Borgnet 12, 136–39) (1258–62)

In this chapter Albert raises the question concerning the efficient and formative cause of the members of the animal body and, more specifically, the question whether this cause is intrinsic to those members of the animal body or else inheres as an intrinsic principle in the sperm itself.

In the first part of the treatment of this issue Albert rejects the idea that there is a soul as an intrinsic formative principle in the sperm, because, he points out, in that case the sperm itself would be an animal with a body and a soul on its own, whereas no animal consists of parts completely similar to each other. On the other hand, the view of

---

[51] *Ibid.*, p. 537b.
[52] Albert, *De caelo et mundo*, II, tr. 3 c. 3 (Geyer, 5, pars 1, p. 147a 45–48).

medically ignorant persons that a principle extrinsic to the sperm is the extrinsic agent of the sperm as well as of some or all the members of the animal body is also completely false and impossible. Aristotle rejected these ideas, Albert points out, on the grounds that a motive principle extrinsic to the sperm could never begin to move the sperm without touching it (*illud extrinsecum spermati non inciperet unquam movere sperma, nisi tangeret ipsum*), because no change of the moved follows the mover unless the mover touches it [*sc.* the moved] (*non sequitur aliquid movens alteratio moti, nisi tangat ipsum*).[53]

Here Albert evidently approves of Aristotle's rejection of the view at hand precisely on ground of the contiguist principle explicitly stated. Thus Albert reveals his physical contiguism in this passage too by using Aristotle as his spokesman.

Since Albert knows that the difficulty with the necessity of an extrinsic agent touching the sperm to cause natural changes in it is not immediately clear, he next commences a detailed explanation.

Some medical experts maintain that the embryo, or the "conceived semen," is first moved to nutrition, growth, and organization by the soul of the mother; but later on a soul is infused into the conceived semen, and then the embryo is moved by the acts of its own, proper soul. But this view is completely absurd (*omnino absurdum*) according to all Peripatetic experts, the most cogent reason for this rejection being the above-stated words of Aristotle. For since there is no medium between the mover and the moved, it is necessary that that which naturally moves should naturally be united (with that which it moves) (*Cum enim inter movens et motum non sit medium, oportet id quod naturaliter movet, naturaliter esse coniunctum*), as nature is united with that of which it is the power and form, because every natural motion comes from an intrinsic and essential principle. Thus, if the soul of the mother moved the embryo, that soul should be both an *extrinsic* and an *essential* principle, which the mother's soul is not.[54] On the basis of this reasoning Albert ultimately concludes that "evidently" (*manifestum est*) the motive power which changes and forms the sperm is in the embryo itself.

The discussion shows that the main argument against the position on which Albert disagrees rests on the Aristotelian principle of causal contiguism and the corresponding theory of the formative principle's being intrinsic to that in which it causes natural changes. Thus, this text contains an additional explicit expression of Albert's contiguist thinking.

[53] Albert, *De animal.* XVI, tr. 1 c. 2 (Borgnet, 12, 136b).
[54] *Ibid.*, pp. 136b–137a.

g) *Metaphysics*, IX, tr. 2 c. 1 (Geyer, 16, pars 2, pp. 414–15) (1261–66)

In this chapter Albert takes up the Megarian error that there is absolutely no potency preceding an act, so that one can operate only when it does operate, and cannot operate when it does not. The Megarians held this view, Albert states, because they were convinced that, in causation, the active potency is the cause of the effect; and that the cause and the caused are simultaneous (*causa et causatum sint simul*). For from this truth it follows, in their opinion, that there is no active potency before its work.

To this allegedly Megarian argument Albert adds another one: If it were true that an active power exists before its effect, then that power would be in potency, since nothing potential is actualized except by the motion of another mover. But if so, the act of another agent would be necessary for the actualization of the active power in question, and that would lead to innumerable absurdities. A third Megarian argument mentioned by Albert reads as follows: That which is always the same, does the same thing either always or never. But the form of a thing from which the active power originates is the nature of the thing and, as such, is always the same. Therefore the thing does something either always or never and, in either case, there is no active power in the thing before the things acts."[55]

Albert commences his reply by pointing out that some potencies are active, others passive and that among the former some are and some are not rational. Next he begins to argue in a way quite relevant to our topic:

> And that [active power] which is without reason does not act, except when it approaches a passive power (*non agit, nisi quando appropinquat passivo*) upon which it acts; and when it does not approach it, it is in [the state of] a habit; and as such, it is before the act.[56]

With this statement, which patently implies the need of causal contact for action, Albert resolved the first and second Megarian objectives, whereas with the immediately following remarks he refutes the third objection:

> And when such a potency becomes actually active, it does not change from one form to another; instead it acts in the same form in which

[55] Albert, *Met.* IX, tr. 2 c. 1 (Geyer, 16, pars 2, p. 414, 23–55). For the "*simul sunt*" doctrine of the agent and patient, cf. Albert, *op. cit.* V, tr. 1 c. 2 (Geyer, 5, pars 1, p. 212, 55).

[56] *Ibid.*, p. 415, 29–34.

it is. And the change takes place not in it as it was not near it and touching it previously (*cum ante non fuerit propinquum et tangens*).[57]

In this reply Albert obviously indicates that the necessary condition of an active power's beginning to act is that the agent and the patient approach and touch each other; and he does so in a matter-of-fact tone, as if stating a self-evident and well-known truth.

Still concerned with the third Megarian argument, Albert continues reasoning this way:

> From this it is also evident that nature does not cease its proper operation; instead, it does not operate, that is, by accident, when it is not near a patient (*non operatur . . . quia non est propinquum patienti*); and nothing operates at all when there is nothing to receive the operation.[58]

This is the third text in the chapter in which Albert displays his contiguistic thinking, even though the topic under discussion is quite different from the contiguist question.

h) *Summa Theologiae* Texts (after 1270)

(1) *Summa Theologiae*, I, tr. 18 q. 70 m. 1 (Borgnet, 31, 727–30)

With this *membrum* we come to the second principal text of Albert's causal contiguism—a text which parallels the article in the *Commentary on the Sentences* dealing with the issue of divine omnipotence. The discussion begins with sixteen[59] arguments for Albert's thesis, seven of which are arguments of authority, and nine *ex ratione*.

The first relevant argument of reason, the fourth in the cited edition, is a mere paraphrase of the first such argument in the corresponding article of the *Sentences* Commentary:[60]

> The world is, and is conserved in existence, and is everywhere conserved in existence; therefore that which conserves the world in existence is [itself] everywhere.[61]

[57] *Ibid.*, p. 415, 36–39.
[58] *Ibid.*, p. 415, 41–45.
[59] The last argument in the Borgnet edition is numbered as the fifteenth. However, this number is incorrect; two separate arguments on pp. 727b and 728a are numbered identically as the fifth.
[60] *In I. Sent.* d. 37, A, a. 1 arg. 1 (Borgnet, 26, 228a).
[61] "Mundus . . . ubique conservatur in esse: ergo conservans mundum in esse est ubique." *Summa Theol.* I, tr. 18 q. 70 m. 1 arg. 4, adhuc (Borgnet, 31, 727b).

The implication of this abbreviated syllogism is as obviously contiguistic as the implication of the explanation offered for this argument: Since it is God who, as a cause, conserves the world everywhere, "it follows that the cause of the conservation of the world is [also] everywhere."

Somewhat similar to this argument is the numerically next one—the first to be numbered as the fifth in the Borgnet edition:

> God conserves the creature in existence either by Himself or through a medium (*per se aut per medium*). If by Himself, I have the proposed thesis. For since He conserves everywhere, it follows that He is everywhere (*cum ubique conservat, sequitur quod ubique est*). If [God conserves the creatures in existence] through a medium, that medium itself needs conservation by another being, as that medium, by supposition, is not God but a created being. Now, the conserver of this medium either is or is not God. In the latter case there may be an infinite series of nondivine conservers, which is absurd; or the first conserver is God Himself. Thus the thesis is proved, because conserving everywhere, God will be everywhere (*ubique conservans, ubique erit*).[62]

Thus this argument both begins and ends with the implicit postulation of the metaphysical principle of causal contact.

The same holds true of the second "fifth" argument, which reads in part: Since God contains and conserves every being in every place, God is immediately present in every being and every place.[63]

The seventh argument, sixth in the Borgnet edition, employs a text of the *Liber de Causis* asserting God's universal efficient causality and contains the following contiguistic lines by Albert: Divine conservation is to be found in every place and every being; and consequently God is in every place and every being.[64]

(2) *Summa Theologiae*, II, tr. 3 q. 12 m. 1 (Borgnet, 32, 149–51)

The topic discussed here is that the "fiery," "shining," or "highest"

---

[62] *Ibid.*, arg. 5, p. 727b–728a.

[63] "Cum ergo in omni re et in omni loco contineat et conservet in esse, sequitur quod Deus in omni re sit, et in omni loco, et immediatus." (*Ibid.* arg. 5, p. 728a.)

[64] "[Deus] continetur autem et conservatur in omni loco et in omni re: ergo Deus actualiter continens et conservans est in omni loco et in omni re." (*Ibid.* arg. 6, p. 728b.) As far as the rest of this *membrum* is concerned, only one other part is relevant to the contiguist question: the objection following the reply to the four counterarguments. (*Ibid.*, Obiicitur, p. 731b.)

heaven (*caelum empyreum, splendidum, summum*),[65] the place where the angels were created, is a body.

In reply to the Aristotelian objection that the place and the placed must be of the same nature, Albert defends this thesis by remarking that this principle holds true only for those things which are in a place circumscriptively, whereas the angel is in place definitively. For, Albert goes on, as John Damascene puts it, the angel "must be where he operates" (*ibi necesse est eum esse, ubi operatur*), "and when he is here, he is not elsewhere" (*et quando est hic, non est alibi*). Thus the angel is created in the highest heaven, and when he is there he is not on earth; and "when he is sent to announce or do something, he is on earth and not in the highest heaven" (*quando in terram aliquid nuntiaturus vel operaturus mittitur, in terra est, et non in caelo empyreo*).[66]

In this passage Albert not only approvingly quotes Damascene's contiguistic principle, changing it into an explicit statement on metaphysical contiguism,[67] but also formally applies it to angelic operation— thus explicitly extending the validity of metaphysical contiguism from the divine to the created spiritual agent.

The same view is implicit in Albert's reply to the second objection, that the angel's place is that toward which he tends, and this is God rather than the highest heaven. Albert approves of the given definition of place, adding a beautiful analogy to it: What is weight in bodies is love in spirits, and thus, whereas a body moves toward the place toward which its weight tends, a spirit moves toward that toward which his love tends. However, Albert continues his reply, the angel has another motion besides the one toward God—the movement of his ministry, and in that respect the angel moves from place to place and through space, is in a place definitively, and needs a corporeal place.[68] The contiguist thinking in this reply is unmistakably obvious.

2. Anticontiguist Texts

In light of the texts discussed above, it may seem completely justified to classify Saint Albert as a casual contiguist who implies the necessity

[65] Cf. "coelum splendidum, quod dicitur empyreum, id est, ignem a splendore, non a calore"—a Peter Lombard quotation in *Summa Theol.* II, tr. 3 q. 12 m. 1, princ. (Borgnet, 32, 149a). Cf. also a Strabus quotation, *ibid.*, in contrarium 2. For *summum caelum* see *ibid.*, solutio, p. 150b.

[66] *Ibid.*, ad 1, p. 150b.

[67] The Damascene text in its original form does not include the adverb *necessarie* (*De fide orthod.* II, c. 3; PG 94, 870B); Albert's text does.

[68] "(Et) hoc modo movetur de loco ad locum et per spatium, et hoc modo definitive continetur in loco, et exigit locum corporalem." (*Ibid.* ad 2, p. 151a).

of causal contact in numerous passages and explicitly states the same in three or four other texts ranging chronologically from the *Summa de Creaturis*, his first major work, to the *Summa Theologiae*, his last and crowning work.

However, there are texts in a few works which seem to render this conclusion or this classification of Albert on the contiguist question either erroneous or, at least, premature. For those texts seem to indicate either that Albert was an inconsistent contiguist or that he compromised between causal contiguism and anticontiguism—thus possibly anticipating Duns Scotus by half a century or so.

For this reason this study would be quite incomplete without attempting to determine whether Albert was, indeed, an inconsistent contiguist or a compromiser, if either one at all. To accomplish this important task, a second set of texts must be carefully considered in a sequence that is determined primarily by topical and logical considerations rather than by the chronology of the works of Albert.

a) The Question of Celestial Influences

Any celestial influence, with the possible exception of solar or stellar light, is prima facie an instance of action at a distance. Therefore, one must carefully consider texts in the *corpus Albertinum* which deal with this generic topic.

> (1) *Quaestiones super "De Animalibus,"*[69] IX, q. 7 (Geyer, 12, 206) (ca. 1258–60)

The question discussed here is "whether the moon dominates the flux of menstruation"—an instance of generically celestial and specifically lunar influence.

First, Albert offers the following reason for a negative answer to this question: If the moon had any such influence, then, as the moon waxes, the menstrual flow should also increase, and the moon should have influence also on the emission of the sperm—and neither of the two consequents is true. Second, Albert invokes Aristotle, who opposed an affirmative answer to the question at hand.[70] Next, Albert states his own Aristotelian position as follows: "One must say that the moon does

[69] This is basically Albert's work, but as reported by Brother Conrad of Austria sometime after 1260, possibly in the 1280s. Cf. the Geyer edition, 12, Prolegomena, p. XLV, 62–90.

[70] "The onset of the catamenia in women takes place towards the end of the month; and on this account the wiseacres assert that the moon is feminine, because the discharge in women and the waning of the moon happen at one at the same time." Aristotle, *De hist. an.* VII, 2, 582a 34-b 3; D'Arcy Wentworth Thompson, tr. in *Works*, Smith and Ross, eds. Vol. IV (Oxford: Clarendon, 1949), p. 582a.

have influence over the flow of menstruum and all humid and cold things" (*luna habet dominium super fluxum menstruum et super omne humidum et frigidum*).[71]

In answering the first objection, based on the analogy of the sperm to menstruation, Albert remarks that the moon influences menstruation more than any other secreted fluid (*egestiones*) of the human body. This reply seems to be anticontiguistic. Albert himself does not offer any clue to the contrary in the *quaestio* at hand, since he fails to explain how the distant moon can act upon human secretions, although no medium between the moon and the human organs is empirically known or even readily thinkable. However, there is another *quaestio* in the same work that seems suitable to determining whether the above position taken by Albert on lunar influences upon the human body is anticontiguistic.

(2) *Quaestiones super "De Animalibus,"* XVII, q. 14 (Geyer, 12, 295)

The topic of this *quaestio* is "whether certain animals stemming from putrefaction are generated by the superior powers of the celestial bodies."

In the preceding question (*quaestio* 13) Albert follows Aristotle[72] in asserting that lower animals can be generated through heat from the decomposition occurring in the depth of the earth. The reason given is that, "just as internal heat predisposes matter for the generation of animate animals, so external heat can dispose matter for the generation of imperfect animals."[73] It is this doctrine which gives rise in *quaestio* 14 to the question whether such generation is caused by celestial bodies.

Despite two objections, Albert follows Aristotle in declaring that lower animals are caused, in addition to the inferior power of the containing matter, by the superior power of the sun. The process is described as follows: First, the inferior power predisposes matter for decomposition. Once this is accomplished, the celestial power of the sun is induced "as the sperm into the menstruum." Therefore, Albert concludes, "just as 'man is begotten by man and the sun,'[74] one may say that such an imperfect animal is also generated by the matter containing it and by the sun."

[71] Albert, *Quaestiones super "De Animalibus,"* IX, q. 7, sol. (Geyer, 12, 206a 12–14). Cf. *Mineralia*, II, tr. 2 c. 17 on the moon influencing the size of the moon stone (*silenites*).

[72] Aristotle, *Met.* IV, 1, 379a 2–8.

[73] *Quaestiones super "De Animalibus,"* XVII, q. 13, sol. (Geyer, 12, 295a 27–30).

[74] Aristotle, *Phys.* II, 2, 194b 13.

Up to this point Albert's view on this issue sounds as anticontiguistic as his position on lunar influence. However, in reply to the first objection ("Cause and effect are proportionate," so that a universal cause causes universal effects; and a particular cause, particular effects), Albert makes it clear that his position is contiguistic. He commences this reply by making a distinction between two kinds of universal cause: one which causes and one which predisposes. With this premise in mind Albert goes on to say that Aristotle's dictum concerning the proportion between cause and effect refers only to a predisposing, not to a producing, universal cause; for it is the lower power which predisposes matter for generation out of putrefaction, so that the sun "can produce a particular effect." This is the reason why, Albert continues, "the universal agent or the celestial body does not act, except through the mediation of the particular agent used as an instrument (*non agit nisi mediante particulari agente instrumentaliter*)."[75]

This reply not only resolves the first objection to the thesis at hand but also makes it clear that solar generation, to Albert's mind, is *not* an action at a distance, because the direct role of the sun consists in sending heat to earth (by means of the light rays),[76] whereas the generation itself of the lower animal in decomposing matter is caused by the distant sun through a particular agent reached by the light rays.

Guided by this explanation of solar generation, we see that the unresolved issue of solar influence upon the menstruum and other bodily secretions can easily be conceived in contiguistic terms. For there is an obvious empirical analogy between the sun and the moon: both emit light to earth. If then, as Albert explicitly states, solar generation consists strictly in the sunlight reaching the earth, warming it up with the heat which the light rays bring along, and thus favorably *predisposing* the earth and making particular agents *cause* certain "imperfect" animals, Albert must have had a similar model in mind for lunar influence upon human secretions. This model is obviously the following: The moon, through its light's reaching the human body, acts as a predisposing and remote moving cause; the human soul and its powers act as the particular causes which produce the physiological changes in the body in which they are present.

With this explanation furnished by Albert indirectly, one may rightly conclude that Albert's doctrine of lunar influences does not represent a deviation from his causal contiguism or an inconsistency in that respect.

[75] Quaestiones super "De animalibus," XVII, q. 14, ad rationes (Geyer, 12, 295b 88–296a 1).

[76] Albert, De caelo et mundo, II, tr. 3 c. 3 (Geyer, 5, pars 1, p. 147a 45–48).

b) The Question of Occult Powers

In a number of his scientific and philosophic works Albert shows a surprisingly great interest in the medical and occult powers of minerals and animate beings, including man[77]—powers, all of which he attributes directly to the substantial form.[78] In fact, Albert goes so far as to defend firmly and solemnly the position that terrestrial beings, such as stones, have such powers, and he does so partly on empirical grounds and partly on the basis of ancient and medieval authorities.[79]

The relevance of this partly scientific and partly philosophic interest of Albert is that many of the occult powers appear, prima facie at least, to cause actions at a distance. It would be impossible in an essay like this to consider every text that deals with occult powers; the number of such texts is simply too large.[80] Besides, it would even be superfluous to

[77] Cf. "For there is nothing in all nature that does not have its own specific action, as sammony purges yellow bile, and the like. This is proved in [the use of] medical simples, and in the science of *Incantations and Ligatures*, where it is shown that parts of many different animals . . . produce wonderful effects. The same [is true] with herbs, roots, and woods." Albert, *Mineralia*, II, tr. 1, c. 1. English tr. by Dorothy Wyckoff, *Albertus Magnus, Book of Minerals* (Oxford: Clarendon Press, 1967), p. 56. *Nota bene*: Since the *Mineralia*, unlike the other works referred to here, is available in English translation, I shall use this translation for quotations instead of the Latin text in the fifth volume of the Borgnet edition.

[78] "We state . . . that the power of stones is caused by the specific substantial form of the stone." (*Min.* II, 1, 4, *tr. cit.* pp. 64–65. Cf. *Min.* II, 3, 6, p. 151.)

[79] "Many indeed seem to doubt whether there are in stones any of the powers which are regarded as belonging to them . . . . But the opposite is proved most convincingly by experience: since we see that the magnet attracts iron and the *adamas* restricts that power in the magnet." Furthermore, it is proved by experience that some *saphirus* cures abscesses, and we have seen one of these with our own eyes. This is a widespread belief; and it is impossible that there should not be some truth at least in what is a matter of common report." (*Min.* II, 1, 1, pp. 55, 56.)

[80] In the *Mineralia* alone Albert speaks of no less than 34 stones (in their natural states or suspended or engraved with certain images), each of which has at least one occult power, causing what appears to be action at a distance. They are *adamas, agathes, alecterius,* (*Min.* II, tr. 2, c. 1, pp. 71–73); *ceraurum, celidonius, corallus* (*ib.* pp. 79–81); *draconites* (c. 4, p. 87); *echites, eliotropia, epistrites* (c. 5, pp. 88–90); *gagates, gerachidem* (c. 7, pp. 93, 95); *hyacinthus* (c. 8, p. 98); *ligurius, lippares* (c. 10, pp. 102–103; II, tr. 3, c. 6, p. 150); *magnes* (II, 2, 11, p. 103; tr. 3, c. 6, p. 150); *melochites* (II, 2, 11, p. 106); *nicomar* (c. 12, p. 107); *sardinus* (c. 17, p. 117; cf. c. 13, p. 109); *silenitas, succinus* (amber) c. 17, pp. 118, 121); *turchois* (c. 18, p. 123); the engraved images of Andromeda, Hydra, Cetus, and Perseus (II, 3, c. 5, pp. 142, 144, 145); in the ligatures and suspensions of *galadides, magnes, naphtha, amethyst, sardonyx, opitistrite,* and red coral (II, tr. 3, c. 6, pp. 147, 148–51); and in white naphtha and the fire of sulphur (II, 3, 6, p. 150). Cf. also the Gorgon story (II, 2, 8, p. 53).

analyze each such text separately, since they all pose basically the same generic problem of how to reconcile Albert's belief in powers which seem to cause actions at a distance with his causal contiguism. For this reason it seems sufficient to deal here with only two groups of occult powers: those of some minerals and the power of "fascination" or "the evil eye."

(1) Occult Mineral Powers

The two examples selected from the *Mineralia* for their representative character involve two stones, called by Albert *ligurius* and *lippares*. About the former, the Ligurian stone, Albert reports, "Experience shows that if rubbed, it attracts straws, which is [a property] of nearly all precious stones" (*fricatus trahit paleas, quod fere convenit omni lapidi pretioso*).[81] On the other hand, the Liparian stone (*lippares*) "is reported," writes Albert, "to have marvelous power: for all wild beasts when harassed by hunters and dogs, run to it, and regard it as a protector. And they say that dogs and hunters cannot [harm] a wild beast so long as it is in the presence of the stone . . ." (*canes et venatores noscere non possunt bestiam quamdiu lapidem habent praesentem . . .*).[82]

Prima facie both stories, like dozens of others in the *Mineralia* alone, represent actions at a distance. This is obvious about the report on the *ligurius,* since it deals with an attractive power analogous in its action to the electric attraction of the amber (*succinus*) and magnetism,[83] and also about the story concerning the *lippares,* because it implies that the stone in question stops the approaching, hence distant, hunters and dogs. On the other hand, Albert offers no explanation for either of the two stories. Thus the question to be answered here is, Are these two, as well as the other stories about occult powers seemingly acting at a distance, reconcilable with Albert's causal contiguism?

One curious fact suggesting a negative answer is that, whether he considers such stories true on empirical grounds or on the basis of someone's authority, Albert does not seem to be disturbed by their anti-contiguist implications, although some remarks indicate that he did realize the physical, if not the metaphysical, problem they raise. At the end of the chapter on the sigils of stones, for example, he concedes that "these things cannot be proved by physical principles, but demand a knowledge of the sciences of astrology and magic and necromancy,"

81 *Min.* II, tr. 2 c. 10 (Borgnet, 5, 40a; *tr. cit.* p. 102).
82 *Ibid.* A variant of this story is related and attributed to Aristotle in *Min.* II, 3, 6, *tr. cit.* p. 150.
83 *Min.* II, 2, 17, *tr. cit.* p. 121.

adding that these sciences "must be considered elsewhere"—a remark amounting to avoiding the answer to the contiguist question.[84]

On the other hand, in the *Mineralia* there are certain positive clues to the contiguist problem with occult powers. One such clue is Albert's doctrine that, while the characteristic powers of the minerals—the medical as well as the occult—are directly rooted in their substantial forms,[85] they originate ultimately from the celestial powers transmitted to them, and transmitted in a contiguist fashion[86]—analogously to celestial heat brought to earth by solar light rays.[87]

A second clue is even more important than the first. Having stated the assertion of the necromancers about the bloodstone (*eliotropia*) that, "if rubbed with the juice of the herb of the same name and placed in a vessel full of water, it makes the sun look blood-red, as if there were an eclipse," Albert immediately adds his own explanation of this apparent instance of action at a distance—an explanation which is patently contiguistic: "And the reason for this is that it makes all the water boil up into a mist, which thickens the air so that the sun cannot be seen except as a red glow in the condensing cloud . . . ."[88]

Admittedly this is probably the only occult phenomenon that is contiguistically explained in the *Mineralia*. Nevertheless, the account clearly shows that Albert is aware of the apparently anticontiguist workings of occult powers and endeavors to explain them contiguistically. That he does not do so in other cases may be due at least partly to the predominantly scientific, i.e., descriptive, character of the alphabetical lapidary and the other chapters of the *Mineralia* listing the occult powers in question.

A third and equally important clue is that the power of the *ligurius*

[84] *Min.* II, 3, 5, p. 145. Cf. the reference to the science of magic, avoiding relevant questions concerning metals in *Min.* III, 1, 1, p. 154.

[85] See n. 78 above.

[86] "(Form) is [intermediate] between two [things]—the heavenly powers by which it is conferred, and the matter of the combination into which it is infused." (*Min.* II, 1, 4, p. 65.) "(The) power of heaven contributes to certain wonderful effects" (*sc.* in the terrestrial bodies). (*Min.* II, 3, 6, p. 147.) "So undoubtedly there is a formative power in nature, poured into the stars of heaven, and this [power] guides towards a specific form the heat that digests the material of metals. For . . . this heat has its right direction and formative power from the Moving Intelligence, and its efficacy from the power of light and heat *emanating* from the light of the starry sphere and from the power that separates things that are alike from things that are different—[that is], the power of Fire." (*Min.* III, 1, 5, pp. 166–67.)

[87] See n. 47 above.

[88] *Min.* II, 2, 5, p. 89.

to attract straws—which is a quality "of nearly all precious stones," [89] as well as of the *gagates*, white naphtha, and sulphur described elsewhere[90] —is evidently analogous to the attractive power of the magnet, for which Albert suggests a contiguist explanation not only in the *De caelo*,[91] as seen, but also in the alphabetical lapidary itself. For there Albert makes it clear that the magnet attracts iron from a distance,[92] so that its power is transferred to the iron.[93] Thus there is no reason why Albert should not have conceived the attractions of the *ligurius*, most precious stones, and the other three chemicals also in terms of contiguistic models—either by emanating particles or by the transmission of the attractive powers through the air. In fact, in the discussion of the amber (*succinus*) this is exactly what Albert formally and explicitly asserts when he remarks, "If rubbed, it [*sc.* the amber] attracts leaves, straws, and threads, as the magnet [attracts] iron."[94] For these reasons it seems fair to say that Albert *indirectly* accounts for all occult powers of attraction in a contiguistic manner.

Finally a nontextual, argumentative point may be made: There is no logical or factual reason to question the *generic* analogy between attractive and protective occult powers—a very important point in light of the large number of the latter type of occult power listed by Albert.[95] The reason for this important assertion is that these two groups of occult powers are related as those pulling to those pushing and that any pushing or pulling power may evidently be transferred to a distant object—two truths so obvious that Albert could not possibly have overlooked them. However, from these principles it follows that Albert could easily conceive the workings of *virtually* all, if not *simply* all,

---

89 *Min.* II, 2, 10, p. 102.

90 *Min.* II, 2, 7, p. 93; II, 3, 6, p. 150.

91 Albert, *De caelo*, I, tr. 3, c. 2 (Geyer, 5, pars 1, pp. 47–48).

92 "Aristotle reports that if two or more magnets of equal power are placed above and below, and a body of *baret*, that is, iron, is placed between, it will hang suspended in the air." (*Min.* II, 3, 6, p. 148.)

93 *Min.* II, 2, 11, p. 103. Cf. "Aristotle in his *Lapidary* says 'the corner of a certain kind of magnet has the power of attracting iron towards *zoron*, that is, the North . . . .' " (*Min.* II, 3, 6, p. 148.)

94 *Min.* II, 2, 17, p. 121.

95 Albert speaks of five minerals having occult attractive powers: the amber (*succinus*), the magnet (*magnes*) (*Min.* II, 2, 17, 121; c. 11, p. 103); *gagates*, white naphtha, and sulphur (*Min.* II, 2, 7, p. 93; 3, 6, p. 150). In contrast, he reports that occult protective powers against enemies, wild beasts, adversity, threats, storms, lightning and hail, sedition, locusts and birds, unhealthy climate, harm in general, misfortunes, and attacks by the envious are possessed by *adamas, agathes, celidonius, corallus, epistrites, hyacinthus, melochites, turchois, opitistrite,* and stones engraved with the image of *Perseus*. (For the text references, see n. 80 above.)

occult powers in ways analogous to the attractive power of the magnet—including even those few which are, or prima facie appear to be, neither attractive nor (simply) protective.[96]

(2) The Question of "Fascination" or "the Evil Eye"

(a) De Animalibus, XXII, tr. l c. 5 (Borgnet, 12, 369–70) (1258–62)

This chapter treats the "natural and divine" properties of man in general and what Albert terms "fascination" in particular.

As the first "natural and divine" property the intellect is mentioned —a quality that makes man the connecting link between the world and God. Through this power, Albert boldly asserts, man has divine intellect in himself (intellectum divinum in se habet), by means of which man is elevated above the world, so much so that the material world conforms to his ideas. This truth can be seen in those exceptional persons who with their minds (suis animabus) so change the bodies of the world that "they are said to do miracles (ut miracula facere dicantur)."[97] For this great power of his, Albert continues, man is not subjugated to the world but rather placed above it as its governor.

After this general introduction Albert suddenly singles out one of the most intriguing topics concerning the human powers—fascination or casting spells by the eye: "This is why fascination is caused [by man], through which the soul of one man acts with his sight or some other sense to the detriment or benefit of another person" (fascinatio, qua anima unius agit ad alterius impedimentum vel expeditionem per visum vel alium sensum).[98]

In this unexpected statement Albert does two things. First, he openly admits his belief in the factuality of a human activity which, being traditionally considered an occult phenomenon, has been both

[96] Occult powers which are neither attractive nor protective are as rare as they are curious. The actions of five such powers are described by Albert as follows: (1) Echites: "If anyone is suspected of poisoning food, and if this stone is placed in the food, it prevents the food from being eaten" (Min. II, 2, 5, p. 88); (2) the image of Andromeda engraved on a stone "brings about lasting love between man and wife," and "is said to reconcile even those who have been adulterous" (II, 3, 5, p. 142); (3) the engraved image of Cetus "is said to . . . restore things that have been lost" (ibid., p. 144); (4) Galadides: "If it is placed near a fire and taken away again, the fire goes out" (II, 3, 6, p. 147); and (5) "If red coral is suspended directly over the seat of pain in the stomach, it soothes the pain" (ibid., p. 151).

[97] Albert, De animalibus, XXII, tr. 1 c. 5 (Borgnet, 12, 369b).

[98] Ibid.

seriously maintained and strongly ridiculed by opposing groups of men throughout history. Second, he expresses his belief in a type of alleged human activity which is generally conceived as affecting other persons at a distance. This aspect of fascination seems to be suggested two sentences later by Albert's remark that a man determined enough in the "high point" of his mind attracts to himself (*trahit ad se*) the body and the world.[99] However, while the action-at-a-distance character of casting a spell is hinted at, no explanation for fascination is given by Albert in this text.

(b) *Metaphysica*, IV, tr. 3 c. 1 (Geyer, 16, pars 1, pp. 186–87) (1261–65)

In this chapter Albert lists three reasons for Protagoras' famous doctrine that contradictories are simultaneously true. The third of the three reasons rests on the analogy of the mechanical mover and the soul. As the mechanical mover is the cause of the form in the mobile being, Albert reasons, so is the form in the soul the cause of the natural form in matter. This analogy means that natural things follow the forms of opinions which are in the soul. Inasmuch, then, as there are simultaneously opposite forms of opinions in the soul, there are simultaneously contradictory things in nature.[100]

At this point Albert mentions the fascination of the eye as being, in Protagoras' view, a sign (*signum*) or instance of simultaneously true opposite things. For fascination, Albert explains, takes place when the soul of one person impedes the activity of another person either simply by a stare at the other person or by some other approach of the imagination or judgment.[101] Thus fascination is a power, Albert goes on to say, which is possessed by the strong mind owing to its similarity to the mover of some of the superior celestial spheres. For this reason every diversity of matter corresponds to the diversity of opinions and estimates of certain minds (souls), so that contrary opinions cause contradictions in things. At the basis of this Protagorean reasoning, Albert concludes, lies the idea that human souls are the images of heavenly movers. For just as matter receives forms only from the movers through the celestial movements, so matter receives changes from the

[99] *Ibid.*, p. 370a.

[100] Albert, *Metaphysica*, IV, tr. 3 c. 1 (Geyer, 16, pars 1, pp. 186, 61–187, 8).

[101] "Est enim fascinatio, quando anima unius per visum vel aliam appropinquationem imaginationis vel aestimationis operationem impedit alterius." (*Ibid.*, p. 187, 10–12.) Cf. "Quidam Philosophi . . . ponunt fascinationem, ita quod anima unius hominis per adspectum vel propinquitatem impediat processum operum alterius hominis . . . ." Albert, *In II. Sent.* d. 7, F, a. 7, sol. (Borgnet, 26, 153a).

forms of opinions which are in the human souls—changes leading to all the diversities of the material things.[102]

Surprisingly to our modern thinking, Albert grants Protagoras' alleged basic principle that the human soul is the obscure or imperfect image (*umbra et resultatio et imago*) of heavenly intelligence. Yet Albert points out also that the soul is the image of heavenly intelligence not in a celestial orbit but in an animal body, and thus its conceived ideas do not necessarily move a body unless that body is united with the soul (*non oportet, quod visa eius . . . moveant nisi corpus illi animae moventi coniunctum*). For with the bodies which are not united with it the soul has no communication, and therefore does not move them (*Cum non coniunctis autem non habent communicantiam, et ideo illa non movent*).[103]

This is Albert's first critical remark on Protagoras' third argument, to be followed by two additional points of criticism. To us, however, this first point is important, for it evidently contains elements of contiguist thinking. Yet in the next paragraph Albert speaks again of the eye as conceived by "the science of incantations":

> With regard to fascination, as the science of incantations teaches, it [*sc.* fascination] certainly stems from the powers which the soul receives from the celestial beings, being the image of the superior movers. For having the power of fascination in that fashion, it need not be [confined] to move only the body which is united with it; instead, [it can] move everything which lies in the sphere of the circle moved by the celestial mover whose image the soul is. . . . And . . . by moving those things with its own proper power, [the soul] hinders their natural operations. This, then, is fascination, and moves mainly those things which follow the lesser or the least power of the celestial movers. And in this regard the science of fascination, which is one among the species of incantations, is the subaltern of astronomy. But let us leave these things at that for the time being.[104]

---

[102] *Ibid.*, p. 187, 12–32.

[103] *Ibid.*, p. 187, 36–41.

[104] "Fascinatio autem, sicut dicit scientia incantationum, pro certo est ex virtutibus animae, quas accipit a caelestibus, secundum quod est imago motorum superiorum. Sic enim habens virtutem illius, non habet movere solum corpus sibi coniunctum, sed totum, quod subiacet sphaerae circuli, quem movet motor, cuius est imago . . . . Et . . . movens ea secundum propriam virtutem impedit ab operatione naturali. Et haec est fascinatio, et movet maxime ea, quae virtutem caelestium minorem aut minimam consecuta sunt, et quoad hoc fascinantium scientia, quae una est de speciebus incantationum, astronomiae subalternatur; sed haec relinquantur ad praesens." (*Ibid.* p. 187, 56–73.)

The characterization in this passage of the soul's power of fascination is likely to suggest that casting a spell represents an action at a distance. However, one must bear in mind that this apparently anti-contiguist description is introduced with the clause "as the science of incantation teaches," and is wound up with the remark that Albert does not wish to say anything more about fascination in this chapter. For the former clause shows that Albert here basically reports the views of those who believe in fascination, whereas the last remark indicates that Albert could say more about the topic, i.e., he has his own ideas about it.

Despite the frustration which Albert causes by his failure to explain his own understanding of fascination in either of the two texts considered heretofore, one thing is unquestionably true: Albert would have no difficulty in finding a contiguist model for fascination (or, for that matter, for any apparent instance of action at a distance). For if the eye of the menstruating woman can be thought of, as it is by both Aristotle and Albert, as emanating blood and transmitting that blood to the mirror and other nearby objects, and if the magnet can be postulated, as it is by Albert, to employ a medium, the person capable of fascination can also and easily be conceived as transmitting his proper power through the air or by some emanation to him who is intended to be the receiver or object of fascination. Indeed, one needs only to consult some Renaissance and early modern thinkers, such as Francis Suárez,[105] Francis Bacon,[106] Sir Kenelm Digby,[107] and Sylvester Maurus,[108] to see that any apparent action at a distance can be conceived in terms of a contiguist model. Consequently, Albert's belief in fascination and his omission formally to account in the consulted texts for fascination in contiguist terms are not sufficient to conclude that Albert has compromised on the principle of causal contiguism—a principle which he unhesitatingly and explicitly applies even to the omnipotent agent.

In attempting to confirm this probable speculative argumentation for Albert's contiguist model of fascination through a text analysis, let

[105] F. Suárez, *Metaphysicae Disputationes* (1597), disp. 18, s. 8, nn. 3–7 and 24–26 (*Opera Omnia*, 25, 651–52, 659–61).

[106] F. Bacon, *Sylva Sylvarum*, Century X, Sections 904–1000. W. Rawley, ed. (London: printed by J. H. for William Lee, 1627), pp. 236–58.

[107] Sir K. Digby, *La Poudre de Sympathie* (1657); English tr. *Of the Sympathetick Powder* (London: printed by S. G. and B. G. for John Williams, 1669), pp. 143–205.

[108] Sylvester Maurus, *Quaestiones Philosophicae* (1658), II, q. 35, obi. 1–7 and ad 1–7 (Cenomani: Leguicheux-Gallienne, 1875), pp. 593–95; 599–601.

us turn now to an article in the second book of the *Commentary on the Sentences*.

(c) *In II. Sent.* d. 7, F, a. 7 (Borgnet, 26, 152–54)

Albert begins his solution of the question whether demons need to assume bodies to cause changes in human bodies by pointing to two historical facts. One is that Saint Augustine took the transmutation of human bodies by demons for granted. The other is that some philosophers, such as Avicenna[109] and Algazel,[110] considered fascination a fact and conceived it as follows:

> The soul of one man, by gazing or [mere] propinquity (*per adspectum vel propinquitatem*), hinders the process of the activities of another man, with the power spiritually going out of one soul and acting on another [soul] (*virtute spiritualiter egrediente de una anima, et operante super aliam*).[111]

Three points need to be considered in this definition of fascination. One is that, apart from the question of how accurately Albert sums up here the notion either Avicenna or Algazel had of fascination, this definition obviously represents Albert's own notion of fascination. For, having stated that some thinkers have posited fascination in a certain sense, Albert immediately proceeds to declare his disapproval of the stated view on fascination; yet his disapproval is directed against the scope of the factuality of fascination rather than against the way in which fascination is conceived by those philosophers:

> This I do not mention as if I approved of this dictum [*sc.* view on fascination]. For I firmly believe that fascination does not harm anyone who has strong faith in the Lord (*bene credo, quod fidem firmam in Domino habenti non nocet fascinatio*), nor can the art of magic do so . . . .[112]

The second point is that, apart from the second clause concerning the spiritual egression of the power from the soul, the above definition of fascination is quite similar to that in the *De animalibus*[113] —which shows that Albert had not changed his concept of fascination after his early work on the *Sentences*.

---

[109] Avicenna, *De anima*, pars 4, cap. 4 (Venetiis; 1509), fol. 20D.
[110] Albert refers here to Algazel's *Physics*. I do not know to which part or passage of the *Makâsid al Falâsifa* by Algazel Albert refers here.
[111] *In II. Sent.* d. 7, F. a. 7, sol. princ. (Borgnet, 26, 153a).
[112] *Ibid.*
[113] Albert, *De animalibus*, XXII, tr. 1 c. 5 (Borgnet, 12, 369b).

The third and most important point is that the definition offered here is richer than that in the *De animalibus* or the description in the *Metaphysics* and that the clause that enriches this definition directly touches on the contiguist question. For, as seen, Albert remarks in this text that the soul of one person impedes the activities of another precisely by having its power of fascination go out (*egrediens*) of the soul and act upon someone else—a description apparently suggesting that the agent of fascination employs a contiguist *modus operandi*.

However, reflection upon the text makes it obvious that Albert fails here to give a clear and unambiguous answer to our question, Precisely how does one person cast a spell on a spatially distant other? For the phrase *virtute spiritualiter egrediente* may mean either that the power of fascination is itself spiritual or, more probably, that the way in which the power of fascination is actuated by the soul is other than the manner in which the power of a subhuman agent is applied to another body. To find a clue to this crucial point of Albert's theory of fascination, we must consider the rest of the article at hand.

As stated before, the subject of the article is whether the demons need to assume bodies in order to cause changes in human beings. Having lined up three arguments in favor of such assumption of bodies, Albert states his position in the *solutio* as follows. For the factuality of demonic influence upon human bodies we have the authority of Augustine, whereas other thinkers assure us that there is also such a thing as fascination, although they have failed to take into consideration that strong faith in God can always frustrate demonic influence upon man. At any rate, if the human soul has the power of fascination, and if even inanimate corporeal agents, like certain minerals, possess various occult powers affecting human bodies, so must spiritual substances. The only significant difference, Albert remarks, is that subhuman corporeal agents use their occult powers with physical necessity whenever an object to which the powers are proportionate is present, whereas the spirits can freely decide whether to keep their occult powers in themselves or open them up to those bodies to which their powers are proportionate.

Interestingly, this *solutio* is incomplete because, on analogous grounds, it merely establishes that demons do have powers causing various changes in human bodies, whereas it fails to answer the real question—*how* the demons cause such changes and whether they need to assume bodies to do so. Albert answers these questions only in the reply to the first objection.

The Aristotelian objection to the reality of demonic influence reads as follows: Since there is no action or change without the agent touching the patient,[114] and since the demons, being spiritual, do not touch anything physical, the demons do not act upon bodies or cause any change in them unless they assume bodies. Albert offers two answers to this argument, the "better" (*melius*) of which is the following: The touch Aristotle speaks of is touch not by substance but by power (*intelligitur non de tactu substantiae agentis, sed de tactu virtutis*), for, "unless the power touches the mobile being, no change will ever follow" (*nisi enim illa tangat mobile, numquam sequitur alteratio*).[115]

This reply is important for two reasons. First, in it Albert finally implies his own position on the real issue of the article: The demons can, indeed, cause changes in human bodies without themselves assuming bodies, because even without assuming bodies they can touch human beings with their occult spiritual powers. Second, in this reply Albert states a doctrine which is not to be found in any of the numerous contiguist texts analyzed above. According to this doctrine no action and no change are possible without the application of the agent's power to the patient; and since the active power of every agent, except God, is an accident that cannot be without a substrate, from the necessity of the application of power it logically follows that either the agent itself or the medium receiving or carrying the active power must be in contact by substance with the patient to which the power is to be applied in order to cause a change.

Having given this significant reply to the first objection, Albert himself finds it necessary to face directly the question concerning the specific manner in which the demonic power touches the human body:

> If, then, one asks, "How does [the power of the demon] touch [the human body]? Does it perhaps multiply itself in the medium up to the mobile [being to be changed], as the heat does?" I reply: It seems to me that it [*sc.* the power of the demon] does not do so. Instead, the active power [in question] comes to be in the body due to the proportion the acting spirit has to that [body] on which it acts according to the order [of the demon's will] (*ex proportione spiritus agentis ad id in quod agit secundum imperium fit virtus transmutans in corpore*). However, with regard to corporeal beings that act through their specific powers, I firmly believe that the power reaches the thing on which they [*sc.* the corporeal agents] act, through a medium (*per medium*).[116]

[114] Aristotle, *De gen. et. corr.* I, 6, 322b 23–25.
[115] Albert, *art. cit.* ad 1, p. 153b.
[116] *Ibid.*

This statement deserves attention for three reasons. One reason is that the second part of this doctrine contains Albert's explicit and solemn testimony to physical contiguism, namely, that the power of every corporeal agent that is spatially distant from the patient needs to be transmitted to that patient by a corporeal medium. The second reason is that, in the first part of this doctrinal declaration, Albert explains the meaning of the ambiguous phrase he previously employed in his definition of fascination. For in the beginning of the *solutio* he merely remarked that the human soul's power of fascination *spiritually* goes out of the soul and operates in another human being, whereas here he tells us that the active power of a spiritual agent, like a demon, comes to be in a spatially distant body not through a material agent that physically carries the power to the patient but in accordance with the order (*imperium*) of the spiritual agent's will.

The third reason why the doctrine at hand is important is that it may well reveal, indirectly at least, the long-sought model Albert conceived of fascination. For, as stated above, the text at hand indicates that, in Albert's opinion, the power of fascination, like the demonic power of causing changes in the human body, is activated by a person's free will in the person to be affected. Undoubtedly this is a reasonable view and conforms to the more or less traditional or customary model of the act of casting a spell on a person. But how does the power of fascination go from the person who casts a spell to the person in whom the spell causes harmful effects? Basically there are only two conceivable alternatives: either through a medium (as Thomas Aquinas, Albert's greatest disciple, explicitly teaches[117]), in case the person who casts

---

117 "(In) fascinatione daemonum non transmutatur materia corporalis ex sola vi apprehensionis, ut Avicenna posuit, sed ex eo quod propter vehementem affectionem invidiae vel irae seu odii, ut plerumque accidit in vetulabus, inficiuntur spiritus; et haec infectio pertingit usque ad oculos, ex quibus inficitur aer circumstans, ex quo corpus alicuius infantis propter teneritudinem recipit aliquam infectionem, per modum quo speculum novum inficitur ad aspectum mulieris menstrualem . . . ." (Thomas, *De malo*, 16, 9, ad 13.) "Et ideo melius dicendum est, quod ex forti imaginatione animae immutantur spiritus corporis coniuncti. Quae quidem immutatio spirituum maxime fit in oculis, ad quos subtiliores spiritus perveniunt. Oculi autem inficiunt aerem continuum usque ad determinatum spatium; per quem modum specula, si fuerint nova et pura, contrahunt quandam impuritatem ex aspectu mulieris menstruatae . . . ." (Thomas, *Summa Theol.* I, 117, 3, ad 2.) Cf. *Summa contra gent.* III, 103, n. 2780; C. Pera, ed. (Taurini: Marietti, 1961), pp. 155–56.

This contiguist interpretation of fascination by Aquinas may well be used as a persuasive historical argument for Albert himself holding a contiguist view on fascination. For Thomas followed Albert in holding explicit contiguist views on a number of apparent actions at a distance, such as celestial influence or terrestrial

the spell is spatially distant, or through direct contact by substance between him who casts the spell and him who suffers from the spell (as John Buridan, a fourteenth-century admirer of Albert, would have it[118]). Yet Albert explicitly rejects the former alternative with regard to the occult power of the spiritual demon, and from this it seems to follow that Albert does the same with regard to the power of fascination, which is a power of the spiritual soul. On the other hand, the latter alternative, that there always is a direct contact by substance between the caster and the sufferer of a spell, is contradicted by Albert's very definition of fascination, since fascination is asserted to take place through the act of gazing or in the propinquity of the one on whom the spell is cast.

There seems to be only one solution to this dilemma: While Albert

---

bodies (De ver. 5, 9, ad 16); lunar influences on the human body in general (Summa Theol. I, 115, 6c.), on the brain (ibid., ad 1), on the sea, thus causing tides (Summa Theol. I, 105, 6, ad 1); De occultis operationibus naturae, n. 442; in Opuscula Philosophica, R. M. Spiazzi, ed. [Taurini: Marietti, 1954], p. 159); menstruating women bloodying spatially distant mirrors (De ver. 26, 3, 4a, ad 4; De malo, 16, 9, ad 13; Summa Theol. I, 117, 3, ad 2); and magnetic attraction and the numbing effect of the torpedo fish (De ver. 5, 9, ad 17; In VII. Phys. lect. 4, n. 909. P. M. Spiazzi, ed. [Taurini: Marietti, 1954], p. 465). Therefore, it is highly probable that Thomas's explicit contiguist position on fascination is also due to Albert's influence. Moreover, like Albert, Thomas does not offer a contiguist model for all the above-listed apparent actions at a distance—the magnet, the torpedo fish, and the bloody mirrors being the only ones specifically explained in contiguist terms; because, again like Albert, Thomas stated the universality of the principle of contact in a number of his works at the physical (In IV. Sent. d. 10 a. 4 q. 1, sol.) as well as the metaphysical level (In I. Sent. d. 37 q. 1 a. 1, sol.; De pot. 6, 7, 11a, 12a, ad 11, ad 12; Quodl. VI, 2, 1, ad 1; Summa Theol. I, 8, 1, ad 3); and explicitly applied that principle to God (In I. Sent. 37, 1, 1, sol.; Summa Theol. I, 8, 1), the angels (Quodl. VI, 2, 1, ad 1; De pot. 6, 7, ad 12), and the celestial bodies (De ver. 5, 9, ad 16). Consequently, Albert's failure to offer a specifically contiguist explanation for fascination should not be construed as an argument for Albert's inconsistency on causal contiguism.

118 "(Malignae) mulieres per fortilegia alterant homines remotos ad infirmitates non praealterando medium." "De illis autem mulieribus ego credo quod non sic agant in homines remotos nisi tetigerunt eos vel per cibos vel per potus vel per herbas aut venena aut huiusmodi et si aliter fiat, hoc est per daemones illis servientes, qui possunt movere se ad illos vel applicare activa sive venena sive alia et agere in illos." Acutissimi philosophi reverendi Magistri Johannis Buridani Subtilissimae Quaestiones super octo Physicorum libros Aristotelis diligenter recognitae et revisae a Magistro Johanne Dullaert de Guadino antea nusquam impressae, lib. VII, q. 4, obi 9, ad 9 (Parisiis: a Magistro Petrile, 1509; repr. Frankfurt a. Main: Minerva, 1964), fols. 95vA and 96rA. The significance of this contiguist view is that, according to his own admission, John Buridan was an admirer and follower of Albert. (Cf. op. cit., obi 3a, ad 3, fol. 95vA, 95vB.)

correctly sees an analogy between fascination and demonic influence on the grounds that both actions flow from powers actuated by the free will, viz., a spiritual power of man and demon respectively, he may not have meant to conceive the analogy so broadly as to extend the explicit denial of demonic influence by a material medium to the act of fascination. If this is the correct interpretation of Albert's text at hand, Albert's model of fascination may be characterized as follows. First, the power of fascination is spiritual according to its proximate cause, the free will of the one who casts a spell, but corporeal entitatively—being the power of doing *corporeal* harm to a person. Second, being a corporeal power, the power of fascination may well be transmitted to the patient of fascination by a corporeal medium, whether effluent or interjacent—just as Thomas Aquinas explicitly teaches. On the other hand, since a demon is entitatively as much a spiritual substance as an angel is (the former differing from the latter in moral quality only), and since, in the same work, Albert maintains angelic locution on the explicit and formal grounds that the angel must be present to that on whom he acts,[119] the demons doing the harm to human bodies must have been conceived by Albert as doing harm by being present with their spiritual powers and, consequently, with their substances to the human being whom the demons harm—a conclusion analogously holding true for the caster of a spell.

(3) *The Problem of Angelic Locution*

Having completed the analysis of the seemingly anticontiguistic texts on *empirical* issues, we must finally turn to the *metaphysical* question of angelic locution to determine whether Albert's doctrine on this question violates causal contiguism.

(a) *Summa de Creaturis*, I, tr. 4 q. 60 a. 2 (Borgnet, 34, 634–38)

As may be recalled, Albert discusses the question of angelic locution on the basis of an interesting analogy—that of two mutually distant physical lights—and he does so in terms of three physical conditions: the absence of any interfering medium, the turning of one light toward the other, and a proportion between active power and distance.

As he applies each of these three physical conditions to the spiritual angels, Albert makes the following important remark:

> The turning (*conversio*) toward another angel, as it orders that this talk become known to the other, completes the locution. For

119 Albert, *In I. Sent.* d. 37, L, a 22 (Borgnet, 26, 257–62).

what is situation in corporeal beings is order in the spiritual beings. From this [analogy] the solution of the possible objection, viz., why not all angels hear when one is talking, is clear. For distance in spiritual beings does not play any role (*cum distantia in spiritualibus nihil operetur*). The reason for this [truth] is, as we have said, that order in spiritual things takes the place of situational distance in the corporeal beings (*in spiritualibus est ordo, loco distantiae in situ in corporalibus*). Thus, inasmuch as the angel who wills communication through his talk is not turned to and ordered toward all angels, not all angels hear him, but only those to whom he talks.[120]

This theory may be summed up as follows: For one light to reach another, three things are required: absence of interfering medium, the turning toward a certain other light, and proportion between their distance and the power to propagate light rays. The situation is similar when one angel talks with another, because angels are both lights (in virtue of their agent intellects) and mirrors (in virtue of their habit of receiving the forms of the intelligible things).[121] The first analogous condition is fulfilled, for no bodily medium can interfere with the angelic will or action. So is the second analogous condition, because to the physical turning of one light in the direction of another there corresponds the angel's will that his thought become known only to a certain other angel rather than to all other angels. However, unlike the first two conditions, the third physical condition is meaningless with reference to the angels, because distances between the angels do not matter; that is, they may will that their thoughts become known to any other angel irrespective of the distance between them. Therefore, angelic locution is possible simply by the will ("order") of one angel that a certain other angel be informed by his thought ("form" or intelligible species).

Now the problem with this theory is that in it Albert seems to maintain the possibility of one angel's acting upon another *at any distance* whatsoever *without* the aid of any medium, i.e., the possibility of angelic action at a distance. In fairness to Albert, it must be emphasized that this theory is not inconsistent with his oft-repeated doctrine that the angel must be where he acts, for angelic talk is an act of one angel on another angel, i.e., of one incorporeal being on another incorporeal being, whereas his Damascenean insistence on the angel's being where he acts concerns the action of an incorporeal agent upon a corporeal patient. Nevertheless, the theory of angelic locution, as presented in

120 *Summa de Creaturis*, I, tr. 4 q. 60 a. 2, sol. (Borgnet, 34, 637a).
121 *Ibid.*, p. 636b.

the *Summa de Creaturis, seems* to be inconsistent with his often-implied and sometimes explicitly pronounced contiguist principle that even God must be where He acts.

The simplest prima facie solution may be that the theory at hand is merely a doctrine in his early work, where he implicitly applies the principle of contact besides angelic locution, only to the operation of physical light[122] and to the theory of bloody mirrors as affected by menstruating women,[123] i.e., to incorporeal or corporeal agents acting on *corporeal* patients. However, this solution is patently wrong for two reasons. One is chronological: the same view on the irrelevance of distance with regard to angelic locution is repeatedly implied also in the *Commentary on the Sentences,*[124] where it is extended even to angelic locomotion.[125] The second reason is doctrinal and can be stated as follows: Albert could not possibly intend to limit the applicability of the contiguist principle to actions involving *corporeal* patients only, at least not without contradicting himself in the treatment of such a fundamental issue as divine omnipresence. For in discussing that issue, he explicitly teaches that, since every creature is contingent, every creature (whether spiritual or corporeal) is conserved by God; and consequently, that God is everywhere.[126]

The proper solution of the problem stemming from Albert's doctrine concerning the irrelevance of distance to angelic locution (and movement) comes from Albert himself in two important works, the *Commentary on the Sentences* and the *Summa Theologiae.* The relevant text in the latter work is addressed more explicitly to our problem, whereas the corresponding text in the former work offers the clearer and final solution of the issue.

(b) *Summa Theologiae,* II, tr. 9 q. 35 m. 3 (Borgnet, 32, 381b–82b)

This *membrum* deals with the organs of the angels who talk to and

---

122 *Ibid.*

123 *Summa de Creat.* II, tr. 40 q. 45 a. 4 (Borgnet, 34).

124 *In I. Sent.* d. 9, I, a. 13, sol. (Borgnet, 25, 293ab); *ibid.* art. 16, ad obi (pp. 296b–297a).

125 *In I. Sent.* d. 37, L, a. 22, ad 1 (Borgnet, 26, 259b) and art. 23, sol., and ad 2 and 3 (p. 261b).

126 *Summa Theol.* I, tr. 18 q. 70 m. 1, arg. 5 (Borgnet, 31, 727b) deals with the conservation of the creature in general: "Deus conservat creaturam in esse . . . quia ubique conservans, ubique erit." Cf. *In I. Sent.* d. 37, A. a. 1, sol., ad 1 (Borgnet, 26, 230b). Objecting to this argument by pointing out that *ubique erit* obviously refers to places in the world would not save Albert from the inconsistency at hand, because Albert assigns the *caelum empyreum* as the natural place of the angels. (*In I. Sent.* d, 37, L, a. 22, obi. 9a [Borgnet, 26, 258b]).

hear each other. Albert states the first reason for the need of "spiritual tongues and ears" for angelic locution as follows:

> For, otherwise, it could not be explained how the word from one [angel] could proceed to the other (*qualiter verbum ab uno procederet in alterum*). For there will be no talk unless words proceed from the one who talks to the listener (*locutio enim non fit nisi verbum procedat a dicente ad audientem*); and he who forms a word has the act of the tongue.[127]

To this argument, which obliquely raises the contiguist question of how a word uttered by an angel reaches a distant other angel who hears it, Albert writes the following important answer:

> The word does not proceed from the talking to the listening angel through some interjacent spirit (*verbum a dicente Angelo non procedit in audientem per aliquem spiritum medium*), who is the vehicle of the word, as is the case in human talk. Instead, [the angelic word] is formed by one [angel] in the other (*ab uno formatur in altero*), when through the intention of communication they direct their concepts toward each other (*sibi suos conceptus dirigunt ad invicem*)—as what is in one mirror is formed by reflection in another, directly opposite to the former, through the spread of light from one mirror to the other situated directly opposite to the first (*sicut quod est in uno speculo, formatur in altero directe sibi opposito, per processum luminis de uno in alterum per reflexionem*). These powers in the angels are called interpretive and auditory, respectively, in the analogous sense.[128]

This text is intriguingly paradoxical in its contents, for it deepens the puzzle about Albert's apparently anticontiguistic model of angelic locution, on the one hand, and explicitly denies any compromise on the contiguist issue, on the other. This text does the latter through the unambiguous, categorical rejection of the idea, expressed in the objection, that in every instance of angelic talk a "word" emanates from the intellect of one angel and enters the intellect of another (the one who listens to the talk). For Albert replies that no word proceeds from the angel who talks to the angel addressed. With this statement Albert effectively puts an end to any anticontiguous interpretation of his model of angelic talk as possibly being an instance of angelic action at a distance. Moreover, Albert denies any anticontiguist implication of his notion of angelic talk by adding that, even if something did pro-

[127] *Summa Theol. II*, tr. 9 q. 35 m 3, obi. 1 (Borgnet, 32, 381b).
[128] *Ibid.*, ad 1 (32, 382).

ceed from the angel who talks to the angel who listens (which is *not* the case), that transmission would naturally take place through a third angel talking as a spiritual medium rather than either through a vacuum or without any suitable medium.

This then is Albert's way of showing that there is no alternative conceivable, such as an anticontiguist one, besides the two listed: angelic talk as not involving a transmission of words from one angel to another and angelic talk involving such transmission through the mediation of a third angel.

However, Albert weakens in two ways the contiguist impact of his denial that any transmission of words is involved in angelic talk, by what he immediately adds to his reply. First, he reiterates his previous characterization of angelic talk as an act of communication by directing concepts toward another angel (*suos conceptus dirigunt ad invicem*). For the idea of directing a concept to another inevitably leads to the original question (How does the word of one angel reach the intellect of another angel?), with its possible anticontiguist implication—especially since Albert ruled out the mediation of a third angel. Second, Albert weakens the impact of his contiguist stance in the reply at hand even more by reverting again to his favorite analogy: The angels direct their concepts toward each other much as the picture in one mirror is formed in another mirror by reflection, with the light radiating from one mirror to the other (*per processum luminis de uno in alterum*). For while two angels engaged in a talk may, indeed, in some respect be analogous to two mirrors reflecting each other's images, the reflection of the mirror image evidently comes about, according to Albert's own admission, by light rays acting as physical media, as they cross the distance between the two light sources, whereas Albert just emphasized the noninvolvement of a third agent at least as a spiritual medium in angelic locution.

Summing up, this *Summa Theologiae* text is at least as misleading and confusing as it is helpful in eliminating the anticontiguist implication from Albert's model of angelic talk. Thus there still is a need for a text which would resolve the basic issue at hand clearly, decisively, and without any misleading element. For such a text we must turn back to the relatively early work of the *Commentary on the Sentences*.

(c) *In I. Sent.* d. 9, I, a. 13, (Borgnet, 25, 295)

This is the text in which Albert employs for a second time the list of the three physical conditions under which alone one light can reach a distant other. However, following the *solutio* containing the discussion about the fact of angelic talk, Albert turns to answering the next

217

question: How do angels talk? Having answered this question with the reply "by decisions and signs" (*nutibus et signis*), Albert writes the following decisive lines:

> But it may still be objected that since it is necessary that something should stimulate the hearer to perceive [the communicated concept], and also that this stimulation should be received from the one [who talks], it follows that the angel who listens receives something from the one who talks; and consequently, something goes out from one into the other [angel] (*aliquid egreditur ab uno in alium*), and one is in potency to the other. To this one must say that [the angel who listens] receives absolutely nothing (*nihil omnino recipit*) that he does not have of the natural things, as is locution. For as we stated before, the turning alone suffices for eliciting [the interest of the other angel]. Hence, by the very fact that he [*sc.* the angel] sees that the other is turned toward him, and since each [of the two angels] is an intelligible light, and the will does not hide that light, the listening [angel] comes to know what he [*sc.* the other angel] wishes to reveal.[129]

A careful consideration of this passage reveals a number of important points. The first is that the objection itself is conceived in the contiguist spirit. For in it is argued that there will be no perception in the angel addressed unless the other who talks to him somehow makes the first perceive what he is saying; therefore, the other angel must receive a stimulation from the angel who talks, and from this, in turn, it follows that a stimulation must go out of the angel who talks and must reach the distant other angel. In brief, the objection conceived by Albert offers a classic contiguist model for angelic locution.

The second point is that Albert's reply in this passage consists of the same two *kinds* of parts of which the *Summa Theologiae* passage considered above consists, namely, of a strong denial that anything emanates from one angel to the other, or is received by the other (*nihil omnino recipit*), and of the explanation of the true nature of angelic talk by the analogy of two physical lights.

---

129 "Sed adhuc obiicitur: quia necesse est quod aliquid excitet audientem ad hoc quod percipiat: et illus excitans oportet eum suscipere a loquente: ergo aliquid recipit ab ipso: et ita *aliquid egreditur ab uno in alium*, et unus est in potentia ad alium. Ad hoc dicendum, quod *nihil omnino recipit*, quod non habet de naturalibus, sicut est locutio: quia sicut prius dicimus, sola conversio sufficit excitationi: unde per hoc ipsum quod videt eum ad se conversum, cum uterque sit lumen intelligibile, et voluntas non est claudens, determinatur in ipso audiente cognitio eius ad hoc, quod ille vult exprimere." (*In I. Sent.* d. 9, I, a. 13, ad quaest., obi. [Borgnet, 25, 295a].)

However, there is a fundamental difference in both the characterization of angelic locution and the utilization of the physical analogy of mutually distant lights. For, first of all, Albert says this time that there is no need for any stimulus to leave the intellect of the speaking angel and going over to the other angel, because the intellectual turning of the former, together with that angel's will to be "heard," suffices for the other angel to notice the conversion and to come to know the communicated concept. Second, Albert continues, the "conversion" and the will to be heard suffice for accomplishing angelic locution precisely because both angels are intellectual lights, so that each one is naturally capable of knowing everything actually intelligible. This is to say, as long as an angel has not decided to reveal to a certain other angel a certain concept, that concept is in that respect and for that reason (*per accidens*) not intelligible or knowable to any other angel. Once, however, the angelic will does not hide or keep secret that concept (*voluntas non est claudens*) from a certain other angel but, instead, decides to render it knowable to the other angel (*vult exprimere*), that concept becomes actually intelligible to that angel. The consequence of this is that the angel comes to know that concept, and to know it through his natural capacity to know everything about the realm of nature (*de naturalibus*).

The basic reason why angels talk this way to each other is, of course, that every angel is like a light source, i.e., an intelligible light (*cum uterque sit lumen intelligible*), as well as the possessor of an intellect capable of knowing everything actually intelligible in reality. Thus the moment an angel decides to communicate rather than to continue hiding a concept in his intellect, the chosen other angel will come to know that thought, and to know it so that the distance between them does not count. To paraphrase this model of angelic locution: Every need for an angelic word traversing the distance between the angelic speaker and the angelic listener either without a medium or with the aid of a third angel and, with that need, every implication of action at a distance is eliminated from angelic locution the moment that the listening angel is conceived of not as a being acted upon by a distant agent but as one who acts on his own, actuating his intellect with respect to a suddenly intelligible object of knowledge; and correspondingly, the angel who initiates the talk is conceived not as an agent acting upon a spatially distant fellow angel but as one who determines himself by deciding to reveal what he has been hiding in his intellect up to that moment. In other words, there are no angelic agents and patients involved in angelic locution; instead, angelic talk involves two independently acting angels: one who changes a hidden and, as such, actually unintelligible concept into an actually intelligible one for a certain other angel, and another angel who suddenly comes to know what was up to that moment actually unintelligible (potentially intelligible) to him.[130]

The key to the proper understanding of Albert's conception of angelic locution is, thus, not to conceive of the angel who hears the talk as a being acted upon or the angel who talks as an agent acting on another angel or angelic locution as involving an agent and a patient but, instead, as consisting of two immanent acts: that of the angelic decision to render a concept actually knowable to a certain other angel and that of another angel suddenly coming to know something that just became actually intelligible to him.

On the basis of this one text, then, one may well conclude the following: First, Albert's model of angelic locution is not anticontiguistic, although some of his statements are definitely misleading and tend to suggest a compromise on causal contiguism by Albert. Second, the reason for Albert's apparent compromise is the severe limitation of the analogy he chooses from the material world. For while the two primary analogues, the mutually distant physical lights, are both agents and patients (as they both emit and receive light rays), each of the secondary analogues, i.e., each of the two angels involved in locution, is only an agent causing an immanent act, and neither is a patient receiving a transient act from the other, although each is an agent differently (one by a decision of his will to reveal, the other by an act of the intellect). Third, Albert is definitely responsible for three things: (1) for giving rise to doubts about his adherence to causal contiguism through his heavy and exclusive reliance on the analogy of physical lights in describing his model of angelic locution, (2) for reverting to a more misleading description of his model at hand in the *Summa Theologiae*, after he succeeded in one passage of an early work in clearing himself of any charge of compromise on the principle of contiguism, and (3) for not drawing a sharp enough line between the *ratio communis* and the uncommon elements of the primary and the secondary analogues in the analogy of light.

3. Classification and Characterization of Albert's Position

The above doctrinal analysis, including Albert's defense of his position against the charge of partial anticontiguism, has already accomplished

[130] Cf. "Qualiter loquuntur? Dico . . . quod nutibus et signis: et nutus vocatur ibi ordo et conversio ad alterum cum voluntate innotescendi, et cum determinatione similitudinis quam habet apud se ad rem." (*In I. Sent.* d. 9, I, a. 13, sol. (Borgnet, 25, 294b].)

the classification of the position Saint Albert takes on the question of action at a distance as being that of causal contiguism—a position which *indirectly* rules out contiguist irrationalism and agnosticism and, *directly*, causal anticontiguism and any compromise between causal contiguism and anticontiguism. Thus there is only one thing left to be done here: to determine the specific characteristics of Albert's causal contiguism.

In terms of the various doctrinal and methodological genera and species of causal contiguism listed in the first, and historical, part of this essay, the following points of classification can be made of Albert's contiguism:

First, one text in the *Commentary on the Sentences* reveals the fundamental metaphysical reason why Albert is a causal contiguist: Since action upon another being means application of an active power to another being, and since no active power can be outside a substrate—the substance either of the agent or of a medium, needs to be in contact with, or present to, the thing that is acted upon.

Second, the texts treating of divine omnipresence and angelic loco-motion in the *Commentary on the Sentences* and the *Summa Theologiae*, as well as the doctrine of the *Physics* concerning the place of the First Mover, make Albert a partly implicit and partly explicit *metaphysical* contiguist with regard to both God and the spiritual creatures. On the other hand, the texts dealing with physical topics, such as the conditions of the spread of physical light in the *Summa de Creaturis* and the *Commentary on the Sentences*, the theory concerning the bloody mirrors in the *Summa de Creaturis*, the statement on causation by natural agents in the *Metaphysics*, the theories of magnetic attraction and solar heat in the *De Caelo et Mundo* and the *De Natura Locorum*, the theory of the torpedo fish in the *De Caelo et Mundo*, and the statement on motion and contact in the *De Animalibus*—all these doctrinal elements establish Albert as a partly implicit and partly explicit physical contiguist.

Third, Albert's *physical* contiguism is *interpretive*, which postulates emanating media (*effluvia*), at least in connection with the bloody mirrors, solar heat, and magnetism, but probably also with regard to celestial generation and lunar influences (the last three in *Quaestiones super "De Animalibus"* and the *De Animalibus*) as well as certain occult phenomena, such as fascination (in the *Mineralia*, the *Metaphysics*, and the *Commentary on the Sentences*). This interpretive physical contiguism also postulates interjacent media at least in regard to the numbing effect of the torpedo fish (in the *De Animalibus* and the *Metaphysics*) in such a way as to distinguish interjacent media that are themselves susceptible to the power they transmit to the patient from interjacent media that are not so susceptible.

Fourth, Albert's physical contiguism is explicitly argumentative on the basis of his detailed empirical demonstration in his *Physics,* whereas his metaphysical contiguism is only implicitly argumentative on grounds of a casual remark made in the *Commentary on the Sentences.*

Fifth, his metaphysical contiguism is, doctrinally, both theistic and angelological (pneumatological): the principle of contact is explicitly as well as implicitly applied to both God and the angels.

Sixth, the contiguist principle is held to apply to corporeal and spiritual agents as well as to God with certainty rather than with some degree of probability only.

Seventh, and finally, while physical and metaphysical contiguism are advocated by Albert as certainly true doctrines, he never leaves any doubt about the applicability of the contiguist principle to God, whereas he often speaks of the acts of the angels and certain corporeal agents in such a way as to leave the impression, however unintentionally, that he represents a limited causal anticontiguism or a compromise between contiguism and anticontiguism.

This much will suffice for the formal classification and characterization of Saint Albert's position on the question of action at a distance. We can turn now to two inevitable historical questions concerning Albert's causal contiguism.

III. *Originality and Influence of Albert's Contiguism*

1. Physical contiguism taken as a basic, generic position on the question of action at a distance, as indicated in the historical review of the various positions listed in Section I, goes back to pre-Platonic times, represented by the pluralists and the atomists, with Aristotle being its first *explicit* advocate (who partly postulated and partly argued for the necessity of causal contact)[131] and Averroes being both its most important nonscholastic interpreter and Albert's greatest authority—next to Aristotle. There were also numerous physical contiguists between Aristotle and Averroes, as well as between Averroes and Albert. Thus, Albert's physical contiguism is far from being an original generic position.

The same holds true for Albert's metaphysical contiguism. Its historical roots in its implicit version go back to Aristotle's theory of the

[131] Aristotle, *Phys.* III, 2, 202a 5–8; VII, 2; *De gen. et corr.* I, 6, 322b 22–25, 27–29; I, 9, 327a 1–6; *De gen. an.* II, 1, 734a 2–4; I, 22, 730b 6–10.

place of the Prime Mover,[132] on the one hand, and to the implicit treatment of divine omnipresence on the basis of divine conservation in the patristic literature,[133] on the other hand, whereas the idea of the necessity of the application of active power as the basic metaphysical reason for causal contiguism has Richard of St. Victor[134] as its proximate source, and Aristotle's doctrine in *Physics*, III, 3, of action taking place *in* the patient, as its original model.

Much the same can be said of Albert's causal contiguism when considered in detail. To mention first his views on his theistic and angelological contiguism, Saint John Damascene is Albert's regularly quoted patristic authority on the reasons for divine omnipresence and angelic locomotion, whereas it was apparently Plotinus's theory of vision containing the particular issue of mirror images[135] that originally inspired Albert's theory of angelic locution, as based on the analogy of mutually distant physical lights.

With regard to the details of Albert's physical contiguism, the story about the electrifying (numbing) effect of the torpedo fish was first mentioned probably by Plato and Aristotle,[136] who, like many subsequent authors of antiquity,[137] make no mention of the anticontiguist

132 Aristotle, *Phys.* VIII, 10, 267b 6–8.

133 Cyrillus Alexandrinus, *In Ioan. Ev.* VI, ad 9, n. 5 (*PG* 73, 960–61). Hilarius, *In Ps.* 124, 6 (Migne, *Patrologia Latina* [henceforth: *PL*] 9, 685A). Fulgentius, *Contra Sermonem Fastidiosi*, c. 4 (*PL* 65, 511B). Anastasius, *De nostris rectis dogmatibus veritates orationes*, II, n. 2 (*PL* 89, 1331D–1332B). Anselmus, *Monologium*, c. 13 (*PL* 158, 161A). Hugh of St. Victor, *Eruditio Didascalica*, VII, 19 (*PL* 176, 828B). Richard of St. Victor, *De Trinitate*, II, 23 (*PL* 196, 913). Alanus ab Insulis, *De arte seu articulis catholicae fidei*, I, theor. 22 (*PL* 210, 602–603). Guillelmus Altissiodorensis, *Summa Aurea*, I, 15, a. 1, arg. 2 et 3 ex ratione and obi to obi. 1 (Parisiis: F. Regnault, 1518), fol. 33v, col. 2 and fol. 34r, col. 1.)

134 "Tenemus . . . quod Deus omnipotens sit . . . . Si ergo vero omnipotens est, consequenter ubique potest. Si ubique potest, potentialiter ubique est. Si ubique potentialiter est, ubique essentialiter." (Richardus, *De Trinitate*, II, 23 [*PG* 196, 913D].) Cf. "Omne quod influit in aliquid, est illi praesens secundum virtutem; nusquam et numquam operatur agens nisi per praesentiam virtutis." (Bonaventura, *In I. Sent.* d. 37 p. 1 a. 1, fund. 2; in *Opera Omnia*, Quaracchi ed. I, 638ab); "anima operatur in toto corpore, ergo in toto corpore est per potentiam" (*In I. Sent.* d. 8, art. un. q. 3, arg. 4, *ed. cit.* I, 170a); and *In I. Sent.* d. 37, p. 1 a. 3 q. 2, ad 4 (I, 639b); and "Oportet enim omne agens coniungi ei in quod immediate agit, et sua virtute contingere." (Thomas, *Summa Theol.* I, 8, 1c.)

135 Plotinus, *Enn.* IV, 5, 7.

136 Plato, *Meno* 80A, C and 84B. Aristotle, *De hist. an.* IX, 620b 19–29.

137 M. T. Varro, *De Lingua Latina*, V, 12, 77. Sextus Empiricus, *Outlines of Pyrrhonism*, I, 93 (Loeb ed., I, 57). Gregorius Naziansis, *Carmina*, II, 1, 1256 (*PG* 37, 1115A). Oppianus, *Alieuticon sive de piscibus*, II, 50–75, III, 149–66. For a list of additional ancient writers mentioning the torpedo fish, see Athanaeus Naucratis, *Deipnosophistai*, VII, 314a–d, 286b (Loeb ed., pp. 411, 413, 285).

aspect of the story. On the other hand, Albert's version of the story, with its anticontiguist implication, and often contiguistically explained, goes back to Theophrastus, Plotinus, and the classical Aristotle commentators, especially Averroes.[138]

Moreover, the apparently anticontiguist story about the bloody mirrors, with its contiguist explanation, originated with Aristotle[139] and had been taken seriously on Aristotle's authority by the classical commentators, including Averroes.

The magnet, whose attractive power Albert explains contiguistically, has been in the philosophical literature ever since Thales,[140] and contiguistic theories of magnetic attraction were expounded by a number of ancient Greek authors known to Albert, the first among them being Empedocles, the conceiver of the prototype of all emanation theories, who was also the first to apply this contiguist theory to magnetism[141]— to be followed by Diogenes of Apollonia, Democritus, Plato, Aristotle, Epicurus, Lucretius,[142] et al.

With regard to the topic of celestial influences, Herodotus was probably the first to speak of the solar "attraction" of water, apparently as an instance of celestial action at a distance,[143] whereas Aristotle was the first to speak of celestial influences in contiguistic terms in connection with solar heat[144] and, together with Theophrastus, in regard to solar generation.[145] Incidentally, it was Aristotle's theory on solar heat in *De caelo*, II, 7, that made Alexander of Aphrodisias initiate a contro-

---

[138] Theophrastus, "Biting and Venomous Animals," in Athanaeus Naucratis, *op. cit.* VII, 314c. Plotinus, *Enn.* IV, 5, 1. Simplicius, *De caelo*, 373, 31–39; 440, 20–28. Themistius, *De caelo*, 110, 20–111, 13. Johannes Philoponus, *Meteorologica*, 48, 7–49, 1. Averroes, *De caelo*, II, comm. 42 (Venetiis: ad Iuntas, 1562), fol. 125DE. The anticontiguist exception seems to be Alexander of Aphrodisias, *Meteor.* 34, 21–28; and, possibly, Olympiodorus, *Meteor.* 33, 7–11.

[139] Aristotle, *De insomniis*, c.2, 459b 27–460a 13.

[140] Thales, in Aristotle, *De an.*, I, 2, 405a 14–22 and Diog. Laertius, *Lives*, I, 24.

[141] Empedocles, in Aetius, *Placita*, A 88.

[142] Diogenes of Apollonia, in Alexander of Aphrodisias, *Quaestiones Naturales*, II, 23, doctrines 89 and 33 in *Diels*, 21 A 171 and A 333. Democritus, in Alexander, *op. cit.* II, 23 (DK 68 a 165). Plato, in Plutarchus, *Quaestiones Platonicae*, q, 7, n. 7; W. W. Goodwin, ed. (Boston: Little, Brown, 1878), V, 436–37—as seen in light of Plato, *Meno* 76 CD, *Theaetetus* 156A–157A, and *Tim.* 45 BC, 67C–68A. Aristotle, *Phys.* VIII, 10, 266b 33–267a 2. Epicurus: in Galen, *On the Natural Faculties*, I, 14, 45 and 47 (Loeb ed., pp. 71–72, 75). Lucretius, *De rerum natura*, VI, 998–1066.

[143] Herodotus, *Historiae*, II, 25.

[144] Aristotle: (1) *De caelo*, II, 4, 287a 6–10; II, 7, 289a 20–32; *Meteor.* I, 3, 340b 34–341a 30. Cf. *De insomniis*, c. 2, 459b 1–4.

[145] Aristotle, *Phys.* II, 2, 194b 13. Theophrastus, *Metaph.* IV, 15, 7a 19–7b 5; IX, 30, 10b 26–11a 1.

versy which eventually involved every commentator on Aristotle, and especially Themistius and Averroes—the two authorities in disagreement with whom Albert eventually partly sided with Alexander. On the other hand, theories about the other principal celestial influence, that of the moon, go back at least to the uncritical *corpus Aristotelicum*.[146]

As far as the occult or magic (*miraculosae*) powers and acts of certain minerals, plants, brutes, and men are concerned, the first, or one of the first, to speak about them are Plato and the unknown author(s) of certain pseudo-Aristotelian works,[147] to be followed by Theophrastus,[148] Plutarch,[149] and a number of Greek and Latin poets, (e.g., Theocritus[150] and Vergil[151]), as well as historians and scientific encyclopedists (e.g., the Elder Pliny,[152] Claudius Aelianus,[153] and Solinus[154]). Clearly Albert had a vast and varied ancient literature to use as

[146] Pseudo-Aristotle, *De mirabilibus auscultationibus*, § 55, in *Aristotle's Minor Works*, W. S. Hett, tr. (Loeb ed., p. 259).

[147] Plato, *Phaedo*, 77E–78A; *Meno* 80A, C; *Euthyd.* 289E–290A; *Theaet.* 149CD; *Rep.* II, 364B, III, 413AC, IV, 426AB, X, 602CD; *Leg.* XI, 932E–933E. Pseudo-Aristotle, *De mirabilibus auscultationibus*, §§ 159, 160; 145, 151 (*ed. cit.*, pp. 319, 313, 317); *Problemata*, VII, 1, 88a 24–25; 2, 886a 29–31 (Loeb ed., pp. 171); 6, 887a 4–5 (p. 175); XX, 34, 926b 20–25 (*ed. cit.* p. 439).

[148] Theophrastus, *Characters*, XXVIII, 2–6, 15–16, 17–20, 28–33. R. C. Jebb, tr., J. E. Sandys, ed. (London: Macmillan, 1909), pp. 141–47. For a parallel text, see Plato, *Rep.* II, 364C.

[149] Plutarchus, "De superstitione," c. 3, 166A in *Moralia* (Loeb ed., II, 460).

[150] Theocritus, *Idyls*; e.g.: (1) No. XIV, 22 in P. E. Legrand, ed., *Bucoliques Grecs*, I: *Theocrite* (Paris: Soc. D'Ed. "Les Belles Lettres," 1953), p. 111; Engl. tr. by A. Holden, *Greek Pastoral Poetry* (Baltimore: Penguin Books, 1974), p. 96; (2) Idyl II, in A. S. Gow, ed., *Bucolici Graeci* (Oxonii: e typographo Clarendoniano, 1952), pp. 9ff.; Holden ed., pp. 51–57; (3) "The Young Herdsman," Gow ed., p. 76, *tr. cit.*, p. 116; (4) Idyl VI, 39–40; Gow ed., p. 29, *tr. cit.*, p. 73.

[151] P. Vergilius Maro, *Ecloga*, III, 102–103; English tr. in T. C. Williams, *The Georgics, and Eclogues of Virgil* (Cambridge: Harvard University Press, 1965), p. 137.

[152] Plinius Secundus C., *Historia Naturalis*, II, 99; L. Ianus & C. Mayhoff, eds. (Lipsiae: B. G. Teubner, 1933), vol. I, 214; also II, 105, 235 (I, 221); VIII, 46, 71 (II, 142); XXIV, 1, 1 (IV, 54); XXIV, 17, 158 (IV, 106); XXXII, 1 (V, 50); XXXII, 38 (V, 51); etc.

[153] Claudius Aelianus, *De natura animalium*, I, 36 (Loeb ed., I, 55); I, 37 (I, 57); I, 38 (I, 59); I, 39 (I, 61); I, 44 (I, 65); I, 54 (I, 73); II, 5 (I, 93); III, 31 (I, 193, 195); V, 45 (I, 341); VI, 14 (II, 27); VI, 31–33 (II, 49, 51): IX, 14 (II, 233, 235); etc.

[154] Caius Iulius Solinus, *Collectanea Rerum Memorabilium*, cc. 7, 11, 30, 39, 42, 44, 54, etc. Moreover, there are more or less isolated data of this kind even in a few church fathers and early schoolmen, such as Ambrosius (*In Ps. David* CXVIII, esp. sermo X, n. 24 [*PL* 15, 1409B]); and Isidorus (*Etymologiae*, XII, 2, 24; 4, 6; 4, 12; 5, 45; 5, 48 [*PL* 82, 438A; 443A; C; 456A, C]).

a source material for alleged instances of occult phenomena, including "fascination."[155]

2. Is there, then, nothing novel or original in Albert's explicit causal contiguism? The answer to this question is that apparently there are at least five more or less important elements of novelty or originality in his causal contiguism.

To begin with, Albert seems to be the first to state explicitly the universality as well as the universal necessity of the contiguist principle in both the physical and the metaphysical contexts. Not even Aristotle qualifies in this respect, because while he explicitly affirms the necessity for causal contact between every corporeal agent and patient, he merely implies the applicability of this principle to the divine First Mover.[156] On the other hand, Saint Thomas later takes the same position as Albert, in his own *Commentary on the Sentences*, and in doing so he walks in the footsteps of his great master, Albert.

The second component of the originality of Albert's causal contiguism concerns the scope of his metaphysical contiguism. For Albert is apparently the first to state explicitly the necessity of causal presence for both divine and angelic activity.[157] John Damascene, who is explicitly quoted by Albert on angelic movement, may seem to have preceded Albert in respect to angelic contiguism. However, unlike Albert, he indicates the fact but not the necessity of angelic presence to the creature the angel acts upon.[158] On the other hand, Alexander of Hales explicitly states the logical consequence of the principle of causal contact (presence) in its application to angelic operation, but not the principle itself as being necessary.[159]

The third doctrinal novelty in Albert's causal contiguism is his theory of angelic locution, which is explicitly so devised, in the *Commentary on the Sentences* at least, as to avoid the appearance that angelic locution is an instance of action at a distance. Genetically this theory of Albert has four historical roots or models. Its analogous basis, the two mutually distant physical lights, goes back to, if it is not inspired by,

---

[155] Albert's most important and direct source is probably Avicenna, *De an.* pars 4, c. 4 (Venetiis, 1509), fol. 20vb. Cf. Albert, *In II. Sent.* d. 7, F, a. 7, sol. (Borgnet, 26, 153a).

[156] Aristotle, *Phys.* VIII, 10, 267b 6–8.

[157] As seen, Albert does the former in *In I. Sent.* d. 37, A, a. 1, arg. 6, item (Borgnet, 26, 229b); and the latter, *ibid.*, L, a. 22, sed contra 2a (26, 259a).

[158] "(Ubi) se conferant, illic spiritualiter adsint et operantur." (Damascenus, *De fide orthodoxa*, II, 3 [PG 94, 870B].)

[159] "(Necesse) est quod ibi sit [*sc.* angelus] ubi operatur . . . . " (Alexander, *Summa Theologica*, I–II, i. 2 tr. 3 s. 2 q. 2 tit. 2 m. 1 c. 1 a. 1, arg. (d) n. 180 [Quaracchi ed., II, 233a]).

Plotinus's theory of mirror images[160] in such an obvious fashion that it is impossible not to see the similarity between the two theories.[161]

A second historical root of Albert's theory at hand is Pseudo-Dionysius's characterization of the angel as a "manifestation of hidden light and pure mirror."[162] A third historical root, Damascene's remark that the angels speak without using words,[163] probably gave rise to Albert's conception of angelic talk as a doubly immanent act.[164] Finally, the model or source closest to Albert's own time is evidently Alexander of Hales's theory of angelic locution, in respect to four of its doctrines.[165]

Despite all these elements borrowed by Albert, especially from Alexander of Hales, Albert's theory of angelic locution not only differs on

---

160 "(It) is simply that, as long as the object stands there, the image is visible, in the form of colour shaped to a certain pattern, and when the object is not there, the reflecting surface no longer holds what it held when the conditions were favourable." (Plotinus, *Enn.* IV, 5, 7; S. MecKenna, tr., revised by B. S. Page [London: Faber and Faber, 1956], p. 336.)

161 A few years before Albert wrote his *Commentary on the Sentences*, Alexander of Hales resorted to a similar analogue, the mirror, in a rather strange form, while discussing the nature of angelic talk: "(Locutio angeli) est per aliquam similitudinem, ut si speculum, cum vellet, daret suam similitudinem alteri speculo, ita angelus, cum vult, communicat suam intelligentiam alteri angelo." (*Summa Theologica* [sc. *Summa fratris Alexandri*], I–II, i. 2 tr. 3 s. 2 q. 1 tit. 3 c. 3, resp. n. 146 [II, 194b]) Nevertheless, it is still true to say that Albert's analogy between two light sources and two angels speaking has, at least objectively, Plotinus's theory of mirror images as its earliest model.

162 "(Imago) est Dei angelus, manifestatio occulti luminis, speculum purum, splendidissimum . . . ." (Pseudo-Dionysius, *De divinis nominibus*, c. 4 Section 22 [*PG* 3, 724B]; tr. by John Scotus Erigena in *PL* 122, 1141C).

163 ". . . quibus nec lingua opus sit, nec auribus; sed sine ulla prolati sermonis ope mutuo sibi sensa sua communicant et consilia." (Damascenus, *De fide orthodoxa*, II, 3 [*PG* 94, 867, 870].)

164 John Damascene's influence may have been direct or indirect; and in the latter case, one coming through Alexander of Hales, who characterizes angelic talk as "*dicere apud se*" by explicitly quoting Damascene's text cited in n. 163 above: *Summa Theologica*, I–II, i. 2, tr. 3 s. 2 q. 1 tit. 3 c. 4, 2a, n. 147 (II, 195a).

165 The four doctrines of Alexander are as follows: (1) The angel engaged in talking is a genuine agent: *Summa Theol.* I–II, i. 2, tr. 3, s. 2, q. 1 tit. 3 c. 5, 3a, n. 148 (II, 196a). (2) The angel who talks is an agent insofar as he wills to manifest some intelligible species (*verbum*) to another angel: *ibid.*, c. 5, ad 5–6, n. 148, p. 197b; *ibid.*, c. 6, sol., n. 149, p. 198ab. (3) There is an analogy between physical light and angels as spiritual lights, insofar as both have self-manifestative powers (*vim manifestandi se*): *ibid.*, c. 5, ad 5–6, n. 148, p. 197b; c. 6, obi. 6a, n. 149, p. 197b. (4) Since angelic talk, as self-manifestation, is the sole effect of angelic will, spatial distance between two angels engaged in talking does not matter: "Distantia vel propinquitas localis nihil facit ibi, immo quantumcumque distent, potest loqui unus alii." (*Ibid.* c.7, qu-la II, resp., n. 150; II, 198b.)

two points from Alexander's[166] but also is more nearly complete in precisely that respect which, in Albert's theory, upholds the principle of causal contiguism despite the stress on the irrelevance of nearness or distance between two angels involved in talk. For Albert makes it clear, in the *Commentary on the Sentences* at least, that an angel can talk to a spatially distant other angel precisely because (and to the extent that) the will to manifest any angelic concept renders that concept actually intelligible to the other angel; and thus the angel addressed immediately comes to know that concept by his innate power of knowing all actually knowable natural things, for intellectual knowledge does not require the spatial presence of the knower to the thing known. This all-important metaphysico-epistemological element is missing from Alexander's corresponding theory—an element that contributes to the originality of Albert's contiguistic theory of angelic locution.

A fourth factor of originality is only indirectly doctrinal. It consists in the fact that Albert is apparently the first to have connected spatial distance with the contiguist issue when, in the *Summa de Creaturis* and the *Commentary on the Sentences*,[167] he uses two mutually distant luminous bodies as the physical analogues of two mutually distant angels engaged in talk, and, in doing so, he lists proportion between distance and active power as one of the three necessary conditions of light rays from one luminous body reaching a distant other luminous body.[168] This element of originality may seem to be insignificant from

---

[166] One such point lies in the intellectualist character of Albert's theory, as opposed to the voluntaristic character of Alexander's theory. According to the former, once an angel decides to make his thought knowable to another angel, the latter angel comes to know that concept with physical necessity, by virtue of his innate power of knowing all actually knowable natural things; whereas Alexander makes this coming-to-know of the latter angel dependent on the will of that angel: "In locutione, quae est per naturam, . . . in voluntate audientis est quod se convertet vel non: unde requiritur voluntas eius ad hoc ut habeat effectum locutio." (*Ibid.,* c. 7, qu–la I, resp. n. 150, p. 198ab.) The other point of disagreement lies in the fact that, in Albert's view, distance matters only if the angel talks to a human being, whereas Alexander opines that spiritual distance or propinquity does make a difference in angelic locution in a way hidden from us: "exigitur tamen propinquitas vel distantia spiritualis quae nos latet adhuc." (*Ibid.,* c. 7, q–la II, resp. n. 150, p. 198b.)

[167] *Summa de creaturis*, I, tr. 4 q. 60 a. 2, sol. (Borgnet, 34, 636a); *In I. Sent.* d. 9, I, a. 13, sol. (Borgnet, 25, 293b).

[168] In contrast to this and two other conditions listed by Albert for the light of one luminous body reaching the other, Alexander of Hales mentions only one such physical condition: "Videmus duo corpora luminose potentia recipere se invicem: unde si sibi obiiciuntur, unum recipit ab alio sine medio, sicut patet in duobus speculis." (*S. Theol.* I–II, i. 3 tr. 3 s. 2 q. 1 tit. 3 c. 6, 6a, n. 149, p. 197b.)

the point of view of the contiguist issue. However, as will be shown below, the post-Albertine history of the idea of action at a distance proves it to be of great importance.

Finally, a partly doctrinal novelty in Albert's causal contiguism lies in the combination of two apparently inconsistent facts which are relevant to the contiguist problem. To understand their relevance, one must realize that being interested in the various kinds and instances of magic powers and activities is natural for a scientist and that any such interest may be expected from a causal anticontiguist much more than from a contiguist, since every magic phenomenon per se tends to suggest the possibility of action at a distance. However, one finds Albert *the scientist* display in a number of his works, mainly in the scientific works of *Mineralia, De Animalibus,* and *Quaestiones super "De Animalibus,"* an unusually great interest in magical or occult powers and activities, for he writes on them or mentions them often, whereas Albert *the philosopher* explicitly advocates causal contiguism at both the physical and the metaphysical levels. True, there had been others before Albert who wrote equally extensively on magical or occult phenomena. However, as already stated, nobody before Albert had explicitly taught the impossibility of every action at a distance, be that action corporeal or incorporeal, angelic or even divine. For this reason the display of great interest in magic or occult phenomena, which appear to be instances of action at a distance, by the first explicit metaphysical contiguist is, indeed, a surprising and truly novel feature.

3. Some of the factors of originality in Albert's causal contiguism lead us over directly to the last question to be discussed here briefly—the question of the historical influence Albert may have exerted with his brand of causal contiguism.

There is a general historical truth that must be borne in mind from the very beginning: One can hardly find a single instance of Albert's influence upon later philosophical thought that is truly independent and really distinct from the influence of Thomas Aquinas, because the influence of Albertism had soon coalesced with the influence of Thomism. The main reason for this historical fact is that Thomas's views on many major issues are similar to Albert's, partly because the thinking of the greatest disciple of Albert had been profoundly influenced by the master. Accordingly, the influence of Albert's partly novel causal contiguism must itself be considered within the framework of the influence Albert exerted by some of his relevant doctrines upon Thomas, who, in turn, influenced later scholastic thinkers. There is room here for mentioning only two specific areas of doctrinal influence, one flowing from

Albert's metaphysical contiguism and the other from his physical contiguism.

The metaphysical theory influencing Thomas concerns angelic locution. As seen, while echoing Plotinus, Pseudo-Dionysius, Damascene, and Alexander of Hales, Albert holds the novel view that angelic locution does not represent an instance of action at a distance because the angel who speaks does not send anything across a distance to the angel addressed; instead, angelic locution consists in two distinct and unilaterally related immanent acts of the angel speaking and the angel spoken to. But this theory is, in virtually all its details, exactly the theory Saint Thomas offers for angelic locution not only in his own commentary on the *Sentences* but also in the *De veritate* and even in his principal work, the *Summa Theologiae*.[169] On the other hand, this Thomistic theory, adopted from Albert, has become the traditional Thomistic doctrine on angelic locution,[170] securing the principle of causal contigu-

[169] (a) On distance: "Cognitio angeli indifferenter se habet ad distans et propinquum secundum locum." (Thomas, *Summa Theol.* I, 55, 2, ad 3.) "Unde in locutione angeli nullum impedimentum facit distantia loci." (*Ibid.* 107, 4c.) Cf. *ibid.* ad 1; I, 89, 7, ad 3; and *De ver.* 9, 6c. (b) On the immanence of angelic talk, not requiring a medium: "cum locutio sit operatio intellectus ipsius [*sc.* angeli], nihil facit ad eam propinquitas vel distantia loci." (*De ver.* 9, 6c.) "(Angelus) ad quem fit locutio, . . . non recipit aliquid a loquente; sed per speciem quam penes se habet, et alium angelum et locutionem eius cognoscit. Unde non oportet ponere aliquod medium per quod deferetur aliquid ab uno in alterum." (*De ver* 9, 6, ad 4.) (Locutio) angeli . . . est locutio interior, quae tamen ab alio percipitur." (*Summa Theol.* I, 107, 4, ad 1.) (c) On the role of the will of the angel who talks and the intellect of the angel addressed: "Ex hoc vero quod conceptus mentis angelicae, ordinatur ad manifestandum alteri per voluntatem ipsius angeli, conceptus mentis unius angeli innotescit alteri, et sic loquitur unus angelus alteri." (*Summa Theol.* I, 107, 1c.) (Cf. *ibid.*, a. 2c. and 3c.; *De ver* 9, 4c. and ad 9, 11, 15.) "Ei ideo quam cito [angelus] vult manifestare suum conceptum, statim alius cognoscit." (*Summa Theol.* I, 107, 1, ad 1.) (d) On angels as spiritual lights analogous to physical lights: "Angeli sunt quaedam naturalia lumina." (*De ver.* 9, 4, 15a.) "Lux corporalis manifestat seipsam ex necessitate naturae . . . . Sed in angelis est voluntas, cuius conceptus manifesti esse non possunt nisi secundum imperium voluntatis." (*Ibid.* ad 15.) Interestingly, the misleading emphasis on the per se true analogy of physical light and angel in Albert's works is missing from Thomas's treatment of angelic talk, although, as seen in this last quotation, Thomas himself concedes the analogy from the point of view of light.

[170] E.g.: (1) *Johannis Capreoli Defensiones Theologiae divi Thomae Aquinatis in secundo Sententiarum*, dist. 11, q. 1 a. 1; C. Paban and T. Pehues, eds. (Turonibus: A. Cattier; reproduced Frankfurt/Main: Minerva, 1967), pp. 489b–497a; (2) Cajetan, *Commentaria in I. Summae Theologiae*, q. 107 a. 1, comm. 1–3; in *S. Thomae Aquinatis Summa Theologiae*, Leonine edition, tom. IV (Romae: ex typographia polyglotta S. Congr. de Propaganda Fide, 1889), p. 489; (3) *Collegii Salmanticensis Fratrum Discalceatorum Cursus Theologicus*, IV, tract. 7: De Angelis, q. 107, disp. 15, dub. 2 Sections 1–2 (Parisiis: V. Palmé; Bruxelles: G.

230

ism with regard to angelic action in direct contrast to Scotus's corresponding and equally influential theory, which explicitly considers angelic talk as an instance of spiritual action at a distance.[171]

4. Even more impressive is the influence Albert has exerted on the *physical* contiguism of later schoolmen with his contiguistically novel emphasis on the necessity of proportion between distance and an active power gradually reaching a distant patient.

Aquinas is the first to imitate Albert in this respect in a contiguist context, by listing two of Albert's three necessary conditions for physical action reaching the distant recipient through a medium. For Thomas points out that the magnet will not attract the iron, except within a proper distance, i.e., a distance proportionate to the attractive power of the magnet *and* in the absence of all impediments.[172] It is also significant that Thomas formally *argues* on the basis of distance that the relation between magnet and iron belongs to the order of efficient rather than final causality—an argument which, indirectly, is likely to show the contiguistic character of magnetic attraction. For when he reasons that if the magnet were the final cause of the iron's motion toward the magnet, as the proper place is for the heavy (i.e., in "gravitational" motion), the iron would move toward the magnet from any

Lebrocquy, 1877), pp. 818b–21b; (4) F. Suárez, *De Angelis*, II, c. 28, n. 37 (*Op. Omn.* II, 269); (5) Joannes a S. Thoma, *Tractatus de Angelis in I. Summae Theologiae*, qq. 106–107 (*Cursus Theologici*, IV, pars 1) disp. 45 art. 1 (Parisiis: Desclée et Socii, 1953), pp. 813–28; (6) Charles R. Billuart, *Summa S. Thomae hodiernis academiarum moribus accommodata*, II, diss. 7a. 1 (Parisiis: V. Palmé; Bruxelles: J. Albanel, 1870 [?]), pp. 68–72.

171 Duns Scotus, *Reportata Parisiensia*, II, d. 9 q. 3, in *Opera Omnia*, XXII (Paris: L. Vivès, 1894), pp. 655a–657b. Cf. Bartholomaeus Mastrius de Meldula (1602–73), *Disputationes Theologicae in I. Sent.*, disp. 2 q. 9 aa. 1–4 (Venetiis: apud J. J. Hertz, 1698), pp. 137–47. For an intermediate position which is contiguistic (unlike Scotus's), but maintains (unlike Albert and Thomas) that angels cannot talk at great distances, see Richard of Middleton, *Super II. Sent.* d. 9 a. 1 q. 1; L. Silvestrius A Sancto, ed., tom. II (Brixiae: de consensu superiorum, 1591), pp. 120–21.

172 "(Magnes) dat aliquam qualitatem ferro, per quam movetur ad ipsum. Et quod sit verum patet ex tribus. Primo quidem quia magnes non trahit ferrum ex quacumque distantia, sed ex propinquo . . . . Secundo, quia si magnes aliis perungatur, ferrum attrahere non potest; quasi aliis vim alterativam ipsius impedientibus . . . ." (Thomas, *In VII. Phys.* lect. 3, Maggiolo ed., n. 903, p. 461a.) With the first reason St. Thomas points here to a feature of magnetism which is left unmentioned in the "Epistle to Sygerus Foncaucurt concerning the Magnet" (1269) by his contemporary, Petrus Peregrinus of Maricourt; although Peter's epistle at hand is praised as *satis pro tempore eruditum* in *De Magnete*, c. 1 (Londini: P. Short, 1600), p. 5, by William Gilbert, the great Renaissance authority on magnetism.

distance,[173] Thomas could as well argue this way more specifically for the magnet's acting upon the iron through the medium which is elsewhere identified as the air.[174]

The first to use precisely this argument is Thomas of Sutton around the end of the thirteenth century, in his *Liber Propugnatorius*. For he takes issue with Scotus's interpretation of solar generation as an instance of physical action at a distance (*non videtur verum*) by arguing that if the sun directly caused things on or in the earth, "there seems to be no reason why it should not be able to act directly at any distance, and equally well at any distance" (*quare non possit agere in quacumque distantia et equaliter in omni distantia*) or why "the imperfect substance should not be able to act at any distance (*in quacumque distantia*) as well as the perfect substance does . . .," and yet "all these things seem to be absurd" (*quae omnia videntur absurda*).[175] Some two decades later Peter Aureolus adopts this argument from Thomas of Sutton, broadens it to cover all physical powers, and adds a significant explanation: If a power could act at a distance, i.e., if distance did not impede action, that power could act even on things infinitely distant; yet it is a fact that neither the sun nor any other physical power can act on an object infinitely distant (*agere non potest in aliquid distans in infinitum*).[176] Moreover, Aureolus continues, the reason why a power cannot act at any distance is that the agent diffuses its action throughout the entire medium (*diffundit actionem suam per totum medium*); and in this manner "the power becomes exhausted at a certain distance" (*in certa distantia deficit*).[177]

Approximately half a century after Aureolus, John Buridan points out—as an anticontiguist objection to his thesis—that the magnet "attracts and moves iron from a distance (*a longinquo*)."[178] Thus he apparently implies what Thomas of Sutton explicitly stated before him, viz., that the power of magnetic attraction becomes exhausted within certain spatial limits. A century or so later, in 1450, Nicholas of Cusa

173 (Si) autem ferrum moveretur ad magnetem solum sicut ad finem, sicut grave ad suum locum, ex qualibet distantia tenderet ad ipsam (Thomas, *loco cit.*, *primo*).

174 (Virtus) magnetis attrehentis ferrum defertur ad ferrum per medium aerem . . . (Thomas, *De ver*, 5, 9, ad 17).

175 Thomas Anglicus, *Liber Propugnatorius super primum Sententiarum contra Johannem Scotum*, dist. 37 (Venedig, 1523), unveränderter Nachdruck (Frankfurt a. Main: Minerva, 1966), fol. 116vB.

176 Aureolus, *In I. Sent.* d. 37 q. un. a. 2 (Romae: ex typographia Vaticana, s. A. Zanetti, 1596), fol. 865aB–C.

177 *Ibid.*, fol. 865bB.

178 Johannes Buridanus, *In VII. Phys.* q. 4, 4a (Parisiis: a Magistro Petrile, 1509), fol. 95va.

232

takes an enormous step forward on the scientific level with regard to magnetism by suggesting a law concerning a definite relation between magnetic force and distance, viz., that magnetic attraction proportionately decreases as the distance from the magnet increases[179]—a law that was empirically confirmed as late as 1750 by John Michell.[180] On the other hand, while Franciscus Toletus in the year of 1573, three centuries after Thomas, expresses his complete agreement with Aquinas's theory of "fascination" as employing an effluvium,[181] Dominic Soto, Toletus's younger contemporary, uses both the argument of Thomas of Sutton and the reasoning of Saint Thomas with regard to magnetism: At certain distances the magnet does not attract iron, and this fact indicates that the iron does not naturally move toward the magnet as toward its final cause; for if the movement of the iron were natural, the iron would move toward the magnet from any distance (*a quacumque distantia*). Thus the iron is moved by a quality imparted to it by the magnet; and when the magnet is large enough, it can impart that quality from a great distance (*a longe*).[182]

A new element in the development of the Albertine idea of distance in physical action comes toward the end of the seventeenth century, from the camp of the anticontiguist schoolmen—from Bartholomew Mastrius of Meldula. He teaches that God wills the corporeal creatures to have a definite sphere of activity, which sphere is proportionate to their limited powers.[183] With this view the Albertine idea spreads over from the Thomistic to the Scotistic school of philosophy.

The last two centuries have witnessed an enormous renaissance of interest in the possibility of action at a distance, and with it a gradually

---

[179] "(Magnete) immoto remanente, puto quod per hoc pondus retrahens virtus magnetis proportionabiliter ponderata dici posset." (N. de Cusa, *Ydiote de staticis experimentis*, n. 175, in [*Neuausgabe des Strassburger Drucks von 1488*], I, Paul Wilpert, ed. [Berlin: W. de Gruyter, 1967], p. 283.)

[180] "The Attraction and Repulsion of Magnets decrease, as the Squares of the Distances from the respective Poles increase." (John Michell, *A Treatise of Artificial Magnets*, conclusion 6 [Cambridge: printed by J. Bentham, 1750], p. 19.)

[181] "Quod autem dicitur de fascinatione oculi, non negamus, sed dicimus, vapores nocivos egredientes per oculos aerem ocendere, et aer nocet aliis . . . ." (Toletus, *In VII. Phys.* c. 2 text. 13 q. 2, ad 3 [Coloniae Agrippinae: apud haeredes A. Brickmann, 1629], fol. 196r.)

[182] D. Soto, *In VII. Phys.* (1545) q. un., a. 1 (Salamanticae: A. a Portonaris, 1551), fol. 92rb.

[183] "Deus voluit iuxta eorum virtutem limitatam, quod usque ad certum terminum, in qua etiam operarentur, non discrete sed continue, ne permiscerentur, out confundarentur actiones diversorum agentium." (B. Mastrius, *Disputationes Theologicae in I. Sent.* [written before 1673], disp. 2 q. 5 a. 2, n. 229 [Venetiis: ex typographia Balleoliana, 1719], p. 71a.)

growing sophistication in the use of Thomas of Sutton's Albert- and Thomas-inspired argument, as perfected by Aureolus, on the one hand; and along the lines of the suggestion of Nicholas of Cusa, on the basis of new scientific discoveries accumulated mainly since Isaac Newton, on the other hand. One needs to consult only such schoolmen as Henry Haan,[184] Tilmann Pesch,[185] Ludovicus de San,[186] Sanctus Schiffini,[187] Albert Stöckl,[188] and J. J. Urráburu,[189] as well as, of the twentieth-century authors, S. Reinstadler,[190] J. A. McWilliams,[191] F. X. Maquart,[192] Kenneth Dougherty,[193] and especially Henry Van Läer,[194] to

[184] "Actio in passum omnino distans physice fieri nequit. Arg. (Ex experientia.) Si corpora naturaliter in passum omnino distans agere possent, et natura mediorum et terminorum distantia relate ad effectum esset indifferens; atqui nullum corpus est, cuius aut actiones medio interposito impediri non possent aut efficacia non decresceret aucta distantia; ergo . . . ." (H. Haan, *Philosophia Naturalis* [*Cursus Philosophicus in usum scolarum*, III], lib. II, c. 1 thesis X, n. 76 [Friburgi Brisgoviae: Herder, 1848], p. 57.) The two conditions listed by Albert are unmistakably present in this argument.

[185] "Si agens non requireret suae virtutis continuationem per intermedium, posset agere in quacunque distantia . . . ." (T. Pesch, *Institutiones Philosophiae Naturalis* [*Philosophia Lacensis*], I, disp. 2 sect. 1, n. 76 [Friburgi Brisgoviae: Herder, 1880], p. 65.) "Die Tatsache, dass bei der verschiedenen Naturwirkungen bei geringerer Entfernung die Intensität grösser ist, und mit wachsender Entfernung abnimmt, weist unverweigerlich darauf hin, dass es nirgends in der Natur ohne irgendwelche Vermittlung eine 'Wirkung in die Ferne' gibt." (Pesch, *Die grossen Welträthsel, Philosophie der Natur allen denkenden Naturfreunden*, I, n. 268 [Freiburg im Breisgau: Herder, 1883], p. 488.)

[186] L. de San, *Cosmologia* (*Institutiones Metaphysicae Specialis*, I), n. 281 (Lovanii: C. Fonteyn, 1881), pp. 351, 354–55.

[187] Sanctus Schiffini, *Principia Philosophica*, n. 633 (Augustae Taurinorum: apud fratres Speirani, 1889), p. 693.

[188] A. Stöckl, *Metaphysik* (*Lehrbuch der Philosophie*, 2. Abtheilung), (1868), § 60, n. 2. Siebente Auflage (Mainz: F. Kirchheim, 1892), p. 127.

[189] J. J. Urráburu points to the fact of obstacles interfering with the action of corporeal agents on distant bodies, and speaks also of the "sphere of activity," beyond which the corporeal agent cannot act, as well as of the role of distance. (*Theodicea*, I [*Institutiones Philosophicae*, VII], disp. 3, c. 2, n. 156 [Vallisoleti: J. E. A. Cuesta, 1899], p. 490.)

[190] S. Reinstadler, *Cosmologia* (*Elementa Philosophiae Scholasticae*, I), (1901) lib. 3 c. 1 sect. 1 a. 2 n. 1, III (Friburgi Brisgoviae: Herder, 1929), p. 491.

[191] J. A. McWilliams argues for the thesis, "The interaction of forces requires an existent medium," by pointing out that the opponents of physical contiguism "cannot explain why a force, e.g. gravitation, even when exerted on a single object, diminishes as the distance increases, and vice versa . . . ." (*Cosmology* [1928], 2d ed. [New York: Macmillan, 1950], p. 85.)

[192] F. X. Maquart, *Philosophia Naturalis* (*Elementa Philosophiae*, II) (Parisiis: A. Blot, 1937), p. 107.

[193] K. Dougherty, *Cosmology* (Peekskill, N. Y.: Graymoor Press, 1952), p. 98.

[194] Henry Van Läer, a professional scientist and scholastic thinker, discusses the

realize the truth of this statement. This is to say that Albert's mention of certain physical facts in a remotely contiguist context has, in seven centuries, grown into the most powerful empirical argument or set of arguments against causal anticontiguism. For this reason the partly material and partly formal influence of Albertine thought upon modern and contemporary thinking about action at a distance is an undeniable fact.

The topic of this study is a relatively minor issue in the thought of Saint Albert and occupies a very modest position among the philosophical, theological, and scientific problems Saint Albert discusses in his works. Moreover, by the time Saint Albert came to deal with it, the contiguist question had been in the philosophical and related literatures for some sixteen or seventeen centuries. Nevertheless, as shown in this essay, Albert succeeded in making his own contribution to the history of this enduring question by way of some originality and in a somewhat novel fashion and succeeded even in influencing thinking about the issue for centuries to come—mainly through his great disciple from Aquino. For these reasons the question of action at a distance is not only one involving all three areas in which Saint Albert excelled but also one whose treatment is a small yet clear sign of the genius of the man who has been reverently and admiringly called *doctor universalis*.

---

role of distance with regard to action at a distance most extensively and persuasively. If there is action at a distance, he reasons, "the collaboration of a medium is eliminated," and "the whole causality of the exercised influence is placed in the properties of the two remaining factors—the agent and the recipient body." For "empty space or inert intermediary matter cannot influence" the action, since neither the action itself nor its effect can pass through the empty space or the intermediary matter. But the cause of a change in the intensity of the action of a force "cannot lie in the agent," because that intensity is "wholly determined by the nature of the acting substance" so that the activity of the substance "will remain fully constant as long as the agent perseveres in the same conditions," whereas the activity cannot be changed by "the mere increase or decrease of the distance" from the influenced body. "Neither can," Van Läer continues, "the cause of a change in intensity lie in the recipient," for "the nature and the intensity of the effect is fully determined, apart from the agent, by the properties of the recipient," whereas these properties "cannot be influenced by the distance from the agent." From all this it follows, he concludes, that the fact that "electric, magnetic and gravitational actions decrease at increasing distance clearly shows that with respect to these phenomena there is no action at a distance," and thus "we must postulate a medium." (*Philosophico-Scientific Problems* [*Duquesne Studies, Philosophical Series*, 3], chap. IV: "The Possibility of Action at a Distance," p. v, a. 5; H. Koren, tr. [Pittsburgh: Duquesne University Press, 1953], pp. 100–101.)

Part V

History

Albertus Magnus and Universal Hylomorphism: Avicebron

A Note on Thirteenth-Century Augustinianism

JAMES A. WEISHEIPL, O.P.
Pontifical Institute of Mediaeval Studies

Labels such as Platonism, Aristotelianism, Augustinianism, Averroism, and even Thomism can be very dangerous and misleading. They can give the impression of being definable doctrines in terms of genus and difference, as though they were species, of which there are many individuals of identical nature. It is even more dangerous to toy with such labels as neo-Augustinianism or "Augustinianism versus Aristotelianism" in the thirteenth century. Yet such labels have commonly been used, perhaps inevitably, by all medievalists of the past one hundred years who have tried to understand the doctrinal issues in medieval controversies. Nowhere has this been more evident than in the innumerable studies "über den Kampf des Augustinismus und Aristotelismus in der 13. Jahrhunderts" or, more generally, in the use of the term "Augustinianism" in the study of medieval thought. Although Gilson himself needed to have recourse to such labels, he carefully pointed out that they "are so many words pointing to groups of facts that are not definable in terms of genus and specific difference. Description applies to them better than definition."[1]

Here I wish to contribute to the scholarly description of Augustinianism, for it was under the flag of "tradition" and of Saint Augustine that the perpetrators of the condemnations of 1277 sailed. John Pecham, who clearly represents the mentality triumphant at the Parisian and Oxford condemnations of 1277, wrote in 1285 that the authority of Saint Augustine and traditional, orthodox Christianity had been challenged by "irreverent innovations (*novitates*) in language, *introduced within the last twenty years* into the depths of theology against philosophical truth, and to the detriment of the Fathers whose positions are disdained and openly held in contempt."[2] But the question is,

[1] E. Gilson, *History of Christian Philosophy in the Middle Ages* (New York: Random House, 1955), p. 655, note 19.

[2] Letter to the bishop of Lincoln, June 1, 1285, in *Registrum epistolarum fratris Johannis Peckham*, ed. C. T. Martin (London: Rolls Series, 1885), 3:901.

What is the Augustinianism that men such as Pecham sought to defend in the face of such "innovations"? Was the so-called Augustinianism cherished by a man like Pecham and his predecessors really the older and more traditional teaching?

Scholars have already done much to answer such questions. Gilson has focused attention on the doctrine of divine illumination as one of the "traditional" and "Augustinian" positions and has shown that it is an Augustinian doctrine substantially altered under the influence of Avicenna, that is, an *Augustinisme avicennisant*.[3] Daniel Callus has proved conclusively that the so-called Augustinian doctrine of the plurality of substantial forms was not the older or more common teaching of Parisian masters but rather was a novelty stemming from Avicebron by way of Gundissalinus.[4] Dom Odon Lottin has examined the lineage of another supposedly "traditional" and "Augustinian" doctrine, that of the unity of the soul with its faculties, and has found the doctrine in its Aristotelian garb to be no older than the teaching of William of Auvergne's *De anima* (1231–36) and that it is an offspring rather of Avicenna and Avicebron than of Augustine.[5]

[3] E. Gilson, "Les sources gréco-arabes de l'augustinisme avicennisant," *Archives d'histoire doctrinale et littéraire du moyen âge* 4 (1929): 5–149; introd. to "The Treatise *De anima* of Dominicus Gundissalinus," ed. J. T. Muckle, *Mediaeval Studies* 2 (1940): 23–27. For a discussion of the background see F. Van Steenberghen, *La Philosophie au XIIIe Siècle* (Louvain: Publ. Univ. "Philosophes Médiévaux, 9, 1966), pp. 9–19.

[4] D. A. Callus, "Introduction of Aristotelian Learning to Oxford," *Proceedings of the British Academy* 19 (1943): 229–81; "Gundissalinus' *De Anima* and the Problem of Substantial Form," *New Scholasticism* 13 (1939): 338–55; "The Origins of the Problem of the Unity of Form," *Thomist* 24 (1961): 257–85 (reprinted in *The Dignity of Science*, ed. J. A. Weisheipl [Washington, D.C.: Thomist, 1961], pp. 121–49). Callus has thus filled out in greater detail an idea originally proposed by M. Wittman, *Die Stellung des hl. Thomas von Aquin zu Avencebrol (Ibn Gebirol)*, in *Beiträge zur Geschichte der Philosophie des Mittelalters*, Bd. 3, heft 3 (1900), pp. 1–32, and largely supported by G. Théry, "L'Augustinisme médiéval et le problème de l'unité de la forme substantielle," *Acta Hebdomadae Augustinianae-Thomisticae* (Taurini: Marietti, 1931), pp. 140–200; and O. Lottin, "L'unité de l'âme humaine avant saint Thomas d'Aquin," *Revue Néo-scolastique de Philosophie* 34 (1932); 449–67 (substantially repr. in *Psychologie et Morale aux XIIe et XIIIe Siècles* [Gembloux: Duculot, 1942], 1:463–79).

[5] O. Lottin, "L'identité de l'âme et des ses facultés pendant la première moitié du XIIIe siècle," *Hommage à Monsieur le professeur Maurice de Wulf* (*Revue néoscolastique de Philosophie*) 36 (1934): 191–210; substantially reprinted in *Psychologie et Morale aux XIIe et XIIIe Siècles*, ed. cit., 1:483–502. This so-called Augustinian thesis was mainly supported by the pseudo-Augustinian *De spiritu et anima* (PL 40, 779–932), written by the Cistercian Alcher of Clairvaux; see G. Théry, "L'authenticité du *Du spiritu et anima* dans S. Thomas et Albert le Grand,"

In agreement with the conclusions of such scholars, I hope to isolate other characteristics of the reputed "Augustinianism" of the thirteenth century and to show that such characteristics are not really the traditional teaching of Christian thinkers, or at least of the older Parisian masters. As I hope to show, Avicebron rather than Augustine is the source of what appeared to the vast majority of thirteenth-century theologians as the traditional and sound doctrine. Also, as we shall see, Saint Albert the Great was one of the first to recognize clearly the influence of Avicebron on this doctrine.

Therefore, in this paper I shall try to develop briefly three main points: (1) the main elements of thirteenth-century Augustinianism; (2) Avicebron and his influence; and (3) the attitude of Albertus Magnus toward Avicebron and his teaching.

I. The Main Elements of Thirteenth-Century Augustinianism

In the same letter, quoted above, to the bishop of Lincoln, Oliver Sutton, written on June 1, 1285, John Pecham, then archbishop of Canterbury, wrote a moving description of what he felt to be the traditional, orthodox doctrines challenged in his day. Although Pecham was very careful not to attack the Friars Preachers as a group, he was deeply convinced that his own Friars Minor were more devoted to the sound, orthodox teaching of Saint Augustine. Toward the end of the long letter he pointedly raised the question that so troubled him:

> Which doctrine is more solid and more sound: the doctrine of the sons of Saint Francis, namely of Friar Alexander [of Hales] of happy memory, of Friar Bonaventure and others like him, who rely on the Fathers and the philosophers in treatises secure against any reproach, or *that very recent and almost entirely contrary doctrine*, which fills the entire world with wordy quarrels, weakening and destroying with all its strength what Augustine teaches concerning the eternal rules and the unchangeable light (*de regulis aeternis et luce incommutabili*), the faculties of the soul (*de potentiis animae*), the seminal reasons imparted to matter (*de rationibus seminalibus inditis materiae*), and innumerable questions of the same kind? Let the Ancients be the judges, since in them is wisdom! Let the God of heaven be judge, and may he remedy it![6]

Revue des sciences philosophiques et théologiques 10 (1921); 373–77. Saint Thomas was well aware of the spurious nature of this work; see *Quaestio de anima*, a.12 ad 1.

[6] Loc. cit. p. 901.

First of all, as Gilson has noted,[7] the "very recent" doctrine "that had been introduced within the last twenty years" (*citra viginti annos*) would definitely implicate the major writings of Saint Thomas Aquinas, such as the *Summa contra gentiles* (1259–65), the *Summa theologiae* (1266–73), and the Aristotelian commentaries (1269–73). One might add that this could also be taken to include the major Aristotelian paraphrases of Albertus Magnus (ca. 1250–ca. 1270), as well as his *De scientia mirabili Dei* (ca. 1272–75). However much Pecham claimed to love the Order of Friars Preachers, he could not help deplore the "novelties" of Thomas and Albert. The basic question, however, is whether the "almost entirely contrary doctrine" of Albert and Thomas was the real "novelty," or was it Pecham's own view of Saint Augustine that was the real "novelty"?

Second, when Pecham wanted to list *some* of the points on which the Augustinianism of the Franciscans opposes the Aristotelianism of the Dominicans, the first that immediately come to his mind are: (1) divine illumination, (2) the real identity of the powers of the soul with its essence, (3) the *rationes seminales* in all matter, "and innumerable questions of the same kind." To anyone familiar with the works of Saint Augustine, these three points would seem to be purely and indisputably "Augustinian" in the true sense of the word. But when we come to examine Pecham's own writings, it becomes abundantly clear that his personal understanding of these terms comes from sources far different from those of Augustine.[8] In fact, the traditionalism Pecham claims for his views cannot be traced back any further in the Latin West than to the Latin translations from Arabic made in the late twelfth century; and in university centers, such as Paris and Oxford, they cannot be traced back any further than the 1220s and 1230s. Gilson is undoubtedly right in saying that "the positions of Pecham conform to the *theologia communis* of the thirteenth century," provided one means by this what was commonly taken to be the Augustinianism of the thirteenth century. It was indeed the "common teaching" of the schools after the 1220s. The question then becomes, What are its origins?

In order to simplify the matter as much as possible, it would seem that the so-called Augustinianism of the thirteenth century can be described by five basic characteristics: (1) voluntarism, (2) universal hylomorphism, (3) plurality of substantial forms in every creature, (4) an Avicennian interpretation of divine illumination, and (5) the

[7] Gilson, *History of Christian Philosophy*, ed. cit., p. 359.

[8] For a summary of Pecham's views, see Gilson, ibid. pp. 359–61 with notes, esp. 80.

identity of the soul with its powers. Enough has already been said by other scholars about the last three characteristics to justify our concentration on the first two, especially since the third is simply a logical consequence of the second, and since the ensemble of the first, second, and third constitutes what was understood as the *rationes seminales inditae materiae*. This is not to say that no further work needs to be done on the fifth characteristic listed. Nor is it to say that further characteristics of thirteenth-century Augustinianism cannot be found. It only means that insufficient attention has been given to the first two as a basis for the third characteristic, especially for the purpose of this paper.

The first basic characteristic of thirteenth-century Augustinianism would seem to be the primacy of will over knowledge, not only in itself, but also, and more especially, in God. Under this heading I would include the emphasis on affectivity over understanding or contemplation, practicality over speculation, *agere* over *intelligere*, as well as a view of *sacra doctrina* as more practical than speculative and "law" as an act of the will rather than an ordination of reason. In the Parisian condemnation of March 7, 1277, it is abundantly clear that the compilers of the list of 219 propositions thought that what was at stake was the omnipotence of God.[9] Over one-third of the propositions were condemned because they seemed either to limit God's omnipotence or to take away man's free will.[10]

This emphasis on God's omnipotence can be traced to the initial Christian reaction in the late twelfth century to the necessary emanationism of Alfarabi, Alkindi, *Liber de causis,* and especially Avicenna. In the necessary emanationism of the Muslim philosophers, all reality flows necessarily (*ex necessitate naturae*) from the First Principle in an eternal descent from the highest to the lowest. Just as all illumination necessarily and immediately flows from Light (*Lux*), the source,

[9] R. Hissette, *Enquête sur les 219 articles condamnés à Paris le 7 mars 1277* (Louvain: Publ. Univ., Philosophes Médiévaux, 21, 1977); J. Wippel, "The Condemnations of 1270 and 1277 at Paris" *Journal of Medieval and Renaissance Studies* (Durham) 7 (1977): 169–201.

[10] The only fundamental exception to this concern over divine omnipotence is the doctrine of the impossibility of an eternal world, the assumption being that if anything were co-eternal with God, it could not have been "created." Thus the clear position of Saint Thomas is condemned: creation *de nihilo,* as such, does not necessarily involve a prior duration of nonbeing, but only the priority of the First Cause by nature (cf. prop. 99). All the condemned propositions dealing with Aristotle's eternity of the world, motion, and time indicate that the compilers of the list identified "being created" with "being created in time," that is, every creature is *factus de novo* by God's free will in such a way that *non esse precessit esse duratione, et non natura tantum;* otherwise, it would not be "created."

with decreased intensity the further brightness is from its source, so all creatures flow necessarily and eternally in a decreasing hierarchy from the One Font of Being, the Supreme Intelligence. In the necessary emanationism of Avicenna, not only is God's free will entirely denied but the emanation of the universe is eternal, though dependent on the First by a priority of nature and thus not "created" *ex nihilo*.

At Paris the first clear rejection of Avicennian determinism and all that it implies is to be found in William of Auvergne, later bishop of Paris (1228–49). His major writings were composed at Paris between 1223 and 1240, coming at the very beginning of thirteenth-century Augustinianism. What was at stake for William was not only the Christian doctrine of creation in time but also the complete dependence of all created things on the omnipotent will of God: *potestas naturarum sola voluntas est conditoris*. Thanks to the identification of creation *ex nihilo* with creation in *principio*, the "ontological indigence of created being affects the whole cosmogony and cosmology of William of Auvergne."[11] But, as Gilson correctly noted, "William's reaction [to the Avicennian thesis of an eternal, necessary emanation] goes far beyond what one could normally foresee."[12] He sees as the crucial issue the absolute omnipotence of God's free and undetermined Will. Besides citing many miracles as manifest proofs of God's liberty with respect to nature, he found in Avicebron's *Fons vitae* the "philosophical justification" of the Christian notion of free creation *ex nihilo* against the necessary emanationism he found in Avicenna. No doubt it was for this reason that William ranked Avicebron as a Christian philosopher[13] and as *unicus omnium philosophorum nobilissimus*.[14] As we shall see, however, the intermediary between Avicebron's philosophy and William of Auvergne was the Spanish archdeacon Dominic Gundisalvi.

The second basic characteristic of thirteenth-century Augustinianism we wish to consider is universal hylomorphism, which stems solely from Avicebron's *Fons vitae* through Gundisalvi's *De anima* and *De processione mundi* and is the ultimate foundation for the so-called Augustinian thesis of plurality of substantial forms in all creatures. The question was usually discussed under the heading of whether angels and the human soul are composed of "matter" and "form" or whether all created things are necessarily constituted by a universal matter and a universal form. At the peak of the controversy the burning question

---

[11] Gilson, *History of Christian Philosophy*, ed. cit., p. 255.
[12] Ibid.
[13] *De universo* I, 1, 26, *Opera Omnia* (Paris 1674), 2:16.
[14] *De trinitate* c.12, *Opera Omnia*, 2:16–17.

was discussed under the heading, "Whether the dead body of Christ retained a *forma corporeitatis* numerically identical with his living body."

To place this second characteristic in proper perspective, however, it would be best to consider it separately, in the context of Avicebron's thought, then in its influence through Gundisalvi.

II. *Avicebron and His Influence*

For our purposes there is little point in calling Avicebron by his real Jewish name, Solomon Bar Jehuda ibn Gabirol (fl. 1020–58), or by the Arabic rendition, Abu Ayyub Soleiman ben-Ya'hya ibn-Djebirul, since this fact was completely unknown until 1845, when Solomon Munk discovered a Hebrew summary of the *Fons vitae* made by Schem-Tob ibn-Falaquera in the thirteenth century.[15] Apparently during his lifetime in the vicinity of Málaga, Córdoba, and Valencia, he enjoyed some fame as a Hebrew poet of mystical and Platonic leanings, who also wrote a Hebrew grammar in verse, and compiled a collection of "Thoughts," a treatise on ethics, and some writings of biblical exegesis. His principal work, however, was composed in Arabic and circulated among the Latins under the title *Liber fontis vitae*, or simply *Fons vitae*, and he was known to the Latins only by the name Avicebron (or Avicembron, Avencebrol, or some other variant). Although William of Auvergne thought he was a Christian, the vast majority of Latin scholastics took him to be an "Arab" of uncertain date, as did Albertus Magnus and Thomas Aquinas.[16] Strangely, Moses Maimonides (1135–1204) never once referred to him, although on one occasion Thomas Aquinas thought one thesis of Avicebron to be of the *Loquentium in lege Maurorum* according to Maimonides.[17] On an earlier occasion Thomas even thought that Avicebron's thesis of plurality of forms had been disproved explicitly by Avicenna (980–1037).[18] We have no idea what his Latin translator, Domingo Gundisalvi, thought were Avicebron's religious leanings, but it is clear that he utilized the doctrines translated for his own Christian philosophy, just as he did those of Avicenna.

[15] S. Munk describes the discovery in his *Mélanges de philosophie juive et arabe*, 1st ed., 1857; 2d enl. ed., 1859; repr. (Paris: Vrin, 1955), pp. 151–32.

[16] See J. I. Saranyan, "Sobre la immaterialidad de las substancias espirituales (Santo Tomás versus Avicebrón)," *Rivista di Filosofia Neo-Scolastica* 70 (1978); 63–97, esp. 63–66.

[17] Saint Thomas, *QQ. Disp. De verit.* q.5, a.9 ad 4.

[18] Saint Thomas, *In II Sent.*, dist. 12, q.1, a.4.

Among modern Jewish scholars there have been some notable studies of Ibn Gabirol's thought and his influence on Jewish thinkers, especially on Abraham ben-David (d. 1180), his abbreviator ibn-Falaquera (thirteenth century), Isaac ibn-Laṭif (thirteenth century), on the formation of the Jewish Kabbala.[19]

Since, however, we are primarily concerned with Avicebron's influence on the formation of thirteenth-century Augustinianism, we can limit our consideration to his *Liber fontis vitae* and his Latin translator, variously known as Dominic Gundisalvi, Gundissalinus, or Domingo Gonzalbo, who seems to have had some assistance from a certain "Johannes." Because of the exceptional importance of Gundisalvi, I will give fuller attention to him than might seem necessary. It is an astonishing fact that we know of only five extant manuscripts of the Latin *Fons vitae*, only one more than was known to the editor of the critical text in 1892, whereas many manuscripts of Gundisalvi's writings are known to exist. It may very well be that the vast number of Latin scholastics of the thirteenth century learned of Avicebron's teaching not through reading the *Fons vitae* but through reading the shorter summaries and adaptations of Gundisalvi.

Despite the strong reluctance of Lynn Thorndike to credit either Gundisalvi or "John" with the translation of *Fons vitae*,[20] M.-T. d'Alverny is undoubtedly correct in claiming that from manuscript evidence alone at least four translations "can be positively ascribed to [Dominic Gundisalvi]":[21]

1. Avicenna's *De anima* (*Liber sextus naturalium*), translated with Avendauth;

2. Avicenna's *Metaphysics*;

3. Algazel's *Summa theoricae philosophiae* (including logic, metaphysics, and physics—a summary of Avicenna), translated with "Magister Johannes"; and

4. Avicebron's *Fons vitae*, translated with "Johannes."

[19] See A. Heschel, "Der Begriff der Einheit in der Philosophie Gabirols," *MGWJ* 82 (1938); 89–111; "Der Begriff des Seins in der Philosophie Gabirols," *Festschrift Jacob Freimann* (Berlin, 1937), pp. 68–77; "Das Wesen der Dinge nach der Lehre Gabirols," *HUCA* 14 (1939): 359–85; Jacques Schlanger, *La Philosophie de Salomon Ibn Gabirol: Étude d'un Neoplatonisme* (Leiden: Brill, 1968); and Sara O. Heller Wilensky, "Isaac Ibn Laṭif—Philosopher or Kabbalist?" *Jewish Medieval and Renaissance Studies*, ed. A. Altmann (Cambridge: Harvard University Press, 1967), pp. 185–224, esp. 201–10.

[20] L. Thorndike, "John of Seville," *Speculum* 34 (1959): 20–38, esp. pp. 29–30, 34–35; *Catalogue of Incipits of Mediaeval Scientific Writings in Latin*, 2d ed. (Cambridge, Mass.: Medieval Academy, 1963), col. 842.

[21] *New Catholic Encyclopedia*, s.v. "Dominic Gundisalvi (Gundissalinus)."

Other possibilities are of no concern to us at the moment, although the personal writings of Dominic are.

Thorndike has done much to clarify some of the confusion among various Spanish authors and translators who were known as "John of Spain," "John of Seville," or "John of Toledo," but we are more concerned with Gundisalvi and his dates, since he was the only source through whom Avicebron reached the Latin scholastics.

From a critical reading of the prefatory letter that accompanied the translation of Avicenna's *De anima*, it is now clear that the work was dedicated to the archbishop of Toledo, John (1151–66), and not to his predecessor, Raymond (1126–51), as previously thought. It is also clear that Gundisalvi was then an archdeacon residing in Toledo, who was associated with a learned Jew (*israelita philosophus*) named Avendauth. From the prefatory letter (written in Latin by Avendauth!) we learn that Avendauth translated verbatim the Arabic text into Castilian, leaving Gundisalvi to translate the Castilian into Latin. The archdeacon Don Domingo Gonzalbo appears again in two Toledan charters dated 1178 and 1181, while in 1190 he signed a charter as a member of the cathedral chapter of Segovia.[22] Thus all of Dominic's activity must be placed in the second half of the thirteenth century, first his translations, then his personal adaptations.

All of Dominic's personal writings, drawn largely from his own translations, are much more than a mere compilation of extracts. They are a sincere effort to render the thought of "Arabic" philosophers (*philosophi*) intelligible to the Latin West and to synthesize their thought in a way that would be acceptable to Christians. Gilson has already shown that the *De anima* of Gundisalvi is a conscious adaptation of Avicennian psychology to Christian teaching, supported by quotations from Augustine, Boethius, and the New Testament.[23] Daniel Callus has shown that, in his *De anima*, Gundisalvi expounds both the unity of form thesis of Avicenna and the plurality thesis of Avicebron.[24] We should note, however, that in the *De anima* Gundisalvi presents not only Avicenna's theory of illumination and unity of substantial form, but also Avicebron's universal hylomorphism. Moreover, Gundisalvi's treatise *De unitate et uno* circulated for centuries in the Latin West under the name of Boethius (PL 63:1075–78), although Aquinas rejected it as spurious: "Dicendum quod liber *De unitate et uno* non est Boetii, ut ipse stilus indicat."[25] While the

22 See d'Alverny, ibid., relying on C. A. González Palencia and D. Mansilla.

23 "The Treatise *De Anima* of Dominic Gundissalinus," ed. J. T. Muckle, intro. by Gilson, *Mediaeval Studies* 2 (1940); 23–103, see pp. 26–27.

24 D. A. Callus, "Origins of the Problem of the Unity of Form," *loc. cit.*

25 St. Thomas, *Quaestio De spirit. creat.* a.1 ad 21.

treatise appears somewhat "Boethian" in its explanation of the various senses in which *unitas* can be said of God and creatures taken singly or in aggregates, it utilizes material drawn from both Avicenna and Avicebron, as the critical edition clearly shows.[26] Far more important is Gundisalvi's *De processione mundi*, which is not only a systematic presentation of Avicebron's universal hylomorphism with Avicennian metaphysics of *fluxus* but also an unsuccessful attempt to render it acceptable to Christians of the Latin West.[27] God is indeed presented as the *Voluntas creatrix* of the universe from all eternity, but what he creates *ex nihilo* is only the first "universal form" and the first "universal matter" from which all things are made. The "formation" of other things, as distinct from "creation," is accomplished by intelligences. Gundisalvi, however, "Christianizes" this unacceptable position by explaining that angels create not by their own authority but as ministers of God's authority (*sic et angeli creant animas ministerio tantum, non auctoritate*). Thus the human soul should not be called a "creature of angels, but of God" (*et ideo anima creatura angeli non dicitur, sed Dei, cuius auctoritate creatur*).[28] Perhaps the last of Gundisalvi's personal writings in his *De immortalitate animae*, in which he defends the incorruptibility of the soul as a form, and seems—according to Gilson—to be indebted to William of Auvergne.[29]

While it is impossible at present to give specific dates for any of the translations or writings of Dominic Gundisalvi, we would not be too far wrong, considering what has already been said, if we put the translation of *Fons vitae* by Gundisalvi and a certain "Johannes" around the year 1165 or a little later.[30] Much further research needs to be done to show how the ideas of Avicebron reached the schools of Paris and Oxford.

Neither Albertus Magnus nor Thomas Aquinas could find anything favorable to say about Avicebron's *Fons vitae*, although clearly both

[26] P. Correns, ed., *Die dem Boethius fälschlich zugeschriebene Abhandlung des Dominicus Gundissalinus De Unitate*, BGPMA 1, 1 (Münster, 1891), see esp. pp. 21–28, where the editor shows that it was composed after the Latin translation of *Fons vitae*.

[27] Georg Bülow, ed., *Des Dominicus Gundissalinus Schrift "Vom dem Hervorgange der Welt" (De processione mundi)* BGPMA 24, 3 (Münster, 1925); i–xxvi, 1–56.

[28] Gundisalvi, *De anima* c.5, ed. cit. p. 51; *De proc. mundi*, ed. cit., pp. 50–52.

[29] Georg Bülow, ed., *Des Dominicus Gundisali Schrift von der Unsterblichkeit der Seele*, BGPMA 2, 3 (Münster 1903); see G. Bülow, ed., *De proc. mundi*, p. xxv; Gilson, *History of Christian Philosophy*, ed. cit., p. 653, note 4.

[30] *Avencebrolis (ibn Gebirol) Fons Vitae ex Arabico in Latinum translatus ab Iohanne Hispano et Dominico Gundissalino*, ed. Clemens Baeumker, BGPMA 1, 2–4 (Münster, 1892–95), 1–339.

had read the entire Latin translation. Thomas, who discussed Avicebron's *Liber fontis vitae* by name at least twenty times,[31] rejected all of his arguments as "frivolous." Albertus Magnus, who seems to have made a progressive study of the work from his Parisian days in the mid-1240s until his paraphrase of *De causis* (before 1271), found the entire work too "fallacious," "improbable," and "ridiculous" to have been written by any serious philosopher at all, but a huge joke perpetrated by undergraduates on an unsuspecting public.

Nevertheless, in this dialogue in five "treatises" (or books) between a Master and a Disciple concerning the "Fountain of life," Avicebron does present a Neo-Platonism based on two main points that are undoubtedly Judaic and directed against Muslim philosophers: (1) God produces everything not by a necessity of nature but by a creative Will (*Voluntas creatrix*); (2) God's infinite and transcendent simplicity (unity) is essentially different from the composed nature of every creature. As such, these two points are biblical enough to be acceptable to all Christians, but what Avicebron makes out of them is somewhat complex and involves many difficulties.

As for the first point, the primacy of God's creative Will (*Voluntas creatrix*), Avicebron clearly wishes to eliminate philosophical emanationism as proposed by Alfarabi, Alkindi, Avicenna, Algazel, and *Liber de causis*, by making the Divine Will the supreme cause in the production of the universe.[32] Avicebron makes the Divine Will the mediating link between God and the universe.[33] Thus the cosmic process is not a necessary and impersonal flow or radiation of all things from the First Principle but a voluntary activity of the Divine Will. There are many difficulties, however, about this divine Will in Avicebron's doctrine. Conceived of as inactive, it is said to be identical with God, while conceived of as active, it is somehow a perfection of the Divine Essence.[34] This would seem to jeopardize the absolute unity of God, as many scholars have pointed out.[35] Further, Avicebron so emphasizes the supremacy of the Divine Will that God's intellectuality and wisdom somehow get buried in his hidden transcendence, and are not even attributed to God. One might object that Avicebron identifies the divine Will with wisdom and with what he calls the divine Word:

31 See C. Vansteenkiste, "Autori Arabi e Giudei nell'opera di San Tommaso," *Angelicum* 37 (1960); esp. pp. 356–65.

32 *Fons vitae* I, 2; II, 13; V, 39 and 41.

33 Ibid., I, 7; III, 38; IV, 19; V, 39.

34 Cf. Ibid., III, 57; IV, 19.

35 See A. Heschel, "Der Begriff der Einheit in der Philosophie Gabirols," *MGWJ* 82 (1938): 89–111.

"Et hoc est quod Verbum, scilicet Voluntas, postquam creavit materiam et formam, ligavit se cum illis, sicut est ligatio animae cum corpore, et effudit se in illis et non discessit ab eis et penetravit a summo usque ad infimum."[36] But this says nothing about divine *intelligence* as such; he speaks only about the binding together of all things through his Will. What has happened to the Supreme Intelligence? the Divine Wisdom? Aristotle's Subsistent Intellection? Avicenna's emphasis on a *Primus intellectus agens* made more sense to Saint Albert than what appears to be a despotic and omnipotent Will, with no recognition of intelligence, presented by Avicebron. Nevertheless, Avicebron's admission of a Divine creative Will was sufficient for William of Auvergne to make him a Christian. The third difficulty, however, concerning the primacy of God's *Voluntas creatrix* was far more serious: all that God could or need create *ex nihilo* was a binary "universal matter" and "universal form." That is to say, instead of granting that an omnipotent will could create a multiplicity of things, Avicebron insisted that from the Supreme Unity there can come only duality: matter and form. Thus Albert is quick to point out that Avicebron in the *Fons vitae* is "the only [philosopher] who says that from one simple principle two [things] must immediately proceed in the order of nature, since the number "two" follows upon unity."[37] And Saint Thomas notes: "Some say that the soul and absolutely every substance besides God is composed of matter and form; indeed the *first author to hold this position is Avicebron*, the author of *Liber fontis vitae*."[38] This is the origin of the later *binarium famosissimum*: after One must come Two.[39]

The second Jewish element in Avicebron's philosophy sounds simple enough at first sight: God alone is absolutely simple; all creatures are composed. William of Auvergne and all the older Parisian theologians followed Boethius in this: God alone is simple (*Omne simplex esse suum et id quod est unum habet*), and all creatures are composed of *quod est* and *esse* (*Omni composito aliud est esse aliud ipsum est*).[40] There were many interpretations of this Boethian distinction between *quod est* and *quo est* (or *esse*), as Gilson has explained on many occasions. The main point is that the admission of some composition of this sort in all creatures was traditional among all older theologians. For Avicebron, on the other hand, the first effect of creation is *materia*

[36] *Fons vitae* V, 36 p. 323, 17–20.

[37] Saint Albert, *Liber de causis* I, tr.4, c.8, ed. Borgnet 10: 428a.

[38] *Quaestio disp. De anima*, a.6.

[39] See D. A. Callus, *Introduction of Aristotelian Learning to Oxford*, (extract from *Proceedings of the Brit. Acad.*), p. 26.

[40] Boethius, *Quomodo Deus Bonus est.* (*De hebdomadibus*), reg. 7 and 8.

universalis and *forma universalis,* of which all created substances are composed.

The first problem here, according to both Albert and Thomas, is that Avicebron has a univocal concept of *matter* and that whatever has the characteristics of "receiving" or "sustaining" anything else, such as form, properties, or activities, must be designated as *matter.*[41] Since, for Avicebron, matter cannot exist without form because its nature is to desire form, then *materia universalis* must be the subject of *forma universalis* in order to constitute a "substance" (*substantia*), whether this substance be the heavens or the earth (Gen. 1:1). The Divine Will creates this duality *ex nihilo,* but everything else is "formed" from this first universal "substance," which necessarily is finite and capable of sustaining other forms. The first division of universal substance (composed of universal matter and form) is into *corporeal,* i.e., three-dimensional bodies, by receiving a *forma corporeitatis,* and *incorporeal,* i.e., intelligent spirits or angels, by receiving a *forma spiritualitatis.* Corporeal and incorporeal substances, for Avicebron, are themselves incapable of generation or corruption. Both corporeal and incorporeal substances, however, need to be further differentiated.

Corporeal substances, made up of universal matter, universal form, and a *forma corporeitatis,* are of three kinds: (1) those which are elements, of which there are only four; (2) those which are made up of elements (*elementatum tantum*), which constitute the sublunar world; and (3) those which are neither elemental bodies nor made up of elements, i.e., celestial bodies. Thus it is fitting that from the Divine Will (the One), should come substance (two), corporeal (three), and elements (four), in such a way that the fourth is divided not only into four elements but also into two parts, matter and form. Consequently, when the element water (*aqua*) becomes stone (*lapis*), the *forma corporeitatis* of "body" does not and cannot change; it must remain numerically the same. All that happens is that the *forma aqueitatis* is corrupted and in its place is generated a *forma lapideitatis.* Most of the sublunar world, however, is made up of the four elements in various ways such that they are "natures," "living," or "animal"; each of these is constituted of a multiplicity of forms, each of which inheres in the preceding. Thus only after universal "substance" is composed of created universal matter and universal form can the Infinite Fountain of Life, the true *Lux,* which is God, illumine all things *per lumen* in the

---

[41] See Saint Thomas, *Sum. theol.* I, q.50, a.2 ad 2; *De pot.* q.3, a.7; *De spirit. creat.* a.3; *De sub. separat.* cc.4–6; Saint Albert, *Sent.* II, dist.1 A art.4, ed. Borgnet, 27:14b–15a; *De causis* I, tr.1, c.6, p. 373.

"formation" of more and more complex substances. All corporeal substances are "formed" by incorporeal substances, or intelligences.

For Avicebron there are not only different kinds of incorporeal substances but also a multiplicity of individuals within each species by reason of *spiritual matter*. There are, in fact, for Avicebron four kinds of incorporeal substances: (1) angels, which contemplate the divine simplicity of God; (2) ministers of the divine plan, such as the "spirits of the planets"; (3) human souls, subject to the human condition because of the body in which they dwell; and (4) demons condemned to eternal damnation. Since, for Avicebron, every matter, being a *subject*, individualizes the form it receives, it is not at all inconsistent for him to allow for many individual angels within any given species.

The usual places where scholastic theologians discussed problems involving Avicebron's universal hylomorphism was in questions such as "whether all creatures are composed," "whether the human soul is like an angelic substance," and "whether there is one matter for all creatures." Such questions were frequently discussed in relation to Book II of the *Sentences,* in questions concerning the human soul or the simplicity of angels or in related questions.

III. *Albertus Magnus and Avicebron*

Considerable research is still needed to draw the connecting lines between Avicebron's Latin *Fons vitae* and the early proponents of universal hylomorphism at Paris and Oxford. In an unpublished doctoral dissertation presented in 1930, E. Kleineidam apparently maintained that the principal defender of the hylomorphic composition of spiritual substances was Alexander of Hales, while among its opponents were William of Auvergne and John of la Rochelle.[42] According to Lottin, Kleineidam rested his main case on the so-called *Summa fratris Alexandri,* a pseudonymous collection posterior to John of la Rochelle's *De anima* (1235) and William of Auvergne's *De universo* (between 1231 and 1235).[43]

Without claiming to have found the original defenders of the hylomorphic composition of spiritual substances, Lottin tried to push the

[42] E. Kleineidam, *Das Problem der hylomorphen Zusammensetzung der geistigen Substanzen im 13. Jahrhundert, behandelt bis Thomas von Aquin,* 1930, reviewed by O. Lottin in *Bulletin de théol. anc. et méd.* (1930), no. 812.

[43] O. Lottin, "La composition hylémorphique des substances spirituelles: Les débuts de la controverse," *Revue néo-scholastique de Philosophie* 34 (1932); 21–41.

investigation to the period before 1235. In an all-too-brief study,[44] he noted the following:

1. Roland of Cremona, the first Dominican master at Paris (1229–30), defended the view that angels are composed of a form and spiritual matter (*materia spiritualis*), as is the rational soul.

2. Roland's successor, Hugh of St.-Cher (1230–35), recognized that some (*quidam*) maintain a hylomorphic composition in human souls and angels, but he rejected it in favor of the older Boethian distinction between *quod est* and *quo est*, intending by this that all creatures are distinct from God in that their being is distinct from the exercise of that being.

3. Philip the Chancellor, writing at the same time as Hugh, recognized the position of those who say that after the monad, which is God, must come the dyad, which is matter and form (the *binarium famosissimum*); but he denied that the word "substance" must be used univocally of material and spiritual things, and held that, although spiritual beings are "subjects" of accidents, that subject should not be called "material." Thus Philip admitted that spiritual substances, or angels, are composed (*binarius*), but their composition is that of *quod est* and *quo est*, potentiality and actuality: *intelligentia est binarius, eius 'quod est' et 'quo est', sive potentiae receptivae et potentiae activae; et ideo dicitur quod est hoc et hoc.*"[45]

4. Finally, Lottin added only one further author, Odo Rigaud, the third Franciscan master at Paris (1245–48) and a contemporary of Saint Albert the Great. Friar Odo, commenting on the *Sentences* (*ca.* 1243–45), makes all the distinctions and utilizes all the terms found in the *Summa fratris Alexandri* and in the entire Franciscan tradition. That is to say, Odo identifies *quod est* and *quo est* with *matter* and *form*, but the kind of "matter" a spiritual substance has is not corporeal nor celestial but *spiritualis et intellectualis*.[46]

The extremely important point buried in Lottin's brief study is twofold: (1) William of Auvergne and all the older theologians explained the composition of all creatures in terms of *quod est* and *quo est* (sometimes *esse*), however diversified their individual understanding was of these Boethian terms; (2) the well-known universal hylomorphism of Saint Bonaventure, Roger Bacon, and John Pecham, is already defended in Friar Odo Rigaud and in the *Summa fratris Alexandri*. The great problem is, How much of this universal hylomorphism can be

[44] Ibid.
[45] Text in Lottin, ibid. p. 29, lines 18–20.
[46] Ibid. p. 38.

traced back to Alexander of Hales himself? His authentic *Glossa* on the four books of *Sentences* and the *Quaestiones "antequam frater esset"* are of no help here.

Before we get to Albert himself, one minor, though significant, point should be made. The earliest known reference to the Avicebron doctrine of universal hylomorphism is found in John Blund, who apparently was teaching in the faculty of arts at Paris or Oxford around 1200. In his *Tractatus de anima*, c.24, John Blund asks "whether the [human] soul is simple or composed." The usual arguments for the composition of the soul from *materia spirituali* and from *forma spirituali* are all taken from Gundisalvi's *De anima* and rejected in favor of simplicity, just as the plurality of souls had been reported by Blund and rejected in favor of unicity.[47]

It should already be clear that the universal hylomorphism, defended by John Pecham and Saint Bonaventure, is the real innovation in Parisian theology. The older explanation of creaturely composition was the Boethian distinction between *quod est* and *quo est* or *esse*. Even William of Auvergne, who welcomed Avicebron's voluntarism, rejected his universal hylomorphism in favor of the Boethian composition of *quod est* and *quo est* in all creatures and their identity in the Godhead. Enough has been written by Gilson and others to show that the traditional Boethian understanding of those terms is very different from that of Saint Thomas. But the point is that no Boethian understanding of *quod est* was ever called *materia spiritualis* until the 1220s.

A statement made by Saint Thomas around 1253–54 in his commentary on the Second Book of the *Sentences* is most illuminating:

> Some say that matter exists in every created substance and that the matter of all things is alike [*una*]. The originator of this position seems to be Avicebron, who wrote the *Liber fontis vitae*, which many people follow [*quem multi sequuntur*].[48]

That is to say, by the early 1250s many Parisian theologians adhered to the teachings of Avicebron's *Fons vitae*. In the scholastic terminology of the 1250s, this position implies: (1) the primacy of God's creative will; (2) universal composition of all created substances from universal matter and universal form; (3) all spiritual substances, including the human soul, are composed of a spiritual matter, which is the subject of a spiritual form; (4) there can be many individual angels of the same

---

[47] *Johannes Blund Tractatus de Anima*, ed. D. A. Callus and R. W. Hunt (London: British Academy, Auctores Britannici Medii Aevi 2, 1970), pp. 89–91.

[48] Saint Thomas, *In II Sent.* dist.3, q.1, a.1.

species without corporeal matter, but not without spiritual matter; (5) the plurality of substantial forms in all created substances; and (6) in all elemental changes the *forma corporeitatis* can be neither generated nor corrupted but remains numerically the same. These not only are the well-known positions of John Pecham,[49] Richard of Mediavilla,[50] Saint Bonaventure,[51] and many other notable theologians but also represent the mentality that triumphed in the condemnations at Paris and Oxford in 1277.

When Albert the Great was sent to Paris in the early 1240s to lecture on the *Sentences* and later become the first German Dominican master in theology from the University of Paris, William of Auvergne was still bishop of Paris (1228–49), Odo Chateaurnoux was chancellor of the University, and Pope Innocent IV was bishop of Rome (1243–54). Although William no longer taught in the University, he continued to write, preach, and exert an influence. Later, Roger Bacon recalled that twice he heard Bishop William of Paris reprove and argue against those who made the *intellectus agens* a faculty of the human soul, a position both Albert and Thomas were to hold. According to Bacon, not only William of Auvergne but also Robert Grossesteste, Adam Marsh, and all wise men of antiquity taught that the *intellectus agens* is God himself.[52] In the early 1240s men like Roger Bacon, Robert Kilwardby, and other masters were actually giving lectures on the philosophy of Aristotle, even though the proscriptions of 1210, 1215, and 1231 had not been officially revoked. Nevertheless, the Aristotelian books of natural philosophy, ethics, and metaphysics were not yet required courses in the University. By that date just about every professor in the University had some acquaintance with the philosophy of Aristotle, oftentimes inadequate. The Neo-Platonic spectacles with which they read the new Aristotle were slowly being corrected by the newly translated literal commentaries of Averroes that arrived in Paris during the 1230s and 1240s.

By the time Albert came to prepare the final copy of his commentary on the second book of the *Sentences* in 1246, he had already read a great deal of Averroes, but we cannot be sure how well acquainted he was with Avicebron's *Fons vitae*. In his first reference to the work Albert associates it with Plato and dismisses it as useless and devoid of proof. In replying to the main question, "Whether Plato's supposi-

[49] See Gilson, *History of Christian Philosophy*, ed.cit. p. 706, note 80.

[50] Ibid. pp. 695–97, with notes.

[51] Ibid. pp. 331–40, with notes.

[52] *Opus tertium* c.23, ed. J. S. Brewer, Fr. Rogeri Bacon, *Opera Quaedam Hactenus Inedita* (London: Rolls Series, 1859), p. 74–75.

tion that there is one kind of matter for all things is true," Albert bluntly replies:

> It never was the opinion of any great philosopher that there is one matter for all things. And if one counters with the example of Plato in the book *Fons vitae*, I reply that those books carry no weight in my opinion, because they do not argue from proper principles of the discipline, namely of natural science. For whoever disregards the evidence of motion and sense experience in nature—since the whole of nature involves motion and sense experience—is ready to deceive himself and others. Therefore I say that something is not a *hoc aliquid* only when it is composed of matter and form, but [also] of potency and act.[53]

Albert had studied natural science long enough to know that the root of potentiality and ability to change is "privation" (*quod non subiacet privationi aliquo modo, ibi nulla est potentia*), and this potentiality is not the same in all things, no more than is privation. Albert therefore admits that all creatures are composed, but not of one universal matter and one universal form. In Albert's view (*meo iudicio*) there is no matter in spiritual substances, but they are composed of *quod est* and *quo est*, meaning by *quod est* the *hoc aliquid* that really exists in nature and by *quo est* the "principium intelligendi et et subsistendi ipsum in tali esse."

Albert's principal objection to "the author of *Fons vitae*" is that he uses the word "matter" univocally of all things that "sustain" or "support," regardless of the many different ways this is done in the real world. Albert expresses his deepest conviction when he concludes his rebuttal of the fourth objection:

> This (in my judgment) has been the entire cause of the controversy between Plato and Aristotle, that he [Plato] wished to utilize arguments of a logical order, and deduced from them principles of the real world. Aristotle, however, does not do this, but looks for principles of real things from within the natures of things.[54]

As far as Albert is concerned, the author of *Fons vitae* not only is a Platonist and guilty of all the errors he sees in Plato[55] but offers no proof for the assertions he gratuitously makes.

In the *Metaphysica* (ca. 1264–67) Albert notes that Avicebron's error in identifying all matter with potentiality "arises from the great-

---

[53] Saint Albert, *Sent.* II, dist. 1 A art.4, ed. Borgnet 27:14b.
[54] Ibid. art.4 ad 4, ed. Borgnet 27:15a.
[55] Cf. ibid., art.5, ed. Borgnet 27:15b–19a.

est ignorance of philosophy, because if intelligence implies matter, then it cannot be proved that any substance exists *secundum se* separated from matter."[56] Positing matter in the intellect and multiplying forms in every creature, for Albert, undermines the very possibility of knowing anything intellectually and so is "most absurd" (*absurdissimum*). "And so," Albert concludes, "that most vile philosophy, which never originated from the ingenuity of the Peripatetics, should be viewed with horror by every man."[57]

The last of Albert's so-called Aristotelian paraphrases was written shortly after the *Metaphysica* and before 1271. It is much more than an explanation of the pseudo-Aristotelian *Liber de causis*. Book I is not a paraphrase of anything but a metaphysician's survey of the whole history of philosophy in its search for God. At the very beginning of the First Book, Albert explains and rejects three schools of philosophy (only the *Epicurei* and *Stoici* are named) before proceeding to the true Peripatetic doctrine concerning the First Principle of all things. First to be considered are the "Epicureans," who are thoroughly materialist, denying all immateriality and identifying God, intelligence, and matter. Neither Albert nor any of the Church Fathers could find anything good to say about them. The second to be considered are called "Stoics," whose Prince was Plato and who stand at almost the opposite end of the philosophical spectrum. Albert lists four main issues that disturb Peripatetics most: (1) Platonists allow for motions without contact of some efficient cause; (2) they identify principles of knowing with principles of being, so that once they have postulated an exemplar they think they have explained the cause of the being of the thing (*de esse rei*); (3) they postulate subsistent numbers as the *per se* principles of physical things; and (4) they even make solids, surfaces, and lines flow from a point to constitute a *corpus mathematicum*, to which they add *corpus naturale*, as though it were an additional *forma*. Albert adds that he has sufficiently refuted the position that makes mathematics to be the principles of natural bodies in his First Philosophy and therefore lets this matter drop.[58]

Then Albert adds after the Stoics, in tr. 1, c. 5, the "strange position" of Avicebron in the book called *Fons vitae* "concerning the Principle of all being" (*circa principium universi esse*), making it clear that Avicebron comes close to Plato in everything except in what he has to

---

[56] Saint Albert, *Metaphysica* XI, tr.2, c.16, ed. Colon. 16/2, p. 502, 53–57.

[57] "Et ideo ab homine omni horrenda est ista vilissima philosophia, quae numquam processit de subtilitate Peripateticorum." ibid., XI, tr.2, c.8, ed. Colon. 16/2, p. 493, 66–68.

[58] Saint Albert, *Liber de causis* I, tr.1, c.4, ed. Borgnet 10:368b–369a.

say about the Will.[59] That Albert should so separate Avicebron from the Platonists and give him special consideration, surely indicates that Avicebron constituted a special problem for Albert's contemporaries in the late 1260s. While it is difficult to summarize Albert's exposition because of the many implications he draws out, four main points will perhaps suffice. First, for Avicebron, all creatures are composed of first matter and a proportionate first form in such a way that the universal "first matter" is the ultimate *per se* subject and recipient of its "first substantial form." Thus even before any further determinations are received by the first "substance," *materia prima* exists in all substances corporeal and intellectual. Second, this "matter," which exists in all things except the First Maker, is of the same genus with all creatures, whether it exists in corporeal substances, intellectual substances, or mixtures of contraries, as a universal substrate for the succession of forms, such that *intelligere fundatur in sentire, sentire in vivere, vivere in esse*—and all rooted in a "matter" that is itself neither corporeal or incorporeal. This peculiar "matter" is called *materia spiritualis*. Third, although the First Maker (*Factor Primus*) is not in any genus, everything that emanates from him—the first intelligence (*intellectualitas prima*), intelligences, the heavens, and elements—are composed of the same antecedent "matter," which is not closed off by the first substantial form, as it were, from becoming either intellectual or corporeal. Finally, while the first agent is indeed most simple (*simplicissimum esse in fine simplicitatis*), his activity must be determined by something: "That determinator he [Avicebron] says is the Will" (*determinans autem illud dicit esse voluntatem*).[60] In this way, according to Avicebron, the first agent is determined in his activity toward first matter to illumine it with first act, which is an intellectual light (*qui est lumen intellectuale*), bursting with a diversity of intelligences that spring from it, as well as all quantified things. The important point here is that the unique principle of Will is *prior to intelligence* and permeates all things by its simplicity. Intelligence and all other forms are really in the potentiality of that first universal matter, "just as in a subject receiving a form in *esse*."

In refuting Avicebron's position, I, tr.1, c.6, Albert briefly gives "five very strong reasons" that Peripatetics would raise, then presents a whole list of his own objections. All of these can perhaps be reduced to three:

1. Avicebron never explains how this ultimate matter receives *esse*.

[59] Ibid. I, tr.1, c.5, ed. Borgnet 10:371b.
[60] Ibid. p. 371a.

It cannot itself be the first principle, since it is deficient in *esse*, which it receives from form; it cannot be derived from a principle unless that principle were the absolutely first principle of *all esse*.

2. Avicebron never explains how the higher, for example, intelligence, can come from the lower, such as first matter.

3. It is completely absurd (*penitus absurdum*) that Will should precede Intelligence, since the will of every agent is determined by intellect. Albert summarily dimisses Avicebron's *Fons vitae* by saying: "Therefore the position of Avicebron is entirely unsatisfactory."

The real genius of Albert's introduction to the paraphrase of *Liber de causis* is in tr. 3 of Book I, where he undermines the necessary emanationism of Muslim philosophers and of the *Liber de causis* itself. After demonstrating that the First Principle (God) must have the full actuality of knowledge, both contemplative and active (tr. 2), he goes on to demonstrate that the First Principle must be omnipotent in all his free and voluntary actions. Here in c.4, Albert freely admits that "Avicebron is the only philosopher who said that the First Principle acts through Will, in a book he deigned to call *The Fountain of Life*." But on examining Avicebron's concept of the Will, Albert found so many questions unanswered on how this Will is determined and indetermined that he ends up by saying:

> For this reason it is absolutely clear that the position of Avicebron is unsatisfactory. Moreover, I do not think that Avicebron wrote this book, but that certain undergraduates (*quidam sophistarum*) perpetrated it under his name.[61]

While much more could be narrated concerning Albert's reaction to Avicebron's universal hylomorphism, enough has been said to show his strong opposition to a position that was of more than historical value to him. Albert did not consider Avicebron's *Fons vitae* a serious work of philosophy. Even in his late *De scientia mirabili Dei* he treated it as a misbegotten Platonism.[62] Yet he devoted considerable space to refuting the many hidden assumptions in Avicebron's voluntarism, a universal hylomorphism that would postulate an underlying "matter" prior to all substance both intellectual and corporeal, and a multiple sequence of "substantial forms" that could be nothing more than

---

[61] Ibid., I, tr.3, c.4, ed. Borgnet 10:407a: "Propter quod pro certo dictum Avicebron inconveniens est: nec puto quod Avicebron hunc librum fecit, sed quod quidam sophistarum confinxerunt eum sub nomine suo."

[62] Saint Albert, *De scientia mirabili Dei* (*Summa theologiae*) P.II, tr.1, q.4, a.1 particula 2, ed. Borgnet 32:60b–67b.

predicamental accidents. All of the *sophismata* and *topicas rationes*,[63] which Avicebron adduced in his *Fons vitae*, were, of course, relevant to the philosophical and theological issues of Albert's day. They were part of the wider context of thirteenth-century Augustinianism.

Conclusion

From what has been said earlier in this paper, three main conclusions seem to emerge. First, the voluntarism basic to the so-called Augustinians of the thirteenth century stemmed from the initial reaction to the necessary emanationism of Muslim philosophers. This initial reaction was made by Ibn Gabirol in the eleventh century, translated and Christianized by Dominic Gundisalvi in the late twelfth, and embraced by William of Auvergne and others at Paris around 1220. It became a fundamental tenet, climaxing in the extreme voluntarism of William of Ockham in the early fourteenth.

Second, the universal hylomorphism of the so-called Augustinians of the thirteenth century is a sheer novelty, stemming from Avicebron by way of Dominic Gundisalvi, who tried to Christianize it. The traditional teaching, however, of Parisian theologians, including William of Auvergne, maintained that all creatures, including angels, are composed of *quod est* and *quo est* (or *esse*), a Boethian distinction variously understood by various theologians. The hylomorphic identification of this composition with "matter" and "form" was certainly made by Odo Rigaud, the third Franciscan master at Paris (1245–48), and perhaps made by Alexander of Hales himself in the 1220s. It certainly cannot be traced earlier than the 1220s.

Third, the plurality of substantial forms in all creatures—especially "spiritual matter" in angels and the numerical immutability of the *forma corporeitatis*—comes directly from Avicebron through Gundisalvi, who rejected it. As Callus has shown, this novelty was not even known in the arts faculties of Paris and Oxford until the first decade of the thirteenth century, and was not even discussed in the faculty of theology until around the 1220s.

What then becomes of "the more solid and more sound doctrines of the sons of Saint Francis, namely Friar Alexander of happy memory, of Friar Bonaventure and others like him" that John Pecham so ardently defended in the name of traditional, orthodox teaching? In the light of our study and others like it, it would seem that the *novitates* decried by John Pecham in 1285 have been attributed to the wrong school in thirteenth-century thought.

[63] Saint Albert, *Liber de causis* I, tr.4, c.8, ed. Borgnet 10:430b.

Galileo's Citations of Albert the Great

WILLIAM A. WALLACE, O.P.
Catholic University of America

Albert the Great is justly regarded as one of the outstanding fore-
runners of modern science in the High Middle Ages. His contributions
to all branches of learning earned for him the title *Doctor universalis,*
and he was heralded as "the Great" even in his own lifetime. Particularly noteworthy was his encyclopedic presentation, in Latin, of the
scientific knowledge of the Greeks deriving especially from Aristotle
and from Aristotle's Greek and Arab commentators. To this corpus
Albert himself added entire treatises based on personal observations
of the heavens and of the mineral, plant, and animal kingdoms. From
our vantage point in time we can therefore see him as a conserver and
transmitter of the scientific knowledge of antiquity and of Islam, who
also contributed to the advancement of science in his day, and who
should, on both counts, be regarded as one of the key figures in the
revival of learning in the thirteenth century.[1]

More difficult to assess is Albert's influence on later centuries and
the role he might have played in the scientific revolution of the seventeenth century. Like many other great thinkers Albert has been over-
shadowed by his students, and especially by his celebrated disciple,
Thomas Aquinas. This fact, coupled with the change of mentality that
is ascribed by intellectual historians to the Renaissance, which is
usually seen as introducing a pronounced cleavage between medieval
and early modern thought, may cause one to wonder whether there is
any continuity whatever between the science cultivated by Albert and
that associated with the names of, say, Galileo Galilei and William
Harvey.[2] Even historians of science who specialize in the Middle Ages

---

[1] For details, see the author's article on Albert the Great in *Dictionary of Scientific Biography* (New York: Charles Scribner's Sons, 1970), 1: 99–103.

[2] Albert and Harvey both studied at Padua, the latter while Galileo was a professor there, so one might suspect that there would be some continuity of thought
among the three. For scholastic and Aristotelian influences on Galileo and Harvey,

are prone to see the fourteenth-century development in mathematical physics as the main medieval contribution to the rise of modern science, and in this development it would appear that Albert the Great had but a small contribution to make.[3]

It is the purpose of this article to shed light on a possible connection between Galileo and a medieval thinker such as Albert by examining in some detail the knowledge that Galileo possessed of the German Dominican and of high-medieval thought generally. Until quite recently Galileo was viewed as a sort of Melchizedek, an innovator without any intellectual forebears who had little or no connection with the university tradition of his day and who established his *nuova scienza* by dint of original investigation—working solely as a craftsman with a penchant for mathematical ways of thinking. Owing to my researches[4] and that of others,[5] however, this picture is gradually being revised. The key to the revision is three sets of notes, or notebooks, written in Latin and in Galileo's hand that date from around 1590, when Galileo was beginning his career as a professor of mathematics in the University of Pisa. The first two notebooks are devoted to questions or problems arising within Aristotle's logic and physical science, respectively, whereas the third contains Galileo's first attempts at constructing a science of local motion. Because of the affinity of its subject matter with that of the *Two New Sciences*, written at the end of Galileo's life, the third notebook has received at least perfunctory notice from scholars, but the first two have been neglected entirely. The editor of the National Edition of Galileo's works, Antonio Favaro, regarded them as *Juvenilia*, or youthful writings, and dated the logical questions from his preuniversity training at the Monastery of Vallombrosa and the physical questions from his student days at Pisa. As a

see William A. Wallace, "Three Classics of Science," in *The Great Ideas Today* 1974 (Chicago: Encyclopaedia Britannica, 1974), pp. 211–72; Albert is not explicitly mentioned, but the influences are typical of Albertine thought.

[3] Albert's discussion of the definition of motion and the way this came to be regarded as a *fluxus formae* or a *forma fluens* in the fourteenth-century debates certainly influenced the rise of mathematical physics in that century. See William A. Wallace, "The Philosophical Setting of Medieval Science," in David C. Lindberg, ed., *Science in the Middle Ages* (Chicago: University of Chicago Press, 1978).

[4] In a series of essays, some of which are cited in the notes that follow and all of which are being edited for publication in a volume to be entitled *Prelude to Galileo: Essays on Medieval and Sixteenth-Century Sources of Modern Science*.

[5] Particularly Adriano Carugo and Alistair Crombie, whose preliminary investigations are reported in the latter's "Sources of Galileo's Early Natural Philosophy," in M. L. Righini Bonelli and W. R. Shea, eds., *Reason, Experiment, and Mysticism in the Scientific Revolution* (New York: Science History Publications, 1975), pp. 157–75.

consequence all three notebooks, and particularly the first two, were seen as trivial, having little or no bearing on the intellectual career of the Pisan physicist.

The later dating of the notebooks and their association with Galileo's career as a university professor, together with the uncovering in them of scholastic expressions that recur in Galileo's later writings,[6] have reopened the question of earlier influences on his thought. Albert the Great is mentioned four times in the notebook dealing with logical questions and nineteen times in that dealing with physical questions. A study of these citations may help us ascertain the extent of Galileo's knowledge of Albert and the source, or sources, from which that knowledge derived. It may also enable us to date more precisely the time of Galileo's composition and perhaps to determine the motivation behind the notebooks. To such a dual objective the present essay is directed.

The Physical Questions and Their Subject

In view of the fact that the notebook dealing with the logical questions has yet to be edited definitively,[7] and the references therein to Albert are far fewer than those in the notebook dealing with the physical questions, we shall restrict attention in what follows to the latter composition. This procedure benefits from the fact that I have recently published an English translation of the physical questions, together with a commentary that indicates some of the sources from which they derive, and thus there exists a work to which the reader can be referred for fuller particulars.[8]

[6] For example, the expression *ex suppositione*, which is frequently used by Galileo to characterize the type of demonstration on which his new science of motion is based. This is discussed in William A. Wallace, "Galileo and Reasoning *Ex suppositione*: The Methodology of the *Two New Sciences*," in R. S. Cohen et al., eds., *Proceedings of the 1974 Biennial Meeting of the Philosophy of Science Association* (Dordrecht-Boston: D. Reidel Publishing Company, 1976), pp. 79–104. The extent to which this expression derives from Albert the Great is analyzed in William A. Wallace, "Albertus Magnus on Suppositional Necessity in the Natural Sciences," forthcoming in J. A. Weisheipl, *Albertus Magnus and the Sciences*, scheduled for publication in 1980 by the Pontifical Institute for Mediaeval Studies, Toronto.

[7] Adriano Carugo has transcribed the Latin text from Galileo's autograph but has not yet published it; some comments on its contents are given by Crombie in the essay cited in note 5 supra.

[8] W. A. Wallace, *Galileo's Early Notebooks: The Physical Questions: A Translation from the Latin, with Historical and Paleographical Commentary* (Notre Dame: University of Notre Dame Press, 1977). The introduction and notes to this volume give biographical information on the Jesuit professors who were the inspiration behind the notebooks. They also contain specific references to the manu-

Twenty-five questions are treated in the notebook under discussion, the first twelve (A through L in my system of reference)[9] being concerned with the matter of Aristotle's *De caelo et mundo*, and the remaining thirteen (M through Y) with topics relating to his *De generatione et corruptione*. Albert the Great is cited nineteen times in all, twelve of these citations occurring in the treatises related to the *De caelo and* the remaining seven in a treatise on the elements that makes up the major portion of Galileo's exposition of the *De generatione*. My previous researches have shown that some 90 percent of the total number of paragraphs making up the physical questions have parallels in the lecture notes of professors teaching at the Collegio Romano, a Jesuit university in Rome, in the years between 1566 and 1597. The vast majority of these parallels can be found in *reportationes* of the lectures of four Jesuits, namely, Antonius Menu, who taught natural philosophy in the academic year 1577–78; Paulus Valla, who taught the same in 1588–89; Mutius Vitelleschi, the same in 1589–90; and Ludovicus Rugerius, the same in 1590–91. Of the nineteen references to Albert, ten have parallels in the lecture notes of these four Jesuits; several of the ten are found in the notes of one author alone, but most are found in two or three sets of notes. It is this circumstance that may shed light on the dating of Galileo's notebook, on the assumption that the closer the similarity of texts the shorter the temporal interval between their respective compositions.

The first treatise of the questions relating to the *De caelo* is made up of two questions, the first (A) inquiring about the subject matter of its various books and the second (B) about their order, connection, and title. Albert the Great is mentioned in two paragraphs of the first question (A4 and A6) and in two paragraphs of the second (B3 and B8). The first citation reads as follows:

> Albertus Magnus makes the subject bodies that are capable of movement to place. His reason is this: the subject of the whole of the *Physics* is bodies that are movable in general; therefore the subject of these four books, which are a part of the *Physics*, should be the first species of movable bodies, i.e., bodies movable to place. [A4]

scripts in which the lecture notes of these Jesuits are recorded, and also outlines of the contents of the manuscripts, which for the most part lack foliation and thus cannot be cited by folio number.

[9] In my translation (note 8, supra) I have used a capital letter to designate each question and Arabic numerals to designate the paragraph numbers within each question. Thus A4 designates the fourth paragraph of question A, which is the first question in the introductory treatise, translated on p. 26 of *Galileo's Early Notebooks*.

No reference is given, but clearly Galileo has in mind Albert's exposition of the first book of *De caelo*, tract 1, chapter 1, where Albert makes the statements that the "mobile ad ubi est subiectum huius libri" and "suum subiectum . . . est simplex corpus mobile ad locum" (Borgnet 4:1a–2b). Parallels for this paragraph are found in the lecture notes of both Vitelleschi and Rugerius, the correspondences for the former being slightly more numerous than those for the latter. The Latin of Galileo's paragraph and of Vitelleschi's parallel account are given below in facing columns, for purposes of comparison:

<table>
<tr><td align="center">Galileo</td><td align="center">Vitelleschi (1590)</td></tr>
<tr><td>Albertus Magnus ponit obiectum corpus mobile ad ubi. Ratio illius haec est: quia obiectum totius Physicae est corpus mobile in communi; horum ergo quatuor librorum, qui sunt una pars Physicae, obiectum debet esse prima species corporis mobilis, quod est corpus mobile ad ubi.</td><td>. . . obiectum esse corpus mobile ad ubi, est . . . Alberti, primo Physicae tr. p° cap. 4° et primo Caeli tr. p° cap. p°, et aliorum. Haec . . . sic explicatur: obiectum totius Physicae est corpus mobile . . . in universum [et] singulis speciebus. . . . Primo modo consideratur in octo libris Physicae, secundo . . . corpus simplex mobile ad ubi.</td></tr>
</table>

Rugerius's exposition, similar to Vitelleschi's, is reproduced below:

Rugerius (1591)

. . . est Alberti, tr. 1 cap. 1, qui ait subiectum horum librorum esse corpus mobile ad ubi, . . . Fundamentum . . . est, quai in octo libris Physicae subiectum est . . . corpus mobile absolute sumptum, . . . ergo debuit post illam tractationem statim agi de mobili ad ubi.

Note in the citations above that of the forty-three words in Galileo's text eighteen have been underlined and that seventeen have correspondences in Vitelleschi's text whereas only eleven are to be found in Rugerius's. It is on this basis that I state that Galileo's exposition is closer to Vitelleschi's than to Rugerius's and possibly dates closer to the former in time of composition.

The remaining three citations of Albert in Galileo's introductory treatise do not have counterparts in the Jesuit *reportationes* and thus are not helpful for dating purposes. They do have interest in another respect, however, and on this account are reproduced below:

Nifo, seeking to find agreement among these four opinions, holds with Alexander that the subject of aggregation is the universe; with Albert, that the subject of predication is bodies movable to place;

with Simplicius, that the subject of attribution is simple bodies; and with Iamblicus and Syrianus, that the subject of principality is the heavens. [A6]

Simplicius and Albertus Magnus, whom we and everyone else follow, hold that these books come after the eight books of the *Physics* and make up the second part of natural philosophy. [B3]

Concerning the title, according to Alexander, Simplicius, and the Greeks, these books are entitled *De caelo* from the more noble portion; according to Albertus Magnus, St. Thomas, and the Latins, they are entitled *De caelo et mundo*. By the term *mundo* they understand the four elements, and this meaning was known also to Aristotle, in the first *Meteors*, chapter 1, saying that the lower world, i.e., the elements, should be contiguous with the movement of the higher. [B8]

With regard to the last two texts, *B3* and *B8*, it is a simple matter to verify that their teaching is found in the place in Albert already referenced (Borgnet 4:2b), and thus one might assume that Galileo himself had made the identification. With regard to the first text (A6), however, the matter is not so straightforward. When we check the teaching of Agostino Nifo contained in his *In quattuor libros de celo et mundo expositio*, printed at Naples in 1517, we find that the teaching ascribed to him by Galileo (fol. 1r) is not completely correct: the concordance of four opinions is there, as stated, but instead of the second opinion being identified as Albert's, in Nifo it is identified as Averroës's! Again, when we check Nifo to find his counterpart for Galileo's paragraph B3, we find that Nifo does not cite Simplicius and Albertus Magnus, as does Galileo, but rather Simplicius and Averroës. What are we to make of these substitutions? It is difficult to understand why Galileo himself would have made them, whereas it is comprehensible that one of the Jesuit professors at the Collegio Romano, who were being viewed with suspicion by their ecclesiastical superiors for being too partial to Averroist teachings, could have done so.[10] Thus I suspect, on the basis of this and other evidences, that Galileo probably did not have reference to original sources in composing his noteboks but based them largely on the citations of others.[11]

[10] For some of the tensions provoked by Averroism in the Collegio Romano, see M. Scaduto, *Storia della Compagnia di Gesu in Italia,* 2 vols. (Rome: Gregorian University Press, 1964), 2:284.

[11] Evidences of Galileo's use of secondary sources in composing the physical questions are described in detail in my commentary on the questions in *Galileo's Early Notebooks,* pp. 253–303.

The bulk of Galileo's questionary on the *De caelo* is made up of two additional treatises, one dealing with the universe as a whole and the other with the heavens. Of these the first is comparatively brief, taking up philosophical and theological queries regarding the origin, unity, perfection, and eternity of the universe. Only one reference is made to Albert the Great in this treatise, and that in the discussion of the unity of the universe. Galileo's citation reads as follows:

> I say, first: there is only one universe. The proof: first, from Plato, there is only one exemplar of the universe; therefore [the universe is one]. Second, from Albertus, on the first *De caelo*, tract 3, chapters 5 and 6: because this is clearly gathered from the first mover, who is only one and cannot be multiplied, not being material, and from the places of the movable objects that are in the universe. Add to this: if there were many universes, a reason could not be given why these would be all and no more.[E2]

The reference to Albert is correct, for in chapter 5 Albert gives the argument based on the immateriality of the prime mover (Borgnet 4:79a) and in chapter 6 he discusses Plato and the problem of the exemplars of the universe (83a). He does not, however, give the argument that follows the words "Add to this." The latter, not unexpectedly, is to be found in the only parallel this text has among the Jesuit *reportationes*, that of Antonius Menu, which is given below, along with the Latin of Galileo's text:

Galileo	Menu (1578)
Dico, primo, unum tantum esse mundum. Probatur, primo, ex Platone: unum tantum est exemplar mundi; ergo . . . . Secundo, ex Alberto, in primo Caeli tr. 3, cap. 5 et 6: quia ex primo motore, qui est tantum unus et non potest multiplicari, cum non sit materia, et ex locis mobilium quae sunt in mundo, id aperte colligitur. Adde, quod si essent plures mundi, non posset assignari ratio cur essent tot et non plures.	Respondeo affirmative unum tantum esse . . . . Probatur . . . . Tertio . . . ad denotandum unitatem sui Creatoris . . . . {De ista materia . . . . Albertus Magnus libro primo De caelo, tr. 3° cap. 6° . . . .} Quarto, si ponerentur plures mundi quam unus non est ratio cur constituuntur duo vel tres et cetera in infinitum.

Here again eighteen of Galileo's seventy-one words are to be found in

Menu's notes, although not in the precise order; this is indicated by our enclosing some of Menu's expression in braces.

The treatise on the heavens shows a heavy dependence on the Jesuit writings, the first two questions, concerned with the number and order of the heavenly orbs, being based almost verbatim on Christopher Clavius's commentary on the *Sphere* of Sacrobosco,[12] and the remaining questions, concerned with the composition, corruptibility, materiality, and animation of the heavens, having many counterparts in lectures given at the Collegio Romano. It would be tedious to reproduce here all of these parallels, so I shall restrict myself in what follows to those with the larger number of coincidences or with readings of special significance.

In the latter category, actually a text for which we have not uncovered a parallel in the Jesuit notes, Galileo references Albert for a teaching that assumes considerable importance in his later treatises *De motu*, where he introduces the idea of a motion that is neither natural nor violent but in some way intermediate between the two. Galileo's citation occurs in the context of his discussion whether the heavens are composed of fire or some other element, and reads as follows:

> The first opinion was that of practically all ancient philosophers before Aristotle, who thought that the heavens are not different in nature from the elements; and this opinion originated with the Egyptians, as Albertus teaches in tract 1, chapter 4, of the first *De caelo*, the Egyptians thinking that the heavens were made of fire. For it is a property of fire to be carried upward, and then, when it can ascend no farther, to go around in a circle—as is seen in flame, which, when it arrives at the top of a furnace, circles around. From this it is apparent that the heavens are fiery, for they have the uppermost place and are moved circularly. [I7]

This teaching is found in Albert pretty much as Galileo states it. To give the reader some idea of the relation of the two teachings we give the respective Latin texts in parallel column:

Galileo	Albertus (Borgnet 4:15b–16a)
Prima opinio fuit veterum fere omnium philosophorum ante Aristotelem, qui putarent caelum non esse	Scias autem quod omnia quae dicuntur, sunt dicta contra Platonem et philosophos Aegypti, qui dixerunt

12 See William A. Wallace, "Galileo Galilei and the *Doctores Parisienses*, in R. E. Butts & J. C. Pitt, eds., *New Perspectives on Galileo* (Dordrecht-Boston: D. Reidel Publishing Company, 1978), pp. 87–138; also Crombie's article cited in note 5 supra.

naturae distinctae ab elementis: et haec sententia promanavit ab Aegyptiis, ut docet Albertus tr. p° cap. 4, primi De caelo, qui existimarunt caelum esse igneum. Nam ignis proprium est ut feratur sursum, deinde ut, cum non potest amplius ascendere, volvatur in girum; ut patet in flamma, quae, ubi pervenit ad summum fornacis, circumvolvitur; ex quo patet, cum caelum supremum locum obtineat et circulariter moveatur, esse igneum.

quod coelum est igneum, et non est motum circulariter nisi per accidens: dicebant enim quod ignis naturaliter ascendat, et quando non habet quo plus ascendat, tunc circumvolvitur in seipso, sicut flamma ignis in fornace: praeter hoc solum quod concavum fornacis circumvolvit flammam, defectus autem ulterioris loci circumvolvit aetherem, ut dicebant.

Words that are similar in the two texts have been underlined, and it would seem that there is sufficient resemblance here to maintain that either Galileo or the source used by him actually had an eye on Albert's exposition when composing this paragraph. The example discussed therein, viz., that of fire or flame having a circular motion when it rises to the top of a furnace, recurs in Galileo's later exposition, for he goes on to inquire whether circular motion would be natural for fire under such circumstances, or, if not natural, then violent. Both possibilities he rejects, leaving only the alternative of a *tertium quid,* namely, a motion that is neither natural nor violent and therefore must be something intermediate between the two. Elsewhere I have argued that this line of reasoning, already adumbrated in the lecture notes of Vitelleschi and Rugerius, could have led Galileo to the idea of circular inertia, which was seminal for his later treatment of local motion in the *Two New Sciences.*[13]

Other references to Albert that do have parallels in the Jesuit *reportationes* occur in paragraphs I10, K37–40, K170, and L11 of Galileo's notebook dealing with the physical questions. Of these I10 and L11 have counterparts in Menu alone, and K170 has a counterpart in Menu but without the explicit citation of Albert's teaching. The line of reasoning advanced in K37–40, however, has parallels in Menu, Vitelleschi, and Rugerius, and thus turns out to be an important text for the comparison of sources on which Galileo's composition could have been based. Galileo's words are as follows:

> The second opinion is that of those who think that the heavens are of an elementary nature, regarding the heavens as a composed body.

[13] In my address to the Second Mid-Atlantic States Conference on Patristic, Medieval, and Renaissance Studies, held at Villanova University in 1977, entitled "Medieval and Renaissance Sources of Modern Science: A Revision of Duhem's Continuity Thesis, Based on Galileo's Early Notebooks," *Proceedings of the PMR Conference* 2 (1977): pp. 1–17.

... [K37] Alexander was also of this opinion. ... Also all the Arabs, with the single exception of Averroës, attributed composition to the heavens; so Avicebron in the book *Fons vitae,* from Albertus and from St. Thomas in the First Part, question 66, article 2; Avempace, from the first *De caelo,* tract 1, chapter 3; Avicenna, in the first of the *Sufficientia,* chapter 3. So did a great number of the Latins, such as Albertus Magnus, in the first *Physics,* as above, the eighth *Physics,* tract 1, chapter 13, and in the book *De quatuor coaequevis,* question 4, article 3, where he teaches that Rabbi Moses was of the same opinion; St. Thomas ... and likewise all Thomists, as Capreolus ... Cajetan ... Soncinas ... Ferrariensis ... [and] St. Bonaventure. ... [K38] However, the cited authors disagree among themselves. First, because some of them wish to define the matter of the heavens differently from the matter of inferior things. So Alexander ... Simplicius ... Albertus, in the first *Physics,* tract 3, chapter 11, and in *De quatuor coaequevis,* question 2, article 6, and St. Thomas in the places cited above. But others contend that heavenly matter is the same in kind as sublunary matter; so Philoponus, Avicenna, Avempace ..., Avicebron, Giles, and Scaliger. ... [K39] Second, they disagree in this ..., as Mirandulanus and Achillini .... [K40].

The Latin text corresponding to this translation is given below on the left and then, in parallel and under Galileo's wording, the corresponding passages in Menu, Vitelleschi, and Rugerius. Any expression in Galileo that has a coincidence in one of these three authors is underlined, and the corresponding expression in one or more of the three is also underlined. Since the ordering of the discussion varies in the different authors, it has been necessary to make some transpositions in the presentations of their texts, and these are indicated, as above, by the use of braces:

Galileo

Secunda opinio est illorum omnium qui putant caelum esse naturae elementaris, sentientum caelum esse corpus compositum. . . . Alexandrum etiam fuisse in hac sententia. . . . Arabes etiam omnes, uno excepto Averroe, compositionem tribuerunt caelo; ut Avicembron in libro Fontis vitae, ex Alberto et ex D. Thoma in Prima Parte, q. 66, art. 2; Avempace, ex primo De caelo tr. p° cap. 3; Avicenna, in p° Sufficientiae cap. 3; et quamplurimi etiam Latinorum, ut

Menu (1578)

Secunda opinio est aliorum qui putant caelum tam secundum Aristotelem quam veritatem esse compositum ex materia et forma. . . .

sic D. Thomas Prima Parte, q. 66, art. 2; octavo Physicorum, lect. 22; primo Caeli, lect. 6 et 8. . . .

Albertus Magnus in primo Physicorum, UBI SUPRA, octavo Physicorum, tr. p° cap. 13, et in libro De quatuor coaequaevis, q. 4, art. 3, ubi etiam docet eandem sententiam fuisse Rabbi Moyses; D. Thomas . . . similiter omnes Thomistae, ut Capreolus . . . Caietanus . . . Soncinas . . . Ferrariensis . . . S. Bonaventura. . . . Verum discrepant inter se citati authores. Primo quidem quia illorum nonnulli volunt materiam caeli esse diversae rationis a materia horum inferiorum, ut Alexander . . . Simplicius . . . Albertus primo Physicorum tr. 3, cap. 11, et in De quatuor coaequaevis, q. 2, art. 6, et D. Thomas, locis citatis supra; at vero alii contendunt esse eiusdem rationis cum materia sublunarium; ut Philoponus, Avicenna, Avempace . . ., Avicembron, Aegidius, et Scaliger . . . . Discrepant secundo in hoc . . . ut Mirandulanus et Achillinus . . . .

{Albertus Magnus, De quatuor coaevis, q. 2, art. 6}

. . . Capreolus, ubi supra, Ferrariensis . . ., Dominicus de Flandria . . . Soncinas . . . Amadeus . . . .

Tertia [opinio] est Aegidii Romani, qui ait caelum esse compositum ex materia et formam et materiam eiusdem rationis cum materia horum inferiorum. Avicenna, Avempace, Avicembron hoc idem senserunt . . . . {Mirandulanus . . . Achillinus . . . .}

Vitelleschi (1590)

Prima sententia vult caelum compositum esse ex materia et forma. . . . {Eiusdem sententia est S. Bonaventura . . . Capreolus . . . Caietanus . . . Ferrariensis . . . Soncinas . . . Flandria . . . Hervaeus . . . Amadeus . . .}
Sed sunt in hac sententia duo modi dicendi . . . . {Secundus . . . qui volunt materiam caeli esse diversae rationis a materia horum inferiorum. . . . Est S. Thomae Prima Parte, loco citato, et alibi saepe, licet in 2° dist. 12, q.   , art. 1, indicatur sequi sententiam Averrois; Albertus, primo Physicorum, tr. 3, cap. 11, primo Caeli, tr. p°, cap. 8, et Prima Parte Summae de quatuor coaevis, q. 4, art. 3} Primus . . . qui dicunt materiam caeli esse eiusdem rationis cum materia horum inferiorum. Ita Aegidius in tractatu De materia caeli compositione, et octavo Metaphysicorum, q. 2 et 7, Scaliger . . . . Idem sentiunt Avicenna . . . Avicebron . . . ut testis

Rugerius (1591)

Unum caput est asserentium caelum ex materia et forma constare . . . {quem sequitur Capreolus . . . Hervaeus . . . Soncinas . . . Ferrariensis . . . Flandria . . . Caietanus . . . et alii Thomistae}
Quo in capite sunt duo modi dicendi: . . . {Alter modus est ponentium materiam diversae rationis a materia inferiorum. . . . Ita Albertus, primo Physicorum, tr. 3, cap. 11, primo Caeli, tr. 1, cap. 8, et Prima Parte Summae quae est de quatuor coaevis, q. 4, a. 3. D. Thomas, Prima Parte, q. 66, a. 2, primo Physicorum, lect. 21 in text. 79, primo Caeli lect. 6 in text. 21 . . .}
Alter ponentium materiam caeli eiusdem rationis cum materia inferiorum. . . . Ita censuit . . . S. Bonaventura . . . Aegidius in proprio tractatu De materia caeli compositione, et octavo Metaphysicorum, q. 2 et 3. Ex philosophis, Avicenna . . .

est <u>Albertus primo Physicorum</u>, tr. ultimo, cap. 11, et S. Thomas, Prima Parte, <u>q. 66, art. 2</u> . . . .

<u>Avicembron</u> . . . . Idem habet <u>Scaliger</u> . . . .

According to my count, in these texts there are 185 Latin words of Galileo's composition that are relevant to our purposes, and, of these, 63 words have counterparts in one or other of the Jesuit notes: 53 coincidences are found in Vitelleschi's lectures, 46 in those of Rugerius, and 33 in those of Menu. The patterns indicate that the content of the lectures remained fairly constant over the period of thirteen years but that the expression varied from year to year. Galileo makes reference to Albertus Magnus three times, and Vitelleschi twice, whereas Menu and Rugerius cite him only once; again, the order of treatment in Vitelleschi and Rugerius is the reverse of that in Galileo's exposition. In Galileo's text, however, it should be pointed out that Galileo's second citation of Albert is a blind reference: he cites Albert's exposition of the first book of the *Physics*, "as above" (*ubi supra*, in capitals in the text), and actually he has no previous reference to that locus! There is a reference to it "below," on the other hand, and so Galileo should have written *ubi infra*. The mistake could be traceable to the fact that Galileo himself reversed the order of treatment from that found in the source from which he worked and neglected to take account of the reversal in his first citation of Albert the Great. On the basis of this reasoning, Vitelleschi would be the closest to Galileo in time of composition.

Before concluding with Galileo's questions on the *De caelo*, I should note that all of his references to Albert in the treatises on the universe and the heavens can be verified in the Borgnet edition. In I10, Galileo states that "Albertus Magnus, in the first *De caelo*, tract 1, chapter 4 . . . maintain[s] that Plato . . . generally disagreed with Aristotle"; this is found in Borgnet 4:15b. The references made in the text cited above, K37–40, are generally correct: the "ubi supra" citation of the first *Physics* should be to tract 3, chapter 11 (Borgnet 3:68); that to the eighth *Physics* is found in Borgnet 3:549–53; and the two citations of the *De quatuor coaevis* are in Borgnet 34:335b and 34:404a, respectively —in Borgnet's division, however, the first would be referenced as tract 1, question 2, article 6, and the second as tract 3, question 7, article 3. In K170 Galileo raises the question whether the matter of the heavenly spheres is one or many, and to that he replies: "We say that if the heavenly spheres differ specifically from each other, the matter of any one sphere is different in kind from the matter of another, as Albert holds in *De quatuor coaequaevis*, question 2, article 6 . . ."; this teaching is verifiable in a general way in Borgnet 34:335, though not in the precise terms given in the text. Finally, in L11 Galileo observes that "some have thought that there ought to exist in the heavens, apart from the intelligences, some kind of proper intellective souls; thus Alexander [of Aphrodisias] . . . ." He goes on to recount that "Algazel, Rabbi Moses, and Isaac seem to feel the same, as Albert mentions in the seventh *Metaphysics*, tract 2, chapter 10" (Borgnet 6:607a). The Latin of the last clause reads: "Idem videntur sentire Algazel, Rabbi Moyses, et Isaac, ut refert Albertus in 11 Metaphysicorum, tr. 2, cap. 10." The same reference is found in Menu, who writes: "Fuit Alexandri Aphrodisias . . . et Algazelli et Rabbi Moysi et Isaac Judaei, referente Alberto 11 Metaphysicorum, cap. 10, tr. 2."

The Elements and Their Qualities

This brings us to Galileo's last tractate of the physical questions, namely, that on the elements, which he divides into two parts or disputations, the first concerned with the elements in general and the second with their qualities. Albertus Magnus is mentioned twice in the first disputation and four times in the second, all four of the latter references being to Albert's teaching on how the primary qualities can be termed active and passive. The two citations in the part dealing with the elements are of some importance for the fact that they permit us to use the lecture notes of a Jesuit professor not discussed thus far, Paulus Valla, the portion of whose lectures on the *De generatione* dealing with the elements has survived, though the remaining portions on that book and the *De caelo* are no longer extant.

Galileo's first mention of Albert occurs in a paragraph wherein he begins to enumerate the various meanings of the term element. He writes:

The first meaning, therefore, is that an element signifies the intrinsic causes composing a thing, i.e., matter and form. These seem especially apt to be called elements because from them a thing is first composed and into them it is ultimately resolved, and they are not in turn composed of others nor are they resolved into others; and this can in no way be said of the other meanings. Such causes, on the authority of Eudemus, based on Simplicius in his introduction to the *Physics*, were first called elements by Plato; the same usage was taken up by Simplicius, Philoponus, Averroës, and Albertus on the first chapter of the first *Physics*. For this reason Averroës, in the third *De caelo*, comment 31, says that Aristotle in the books of the *Physics* treated of the universal elements of all simple and composed bodies.

Thus Philoponus, in the first text of the second *De generatione*, gives the reason why Aristotle, in the third *Physics*, 45, the second *De generatione*, first text, and the second *De partibus* [*animalium*], chapter 1, calls the four simple bodies elements. He gives the reason: because, he says, these bodies are not really elements themselves, since they are composed of other things that are prior, i.e., matter and form, which are most properly elements. For, although elements in this sense are said of any intrinsic cause, more commonly and more properly they are said of matter, as is apparent from Alexander, Eudemus, Simplicius, and St. Thomas on the first chapter of the first *Physics*. Since, however, matter is manifold, the first and most common matter of all, says Averroës, third *De caelo*, 31, second *De generatione*, text 6, first *Metaphysics*, text 4, and tenth *Metaphysics*, text 2, is primarily and most properly said to be an element, for elements are like the material parts of a thing; and this is the first meaning. [P8]

The Latin for this passage is reproduced below, and placed opposite it is the corresponding passage from the undated "Tractate on the Elements," composed by Valla probably in 1589:

Galileo	Valla (1589)
Prima igitur est, ut elementum significet causas intrinsecas rem componentes, idest materiam et formam: quae maxime videntur posse dici elementa, quia ex his primo componitur res et in haec ultimo resolvitur, et ipsa non amplius ex aliis componuntur neque in alia resolvuntur; quod non omnino caeteris significationibus aptari potest. Et haec, authore Eudemo apud Simplicium in prooemio Physicorum, a Platone primo fuerunt dicta elementa; et idem etiam usurpavit Simplicius, Philoponus, Averroes, et Albertus, primo Physicorum, primo. Et hac ratione Averroes, tertio Caeli, com. 31, ait, Aristotelem in primis Physicorum egisse de elementis universalibus omnium corporum simplicium et compositorum: unde Philoponus, in textum primum secundi De generatione, reddit rationem quare Aristoteles, tertio Physicorum 45, secundo De generatione t. p°, et	{tertio sumitur elementum pro causis tantum intrinsecis, materia scilicet et forma....}

Eudemus, ex Simplicio, primo Physicorum in proemio ait Platonem ... ita appellasse elementum .... Hoc tertio modo sumuntur elementum Simplicio, Philopono, Alberto, et aliis primo Physicorum, textu primo .... Avicenna, prima primi, elementa definit esse corpora, et videtur hoc colligi ex Averroe, quinto Metaphysicorum t. 4 ... ut videtur indicasse elementum dicere esse speciem aliquam, i.e., corpus aliquod completum, ex quo sequitur nomen elementum primo dici de quatuor |

secundo De partibus, capite primo, quatuor corpora simplicia appellet vocata elementa: reddit rationem, quia, inquit, non sunt ipsa vere elementa, siquidem ex aliis prioribus componuntur, idest materia et forma quae sunt propriisime elementa. Quamvis autem elementa in hoc sensu dicantur de utraque causa intrinseca, communius tamen et proprius dicitur de materia; ut patet ex Alexandro, Eudemo, Simplicio, et D. Thoma primo Physicorum, primo. Cum autem materia sit multiplex, ideo, primam et communissimam omnium, inquit Averroes, tertio Caeli 31 et secundo De generatione t. 6, et quinto Metaphysicorum t. 4, et decimo Metaphysicorum t. 2, primo et propriisime dici elementum ipsam materiam; elementa enim sunt quasi partes materiales rei: et haec est prima acceptio.

elementis. Alii vero asserunt elementum primo dici de materia; ita Eudemus et Alexander, primo Physicorum, t. p°, referente Simplicio, et Averroes, tertio Metaphysicorum, com. 4, Philoponus, secundo De generatione in t. p°, et aliis communiter, primo Physicorum, t. p°, primo De generatione, t. p°, et primo Meteororum in principio, et hanc ob causam sequisse Averroem: quatuor elementa vocat vocata elementa, non autem simpliciter elementa. Ita habet tertio Physicorum, t. 45, secundo De generatione, t. p°, 4° et 6°, secundo De partibus animalium, cap. p°, et primo Physicorum, t. 22, quia quatuor elementa non sunt communia omnibus rebus, cuiusmodi est materia prima, et quia elementa debent esse prima et simplicissima, quod magis videtur convenire materiae primae.

There are no corresponding passages in the notes of Menu and Vitelleschi, but Rugerius discusses approximately the same matter and in so doing has wording that is somewhat closer to Galileo's, as can be seen from the following text:

Rugerius (1591)

{Solet autem nomen hoc elementi variis significationibus usurpari . . . . Aristoteles, quinto Metaphysicorum, quod quia elementum est id ex quo primo componitur aliquid inexistens indivisibile specie in aliam speciem . . . .}

Primo advertendum quod Eudemus, referente Simplicio in prologo Physicorum, elementaria principia, id est, intrinseca, materiam et formam ait primo a Platone appellata fuisse elementa . . . .

Simplicius vero, Philoponus, Albertus, Averroes, et alii intelligunt duas causas intrisecas, materiam et formam . . .

et Philoponus hic docet Aristotelem dixisse vocata elementa, quia non sunt ipsa vere elementa, siquidem ex aliis prioribus componuntur, materia scilicet et forma, quae sunt propriisime elementa . . . .

Quamvis autem proprie elementum dicatur de utraque causa intrinseca, magis tamen proprie dici solet de materia, et propriisime quidem de prima; elementa enim sunt quasi partes materiales rei, et sic proprie

videntur causae materiali convenire definitiones
illae . . . .
primum enim est materia prima, vel materia et forma
ut modo dicebamus, immo haec propriissime sunt
elementa . . . .

Comparing all three passages, we note that Galileo's use of Albert is merely to list him among those who give the common interpretation to the use of the term element by Plato; this is verifiable in Albert's exposition of the first book of the *Physics*, tract 1, chapter 5 (Borgnet 3:12a). Of the 233 Latin words in Galileo's paragraph, 96 have counterparts in either Valla or Rugerius, 54 being coincident in Valla and 65 in Rugerius. Noteworthy perhaps is the fact that Valla has a fuller enumeration of texts and authorities whereas Rugerius duplicates more of the content of Galileo's exposition; again, with Galileo and Rugerius this is the first meaning of element, whereas with Valla it is the third meaning. These indications perhaps favor Rugerius over Valla slightly; between the two, however, they can account for over 40 percent of the wordage actually used by Galileo.

The remaining citation of Albert in the general tractate on the elements is of special interest because it occurs in a passage where there are two lacunae in Galileo's exposition. As we have suggested in our commentary on this passage[14] these are probably explicable from the fact that Galileo used a secondary handwritten source in composing the passage and had difficulty deciphering either the words or their meaning. Fortunately similar passages occur in the lecture notes of Menu, Valla, and Rugerius, and they are all helpful for reconstructing the sense of Galileo's statement. As we reconstruct his meaning, the passage reads as follows in English translation:

The fourth opinion is that of those saying that the forms of the elements are substantial forms hidden from us [but knowable through their] qualities. This is the position of St. Thomas, Albert, and the Latins, in the second *De generatione*, 16, and the third *Metaphysics*, 27; likewise the Conciliator, [clarification of] difference 13; Giles, on the first *De generatione*, question 19; Jandun, *De sensu*, question 25, and the fifth *Physics*, question 4; Zimara in the *Table*; and Contarenus in the first and seventh *De elementis*. [S8]

Here the two passages enclosed in brackets replace spaces left blank in Galileo's Latin composition. His Latin text, together with the corresponding texts of Menu, Valla, and Rugerius, are given below in parallel column:

14 Wallace, *Galileo's Early Notebooks*, pp. 286–87.

Galileo

Quarta opinio est dicentium formas elementorum esse formas substantiales [space for three words] qualitates nobis occultas. Est D. Thomae, Alberti, et Latinorum, secundo De generatione 16 et tertio Metaphysicorum 27; item Conciliatoris [space for one word] differentiae 13, Aegidii, primo De generatione, quaestione 19, Ianduni De sensu, quaestione 25 et quinto Physicorum, quaestione 4, Zimara in Tabula, Contareni, primo et septimo De elementis.

Menu (1578)

Tertia opinio est communis aliorum qui asserunt formas elementorum esse quasdam substantias occultas qui explicantur per qualitates motivas et alterativas. Ita Albertus Magnus, secundo De generatione, tr. 2, cap. 7, et D. Thomas, primo De generatione super t. 18, Conciliator, differentia 13, Iandunus, libro de sensu et sensili, quaestione 25.

Valla (1589?)

Tertia sententia est communis omnium fere Perepateticorum, quia asserunt formas substantiales elementorum esse substantias quasdam occultas, quae interdum explicant per qualitates motivas, interdum per alterativas. Ita tenent . . . D. Thomas, secundo De generatione in t. 24 et primo De generatione, lect. 8, Conciliator, differentia 13, Albertus Magnus, secundo De generatione, tr. 2, cap. 7, Iandunus, De sensu et sensili, quaestione 15 . . . .

Rugerius (1591)

Altera sententia est communis, differentias essentiales elementorum esse veras et proprias formas substantiales, qualitates vero tam motivas quam alterativas fluere ex illis tanquam passiones proprias. Haec sententia . . . Alberti hic, tr. 2, cap. 7, D. Thomae, primo De generatione 18 et secundo De generatione 6. Legite Conciliatorem, differentia 13, Iandunum, De sensu et sensili, quaestione 28 et quinto Physicorum, quaestione 4, Zimaram in Tabula . . . Contarenum in primo libro De elementis, et alios . . . .
Propositio: formae elementorum sunt vere formae substantiales. . . . Illa ratio est quod quia rerum differentiae ignotae sunt, ideo maluerunt per qualitates tanquam notiores explicare naturas illorum . . . .

With regard to Galileo's text, it should be noted, first, that his reference to the "third Metaphysics" is doubtful; the abbreviation he uses is "Met.," which he usually employs for *Metaphysics*, and not "Mete.," which is customary for the *Meteors*; since this reference does not occur in any of the Jesuit authors, however, it assumes no importance for our purposes. Again, Galileo's reference to the "seventh" book of Contarenus's *De elementis* is erroneous: there are only five books in this work. The lacunae, on the other hand, are fairly important, since they offer a primary indication that the notebooks are derivative but at the same time represent some thought and reconstruction by Galileo. It seems clear that the missing sense of the first lacuna in the passage is that conveyed in the English translation, with its substitution, but when we compare Galileo's Latin with the corresponding passages in the three Jesuit authors, we discover that it is almost impossible to find three Latin words that can be put in the empty space! This undoubtedly explains why Galileo left it blank. The second lacuna is also puzzling, but it does permit of solution. The Jesuit professors cite the Conciliator frequently, and in one of these citations (though not in the passage above) Rugerius writes out his citation more fully as "Conciliator in dilucidario ad differentiam 10." It is probable that Galileo saw the abbreviation for "in dilucidario" and was unable to decipher it (the expression being fairly unusual in scholastic texts); as a consequence he left a space, possibly to be filled in later. Note that Galileo's reference to Albert, moreover, is not specific, whereas it is clearly indicated in all three *reportationes* and can be readily verified in the Borgnet edition (4:433a), where Albertus Magnus writes: ". . . et ideo [primae qualitates] sunt substantiales elementis alio modo quam formae substantiales, quia sunt substantiales sicut passiones quae fluunt a substantia." Rugerius incorporates Albert's expression into his own exposition, and it is noteworthy that his passage has the most coincidences with Galileo, namely, twenty-five words, as compared to eighteen each for Menu and Valla, and on this basis may be regarded as the closest to Galileo's.

The last four mentions of Albert the Great by Galileo all occur in the question wherein the Pisan professor is discussing the active and passive character of the primary qualities of the elements and refers to Albert as providing the best explanation of how heat assists dryness in producing the latter's proper effects. The specific references occur in paragraphs X_7, X_{13}, and twice in X_{15}, and additional material is contained in paragraphs $X8–10$ and $X16–17$; all of them are further developments of a teaching of Albert in his exposition of the fourth book of the *Meteors*, tract 1, chapter 2 (Borgnet 4:708b). Counterparts for these passages are found in Vitelleschi, and to a lesser extent in Rugerius, but not in Menu or Valla. For our purposes it may suffice to give only one paragraph in English translation, followed by the Latin texts of Galileo and Vitelleschi in parallel column:

On this account I assign the following reasons for these statements of Aristotle. . . . The third reason is that given by Philoponus, second *De generatione* on text 8, St. Thomas, Averroës in the beginning of the fourth *Meteors*, and Pomponatius in the same place, third doubt, and Albert, same place, first treatise, chapter 2: namely, that Aristotle said this not absolutely but only with regard to compounds, wherein heat and cold act most effectively and wetness and dryness receive most effectively, though the former also receive a little and the latter act, as Albert and Buccaferrus have correctly noted. Yet they add that wetness and dryness act only with the aid of the other two, and particularly with heat; since wetness, for example, does not act in a compound per se, except insofar as previously, by virtue of the heat, a humid vapor is raised that can be mixed with the humidifying body; then, in virtue of the same heat, the body will be opened up so that the vapor can penetrate it and moisten it. Thus heat is said to aid the action of wetness, and in a similar way it aids the action of dryness also. [X15]

Galileo	Vitelleschi (1590)
Quare ego assigno has causas illorum dictorum Aristotelis. . . . Tertia est quam reddit Philoponus, secundo De generatione in t. 8, D. Thomas, Averroes in initio quarti Meteororum, et Pomponatius, ibidem dubitatione 3, et Albertus, ibidem tr. p° cap. 2°: nimirum, Aristotelem illud dixisse non simpliciter, sed in ordine ad mixtionem, in qua calor et frigus potissimum agunt, humor et siccitas potissimum patiuntur; licet etiam illae aliquantulum patiantur et hae agant, ut recte notavit Albertus et Buccaferrus. Qui tamen addunt, humorem et siccitatem non agere nisi iuvantibus aliis duabus et praecipue calore: nam humor, verbi gratia, in mixtione per se non agit, nisi prius, vi caloris, elevetur vapor humidus, qui possit admisceri corpori humefaciendo; deinde, vi eiusdem caloris, aperiatur ipsum corpus, ita ut illud penetrare possit et humefacere. Et sic dicitur calor iuvare actionem humidi; et simili modo etiam iuvat actionem sicci.	S. Thomas, quarto Meteororum initio, Bannes hic, quaestione 4, Pomponatius loco citato, Turris primo Tegni, com. 18, et alii dicunt Aristotelis dictum non esse intelligendum simpliciter considerando eas qualitates secundum se quatenus per illas elementa agunt ad invicem sed respectu mixtionis, quia enim calor et frigus . . . dicuntur activae, reliquae passivae. . . . Albertus, quarto Meteororum, tr. p° cap. 2°, et Buccaferrus ibidem, initio et hic in t. 8, explicant Aristotelem eodem modo quo praecedentes, sed addunt etiam in mixtione omnes qualitates agere et omnes pati; calorem tamen et frigus plurimum agere et ideo dici activas, alias plurimum pati et ideo dici passivas, cum praesertim actio humoris et siccitatis iuvetur actione caloris, qui et elevat vaporem humidum et exalationem siccam, quae debent admisceri corpori humectando et exiccando. Item corpus ipsum rarefacit et attenuat, et ita illud agit vapori et exaltationi, ut possunt penetrare ad illud humectandum et exiccandum.

Of the 140 relevant Latin words in Galileo's composition, 35 have coincidences with the terms employed by Vitelleschi. This in itself does not convey how important the notions deriving from Albert via this Jesuit and his confreres are for Galileo's treatment of primary qualities and their role in explaining the activities and passivities of the elements. The ideas presented by Vitelleschi (and also contained, in some instances in more detail, in the exposition of Rugerius) form the key to Galileo's understanding of the sublunary region, which he was to use to good effect in his later discussions of the comets and other heavenly appearances, and often in debate with other Jesuits whose intellectual formation (we now know) was not far different from his own.

Albert's Importance for Galileo Studies

This brief study of Albert the Great as seen through the use made of him by Galileo in his early notebooks is helpful on two counts: it furnishes a large amount of incidental information that can be used to date Galileo's writings, and it shows how seriously philosophers in the late sixteenth century took their thirteenth-century sources, and particularly the writings of Albert on physical science, when they were addressing the problems whose solutions were to come only in the early modern period.

With regard to the first point, it is possible to summarize all of the information on word coincidences in Galileo's Latin text and in the corresponding passages in the *reportationes* of lectures given at the Collegio Romano. A tabulation of the results of these word counts is given in Table 1. Of the total number of words in passages relating in one way or another to Albert the Great, 37 percent have counterparts in lecture notes of Jesuits teaching at the Collegio Romano between 1578 and 1591. Only four sets of notes are available for this period, and of these only two sets are complete, viz., those of Vitelleschi and Rugerius, who taught in 1590 and 1591, respectively. Of these two authors Vitelleschi has 21 percent coincidences with Galileo's composition, and Rugerius has 20 percent; these are far in excess of the 7 percent and the 4 percent coincidences to be found in the notes of Menu and Valla, respectively. Valla's low percentage is perhaps explicable by the fact that only a small portion of his notes have survived, but Menu's notes are fairly complete, and his coincidences are particularly sparse in the latter parts of Galileo's notebooks, even though he does treat the same subject matter as Galileo. The larger number of coincidences for the Jesuits writing in 1590 and 1591 would seem to confirm the dating of Galileo's composition as "around 1590," an inscription written on the notebook by one of the curators who

Table 1

Number of Latin Words Coincident in Galileo's Composition and in the Notes of Jesuits Teaching at the Collegio Romano Between 1578 and 1591

(The last column gives the number of words in Galileo's text that have counterparts in one or more of the four notebooks indicated.)

Par. No.	Total No. Relevant Words	Menu (1578)	Valla (1589)	Vitelleschi (1590)	Rugerius (1591)	Galileo (ca. 1590)
A4	43	..	..	17	11	18
E2	71	18	..	..	..	18
I10	137	22	..	..	..	22
K37–40	185	33	..	53	46	63
L10–11	82	30	..	..	..	30
P8	233	..	54	..	65	96
S8	55	18	18	..	25	28
X7	63	..	..	15	22	22
X8	60	..	..	9	20	20
X9	37	..	..	17	23	25
X10	214	..	..	63	27	73
X13	108	..	..	32	..	32
X15	140	..	..	35	..	35
X16	90	..	..	33	53	61
X17	146	..	..	70	38	79
Totals	1,664	121	72	344	330	622
Percent of total no.		7	4	21	20	37

bound together the folios as they are now found in the Galileo Archives.[15]

It should be pointed out that this evidence is not being adduced to suggest that Galileo actually used the notes of either Vitelleschi or Rugerius when composing the physical questions. This would have been impossible if he composed them in 1589 or 1590, because Vitelleschi's lectures were just being given at that time in Rome, and we know that Galileo was not there then to hear them; *a fortiori* he would not have had Rugerius's notes, because they were not yet written. It is probable that Galileo had access to an earlier set of notes deriving from the Collegio Romano, possibly those of Valla, which we know existed at

[15] For this and other evidences bearing on the dating of the physical questions, see ibid., pp. vi, 21–24, 258–59.

one time, [16] or, even more likely, those of Mutius de Angelis, who last taught in 1587 but whose notes also are no longer extant.[17] Examination of notes coming from the Collegio in successive years shows that there is very little evidence of verbatim copying from one year to another, but similar phrases recur, and it is this kind of repetition that could well explain the coincidences of words I have pointed out in this essay.

With regard to my second point, this relationship between the young Galileo and the Jesuits of the Collegio Romano helps explain a curious fact about the Pisan notebooks, namely, that they consistently pay as much attention to philosophers and theologians of the thirteenth century as they do to writers of the fourteenth and fifteenth centuries, including those of nominalist leanings. The standard account of medieval influences on the rise of modern science is that all these surfaced after the Condemnation of 1277 and particularly in the nominalist schools of Bradwardine at Oxford and Buridan at Paris. Galileo's citations of such authors is minimal, whereas his use of authors such as Albert the Great and Thomas Aquinas is substantial. The explanation of this fact is now clear: Galileo was influenced in his choice of philosophical authorities by Jesuit professors who, while taking a glance at these nominalist contributions, were much more influenced by the scholastic syntheses of the High Middle Ages. They were pronouncedly realist in their options, moreover, and this perhaps explains why Galileo himself turned out to be so doggedly realist in his ill-fated attempt to establish the truth of the Copernican system in his later years. The Jesuits, too, were not adverse to studying Averroes, though the effect of the Condemnation of 1277 was still felt in their day, and so occasionally they had to resort to someone such as Albert the Great as a cover for their explorations of Averroist teachings.

The substantive doctrine deriving from Galileo's citations of Albert is not extensive, but two points are worthy of mention, and with these we must conclude. The first is Albert's discussion of the circular motion of fire after it rises as far as it can through rectilinear motion. This phenomenon raised the question whether such circulation is natural for fire in these circumstances or whether it is violent and ultimately led to the proposal that it is neither natural nor violent but inter-

[16] In the preface to his two-volume *Logica* published at Lyons in 1622, Valla indicated that he had commented on all the philosophical works of Aristotle and had these ready for publication; these are undoubtedly the lecture notes from his teaching at the Collegio Romano, which he probably reworked for later publication but which are not known to have survived.

[17] On Mutius de Angelis, see Wallace, *Galileo's Early Notebooks*, pp. 22–23.

mediate between the two. Such a proposal, explicit in Galileo's later writings but already adumbrated in Jesuit lecture notes, was seminal for the concept of circular inertia, from which it is a simple matter to trace the rise of modern mechanics from Galileo to Newton. The second area is the use made by Galileo of Albert's teaching on primary qualities in his attempt to unravel the activities and passivities of elemental bodies. Remotely, a study such as this undoubtedly influenced the new theories of primary and secondary qualities that would emerge as distinctive of modern philosophy from Galileo through Descartes to Locke and Berkeley. More proximately, it led to a development of scholastic teachings on qualities and powers and on ways of quantifying these and ultimately to the employment of the force concept as more fruitful for analyzing elemental interactions. I have explored this point elsewhere,[18] but for purposes here it may suffice to note that Albert the Great was the author Galileo recognized as having made the most significant contributions in these areas and thus as influencing at least indirectly the *nuova scienza* he was soon to originate.

[18] See William A. Wallace, "Causes and Forces in Sixteenth-Century Physics," *Isis* 69 (1978): pp. 400–12.

Contributors

McInerny, Ralph M. Michael P. Grace Professor of Mediaeval Studies, University of Notre Dame, Notre Dame, Indiana. Appointed Director of Medieval Institute at Notre Dame. Editor of *New Scholasticism*. President of American Catholic Philosophical Association (1972). Member of American Philosophical Association, American Catholic Philosophical Association, Metaphysical Society of America, Medieval Academy, Author's Guild, Mystery Writers of America, and Sören Kierkegaard Society. Author of seven books, including *Logic of Analogy, History of Western Philosophy, Studies in Analogy, Thomism in an Age of Renewal, New Themes in Christian Philosophy and St. Thomas Aquinas;* twelve novels (*Jolly Rogerson, A Narrow Time, The Priest,* and the Father Dowling mystery series); and 33 articles in journals and books, including the Acts of 1955 and 1959 International Thomistic Congresses, *Filosofia della Natura nel Medioevo, Laval Théologique et Philosophique, Modern Schoolman, New Scholasticism, Proceedings of the American Catholic Philosophical Association, Revista di Filosofia Neoscolastica, Revue Philosophique de Louvain, Science Ecclesiastique, Studies in Honor of Charles De Koninck, Studies in Medieval Philosophy,* and *Thomist.*

Quinn, (Rev.) John M., O.S.A. Professor of Philosophy, Villanova University, Villanova, Pennsylvania. Secretary-Treasurer and Associate Director of Augustinian Historical Institute, Villanova University, and President of Florida Philosophical Association (1972). Member of American Catholic Philosophical Association and American Maritain Association. Author of three books (*The Doctrine of Time in St. Thomas Aquinas, The Concept of Time in St. Augustine,* and *The Thomism of Etienne Gilson: A Critical Study*) and articles in *Augustiniana, Augustinianum, International Philosophical Quarterly, New Scholasticism, Thomist, New Catholic Encyclopedia,* and *Proceedings* of the American Catholic Philosophical Association.

Craemer-Ruegenberg, Ingrid. Professor of Philosophy, University of Cologne, Cologne, West Germany, and staff member of Thomas Institute (connected with the same university) since 1968. Author of *Moralsprache und Moralität: Zu Thesen der sprachanalytischen Ethik-Diskussion, Kritik, Gegenmodell* (Freiburg-München: Karl Albert Verlag, 1975), translated into Spanish under the title *Lenguaje Moral y Moralidad* (Buenos Aires: Editorial Alfa Argentina, 1976) and of a number of articles concentrating on ancient, Islamic, and medieval psychology.

Sweeney, (Rev.) Leo, S.J. Adjunct Professor (Research) of Philosophy, Loyola University of Chicago; previously of St. Louis University; Creighton University, Omaha; and Catholic University of America. Secretary (1960–63) and President (1965–66) of Jesuit Philosophical Association of America. Vice-President and President-elect of the American Catholic Philosophical Association (1979). Member of Executive Council, American Catholic Philosophical Association (1969–71). Recipient of Fellowship from American Council of Learned Societies (1963–64); Research Grant-in-Aid in USOE Humanities and Social Sciences Development Program (1969–70). Member of Metaphysical Society of America, Mediaeval Academy of America, Société Internationale pour L'Etude de la Philosophie Médiévale, American Philosophical Association, Society for Ancient Greek Philosophy, International Society for Neoplatonic Studies, Jesuit Philosophical Association, American Catholic Philosophical Association, Society for Christian Philosophy, and Maritain Association of America. Editor of four books for *Modern Schoolman*. Author of *A Metaphysics of Authentic Existentialism* and *Infinity in the Presocratics* and of 32 articles in the journals *Gregorianum, International Philosophical Quarterly, Journal of History of Philosophy, Manuscripta, Mediaeval Studies, The Modern Schoolman, New Scholasticism, Revue philosophique de Louvain, Southern Journal of Philosophy, Southwestern Journal of Philosophy,* and *Speculum;* in *Collier's Encyclopedia, Encyclopedia Americana, Encyclopedia of Christian Doctrine, Encyclopedia of Philosophy,* and *New Catholic Encyclopedia* and in the books *Arts Liberaux et Philosophie au moyen Age, Bonaventure and Aquinas: Enduring Philosophers, Etienne Gilson Tribute, Great Events from History, Miscellanea Mediaevalia, Proceedings of Jesuit Philosophical Association, Proceedings of the American Catholic Philosophical Association, Studia Patristica,* and *Wisdom in Depth.*

Catania, Francis J. Professor of Philosophy and Dean of the Graduate School, Loyola University, Chicago. Author of seven articles in *Ency-*

clopedia of Philosophy, Listening, Masterpieces of Catholic Literature, Mediaeval Studies, Modern Schoolman, Rechérchés de Theologie Ancienne et Medievale, and *Studies in Medieval Culture.*

Ducharme, (Rev.) Léonard, O.M.I. Professor of Philosophy, University of Ottawa, Canada. Member of Canadian Philosophical Association and Société de Philosophie du Quebec. Author of various articles in *Revue de l'Université d'Ottawa* and *Eglise et Theologie* (Saint Paul University, Ottawa).

Kovach, Francis J. Professor of Philosophy, University of Oklahoma, Norman, Oklahoma. Editorial consultant to *New Scholasticism.* Member of American Catholic Philosophical Association, American Society for Aesthetics, British Society for Aesthetics, Societas Internationalis Scotistica, Société Internationale pour l'Étude de la Philosophie Médiévale, Società Internazionale Tommaso d'Aquino, and Southwestern Philosophical Society. Representative of American Council of Learned Societies at Fifth International Congress of Aesthetics, Amsterdam, 1964. Author of two books (*Die Aesthetik des Thomas von Aquin. Eine genetische und systematische Analyse* and *Philosophy of Beauty*) and 27 articles in the journals *American Benedictine Review, American Journal of Jurisprudence, Archiv für Geschichte der Philosophie, Benedictine Review, New Scholasticism, Revista Portuguesa de Filosofia, Review of Metaphysics, Southwestern Journal of Philosophy* and *Zeitschrift der Geschichte der Philosophie* and in nine books (*Actes du IV et V Congres Internationale d'Esthetique, Art Liberaux et Philosophie au Moyen Age, Deus et Homo ad mentem I. Duns Scoti, Die Metaphysik im Mittelalter, Filosofia della Natura nel Medioevo, New Catholic Encyclopedia, Regnum Hominis et Regnum Dei* ([*Studia Scholastico-Scotistica,* 6]). Coeditor of two books (*Bonaventure and Aquinas: Enduring Philosophers* and the present book).

Weisheipl, (Rev.) James A., O.P. Professor of Patristic and Medieval Thought, Pontifical Faculty of Philosophy, Dominican House of Studies, River Forrest, Illinois (1957–65). Founder and first Director of the Leonine Commission for the critical editing of the works of Saint Thomas Aquinas, American Section, Yale (1965–68); Visiting Lecturer (1963); Associate Professor (1964–68); Professor of History and Philosophy of Medieval Science, University of Toronto (1968–); Senior Fellow of Pontifical Institute of Mediaeval Studies, Toronto (1968–); Master in Sacred Theology from Master General of the Order of Preachers (1978). President of the American Catholic Philosophical Association (1963–64) and Secretary General of the Thomist Association (1960–64). Member of the History of Science Society, Mediaeval Academy of America, American Catholic Philosophical Association,

Renaissance Society of America, and Societé internationale pour l'étude de la philosophie médiévale. Author of *Nature and Gravitation* (1955, 1961); *Development of Physical Theory in the Middle Ages* (1959, 1960, 1971); (ed.) *The Dignity of Science* (1961); *Friar Thomas d'Aquino: His Life, Thought and Works* (1974, 1975); (ed.) *Albertus Magnus and the Sciences: Commemorative Essays 1980*, 2 vols. (1980); translator and editor of Saint Thomas's *Commentary on St. John*, 2 vols. (1979–); author of more than 56 articles in various American, Argentinian, British, French, Italian, Polish, and Portuguese journals and more than 70 articles for various encyclopedias, including *The New Catholic Encyclopedia*. One of the editors of the critical Cologne edition of *Opera Omnia S. Alberti Magni*.

Wallace, William A., O.P. Professor of Philosophy and History, Catholic University of America, Washington, D.C. Associate Editor of *Thomist*, Philosophy Editor of *New Catholic Encyclopedia*, president of American Catholic Philosophical Association (1970), Councillor of History of Science Society (1974–77), Philosophy of Science Association, Renaissance Society of America, Trustee of Providence College, Director General of Leonine Commission. Author of eight books (*Scientific Methodology of Theodoric of Freiberg, Role of Demonstration in Moral Theology, Cosmogony, Causality and Scientific Explanation* [2 vols.], *Elements of Philosophy, Galileo's Early Notebooks*, and *From a Realist Point of View*); 70 articles or chapters in scholarly journals and books, including *Thomist, New Scholasticism, Review of Metaphysics, Isis, Boston Studies in the Philosophy of Science, Journal of the History of Ideas, Science in the Middle Ages, Source Book in Medieval Science*, and *New Perspectives on Galileo* and 56 articles in encyclopedias, including *New Catholic Encyclopedia, Dictionary of Scientific Biography*, and *Dictionary of the History of Ideas*.

Index

Aa, J. Van der: 166
Abraham ben-David: 246
Achillini: 270, 271
Acts of "sympathy": 167
Action at a distance: xvi, xvii, 161–235, 257; Albert's position on, 220–22; apparent, 165; compromising positions on, 168–71; see Compromising positions; empirical origin of the idea of, 161–62; enduringness of the idea of, 161–71; physical conditions of apparent, 172–73, 176, 199, 213–14, 219, 220, 223, 226–28, 230–35; psychic, 168, 169; "transnatural," 169; views on, 162–71; see Causal anticontiguism, Causal contiguism, compromising views, and Contiguist
Adam, Marsh: 255
Aegidius, Romanus: see Giles of Rome
Aelianus, C.: 167, 225
Aenesidimus: 164
Aether: 165
Aetius: 173
Alan de Lille (Alanus of Insulis): viii, 166, 223
Albert the Great (Albertus Magnus): birthplace of, vii; chronicles naming or praising, xvii–xix; commemorative essays on, xvi–xvii; date of birth of, vii–viii; date of death of, viii, xiv, xv, 161; editions of the works of, see Editions; historical events in Albert's lifetime, viii–xv; length of life, vii; names of, viii, xvii–xix, 21, 235, 261; praise of, xvii–xix, 17–18, 21, 47, 62, 95, 159–61, 235, 241, 261, 280, 283;

relative neglect of, vii; works of, xiii, xv–xvi, 3–4, 12, 16, 17, 50n.5, 172n.6, 197; as arbitrator, xi–xiv; as apparent causal contiguist, 196–220; as bishop, xi, xii; as causal contiguist, 171–97, 220–22; as philosopher, 229; as preacher of the Crusade, xii; as prior provincial, xi, xii; as traveler, xi, xii, xiii, xiv; and Avicebron, 239–60, especially 252–60; and Galileo, 261–83; and Thomas Aquinas, vii, 97, 229–31; see also Action at a distance, Four creata, and Soul
Alcher of Clairvaux: 240
Alexander of Aphrodisias: 23, 29, 51, 52, 167, 186–88, 224, 225, 270, 273–75
Alexander of Hales: ix, x, 23, 170, 226–28, 230, 241, 252, 253, 260
Alfarabi: 23, 243, 249
Alfredus Anglicus: 51
Algazel: 164, 208, 246, 249, 273
Alkindi: 243, 249
Altmann, A.: 246
Amadeus: 271
Amalric of Bene: ix
Ambrosius, St.: 167, 225
Analogous: 98, 108, 109, 125–26, 202, 203, 209, 213, 214, 226; causality, 125; kinds of causality, 125–26
Analogy: 97, 98, 108, 125, 198, 203, 205, 213, 219, 220, 227, 228, 230,
Anastasius, St.: 223
Anawati, G. C.: 70
Anaxagoras: 164
Anselm of Canterbury, St.: 166, 223

Arcesilaus: 164
Aristotle ("the Philosopher"; Aristotelian): ix–xiii, xvi–xix, 12, 17, 23, 25,
26, 29, 37, 40, 44, 46, 49, 50, 52–59,
61, 62, 70, 71, 73, 75, 77, 79, 81–85,
106, 134, 135, 143, 145–47, 152, 156,
159, 165, 173–75, 179, 183–86, 188,
192, 196–99, 201, 203, 209, 210,
222–26, 240, 242, 243, 250, 255,
256, 261, 262, 264, 268, 270, 273–
75, 279, 282
Aristotelianism: 21, 79, 134–36, 239
Athanaeus Naucratis: 223, 224
Atomists, pre-Platonic: 222
Augustine, St. (Augustinian): 27, 46,
78, 81, 82, 88, 91, 135, 158, 169,
208, 239–42, 260
Augustinianism: 239–44; elements of
thirteenth-century, 241–45
Aureolus: see Petrus Aureolus
Avempace: 270, 271
Avendauth: 247
Averroes ("the Commentator"): xii,
xix, 22, 23, 25–28, 31, 37, 39–41, 51,
52, 76, 84, 139, 143, 165, 185, 187,
188, 222, 224, 225, 255, 266, 270,
271, 273–75, 278, 279, 282
Averrorists: xiii, 266, 271, 282
Averrorism: 239, 266
Avicebron (Avencebrol, Ibn Gabirol):
xvi, 240, 241, 243, 245–52, 254, 256–
60, 270–72; influence of, 245–52; and
Albert, see Albert
Avicenna (Avicennian): xix, 10, 23, 25–
27, 31, 32, 36, 37, 106, 135, 139,
142–44, 147, 152, 159, 167, 189, 208,
211, 226, 240, 243–50, 270, 271, 274

Bacon, Francis: 21, 167, 207
Bacon, Roger: ix, xi–xv, xix, 51, 253, 255
Badawi, A.: 70
Baeumker, C.: 248
Banez, D.: 166, 279
Bardenhewer, O.: 70
Bartholomew of Bologna: xv
Beauregard, O. C. De: 22
Bédoret, H.: 70
Benedetto, A. J.: 166
Berkeley, G.: 283
Bernoulli, D.: 167
Bernoulli, J., Jr.: 165

Billingham, R.: ix
Billot, L.: 166
Billuart, C. R.: 166, 231
Binarium famosissimum: 250, 253
Boedder, B.: 166
Boethius (Boethian): 9, 43, 71, 84, 85,
99, 105, 120, 133, 151–54, 247, 248,
250, 254, 260
Boethius of Sweden (de Dacia): xiv
Bolzano, B.: 168
Bonaventure, St.: vii–xiii, 66, 106, 161,
170, 223, 241, 253–55, 260, 270, 271
Boskovich, R.: 168
Boucat Biturico, A.: 166
Boussinesq, J.: 165
Boyer, C.: 166
Boyle, R.: 165
Bradley, F. H.: 163
Brady, I.: 72
Brossnan, W. J.: 168
Brown, T.: 165
Browne, W. R.: 167
Buccaferrus: 279
Bulletin: de théologie, 66; *Thomiste*, 66
Bülow, G: 248
Bunger, M.: 164
Burrell, D.: 97

Cajetan (Thomas de Vio): 166, 230,
270, 271
Callus, D. A.: 240, 247, 250, 254, 260
Campanella, T.: 169
Capec, M.: 22
Capreolus: see Johannes Capreolus
Carneades: 164
Carugo, A.: 262, 263
Catania, F. J.: viii, xvii, 65, 72, 78, 97–
99, 117, 120, 286–87
Causal anticontiguism: 167–68, 221,
235; doctrinal, 167, 168; empirical,
167; explicit, 167, 168; immoderate,
167, 168; implicit, 167, 168; metaphysical, 168; moderate, 167; physical, 167
Causal contiguism: argumentative: 166,
222; descriptive, 164; direct, 163; explicit, 163, 164, 166, 221, 222, 226;
generic, 163, 222; historical models
(sources) of Albert's, 222–26; historical role of Albert's, 222, 229–35;
implicit, 162, 164, 166, 221, 222;

Torpedo fish: 165, 167, 187, 188, 212, 221, 223
Transcendentals (*unum, verum, bonum*): x, 79–85, 127

Ueberweg, F.: viii
Ulrich Engelberg of Strasbourg: xiii, xiv, xix
Universal hylomorphism: 239, 242–45, 248, 250–56, 259
Universal(s): 3–18, 160; *ante rem, in re*, and *post rem*: 13; called first and second intentions: 10, 157; unlike proper names: 8; views on, 5, 6, 11–17
University: Collegio Romano, Rome, 264, 266, 268, 280–82; St. John's, 66; of Oxford, ix, xii, 242, 248, 250, 252, 254, 260, 282; of Padua, ix, 261; of Paris, *see* Paris; of Pisa, 262
Urràburu, J. J.: 170, 234

Vaissière, J. de la: 169
Valla, P.: 264, 273–78, 280–82
Van Steenberghen, F.: 240
Van Steenkiste, C.: 97, 99, 249
Varro, M. T.: 223
Vásquez, G.: 164
Vergilius Maro, P.: 225
Vitelleschi, M.: 264, 265, 269–72, 275, 278–81
Voltaire, F. M. A.: 164
Voluntarism (Primacy of Will): 242–44, 254, 258–60
Vorstius, C.: 168

Wallace, W. A.: xvii, 261–64, 266, 268, 269, 282, 283, 288

Walter of Bruges: xiv
Washell, R. F.: 5, 6, 9
Watson, W.: 165
Weber, W.: 167
Weisheipl, J. A.: viii, xvii, 22, 72, 172, 239, 240, 263, 287–88
Werkmeister, W. H.: 47
Whitehead, A. N.: 95
Wieland, G.: 49, 69–71, 73, 74, 82, 89, 92
William of Auvergne: x, xi, 240, 244, 245, 248, 250, 252–55, 260
William of Auxerre (Altissiodorensis): 166, 223
William of la Mare: xiii, xiv
William of Melitva: x
William of Moerbeke: ix, xii, xiii
William of Paris: 255
William of St. Amour: xi
Williams, T. C.: 225
Wilms, vii, viii, xviii
Wilpert, P. 70, 233
Wippel, J.: 243
Wittgenstein, L.: 163
Wittman, M.: 240
Wolff, C.: 165
Wundt, W.: 168
Wyckoff, D.: viii, 200

Young, T.: 165

Zeno: 163
Zigliara, F. T. M.: 166
Zimara, M. A.: 165, 276, 277
Zimmerman, E. J.: 21
Zöllner, F.: 163, 168
Zubizaretta, V.: 166